# Contemporary
# Supreme Court Cases

# Contemporary Supreme Court Cases

## Landmark Decisions since *Roe v. Wade*

### Volume 1

*Second Edition*

DONALD E. LIVELY AND D. SCOTT BROYLES

 ABC-CLIO™

An Imprint of ABC-CLIO, LLC
Santa Barbara, California • Denver, Colorado

**Library of Congress Cataloging-in-Publication Data**

Names: Lively, Donald E., 1947– author. | Broyles, D. Scott, author.
Title: Contemporary Supreme Court cases : landmark decisions since Roe v.
    Wade / Donald E. Lively and D. Scott Broyles.
Description: Second edition. | Santa Barbara, California : ABC-CLIO, 2016. |
    Includes bibliographical references and index.
Identifiers: LCCN 2015024843 | ISBN 9781440837128 (set) | ISBN 9781440837135
    (e-book : set) | ISBN 9781440845390 (volume 1) | ISBN 9781440845406
    (volume 2)
Subjects: LCSH: Constitutional law—United States—Popular works. |
    Constitutional law—United States—Cases. | United States. Supreme
    Court—Popular works. | Judgments—United States—Popular works.
Classification: LCC KF4550.Z9 L58 2016 | DDC 342.73—dc23
LC record available at http://lccn.loc.gov/2015024843

ISBN:  978-1-4408-3712-8 (set)
ISBN:  978-1-4408-4539-0 (vol. 1)
ISBN:  978-1-4408-4540-6 (vol. 2)
EISBN: 978-1-4408-3713-5 (set)

20 19 18 17 16    1 2 3 4 5

This book is also available on the World Wide Web as an eBook.
Visit www.abc-clio.com for details.

ABC-CLIO
An Imprint of ABC-CLIO, LLC

ABC-CLIO, LLC
130 Cremona Drive, P.O. Box 1911
Santa Barbara, California 93116-1911

This book is printed on acid-free paper ∞

Manufactured in the United States of America

# Contents

# Preface

The power of judicial review is not specifically enumerated by the Constitution. It is a function that the Supreme Court secured in its first landmark decision, *Marbury v. Madison* (1803). Since establishing its "power to say what the law is," and thus make its interpretation of the Constitution binding on the political branches of government, the Court has rendered many more landmark rulings. This book's predecessors, *Landmark Supreme Court Cases* and the first edition of *Contemporary Supreme Court Cases: Landmark Decisions since* Roe v. Wade, catalogued more than two centuries worth of essential Supreme Court decisions.

Determining landmark status is even trickier when the focus is upon cases that have been decided in the recent past. A century ago, Supreme Court jurisprudence was defined by an emphasis upon economic rights, and those rights were generally considered to be fundamental in nature. With the advent of the New Deal and the rise of Progressivism, the Supreme Court changed its philosophy and economic rights were no longer deemed fundamental. Short-term landmark status thus is not necessarily a precursor of long-term significance.

This book identifies landmark cases on the basis of their societal impact, specifically the extent to which they adjust the boundaries of government power and individual rights and liberties. It is conceivable that the force of some of these cases will be diminished or undone by future decisions. Such a development does not minimize their significance, however, as a landmark of the time in which they were crafted.

The book is subdivided into four primary sections that reflect divisions of traditional constitutional law text books and case books. The first section, "Separation and Distribution of Powers," examines cases that have charted boundaries among the three branches of the federal government. The second section, "Power to Regulate or Affect the Economy," consists of cases concerning the federal commerce power and the states' sometimes conflicting authority to exercise their police powers. The third section, "Equality Concepts," includes cases relating to constitutionally prohibited forms of discrimination including classifications based upon race and gender. The final and largest section pertains to individual rights and liberties, including those enumerated by the Constitution and those developed by the judiciary through its interpretation of the Due Process Clause. These substantive sections are augmented by two tables of cases (in alphabetical and chronological order), the complete text of the United States Constitution, a glossary of key terms, general bibliography, and subject index.

This revised and expanded edition of *Contemporary Supreme Court Cases: Landmark Decisions since* Roe v. Wade features 109 important Supreme Court decisions—37 more than were included in the first edition. New cases featured include major decisions on abortion, climate change, voting rights, immigration, campaign financing, gay marriage, and the Affordable Care Act, among other subjects.

The revised edition also includes a brand new feature not included in the first edition: extensive excerpts from Supreme Court opinions for all 109 cases. These excerpts from majority opinions, concurrences, and dissents provide readers with a close look at the legal reasoning employed by the Justices in their deliberations—as well as a ringside seat for following their oft-colorful clashes over their differing interpretations of U.S. law and the Constitution.

The use of *Roe v. Wade* (1973) as a starting time line for modern landmark decisions is not an arbitrary choice. Many observers view the Warren Court, and its decisions concerning civil rights, First Amendment freedoms, and rights of the accused, as the primary source of landmark decisions that continues to this day. It is against this backdrop of perception that *Roe v. Wade* becomes a compelling starting point. The decision in this case, establishing a woman's freedom to choose an abortion, is a post-Warren Court ruling. It represents a model of review that is characterized by critics as activist and that takes the Court beyond the boundaries of interpreting the Constitution and into the zone of creating new Constitutional rights, rights arguably not contemplated by the Constitution's framers. Since then, conflicting arguments among the justices of the Supreme Court about interpretations of the Constitution have further intensified.

The authors have developed this book with the aim of making it relevant and accessible to a wide variety of audiences. Toward this end, it identifies not only the Court's rulings on "what the law is" but offers competing perspectives on "what the law should be." In this regard, the book is different from many casebooks, which are generally in the nature of an historical survey. The hope is that readers will gain not only insight into the nation's highest law, but awareness that the Constitution is a work in progress subject to highly competitive perspectives on how it should be understood.

# Alphabetical Table of Cases

# Chronological Table of Cases

# Part I
# Separation and Distribution of Powers

Federal power under the Constitution is distributed among three branches of government. The principle of separation of powers is not set forth in the text of the Constitution but is evident in its structure. Articles I, II, and III of the Constitution enumerate, respectively, the authority of Congress, the President, and the judiciary. These coordinate branches function independently but also interact on the basis of checking and balancing each other's power. The consequent relationship reflects the framers' sense that authority should not be centralized and effective governance could be achieved through a convergence of their roles.

Constitutional doctrine has been driven by conflict among the branches with respect to their respective roles. Separation of powers decisions typically have resulted from conflicts between branches of government over how far their respective authorities extend. The first significant separation of powers decision was *Marbury v. Madison* (1803), which established the Supreme Court as the final authority in interpreting the Constitution. This decision resolved a conflict between the Court and President Jefferson, who had argued that the judiciary's rulings did not bind him in the exercise of his power. Boundaries of power within the federal system have been tested periodically since.

The departure point for this section is the power of judicial review which, pursuant to *Marbury v. Madison*, gives federal courts the authority to determine conclusively the Constitution's meaning. The balance of this section relates to the boundaries of presidential and congressional power.

# Chapter 1

# The Power of Judicial Review

The Supreme Court's status as the final arbiter of the Constitution's meaning is established not by constitutional text but by the Court's interpretation of it. The usual starting point for any discussion of judicial review is *Marbury v. Madison* (1803). This case arose from President Jefferson's refusal to deliver the commission of a judge appointed by President Adams. Although the Court did not require the President to deliver the commission in this case, it declared the power to do so. More than a century and a half later, President Richard Nixon confronted the Court with a claim that raised similar issues with respect to the judiciary's power over the presidency. This case concerned whether the President, on the basis of executive privilege, was immune from having to participate in the criminal justice process. In *United States v. Nixon* (1974), the Court determined that the President was accountable to the judicial process and ordered him to comply with an order compelling production of evidence in a criminal proceeding.

## United States v. Nixon

**Citation: 418 U.S. 683.**

**Issue: Whether executive privilege enables the President to resist a judicial order directing him to provide evidence in a criminal proceeding.**

**Year of Decision: 1974.**

**Outcome: It is the role of the judiciary to determine whether the executive privilege claim or needs of the criminal justice process should prevail.**

**Author of Opinion: Chief Justice Warren Burger.**

**Vote: 8-0.**

The power of judicial review was established as a general proposition early in the nation's history. Its specific implications have been developed, however, through subsequent case law. In the 1950s, for instance, some states challenged the Court's authority to order desegregation of public schools. Citing *Marbury v. Madison* (1803), the Court in *Cooper v. Aaron* (1957) reaffirmed that it had "the power to say what the law is" and ordered the implementation of desegregation. The *Cooper* decision established the Court's constitutional authority in relationship not only to the federal government but also to the states.

The next significant constitutional challenge to the scope of judicial review arose in circumstances that, like those in Marbury, concerned the President and the Court. It arose following a politically inspired burglary of Democratic Party national headquarters during the 1972 presidential election campaign. Two years later, in the course of a special prosecutor's investigation, a grand jury indicted several executive aides and advisers and named President Nixon as an unindicted coconspirator. The district court, at the special prosecutor's request, subpoenaed documents and tapes relating to conversations between the President and his aides and advisers. Although providing edited transcripts of those conversations, the President moved to quash the subpoena on grounds the tapes and other materials were protected by executive privilege. After the district court rejected the President's arguments, the controversy was presented to the Supreme Court.

The Constitution does not mention executive privilege in specific terms. President Nixon argued, however, that it was implicit in executive power. Without such protection, he maintained that it would be impossible for policy makers in the executive branch to engage in open and frank discussion. The Court agreed with the President, as evidenced by its observation that "government . . . needs open but protected channels for the kind of plain talk that is essential to the quality of its functioning." Without the ability to keep internal communications confidential, members of the executive branch would be chilled in their discourse. If the risk of public disclosure had to be assumed, they would be less willing to assume the intellectual risks necessary for dynamic and fully reasoned policy making. Although not disagreeing with this premise, the Court ruled against the President with respect to his conceptualization of the privilege and its applicability in this case. Specifically, it rejected the contentions that (1) his claim was beyond the scope of judicial review and (2) executive privilege was an absolute barrier to the Court.

In rejecting the argument that the privilege claim was beyond its power of review, the Court restated the central premise of Marbury v. Madison—that the judiciary has the ultimate power to decide "what the law is." From the Court's perspective, "an absolute, unqualified privilege" would undermine significantly the "primary constitutional duty of the Judicial Branch to do justice in criminal prosecutions." Such an impediment "would plainly conflict with the function of the courts" under the Constitution. The Court, however, made a significant allowance for the presidency by finding that a presidential claim of confidentiality is presumptively privileged. What this determination means is that the chief executive could prevail upon a claim of privilege when a court finds that the interest of confidentiality outweighs the interests of the criminal justice system.

In striking this balance, the Court found that the privilege sought by President Nixon was based upon a very general claim that it was in "the public interest." The Court was unmoved by this argument at least for purposes of finding a basis for confidentiality: "[N]either the doctrine of separation of powers, nor the need for confidentiality of high-level communications, without more, can sustain an absolute, unqualified Presidential privilege of immunity from judicial process under all circumstances. The President's need for complete candor and objectivity from advisers calls for great deference from the courts. However, when the privilege depends solely on the broad, undifferentiated claim of public interest in the confidentiality of such conversations, a confrontation with other values arises. Absent a claim of need to protect military, diplomatic, or sensitive national security secrets, we find it difficult to accept the argument that even the very important interest in confidentiality of Presidential communications is significantly diminished by production of such material for *in camera* inspection with all the protection that a district court will be obliged to provide."

Given the criminal justice system's dependence upon pertinent and admissible evidence, the generalized interest in confidentiality was not sufficiently compelling. Another factor in support of the outcome was the judiciary's ability to review the materials privately and limit public disclosure only to those evidentiary materials relevant to the criminal proceeding. The President's interest thus was subordinated to "the legitimate needs of the judicial process."

The Court's ruling thus drew upon "the ancient proposition of law . . . 'that the public . . . has a right to every man's evidence.'" Although disfavoring operation of executive privilege in the specific instance, the interests of the chief executive were not entirely disregarded. Rather, the Court affirmed that the "confidentiality of Presidential communications has . . . constitutional underpinnings." It follows from this premise that the President may have a protected confidentiality interest when a court finds that, under the circumstances, the need for secrecy is compelling. The interests of the judicial process also may be diminished in settings outside the criminal justice system. In the context of civil litigation, when the parties represent private concerns, public interest may be less of a factor. The need for presidential participation also may abate when the evidence is relatively inconsequential and available from other sources. The balance tilts more against the President, however, insofar as the government is suing a private party. As in a criminal prosecution, there are fairness concerns if government can use the litigation process to its advantage by denying the other party access to relevant information.

Despite acknowledging the constitutional basis of a conditional presidential privilege, the ruling is most notable for reaffirming the power of judicial review. The *Nixon* case, like its landmark antecedent *Marbury v. Madison*, represented a constitutional clash between the President and judiciary. President Jefferson, when thrust into this showdown context, threatened to resist the Court. Contrary to this belligerent tone, President Nixon promptly complied with the Court's order to turn over documents and tapes. Shortly thereafter he resigned the presidency. Nearly a quarter of a century later, the Court revisited the issue of executive privilege in *Clinton v. Jones* (1997). In this case, President William Clinton argued that the "character of the office" justified postponement of a civil lawsuit until his term in office expired. Referencing its decision in *Nixon,* the Court rejected the claim that litigation would impose an unacceptable burden upon him and impair his performance in office. It also restated the proposition "that the President is subject to judicial process in appropriate circumstances."

## Mr. Chief Justice BURGER delivered the opinion of the Court.

. . . In the performance of assigned constitutional duties each branch of the Government must initially interpret the Constitution, and the interpretation of its powers by any branch is due great respect from the others. The President's counsel, as we have noted, reads the Constitution as providing an absolute privilege of confidentiality for all Presidential communications. . . .

In support of his claim of absolute privilege, the President's counsel urges two grounds, one of which is common to all governments and one of which is peculiar to our system of separation of powers. The first ground is the valid need for protection of communications between high Government officials and those who advise and assist them in the performance of their manifold duties; the importance of this confidentiality is too plain to require further discussion. Human experience teaches that those who expect public dissemination of their remarks may well temper candor with a concern for appearances and for their own interests to the detriment of the decisionmaking process. Whatever the nature of the privilege of confidentiality of Presidential communications in the exercise of Art. II powers, the privilege can be said to derive from the supremacy of each branch within its own assigned area of constitutional duties. Certain powers and privileges flow from the nature of enumerated powers; the protection of the confidentiality of Presidential communications has similar constitutional underpinnings.

The second ground asserted by the President's counsel in support of the claim of absolute privilege rests on the doctrine of separation of powers. Here it is argued that the independence of the Executive Branch within its own sphere insulates a President from a judicial subpoena in an ongoing criminal prosecution, and thereby protects confidential Presidential communications.

However, neither the doctrine of separation of powers, nor the need for confidentiality of high-level communications, without more, can sustain an absolute, unqualified Presidential privilege of immunity from judicial process under all circumstances. The President's need for complete candor and objectivity from advisers calls for great deference from the courts. However, when the privilege depends solely on the broad, undifferentiated claim of public interest in the confidentiality of such conversations, a confrontation with other values arises. Absent a claim of need to protect military, diplomatic, or sensitive national security secrets, we find it difficult to accept the argument that even the very important interest in confidentiality of Presidential communications is significantly diminished by production of such material for in camera inspection with all the protection that a district court will be obliged to provide.

The impediment that an absolute, unqualified privilege would place in the way of the primary constitutional duty of the Judicial Branch to do justice in criminal prosecutions would plainly conflict with the function of the courts under Art. III. In designing the structure of our Government and dividing and allocating the sovereign power among three co-equal branches, the Framers of the Constitution sought to provide a comprehensive system, but the separate powers were not intended to operate with absolute independence.

To read the Art. II powers of the President as providing an absolute privilege as against a subpoena essential to enforcement of criminal statutes on no more than a generalized claim of the public interest in confidentiality of nonmilitary and nondiplomatic discussions would upset the constitutional balance of 'a workable government' and gravely impair the role of the courts under Art. III . . . .

Since we conclude that the legitimate needs of the judicial process may outweigh Presidential privilege, it is necessary to resolve those competing interests in a manner that preserves the essential functions of each branch. The expectation of a President to the confidentiality of his conversations and correspondence, like the claim of confidentiality of judicial deliberations, for example, has all the values to which we accord deference for the privacy of all citizens and, added to those values, is the necessity for protection of the public interest in candid, objective, and even blunt or harsh opinions in Presidential decisionmaking. A President and those who assist him must be free to explore alternatives in the process of shaping policies and making decisions and to do so in a way many would be unwilling to express except privately. These are the considerations justifying a presumptive privilege for Presidential communications. The privilege is fundamental to the operation of Government and inextricably rooted in the separation of powers under the Constitution. But this presumptive privilege must be considered in light of our historic commitment to the rule of law. This is nowhere more profoundly manifest than in our view that 'the twofold aim (of criminal justice) is that guilt shall not escape or innocence suffer.' We have elected to employ an adversary system of criminal justice in which the parties contest all issues before a court of law. The need to develop all relevant facts in the adversary system is both fundamental and comprehensive. The ends of criminal justice would be defeated if judgments were to be founded on a partial or speculative presentation of the facts. The very integrity of the judicial system and public confidence in the system depend on full disclosure of all the facts, within the framework of the rules of evidence. To ensure that justice is done, it is imperative to the function of courts that compulsory process be available for the production of evidence needed either by the prosecution or by the defense. . . .

In this case the President challenges a subpoena served on him as a third party requiring the production of materials for use in a criminal prosecution; he does so on the claim that he has a privilege against disclosure of confidential communications. He does not place his claim of privilege on the ground they are military or diplomatic secrets. As to these areas of Art. II duties the courts have traditionally shown the utmost deference to Presidential responsibilities. . . .

No case of the Court, however, has extended this high degree of deference to a President's generalized interest in confidentiality. Nowhere in the Constitution, as we have noted earlier, is there any explicit reference to a privilege of confidentiality, yet to the extent this interest relates to the effective discharge of a President's powers, it is constitutionally based. The right to the production of all evidence at a criminal trial similarly has constitutional dimensions. The Sixth Amendment explicitly confers upon every defendant in a criminal trial the right 'to be confronted with the witnesses against him' and 'to have compulsory process for obtaining witnesses in his favor. Moreover, the Fifth Amendment also guarantees that no person shall be deprived of liberty without due process of law. It is the manifest duty of the courts to vindicate those guarantees, and to accomplish that it is essential that all relevant and admissible evidence be produced.

In this case we must weigh the importance of the general privilege of confidentiality of Presidential communications in performance of the President's responsibilities against the inroads of such a privilege on the fair administration of criminal justice. The interest in preserving confidentiality is weighty indeed and entitled to great respect. However, we cannot conclude that advisers will be moved to temper the candor of their remarks by the infrequent occasions of disclosure because of the possibility that such conversations will be called for in the context of a criminal prosecution. On the other hand, the allowance of the privilege to withhold evidence that is demonstrably relevant in a criminal trial would cut deeply into the guarantee of due process of law and gravely impair the basic function of the courts. . . . We conclude that when the ground for asserting privilege as to subpoenaed materials sought for use in a criminal trial is based only on the generalized interest in confidentiality, it cannot prevail over the fundamental demands of due process of law in the fair administration of criminal justice. The generalized assertion of privilege must yield to the demonstrated, specific need for evidence in a pending criminal trial.

## Bibliography

Berger, Raoul. *Executive Privilege: A Constitutional Myth.* Cambridge, MA: Harvard University Press, 1974.

Cox, Archibald. "Executive Privilege." *University of Pennsylvania Law Review* 122 (1974): 1383.

Lane, Eric, and Frederick A.O. Schwarz. "Too Big a Canon in the President's Arsenal: Another Look at United States v. Nixon." *George Mason Law Review* 17 (2010): 737.

Warren, Charles. *The Making of the Constitution.* Boston, MA: Little, Brown and Company, 1937.

# Chapter 2

# The Power of the President

The boundaries of presidential authority initially were tested in *Marbury v. Madison* (1803), when the Court determined that not even the chief executive was beyond its power "to say what the law is." The *Marbury* decision, like the Court's ruling in *United States v. Nixon* (1974), drew a line between presidential and judicial power.

Turf issues also have arisen between the President and Congress. In *Youngstown Sheet and Tube Co. v. Sawyer* (1952), the Court ruled against President Truman's seizure of the steel industry. The President had justified his action on grounds that it was essential for successful execution of the Korean War. The Court determined that, absent any specific constitutional provision or congressional authorization, the President had exceeded his authority. In *Dames and Moore v. Regan* (1981), the Court revisited the boundaries between the President and Congress. This case concerned the resolution of a conflict between the United States and Iran and provided more flexibility for the chief executive to act in foreign affairs. The President's power to appoint officers of the United States was examined in *Morrison v. Olson* (1988), when the Court upheld congressional authority to appoint independent counsel to investigate and prosecute government misconduct. The post-9/11 war on terror brought new questions about executive power.

Executive authority to detain "enemy combatants" was the issue in *Hamdi v. Rumsfeld* (2004). In this case, the Court determined that an American citizen in an allegedly "enemy" relationship with the United States could not be detained through the duration of a war without due process. An uneasy relationship developed between the Court and Congress, particularly over the rights of enemy combatants held at Guantanamo Bay. In 2005 Congress passed the Detainee Treatment Act, which provided that federal courts could not hear writs of habeas corpus by "enemy combatants." However, in *Hamdan v. Rumsfeld* (2006), the Court held that the Detainee Treatment Act did not apply retroactively to those held in custody prior to the Act's enactment.

In response to *Hamdan*, Congress passed the Military Commission Act, which provided that noncitizens held as enemy combatants could not have access to federal courts, except in the limited circumstance where a military proceeding had occurred, in which case the detainee could seek review of its decision in the U.S. Court of Appeals for the District of Columbia. The back and forth continued with the Court's ruling in *Boumediene v. Bush* (2008). In *Boumediene*, the Court, in a 5-4 decision, ruled that the writ of habeas corpus could only be suspended in times of rebellion or invasion, and that neither of those conditions existed at the time to justify Congress's action.

## Dames and Moore v. Regan

> **Citation: 453 U.S. 654.**
>
> **Issue: The scope of presidential power to make law in the context of an infringement of individual property rights.**
>
> **Year of Decision: 1981.**
>
> **Outcome: The scope of presidential powers depends on an assessment of a variety of factors including the President's explicit powers and those powers delegated to the President by Congress.**
>
> **Author of Opinion: Justice William Rehnquist.**
>
> **Vote: 8-1.**

Relying on eighteenth-century European political philosophy, the framers of the United States Constitution created a system of divided powers. Influenced by the adage that power corrupts, and absolute power corrupts absolutely, the framers chose to divide power between three separate and independent branches of government (the legislative, the executive, and the judicial). The framers hoped that the three branches would compete with each other for power and would thereby limit the power of the other branches. As the Court put it in *Mistretta v. United States* (1989), the Constitution created "a carefully crafted system of checked and balanced power within each Branch [to avoid tyranny in a Branch]."

The concepts of separated powers, and of "checked and balanced" power, are reflected in various provisions of the Constitution. Even though Congress has the power to pass legislation, a bill does not become law unless it is signed by the President (or unless a presidential veto is overridden by a supermajority). In the area of foreign affairs, whereas the President is given broad authority over foreign affairs and is denominated as the commander in chief of the armed forces, Congress is given the power to regulate foreign commerce, to spend money to raise armies, to declare wars, and to consent to treaties.

The clash between the President's power and Congress's power over foreign affairs has played out in several dramatic cases. One of the most famous cases, *Youngstown Sheet and Tube Co. v. Sawyer* (1952), arose during the Korean War. Facing a strike at United States steel mills, President Truman seized them in order to preserve the continuity of steel production during the war. The President claimed that a national emergency existed because "steel is an indispensable component of substantially all of such weapons and materials." Truman declared that "to assure the continued availability of steel and steel products during the existing emergency, it is necessary that the United States take possession of and operate the [steel] plants."

In an opinion by Justice Hugo Black, the Court concluded that President Truman had acted illegally. Viewing the President's power formalistically, the Court concluded that the President was required to point to "express constitutional language" supporting his right to seize the mills. In other words, the President's power, if any, to issue the order must stem either from an act of Congress or from the Constitution itself. Since no constitutional provision explicitly authorized the seizure, the authority could not be implied. The Court rejected the argument that the President's explicit powers included his obligation to "take Care that the Laws be faithfully executed" and his power as "Commander in Chief of the Army and Navy of the United States." The Court ultimately concluded that the "Founders of this Nation entrusted the law making power to the Congress alone in both good and bad times. [T]his seizure order cannot stand."

The Court departed from Youngstown's formalistic approach in *Dames and Moore v. Regan.* In this case, which arose after Iranian students had held Americans hostage for more than a year, President Carter entered into an executive agreement with Iran that obtained the hostages' release. The agreement provided that attachments and liens on Iranian assets in the United States would be nullified, and those assets would be transferred to Iran. The agreement also provided for a suspension of claims against Iran and presentation of those claims to an International Claims Tribunal. After the Executive Agreement was finalized, the Treasury Department promulgated a regulation providing that "[u]nless licensed or authorized . . . any attachment, judgment, decree, lien, execution, garnishment, or other judicial process is null and void with respect to any property in which on or since [November 14, 1979,] there existed an interest of Iran."

The case arose when Dames and Moore challenged the Executive Agreement and the regulation. Dames and Moore claimed that it was a beneficiary under a contract to conduct site studies for a proposed nuclear power plant in Iran and sought damages for services provided as well as interest. Although the trial court entered orders of attachment, the regulation required disallowance of the claim.

Had the Court applied Youngstown's more formalistic view of presidential power, it should have struck down the Executive Agreement and the regulation because the President's actions were not explicitly authorized. Instead, eschewing Youngstown's formalistic approach to presidential power, the Court relied on Justice Robert Jackson's concurring opinion in Youngstown. In that concurrence, Justice Jackson articulated a flexible approach to presidential power that focused on the relationship between the President and Congress. When the President acts pursuant to express or implied congressional authorization, "the President's power is at its zenith because he exercises both his own power and Congress' power." In such a situation, the President's action "would be supported by the strongest presumptions and the widest latitude of judicial interpretation, and the burden of persuasion would rest heavily upon any who might attack it." By contrast, when the President acts without congressional authorization, he enters "a zone of twilight in which he and Congress may have concurrent authority, or in which its distribution is uncertain." In this second situation, the analysis is more complex, and "the validity of the President's action, at least so far as separation-of-powers principles are concerned, hinges on a consideration of all the circumstances which might shed light on the views of the Legislative Branch toward such action, including 'congressional inertia, indifference or acquiescence.'" Finally, when the President acts contrary to Congress's will, "his power is at its lowest ebb," and the Court "can sustain his actions 'only by disabling the Congress from acting upon the subject.'"

In *Dames and Moore,* President Carter asserted that his authority to nullify attachments fit within Justice Jackson's first category because he was acting with congressional authorization. President Carter relied on a federal statute that allowed him to "investigate, regulate, direct and compel, nullify, void, prevent or prohibit, any acquisition, holding, withholding, use, transfer, withdrawal, transportation, importation or exportation of, or dealing in, or exercising any right, power, or privilege with respect to, or transactions involving, any property in which any foreign country or a national thereof has any interest; by any person, or with respect to any property, subject to the jurisdiction of the United States."

In accepting President Carter's argument, the Court concluded that, because "the President's action in nullifying the attachments and ordering the transfer of the assets was taken pursuant to specific congressional authorization," it was "supported by the strongest of presumptions and the widest latitude of judicial interpretation, and the burden of persuasion would rest heavily upon any who might attack it." As a result, the Court concluded that, "[u]nder the circumstances of this case, we cannot say that petitioner has sustained that heavy burden."

The Court also upheld the President's authority to suspend pending claims in United States courts. Although Congress did not explicitly authorize the suspension, Congress arguably approved it when it enacted the *International Claims Settlement Act of 1949.* Congress had amended the *International Claims Settlement Act* to provide for its application to settlement agreements, and the Court viewed this fact as demonstrating Congress's acceptance of the President's claim authority. The Court concluded that "[i]n light of . . . the inferences to be drawn from the character of the legislation Congress has enacted in the area, such as the IEEPA and the Hostage Act, and from the history of acquiescence in executive claims settlement—we conclude that the President was authorized to suspend pending claims pursuant to Executive Order No. 12294. *Dames and Moore* is one of those landmark decisions that reshape the Court's approach to a constitutional problem. The decision rejected *Youngstown's* more formalistic approach to presidential power and substituted a flexible approach that examines both congressional and presidential action. The net result was an expansion of presidential power. No longer must the President point to a specific constitutional provision that explicitly authorizes his actions. Moreover, especially when Congress has explicitly or implicitly signaled its assent to the presidential actions, the President can rely on both his constitutional prerogatives and Congress's as well.

## Mr. Justice REHNQUIST delivered the opinion of the Court.

. . . When the President acts pursuant to an express or implied authorization from Congress, he exercises not only his powers but also those delegated by Congress. In such a case the executive action "would be supported by the strongest of presumptions and the widest latitude of judicial interpretation, and the burden of persuasion would rest heavily upon any who might attack it." When the President acts in the absence of congressional authorization he may enter "a zone of twilight in which he and Congress may have concurrent authority, or in which its distribution is uncertain." In such a case the analysis becomes more complicated, and the validity of the President's action, at least so far as separation-of-powers principles are concerned, hinges on a consideration of all the circumstances which might shed light on the views of the Legislative Branch toward such action, including "congressional inertia, indifference or quiescence." Finally, when the President acts in contravention of the will of Congress, "his power is at its lowest ebb," and the Court can sustain his actions "only by disabling the Congress from acting upon the subject."

Because the President's action in nullifying the attachments and ordering the transfer of the assets was taken pursuant to specific congressional authorization, it is "supported by the strongest of presumptions and the widest latitude of judicial interpretation, and the burden of persuasion would rest heavily upon any who might attack it. Under the circumstances of this case, we cannot say that petitioner has sustained that heavy burden. A contrary ruling would mean that the Federal Government as a whole lacked the power exercised by the President, and that we are not prepared to say.

Although we have concluded that the IEEPA constitutes specific congressional authorization to the President to nullify the attachments and order the transfer of Iranian assets, there remains the question of the President's authority to suspend claims pending in American courts. We conclude that although the IEEPA authorized the nullification of the attachments, it cannot be read to authorize the suspension of the claims. The claims of American citizens against Iran are not in themselves transactions involving Iranian property or efforts to exercise any rights with respect to such property. An *in personam* lawsuit, although it might eventually be reduced to judgment and that judgment might be executed upon, is an effort to establish liability and fix damages and does not focus on any particular property within the jurisdiction. The terms of the IEEPA therefore do not authorize the President to suspend claims in American courts. This is the view of all the courts which have considered the question.

Although we have declined to conclude that the IEEPA or the Hostage Act directly authorizes the President's suspension of claims for the reasons noted, we cannot ignore the general tenor of Congress' legislation in this area in trying to determine whether the President is acting alone or at least with the acceptance of Congress. . . . At least this is so where there is no contrary indication of legislative intent and when, as here, there is a history of congressional acquiescence in conduct of the sort engaged in by the President. . . .

In addition to congressional acquiescence in the President's power to settle claims, prior cases of this Court have also recognized that the President does have some measure of power to enter into executive agreements without obtaining the advice and consent of the Senate. . . .

In light of all of the foregoing—the inferences to be drawn from the character of the legislation Congress has enacted in the area, such as the IEEPA and the Hostage Act, and from the history of acquiescence in executive claims settlement—we conclude that the President was authorized to suspend pending claims pursuant to Executive Order No. 12294. . . .

Finally, we re-emphasize the narrowness of our decision. We do not decide that the President possesses plenary power to settle claims, even as against foreign governmental entities. As the Court of Appeals for the First Circuit stressed, "[t]he sheer magnitude of such a power, considered against the background of the diversity and complexity of modern international trade, cautions against any broader construction of authority than is necessary." But where, as here, the settlement of claims has been determined to be a necessary incident to the resolution of a major foreign policy dispute between our country and another, and where, as here, we can conclude that Congress acquiesced in the President's action, we are not prepared to say that the President lacks the power to settle such claims.

## Justice STEVENS, concurring in part.

In my judgment the possibility that requiring this petitioner to prosecute its claim in another forum will constitute an unconstitutional "taking" is so remote that I would not address the jurisdictional question considered in Part V of the Court's opinion. However, I join the remainder of the opinion.

## Justice POWELL, concurring and dissenting in part.

I join the Court's opinion except its decision that the nullification of the attachments did not effect a taking of property interests giving rise to claims for just compensation. The nullification of attachments presents a separate question from whether the suspension and proposed settlement of claims against Iran may constitute a taking. I would leave both "taking" claims open for resolution on a case-by-case basis in actions before the Court of Claims. The facts of the hundreds of claims pending against Iran are not known to this Court and may differ from the facts in this case. I therefore dissent from the Court's decision with respect to attachments. The decision may well be erroneous, and it certainly is premature with respect to many claims.

I agree with the Court's opinion with respect to the suspension and settlement of claims against Iran and its instrumentalities. The opinion makes clear that some claims may not be adjudicated by the Claims Tribunal and that others may not be paid in full. The Court holds that parties whose valid claims are not adjudicated or not fully paid may bring a "taking" claim against the United States in the Court of Claims, the jurisdiction of which this Court acknowledges. The Government must pay just compensation when it furthers the Nation's foreign policy goals by using as "bargaining chips" claims lawfully held by a relatively few persons and subject to the jurisdiction of our courts. The extraordinary powers of the President and Congress upon which our decision rests cannot, in the circumstances of this case, displace the Just Compensation Clause of the Constitution.

## Bibliography

Bradley, Curtis A., and Trevor W. Morrison. "Presidential Power, Historical Practice, and Legal Constraint." *Columbia Law Review* 113 (2013): 1097.

Morrison, Alan B. "The Sounds of Silence: the Irrelevance of Congressional Inaction in Separation of Powers Litigation." *George Washington Law Review* 81 (2013): 1211.

Tribe, Laurence H. "Taking Text and Structure Seriously." *Harvard Law Review* 108 (1995): 1221.

Yoo, John C. "Laws as Treaties: The Constitutionality of Congressional-Executive Agreements." *Michigan Law Review* 99 (2001): 757.

## *Morrison v. Olson*

**Citation: 487 U.S. 654.**

**Issue: Whether an independent counsel, whose role is to investigate government misconduct, is an "officer" of the United States and thus appointable only by the President.**

**Year of Decision: 1988.**

**Outcome: An independent counsel is an "inferior officer" and thus may be appointed by department heads or the judiciary.**

**Author of Opinion: Justice William Rehnquist.**

**Vote: 7-1.**

In drafting the United States Constitution, the framers divided power between three separate and independent branches of government, but also provided for overlapping and intertwined relation- ships between the three branches. Examples of this intertwinement are evident throughout the Constitution. The decision to enter into a treaty requires combined presidential and Senate action. Likewise, even though Congress is vested with the power to pass legislation, the President must approve it before the legislation becomes law (unless two-thirds of the Congress override the President's veto). As the Court observed in *Youngstown Sheet and Tube Co. v. Sawyer* (1952), "[w]hile the Constitution diffuses power the better to secure liberty, it also contemplates that practice will integrate the dispersed powers into a workable government. It enjoins upon its branches a separateness but interdependence, autonomy but reciprocity."

Under the appointments clause of the United States Constitution, the Constitution generally vests the appointment power in the President subject to the advice and consent of the Senate. The clause provides that the President "shall nominate, and by and with the Advice and Consent of the Senate, shall appoint . . . .all other Officers of the United States, whose Appointments are not herein otherwise provided for, and which shall be established by Law: but the Congress may by Law vest the Appointment of such inferior Officers, as they think proper, in the President alone, in the Courts of Law, or in the Heads of Departments" (U.S. Const., Art. II, s 2, cl. 2).

In general, the appointments clause has been construed to place the appointment power with the President. For example, in *Buckley v. Valeo* (1976), the Court struck down portions of the *Federal Election Campaign Act of 1971*, in which Congress established the Federal Election Commission (FEC) and vested it with the power to administer federal election laws. Congress provided that commissioners were to be appointed by the President (subject to confirmation by both houses of Congress), the President pro tempore of the Senate, and the Speaker of the United States House of Representatives. The Court concluded that "any appointee exercising significant authority pursuant to the laws of the United States is an 'Officer of the United States,' and must, therefore, be appointed by the President." The Court concluded that all of the FEC commissioners were "officers" because they exercised discretionary enforcement power.

The Court has construed the President's removal power similarly. In *Myers v. United States* (1925), the Court held that the President had the right, without Senate approval, to remove a postmaster. However, a decade later, in *Humphrey's Executor v. United States* (1935), the Court qualified *Myers* in holding that the President did not have discretionary authority to remove a Federal Trade commissioner. The Court held that a statutory provision, providing that the President could remove commissioners only "for inefficiency, neglect of duty, or malfeasance in office," was constitutional. The Court distinguished *Myers*, reaffirming its holding that "congressional participation in the removal of executive officers is unconstitutional."

*Morrison* arose in the wake of the Watergate break-in and cover-up that ultimately led to President Nixon's resignation. The Ethics in Government Act of 1978 provided for the appointment of an "independent counsel" with the authority to investigate, report, and prosecute governmental misconduct against the law. While a panel of three federal judges appointed independent counsels, the executive branch retained the removal power. This power was vested in the attorney general, who was required to show "good cause" for removal and report those reasons to the appointing judges.

In upholding the Ethics in Government Act's appointment provisions, *Morrison* held that the critical question is whether the independent counsel is an "officer" of the United States (in which case the President must retain the power to appoint) or is an "inferior officer." Under the appointments clause, Congress may vest the appointment of these "inferior officers" in the President alone, the heads of departments, or the Judiciary. The Court concluded that an independent counsel is an "inferior officer" of the United States. The Court did not attempt to draw a bright line between "officers" and "inferior officers," but it did offer four factors to use as helpful guides in making the distinction.

*Morrison* did not hold that Congress has unlimited power to vest the appointment power over "inferior federal officers" outside the Executive Branch. The Court suggested that it might invalidate such appointments if "there was some 'incongruity' between the functions normally performed by the courts and the performance of their duty to appoint." However, the Court held that independent counsel appointments did not raise these concerns.

Justice Antonin Scalia dissented, arguing that the independent counsel's function is essentially executive in nature "in the sense that they are law enforcement functions that typically have been undertaken by officials within the Executive Branch." As a result, he would have invalidated the statute because it reduced "the amount of control or supervision that the Attorney General and, through him, the President exercises over the investigation and prosecution of a certain class of alleged criminal activity."

*Morrison* is an important decision because it helps define the scope of the President's appointment power. While the President is vested with the power to appoint "officers" of the United States, *Morrison* makes it clear that Congress can vest the appointment of "inferior officers" in the courts.

### Mr. Chief Justice REHNQUIST delivered the opinion of the Court.

. . . The Appointments Clause of Article II reads as follows:

"[The President] shall nominate, and by and with the Advice and Consent of the Senate, shall appoint Ambassadors, other public Ministers and Consuls, Judges of the Supreme Court, and all other Officers of the United States, whose Appointments are not herein otherwise provided for, and which shall be established by Law: but the Congress may by Law vest the Appointment of such inferior Officers, as they think proper, in the President alone, in the Courts of Law, or in the Heads of Departments." The line between "inferior" and "principal" officers is one that is far from clear, and the Framers provided little guidance into where it should be drawn. . . . We need not attempt here to decide exactly where the line falls between the two types of officers, because in our view appellant clearly falls on the "inferior officer" side of that line. Several factors lead to this conclusion.

First, appellant is subject to removal by a higher Executive Branch official. Although appellant may not be "subordinate" to the Attorney General (and the President) insofar as she possesses a degree of independent discretion to exercise the powers delegated to her under the Act, the fact that she can be removed by the Attorney General indicates that she is to some degree "inferior" in rank and authority. Second, appellant is empowered by the Act to perform only certain, limited duties. An independent counsel's role is restricted primarily to investigation and, if appropriate, prosecution for certain federal crimes. . . .

Third, appellant's office is limited in jurisdiction. Not only is the Act itself restricted in applicability to certain federal officials suspected of certain serious federal crimes, but an independent counsel can only act within the scope of the jurisdiction that has been granted by the Special Division pursuant to a request by the Attorney General. Finally, appellant's office is limited in tenure. There is concededly no time limit on the appointment of a particular counsel. Nonetheless, the office of independent counsel is "temporary" in the sense that an independent counsel is appointed essentially to accomplish a single task, and when that task is over the office is terminated, either by the counsel herself or by action of the Special Division. Unlike other prosecutors, appellant has no ongoing responsibilities that extend beyond the accomplishment of the mission that she was appointed for and authorized by the Special Division to undertake. . . .

This does not, however, end our inquiry under the Appointments Clause. Appellees argue that even if appellant is an "inferior" officer, the Clause does not empower Congress to place the power to appoint such an officer outside the Executive Branch. They contend that the Clause does not contemplate congressional authorization of "interbranch appointments," in which an officer of one branch is appointed by officers of another branch. The relevant language of the Appointments Clause is worth repeating. It reads: ". . . but the Congress may by Law vest the Appointment of such inferior Officers, as they think proper, in the President alone, in the courts of Law, or in the Heads of Departments." On its face, the language of this "excepting clause" admits of no limitation on interbranch appointments. Indeed, the inclusion of "as they think proper" seems clearly to give Congress significant discretion to determine whether it is "proper" to vest the appointment of, for example, executive officials in the "courts of Law." . . .

We do not mean to say that Congress' power to provide for interbranch appointments of "inferior officers" is unlimited. . . . In this case, however, we do not think it impermissible for Congress to vest the power to appoint independent counsel in a specially created federal court. We thus disagree with the Court of Appeals' conclusion that there is an inherent incongruity about a court having the power to appoint prosecutorial officers. . . . Congress, of course, was concerned when it created the office of independent counsel with the conflicts of interest that could arise in situations when the Executive Branch is called upon to investigate its own high-ranking officers. If it were to remove the appointing authority from the Executive Branch, the most logical place to put it was in the Judicial Branch. In the light of the Act's provision making the judges of the Special Division ineligible to participate in any matters relating to an independent counsel they have appointed, we do not think that appointment of the independent counsel by the court runs afoul of the constitutional limitation on "incongruous" interbranch appointments.

## Justice SCALIA, dissenting.

It is the proud boast of our democracy that we have "a government of laws and not of men." Many Americans are familiar with that phrase; not many know its derivation. It comes from Part the First, Article XXX, of the Massachusetts Constitution of 1780, which reads in full as follows:

"In the government of this Commonwealth, the legislative department shall never exercise the executive and judicial powers, or either of them: The executive shall never exercise the legislative and judicial powers, or either of them: The judicial shall never exercise the legislative and executive powers, or either of them: to the end it may be a government of laws and not of men."

The Framers of the Federal Constitution similarly viewed the principle of separation of powers as the absolutely central guarantee of a just Government. In No. 47 of The Federalist, Madison wrote that "[n]o political truth is certainly of greater intrinsic value, or is stamped with the authority of more enlightened patrons of liberty." The Federalist No. 47 (hereinafter Federalist). Without a secure structure of separated powers, our Bill of Rights would be worthless, as are the bills of rights of many nations of the world that have adopted, or even improved upon, the mere words of ours.

The principle of separation of powers is expressed in our Constitution in the first section of each of the first three Articles. Article I, § 1, provides that "[a]ll legislative Powers herein granted shall be vested in a Congress of the United *698 States, which shall consist of a Senate and House of Representatives." Article III, § 1, provides that "[t]he judicial Power of the United States, shall be vested in one supreme Court, and in such inferior Courts as the Congress may from time to time ordain and establish." And the provision at issue here, Art. II, § 1, cl. 1, provides that "[t]he executive Power shall be vested in a President of the United States of America."

But just as the mere words of a Bill of Rights are not self-effectuating, the Framers recognized "[t]he insufficiency of a mere parchment delineation of the boundaries" to achieve the separation of powers. Federalist No. 73 (A. Hamilton). "[T]he great security," wrote Madison, "against a gradual concentration of the several powers in the same department consists in giving to those who administer each department the necessary constitutional means and personal motives to resist encroachments of the others. The provision for defense must in this, as in all other cases, be made commensurate to the danger of attack." Federalist No. 51. . . .

The major "fortification" provided, of course, was the veto power. But in addition to providing fortification, the Founders conspicuously and very consciously declined to sap the Executive's strength in the same way they had weakened the Legislature: by dividing the executive power. Proposals to have multiple executives, or a council of advisers with separate authority were rejected. Thus, while "[a]ll legislative Powers herein granted shall be vested in a Congress of the United States, which shall consist of a Senate *and* House of Representatives," U.S. Const., Art. I, § 1 (emphasis added), "[t]he executive Power shall be vested in *a President of the United States,*" Art. II, § 1, cl. 1 (emphasis added).

That is what this suit is about. Power. The allocation of power among Congress, the President, and the courts in such fashion as to preserve the equilibrium the Constitution sought to establish—so that "a gradual concentration of the several powers in the same department," Federalist No. 51, p. 321 (J. Madison), can effectively be resisted. Frequently an issue of this sort will come before the Court clad, so to speak, in sheep's clothing: the potential of the asserted principle to effect important change in the equilibrium of power is not immediately evident, and must be discerned by a careful and perceptive analysis. But this wolf comes as a wolf.

The present case began when the Legislative and Executive Branches became "embroiled in a dispute concerning the scope of the congressional investigatory power,"—as is often the case with such interbranch conflicts—became quite acrimonious. In the course of oversight hearings into the administration of the Superfund by the Environmental Protection Agency (EPA), two Subcommittees of the House of Representatives requested and then subpoenaed numerous internal EPA documents. The President responded by personally directing the EPA Administrator not to turn over certain of the documents, and by having the Attorney General notify the congressional Subcommittees of this assertion of executive privilege. In his decision to assert executive privilege, the President was counseled by appellee Olson, who was then Assistant Attorney General of the Department of Justice for the Office of Legal Counsel, a post that has traditionally had responsibility for providing legal advice to the President (subject to approval of the Attorney General). The House's response was to pass a resolution citing the EPA Administrator, who had possession of the documents, for contempt. Contempt of Congress is a criminal offense. The United States Attorney, however, a member of the Executive Branch, initially took no steps to prosecute the contempt citation. Instead, the Executive Branch sought the immediate assistance of the Third Branch by filing a civil action asking the District Court to declare that the EPA Administrator had acted lawfully in withholding the documents under a claim of executive privilege. The District Court declined (in my view correctly) to get involved in the controversy, and urged the other two branches to try "[c]ompromise and cooperation, rather than confrontation." After further haggling, the two branches eventually reached an agreement giving the House Subcommittees limited access to the contested documents. . . .

As a general matter, the Act before us here requires the Attorney General to apply for the appointment of an independent counsel within 90 days after receiving a request to do so, unless he determines within that period that "there are no reasonable grounds to believe that further investigation or prosecution is warranted." As a practical matter, it would be surprising if the Attorney General had any choice (assuming this statute is constitutional) but to seek appointment of an independent counsel to pursue the charges against the principal object of the congressional request, Mr. Olson. Merely the political consequences (to him and the President) of seeming to break the law by refusing to do so would have been substantial. How could it not be, the public would ask, that a 3,000–page indictment drawn by our representatives over 2 ½ years does not even establish "reasonable grounds to believe" that further investigation or prosecution is warranted with respect to at least the principal alleged culprit? But the Act establishes more than just practical compulsion. Although the Court's opinion asserts that the Attorney General had "no duty to comply with the [congressional] request," that is not entirely accurate. He *had* a duty to comply unless he could conclude that there were "*no reasonable grounds to believe,*" not that prosecution was warranted, but merely that "*further investigation*" was warranted, after a 90–day investigation in which he was prohibited from using such routine investigative techniques as grand juries, plea bargaining, grants of immunity, or even subpoenas. The Court also makes much of the fact that "the courts are specifically prevented from reviewing the Attorney General's decision not to seek appointment. Yes, but *Congress* is not prevented from reviewing it. The context of this statute is acrid with the smell of threatened impeachment. Where, as here, a request for appointment of an independent counsel has come from the Judiciary Committee of either House of Congress, the Attorney General must, if he decides not to seek appointment, explain to that Committee why.

Thus, by the application of this statute in the present case, Congress has effectively compelled a criminal investigation of a high-level appointee of the President in connection with his actions arising out of a bitter power dispute between the President and the Legislative Branch. Mr. Olson may or may not be guilty of a crime; we do not know. But we do know that the investigation of him has been commenced, not necessarily because the President or his authorized subordinates believe it is in the interest of the United States, in the sense that it warrants the diversion of resources from other efforts, and is worth the cost in money and in possible damage to other governmental interests; and not even, leaving aside those normally considered factors, because the President or his authorized subordinates necessarily believe that an investigation is likely to unearth a violation worth prosecuting; but only because the Attorney General cannot affirm, as Congress demands, that there are *no reasonable grounds to believe* that further investigation is warranted. The decisions regarding the scope of that further investigation, its duration, and, finally, whether or not prosecution should ensue, are likewise beyond the control of the President and his subordinates. . . .

## Bibliography

Croner, Andrew. "Morrison, Edmond, and the Power of Appointments," *George Washington Law Review* 77 (2009): 1002.

Fisher, Louis. *Constitutional Conflicts between the Congress and the President.* Lawrence, KS: University Press of Kansas, 1997.

Lessig, Lawrence, and Cass R. Sunstein. "The President and the Administration." *Columbia Law Review* 94 (1994): 1.

## Hamdi v. Rumsfeld

**Citation: 124 S.Ct. 2633.**

**Issue: Whether the military may detain a United States citizen on enemy soil as an enemy combatant without a hearing.**

**Year of Decision: 2004.**

**Outcome: A citizen cannot be held indefinitely without being given the opportunity to challenge the government's conclusion that he/she is an "enemy combatant."**

**Author of Opinion: Justice Sandra Day O'Connor.**

**Vote: 6-3.**

The terrorist attack on the World Trade Center buildings in 2001 triggered a rapid review and restructuring of national security. Consistent with historical experience when national security risks have been elevated, the role of the President became a focal point of debate. In this particular instance, a key issue was whether the President's power to combat terrorism included the authority to detain enemy combatants. Few doubted that the United States legitimately could take steps to improve security and to prevent future terrorist attacks.

Indeed, Congress responded to the attack by creating a new cabinet-level agency, the Department of Homeland Security, and enacting the *USA Patriot Act. Hamdi v. Rumsfeld* concerned another aspect of antiterrorism policy: whether a United States citizen, who was captured as an "enemy combatant" during the conflict in Afghanistan, could be detained indefinitely on American soil with no opportunity to challenge the legality of his detention.

Prior to *Hamdi,* the Court had rendered a number of decisions regarding governmental power to detain citizens during wartime. In *Ex parte Milligan* (1866), decided shortly after the Civil War, the Court limited governmental power by holding that United States military officers had improperly imprisoned United States citizens. By contrast, in *United States v. Korematsu* (1944), which arose during World War II, the Court adopted a more expansive view of federal power. In that case, the United States established military areas from which persons of Japanese ancestry were excluded and also provided for their detention and resettlement. Under this system, Fred Korematsu was ordered to report to a detention camp. When he refused to report, Korematsu was ultimately convicted of remaining in a military area from which persons of Japanese ancestry had been excluded. The Court upheld his conviction in a decision that was deferential to legislative authority. In another decision from the same era, *Ex Parte Quirin* (1942), the Court recognized broad presidential authority to treat enemy combatants differently. In that case, petitioners traveled by submarine across the Atlantic Ocean and landed on Long Island, New York, in the middle of the night. After they landed, they changed to civilian dress and buried their German military uniforms. After they were captured, the President appointed a military commission to try petitioners for offenses against the laws of war.

Decisions like *Korematsu* and *Ex Parte Quirin* were effectively overruled by a 1971 act, the *Non-Detention Act,* which limited the power of the President to detain individuals unless authorized by the legislative branch. Many believed that this act was passed to prohibit internment camps for citizens like the one in which Korematsu was detained.

*Hamdi's* inception can be traced to the terrorist assault on the World Trade Center and Pentagon in 2001. After that attack, Congress authorized the President to "use all necessary and appropriate force against those nations, organizations, or persons he determines planned, authorized, committed, or aided the terrorist attacks," as well as against any persons or groups that "harbored such organizations or persons." In addition, the President was given the power "to prevent any future acts of international terrorism against the United States by such nations, organizations or persons." The Act did not explicitly authorize the detention of persons. However, Congress also enacted the Authorization for Use of Military Force (AUMF), which gave the President the power to use all "necessary and appropriate force" against the al Qaeda terrorist network, the Taliban, and any nation harboring terrorists. In November 2001, the President issued an order directing the military to identify and detain "enemy combatants," those persons fighting for or supporting terrorist organizations opposing the United States.

Following United States intervention in Afghanistan and Iraq, the United States detained individuals that it believed to be members of the al Qaeda terrorist organization or the Taliban regime of Afghanistan. Within a short period of time, the United States held nearly 600 purported "enemy combatants" at the United States Naval Base located in Guantanamo Bay, Cuba. By labeling the detainees as "enemy combatants," the President endeavored to subject the detainees to a military process rather than a civilian process.

Yaser Esam Hamdi, a United States citizen who was born in the United States but who grew up in Saudi Arabia, was captured by United States military forces in Afghanistan and labeled an enemy combatant. At the time, he was fighting with the Taliban. Hamdi was first detained at Guantanamo Bay, but was later transferred to the continental United States where he was held without formal charges or access to counsel. Hamdi's father filed a habeas corpus petition challenging the government's right to hold his son without charges or an opportunity to rebut the charges.

In *Hamdi,* the United States Supreme Court held that the AUMF allowed the United States government to detain enemy combatants for the duration of the Afghanistan conflict. The Court recognized that the government has broad power to detain enemies during wartime. Otherwise, these "enemy combatants" might return to the battlefield and inflict injury on United States forces. As a result, the Court held that detention was an appropriate remedy: "detention of individuals falling into the limited category we are considering, for the duration of the particular conflict in which they were captured, is so fundamental and accepted an incident to war as to be an exercise of the 'necessary and appropriate force' Congress has authorized the President to use."

The Court then considered whether, despite the government's power, Hamdi was entitled to challenge the government's determination that he was an "enemy combatant." In other words, the government could not hold Hamdi indefinitely without the opportunity to challenge the designation concluding that the writ of habeas corpus has historically provided "a critical check on the Executive, ensuring that it does not detain individuals except in accordance with law." In reviewing the Act, the Court concluded that Congress assumed that habeas petitioners "would have some opportunity to present and rebut facts and that courts in cases like this retain some ability to vary the ways in which they do so as mandated by due process." In other words, Hamdi was entitled to contest the issue of whether he was an "enemy combatant."

However, the Court did not hold that alleged "enemy combatants" were entitled to "hearings" in the same sense as ordinary citizens. In assessing the process that was due Hamdi, the Court balanced a variety of factors and ultimately engaged in "an analysis of 'the risk of an erroneous deprivation' of the private interest if the process were reduced and the 'probable value, if any, of additional or substitute safeguards.'" In concluding that Hamdi was entitled to a hearing, the Court affirmed the "fundamental nature of a citizen's right to be free from involuntary confinement by his own government without due process of law," and balanced it against the "weighty and sensitive governmental interests in ensuring that those who have in fact fought with the enemy during a war do not return to battle against the United States." The Court concluded that a citizen-detainee must be given the opportunity to challenge his classification as an enemy combatant. As part of that challenge, the citizen must be given notice regarding the factual basis for his classification, and a fair opportunity to rebut the Government's factual assertions before a neutral decision maker.

Justice David Souter, joined by two other justices, concurred on the basis that Hamdi's detention was forbidden by federal law. Justice Scalia, joined by Justice John Stevens, dissented, arguing that, when the Government accuses a citizen of waging war against it, "our constitutional tradition has been to prosecute him in federal court for treason or some other crime." In his view, this tradition can be relaxed only as demanded by the exigencies of war and then only temporarily. "The very core of liberty secured by our Anglo-Saxon system of separated powers has been freedom from indefinite imprisonment at the will of the Executive. The gist of the Due Process Clause [was] to force the Government to follow those common-law procedures traditionally deemed necessary before depriving a person of life, liberty, or property. Where the citizen is captured outside and held outside the United States, the constitutional requirements may be different."

Justice Clarence Thomas, dissenting, argued that Hamdi's "detention falls squarely within the Federal Government's war powers, and we lack the expertise and capacity to second-guess that decision. As such, petitioners' *habeas corpus* challenge should fail."

*Hamdi* is an important decision because it rejects the notion that citizens can be detained on American soil without an opportunity to rebut the allegations against them. The constitutional requirement of due process demands that the citizen be informed of the allegations against him and be given an opportunity to rebut those allegations. Only if the court concludes that the government's allegations, that the citizen is an "enemy combatant," are sustained can the citizen be detained for the remainder of the conflict.

### Justice O'CONNOR announced the judgment of the Court, and delivered an opinion, in which CHIEF JUSTICE REHNQUIST, Justice KENNEDY, and Justice BREYER joined.

. . . We therefore hold that a citizen-detainee seeking to challenge his classification as an enemy combatant must receive notice of the factual basis for his classification, and a fair opportunity to rebut the Government's factual assertions before a neutral decisionmaker. . . .

These essential constitutional promises may not be eroded. At the same time, the exigencies of the circumstances may demand that, aside from these core elements, enemy-combatant proceedings may be tailored to alleviate their uncommon potential to burden the Executive at a time of ongoing military conflict. Hearsay, for example, may need to be accepted as the most reliable available evidence from the Government in such a proceeding. Likewise, the Constitution would not be offended by a presumption in favor of the Government's evidence, so long as that presumption remained a rebuttable one and fair opportunity for rebuttal were provided. Thus, once the Government puts forth credible evidence that the habeas petitioner meets the enemy-combatant criteria, the onus could shift to the petitioner to rebut that evidence with more persuasive evidence that he falls outside the criteria. A burden-shifting scheme of this sort would meet the goal of ensuring that the errant tourist, embedded journalist, or local aid worker has a chance to prove military error while giving due regard to the Executive once it has put forth meaningful support for its conclusion that the detainee is in fact an enemy combatant. In the words of *Mathews,* process of this sort would sufficiently address the "risk of an erroneous deprivation" of a detainee's liberty interest while eliminating certain procedures that have questionable additional value in light of the burden on the Government.

We think it unlikely that this basic process will have the dire impact on the central functions of warmaking that the Government forecasts. The parties agree that initial captures on the battlefield need not receive the process we have discussed here; that process is due only when the determination is made to *continue* to hold those who have been seized. The Government has made clear in its briefing that documentation regarding battlefield detainees already is kept in the ordinary course of military affairs. Any factfinding imposition created by requiring a knowledgeable affiant to summarize these records to an independent tribunal is a minimal one. Likewise, arguments that military officers ought not have to wage war under the threat of litigation lose much of their steam when factual disputes at enemy-combatant hearings are limited to the alleged combatant's acts. This focus meddles little, if at all, in the strategy or conduct of war, inquiring only into the appropriateness of continuing to detain an individual claimed to have taken up arms against the United States. While we accord the greatest respect and consideration to the judgments of military authorities in matters relating to the actual prosecution of a war, and recognize that the scope of that discretion necessarily is wide, it does not infringe on the core role of the military for the courts to exercise their own time-honored and constitutionally mandated roles of reviewing and resolving claims like those presented here. . . .

In sum, while the full protections that accompany challenges to detentions in other settings may prove unworkable and inappropriate in the enemy-combatant setting, the threats to military operations posed by a basic system of independent review are not so weighty as to trump a citizen's core rights to challenge meaningfully the Government's case and to be heard by an impartial adjudicator.

## Mr. Justice THOMAS, dissenting.

The Executive Branch, acting pursuant to the powers vested in the President by the Constitution and with explicit congressional approval, has determined that Yaser Hamdi is an enemy combatant and should be detained. This detention falls squarely within the Federal Government's war powers, and we lack the expertise and capacity to second-guess that decision. As such, petitioners' habeas challenge should fail, and there is no reason to remand the case. The plurality reaches a contrary conclusion by failing adequately to consider basic principles of the constitutional structure as it relates to national security and foreign affairs and by using the balancing scheme of *Mathews v. Eldridge.* I do not think that the Federal Government's war powers can be balanced away by this Court. . . .

### Bibliography

Beery, Ryan H. "Modern Use of Military Tribunals: A Legal 'Can' and a Political 'Should'?" *Ohio Northern University Law Review* 28 (2002): 789.

Berkowitz, Peter. *Terrorism, the Laws of War, and the Constitution: Debating the Enemy Combatant Cases.* Stanford, CA: Hoover Institution, 2005.

Martinez, Jenny S. "Availability of U.S. Court to Review Decision to Hold U.S. Citizen as Enemy Combatant—Executive Power in War on Terror." *American Journal of International Law* 98 (2004): 782.

Nowak, John E., and Ronald D. Rotunda. *Principles of Constitutional Law.* St. Paul, MN: Thomson/West, 2004, 114–16.

## Hamdan v. Rumsfeld

**Citation: 548 U.S. 557.**

**Issue: Whether the military tribunal established to try terrorists for alleged war crimes in the War on Terror was authorized by the Congress or the inherent powers of the President.**

**Year of Decision: 2006.**

**Outcome: No. Neither an act of Congress nor the inherent Constitutional powers of the Executive expressly authorized these sorts of military tribunals.**

**Author of Opinion: John Paul Stevens.**

**Vote: 5-3.**

Unlike Yaser Hamdi, the plaintiff in *Hamdi v. Rumsfeld,* who was a United States citizen, Salim Ahmed Hamdan was a Yemeni national. He was also Osama bin Laden's former chauffeur. Like Hamdi, Hamdan was captured in Afghanistan while fighting for the Taliban against United States forces and imprisoned by the United States military in Guantanamo Bay. He filed a petition for a writ of habeas corpus in federal district court to challenge his detention. Before the district court ruled on his petition, a military tribunal designated him an enemy combatant.

Salim Hamdan faced a different legal landscape than did Yaser Hamdi because Congress had passed the Detainee Treatment Act (DTA) in 2005, partly in reaction to the *Hamdi* decision. The DTA appeared to deny detainees in Guantanamo any right to habeas corpus relief. Instead, military tribunals, where a defendant could be excluded during the presentation of evidence against him, were the only courts available to determine whether detainees were in fact enemy combatants. Accordingly, the Court in *Hamdan* confronted the question whether the military tribunal established to try Hamdan and others for alleged war crimes in the War on Terror was authorized by the Congress or the inherent powers of the President.

The Supreme Court, in a 5-to-3 decision, held that neither an act of Congress (including the DTA) nor the inherent Constitutional powers of the Executive expressly authorized these sorts of military tribunals. In addition, the Court ruled that the tribunals violated certain provisions of the Geneva Conventions. Finally, the Court held that Hamdan had not been charged with a violation of the "law of war," but rather with an ordinary crime (conspiracy). Because Hamdan had been charged with an ordinary crime, he was entitled to habeas corpus relief in an Article III court of law. The Court further argued that it was fully aware of the danger individuals like Hamdan posed to innocent civilians, but that upholding the rule of law could deal with the danger.

### Justice STEVENS announced the judgment of the Court, and delivered the opinion of the Court.

. . .The Court of Appeals relied on [our earlier decision] *Johnson v. Eisentrager,* to hold that Hamdan could not invoke the Geneva Conventions to challenge the Government's plan to prosecute him in accordance with Commission Order No. 1. *Eisentrager* involved a challenge by 21 German nationals to their 1945 convictions for war crimes by a military tribunal convened in Nanking, China, and to their subsequent imprisonment in occupied Germany. The petitioners argued, *inter alia,* that the 1929 Geneva Convention rendered illegal some of the procedures employed during their trials, which they said deviated impermissibly from the procedures used by courts-martial to try American soldiers. We rejected that claim on the merits because the petitioners (unlike Hamdan here) had failed to identify any prejudicial disparity "between the Commission that tried [them] and those that would try an offending soldier of the American forces of like rank," and in any event could claim no protection, under the 1929 Geneva Convention, during trials for crimes that occurred before their confinement as prisoners of war.

Buried in a footnote of the opinion, however, is this curious statement suggesting that the Court lacked power even to consider the merits of the Geneva Convention argument:

"We are not holding that these prisoners have no right which the military authorities are bound to respect. The United States, by the Geneva Convention of July 27, 1929, 47 Stat.2021, concluded with forty-six other countries, including the German Reich, an agreement upon the treatment to be accorded captives. These prisoners claim to be and are entitled to its protection. It is, however, the obvious scheme of the Agreement that responsibility for observance and enforcement of these rights is upon political and military authorities. Rights of alien enemies are vindicated under it only through protests and intervention of protecting powers as the rights of our citizens against foreign governments are vindicated only by Presidential intervention."

The Court of Appeals, on the strength of this footnote, held that "the 1949 Geneva Convention does not confer upon Hamdan a right to enforce its provisions in court."

Whatever else might be said about the *Eisentrager* footnote, it does not control this case. We may assume that "the obvious scheme" of the 1949 Conventions is identical in all relevant respects to that of the 1929 Geneva Convention, and even that that scheme would, absent some other provision of law, preclude Hamdan's invocation of the Convention's provisions as an independent source of law binding the Government's actions and furnishing petitioner with any enforceable right. For, regardless of the nature of the rights conferred on Hamdan, they are, as the Government does not dispute, part of the law of war. And compliance with the law of war is the condition upon which the authority set forth in Article 21 is granted.

For the Court of Appeals, acknowledgment of that condition was no bar to Hamdan's trial by commission. As an alternative to its holding that Hamdan could not invoke the Geneva Conventions at all, the Court of Appeals concluded that the Conventions did not in any event apply to the armed conflict during which Hamdan was captured. The court accepted the Executive's assertions that Hamdan was captured in connection with the United States' war with al Qaeda and that that war is distinct from the war with the Taliban in Afghanistan. It further reasoned that the war with al Qaeda evades the reach of the Geneva Conventions. We, like Judge Williams, disagree with the latter conclusion. . . .

We need not decide the merits of this argument because there is at least one provision of the Geneva Conventions that applies here even if the relevant conflict is not one between signatories. Article 3, often referred to as Common Article 3 because, like Article 2, it appears in all four Geneva Conventions, provides that in a "conflict not of an international character occurring in the territory of one of the High Contracting Parties, each Party to the conflict shall be bound to apply, as a minimum," certain provisions protecting "[p]ersons taking no active part in the hostilities, including members of armed forces who have laid down their arms and those placed *hors de combat* by ... detention." One such provision prohibits "the passing of sentences and the carrying out of executions without previous judgment pronounced by a regularly constituted court affording all the judicial guarantees which are recognized as indispensable by civilized peoples." . . .

Although the official commentaries accompanying Common Article 3 indicate that an important purpose of the provision was to furnish minimal protection to rebels involved in one kind of "conflict not of an international character," *i.e.,* a civil war, the commentaries also make clear "that the scope of application of the Article must be as wide as possible," In fact, limiting language that would have rendered Common Article 3 applicable "especially [to] cases of civil war, colonial conflicts, or wars of religion," was omitted from the final version of the Article, which coupled broader scope of application with a narrower range of rights than did earlier proposed iterations.

Common Article 3, then, is applicable here and, as indicated above, requires that Hamdan be tried by a "regularly constituted court affording all the judicial guarantees which are recognized as indispensable by civilized peoples." While the term "regularly constituted court" is not specifically defined in either Common Article 3 or its accompanying commentary, other sources disclose its core meaning. . . .

The Government offers only a cursory defense of Hamdan's military commission in light of Common Article 3. As Justice KENNEDY explains, that defense fails because "[t]he regular military courts in our system are the courts-martial established by congressional statutes." At a minimum, a military commission "can be 'regularly constituted' by the standards of our military justice system only if some practical need explains deviations from court-martial practice." As we have explained, no such need has been demonstrated here.

Inextricably intertwined with the question of regular constitution is the evaluation of the procedures governing the tribunal and whether they afford "all the judicial guarantees which are recognized as indispensable by civilized peoples." Like the phrase "regularly constituted court," this phrase is not defined in the text of the Geneva Conventions. But it must be understood to incorporate at least the barest of those trial protections that have been recognized by customary international law. . . .

We agree with Justice KENNEDY that the procedures adopted to try Hamdan deviate from those governing courts-martial in ways not justified by any "evident practical need," and for that reason, at least, fail to afford the requisite guarantees. We add only that, various provisions of Commission Order No. 1 dispense with the principles, articulated in Article 75 and indisputably part of the customary international law, that an accused must, absent disruptive conduct or consent, be present for his trial and must be privy to the evidence against him. That the Government has a compelling interest in denying Hamdan access to certain sensitive information is not doubted. But, at least absent express statutory provision to the contrary, information used to convict a person of a crime must be disclosed to him.

Common Article 3 obviously tolerates a great degree of flexibility in trying individuals captured during armed conflict; its requirements are general ones, crafted to accommodate a wide variety of legal systems. But *requirements* they are nonetheless. The commission that the President has convened to try Hamdan does not meet those requirements.

We have assumed, as we must, that the allegations made in the Government's charge against Hamdan are true. We have assumed, moreover, the truth of the message implicit in that charge—viz., that Hamdan is a dangerous individual whose beliefs, if acted upon, would cause great harm and even death to innocent civilians, and who would act upon those beliefs if given the opportunity. It bears emphasizing that Hamdan does not challenge, and we do not today address, the Government's power to detain him for the duration of active hostilities in order to prevent such harm. But in undertaking to try Hamdan and subject him to criminal punishment, the Executive is bound to comply with the rule of law that prevails in this jurisdiction.

The judgment of the Court of Appeals is reversed, and the case is remanded for further proceedings.

### Justice THOMAS, with whom Justice SCALIA joins, and with whom Justice ALITO joins in all but Parts I, II–C–1, and III–B–2, dissenting.

For the reasons set forth in Justice SCALIA's dissent, it is clear that this Court lacks jurisdiction to entertain petitioner's claims. The Court having concluded otherwise, it is appropriate to respond to the Court's resolution of the merits of petitioner's claims because its opinion openly flouts our well-established duty to respect the Executive's judgment in matters of military operations and foreign affairs. The plurality's evident belief that *it* is qualified to pass on the "military necessity," of the Commander in Chief's decision to employ a particular form of force against our enemies is so antithetical to our constitutional structure that it simply cannot go unanswered. I respectfully dissent.

Our review of petitioner's claims arises in the context of the President's wartime exercise of his Commander in Chief authority in conjunction with the complete support of Congress. Accordingly, it is important to take measure of the respective roles the Constitution assigns to the three branches of our Government in the conduct of war.

As I explained in *Hamdi v. Rumsfeld,* the structural advantages attendant to the Executive Branch—namely, the decisiveness, " 'activity, secrecy, and dispatch'" that flow from the Executive's " 'unity,' " (quoting The Federalist No. 70) (A.Hamilton))—led the Founders to conclude that the "President ha[s] primary responsibility—along with the necessary power—to protect the national security and to conduct the Consistent with this conclusion, the Constitution vests in the President "[t]he executive Power," Art. II, § 1, provides that he "shall be Commander in Chief" of the Armed Forces, § 2, and places in him the power to recognize foreign governments, § 3. This Court has observed that these provisions confer upon the President broad constitutional authority to protect the Nation's security in the manner he deems fit.

Congress, to be sure, has a substantial and essential role in both foreign affairs and national security. But "Congress cannot anticipate and legislate with regard to every possible action the President may find it necessary to take or every possible situation in which he might act," and "[s]uch failure of Congress ... does not, 'especially ... in the areas of foreign policy and national security,' imply 'congressional disapproval' of action taken by the Executive." *Dames & Moore v. Regan.* In these domains, the fact that Congress has provided the President with broad authorities does not imply—and the Judicial Branch should not infer—that Congress intended to deprive him of particular powers not specifically enumerated.

When "the President acts pursuant to an express or implied authorization from Congress," his actions are " 'supported by the strongest of presumptions and the widest latitude of judicial interpretation, and the burden of persuasion ... rest[s] heavily upon any who might attack it.'" Accordingly, in the very context that we address today, this Court has concluded that "the detention and trial of petitioners—ordered by the President in the declared exercise of his powers as Commander in Chief of the Army in time of war and of grave public danger—are not to be set aside by the courts without the clear conviction that they are in conflict with the Constitution or laws of Congress constitutionally enacted."

Under this framework, the President's decision to try Hamdan before a military commission for his involvement with al Qaeda is entitled to a heavy measure of deference. In the present conflict, Congress has authorized the President "to use all necessary and appropriate force against those nations, organizations, or persons *he determines* planned, authorized, committed, or aided the terrorist attacks that occurred on September 11, 2001 ... in order to prevent any future acts of international terrorism against the United States by such nations, organizations or persons." As a plurality of the Court observed in *Hamdi,* the "capture, detention, and *trial* of unlawful combatants, by 'universal agreement and practice,' are 'important incident[s] of war,' " and are therefore "an exercise of the 'necessary and appropriate force' Congress has authorized the President to use," *Hamdi's* observation that military commissions are included within the AUMF's authorization is supported by this Court's previous recognition that "[a]n important incident to the conduct of war is the adoption of measures by the military commander, not only to repel and defeat the enemy, but to seize and subject to disciplinary measures those enemies who, in their attempt to thwart or impede our military effort, have violated the law of war." . . .

## Bibliography

Kmiec, Douglas W. "The Separation of Powers: Hamdan v. Rumsfeld—The Anti-Roberts." *Pepperdine Law Review* 34 (2006–2007): 573.

Rudko, Frances Howell. "Searching for Remedial Paradigms: Human Rights in the Age of Terrorism." *University of Massachusetts Roundtable Symposium Law Journal* 5 (2010): 116.

Shamir-Borer, Eran. "Revisiting Hamdan v. Rumsfeld's Analysis of the Laws of Armed Conflict." *Emory International Law Review* 21 (2007): 601.

## *Boumediene v. Bush*

**Citation: 553 U.S. 723.**

**Issue: Whether Suspected Terrorists held at Guantanamo Bay may be denied habeas corpus relief in federal courts.**

**Year of Decision: 2008.**

*(Continued)*

**Outcome: No. The Constitution provides habeas corpus relief to detainees, except in times of rebellion or invasion.**
**Author of Opinion: Anthony Kennedy.**
**Vote: 5-4.**

Just as it had reacted to the *Hamdi* case by passing the Detainee Treatment Act, Congress now reacted to the *Hamdan* case by passing the Military Commission Act (MCA), which amended the federal habeas statute to deny to Guantanamo detainees the right to bring a habeas action in federal courts. The MCA did allow detainees the right to seek review of *military* court decisions in the United States Court of Appeals for the District of Columbia.

In a 5-to-4 decision, the Court held that the denial of habeas corpus relief in federal courts was unconstitutional. Writing for the majority, Justice Kennedy wrote that "petitioners may invoke the fundamental procedural protections of habeas corpus. The laws and Constitution are designed to survive, and remain in force, in extraordinary times. Liberty and security can be reconciled; and in our system they are reconciled within the framework of the law." Moreover, Kennedy contended, Article I, §9, of the Constitution allows Congress to suspend habeas corpus in times of rebellion or invasion, but that neither of these situations were present.

In dissent, Chief Justice Roberts, joined by Justices Scalia, Thomas, and Alito, argued that in such times of war the Court should defer to the choices made by Congress and the President. In particular, Justice Roberts maintained that the "political branches crafted these procedures amidst an ongoing military conflict, after much careful investigation and thorough debate."

*Hamdi*, *Hamdan*, and *Boumediene* are important cases involving the delicate question of the proper role of the federal courts during times of war, and the war on terror in particular. The difficult question of balancing the nation's security (by granting greater authority to the President and Congress in order to deal with wartime realities) and the rule of law (circumscribing that authority in order to protect the rights of individuals by providing more extensive judicial procedural protections) is at the center of the Supreme Court's deliberations.

## Majority opinion of Justice KENNEDY:

. . . In cases involving foreign citizens detained abroad by the Executive, it likely would be both an impractical and unprecedented extension of judicial power to assume that habeas corpus would be available at the moment the prisoner is taken into custody. If and when habeas corpus jurisdiction applies, as it does in these cases, then proper deference can be accorded to reasonable procedures for screening and initial detention under lawful and proper conditions of confinement and treatment for a reasonable period of time. Domestic exigencies, furthermore, might also impose such onerous burdens on the Government that here, too, the Judicial Branch would be required to devise sensible rules for staying habeas corpus proceedings until the Government can comply with its requirements in a responsible way. Here, as is true with detainees apprehended abroad, a relevant consideration in determining the courts' role is whether there are suitable alternative processes in place to protect against the arbitrary exercise of governmental power.

The cases before us, however, do not involve detainees who have been held for a short period of time while awaiting their CSRT determinations. Were that the case, or were it probable that the Court of Appeals could complete a prompt review of their applications, the case for requiring temporary abstention or exhaustion of alternative remedies would be much stronger. These qualifications no longer pertain here. In some of these cases six years have elapsed without the judicial oversight that habeas corpus or an adequate substitute demands. And there has been no showing that the Executive faces such onerous burdens that it cannot respond to habeas corpus actions. To require these detainees to complete DTA review before proceeding with their habeas corpus actions would be to require additional months, if not years, of delay. The first DTA review applications were filed over two years ago, but no decisions on the merits have been issued. While some delay in fashioning new procedures is unavoidable, the costs of delay can no longer be borne by those who are held in custody. The detainees in these cases are entitled to a prompt habeas corpus hearing.

Our decision today holds only that petitioners before us are entitled to seek the writ; that the DTA review procedures are an inadequate substitute for habeas corpus; and that petitioners in these cases need not exhaust the review procedures in the Court of Appeals before proceeding with their habeas actions in the District Court. The only law we identify as unconstitutional is MCA § 7, 28 U.S.C. § 2241(e). Accordingly, both the DTA and the CSRT process remain intact. Our holding with regard to exhaustion should not be read to imply that a habeas court should intervene the moment an enemy combatant steps foot in a territory where the writ runs. The Executive is entitled to a reasonable period of time to determine a detainee's status before a court entertains that detainee's habeas corpus petition. The CSRT process is the mechanism Congress and the President set up to deal with these issues. Except in cases of undue delay, federal courts should refrain from entertaining an enemy combatant's habeas corpus petition at least until after the Department, acting via the CSRT, has had a chance to review his status.

Although we hold that the DTA is not an adequate and effective substitute for habeas corpus, it does not follow that a habeas corpus court may disregard the dangers the detention in these cases was intended to prevent. *Felker, Swain,* and *Hayman* stand for the proposition that the Suspension Clause does not resist innovation in the field of habeas corpus. Certain accommodations can be made to reduce the burden habeas corpus proceedings will place on the military without impermissibly diluting the protections of the writ.

In the DTA Congress sought to consolidate review of petitioners' claims in the Court of Appeals. Channeling future cases to one district court would no doubt reduce administrative burdens on the Government. This is a legitimate objective that might be advanced even without an amendment to § 2241. If, in a future case, a detainee files a habeas petition in another judicial district in which a proper respondent can be served, the Government can move for change of venue to the court that will hear these petitioners' cases, the United States District Court for the District of Columbia.

Another of Congress' reasons for vesting exclusive jurisdiction in the Court of Appeals, perhaps, was to avoid the widespread dissemination of classified information. The Government has raised similar concerns here and elsewhere. We make no attempt to anticipate all of the evidentiary and access-to-counsel issues that will arise during the course of the detainees' habeas corpus proceedings. We recognize, however, that the Government has a legitimate interest in protecting sources and methods of intelligence gathering; and we expect that the District Court will use its discretion to accommodate this interest to the greatest extent possible.

These and the other remaining questions are within the expertise and competence of the District Court to address in the first instance.

In considering both the procedural and substantive standards used to impose detention to prevent acts of terrorism, proper deference must be accorded to the political branches. Unlike the President and some designated Members of Congress, neither the Members of this Court nor most federal judges begin the day with briefings that may describe new and serious threats to our Nation and its people. The law must accord the Executive substantial authority to apprehend and detain those who pose a real danger to our security.

Officials charged with daily operational responsibility for our security may consider a judicial discourse on the history of the Habeas Corpus Act of 1679 and like matters to be far removed from the Nation's present, urgent concerns. Established legal doctrine, however, must be consulted for its teaching. Remote in time it may be; irrelevant to the present it is not. Security depends upon a sophisticated intelligence apparatus and the ability of our Armed Forces to act and to interdict. There are further considerations, however. Security subsists, too, in fidelity to freedom's first principles. Chief among these are freedom from arbitrary and unlawful restraint and the personal liberty that is secured by adherence to the separation of powers. It is from these principles that the judicial authority to consider petitions for habeas corpus relief derives.

Our opinion does not undermine the Executive's powers as Commander in Chief. On the contrary, the exercise of those powers is vindicated, not eroded, when confirmed by the Judicial Branch. Within the Constitution's separation-of-powers structure, few exercises of judicial power are as legitimate or as necessary as the responsibility to hear challenges to the authority of the Executive to imprison a person. Some of these petitioners have been in custody for six years with no definitive judicial determination as to the legality of their detention. Their access to the writ is a necessity to determine the lawfulness of their status, even if, in the end, they do not obtain the relief they seek.

Because our Nation's past military conflicts have been of limited duration, it has been possible to leave the outer boundaries of war powers undefined. If, as some fear, terrorism continues to pose dangerous threats to us for years to come, the Court might not have this luxury. This result is not inevitable, however. The political branches, consistent with their independent obligations to interpret and uphold the Constitution, can engage in a genuine debate about how best to preserve constitutional values while protecting the Nation from terrorism.

It bears repeating that our opinion does not address the content of the law that governs petitioners' detention. That is a matter yet to be determined. We hold that petitioners may invoke the fundamental procedural protections of habeas corpus. The laws and Constitution are designed to survive, and remain in force, in extraordinary times. Liberty and security can be reconciled; and in our system they are reconciled within the framework of the law. The Framers decided that habeas corpus, a right of first importance, must be a part of that framework, a part of that law.

### Chief Justice ROBERTS, with whom Justice SCALIA, Justice THOMAS, and Justice ALITO join, dissenting:

Today the Court strikes down as inadequate the most generous set of procedural protections ever afforded aliens detained by this country as enemy combatants. The political branches crafted these procedures amidst an ongoing military conflict, after much careful investigation and thorough debate. The Court rejects them today out of hand, without bothering to say what due process rights the detainees possess, without explaining how the statute fails to vindicate those rights, and before a single petitioner has exhausted the procedures under the law. And to what effect? The majority merely replaces a review system designed by the people's representatives with a set of shapeless procedures to be defined by federal courts at some future date. One cannot help but think, after surveying the modest practical results of the majority's ambitious opinion, that this decision is not really about the detainees at all, but about control of federal policy regarding enemy combatants. . . .

For all its eloquence about the detainees' right to the writ, the Court makes no effort to elaborate how exactly the remedy it prescribes will differ from the procedural protections detainees enjoy under the DTA. The Court objects to the detainees' limited access to witnesses and classified material, but proposes no alternatives of its own. Indeed, it simply ignores the many difficult questions its holding presents. What, for example, will become of the CSRT process? The majority says federal courts should *generally* refrain from entertaining detainee challenges until after the petitioner's CSRT proceeding has finished. But to what deference, if any, is that CSRT determination entitled?

There are other problems. Take witness availability. What makes the majority think witnesses will become magically available when the review procedure is labeled "habeas"? Will the location of most of these witnesses change—will they suddenly become easily susceptible to service of process? Or will subpoenas issued by American habeas courts run to Basra? And if they did, how would they be enforced? Speaking of witnesses, will detainees be able to call active-duty military officers as witnesses? If not, why not?

The majority has no answers for these difficulties. What it does say leaves open the distinct possibility that its "habeas" remedy will, when all is said and done, end up looking a great deal like the DTA review it rejects. But "[t]he role of the judiciary is limited to determining whether the procedures meet the essential standard of fairness under the Due Process Clause and does not extend to imposing procedures that merely displace congressional choices of policy."

The majority rests its decision on abstract and hypothetical concerns. Step back and consider what, in the real world, Congress and the Executive have actually granted aliens captured by our Armed Forces overseas and found to be enemy combatants:

- The right to hear the bases of the charges against them, including a summary of any classified evidence.
- The ability to challenge the bases of their detention before military tribunals modeled after Geneva Convention procedures. Some 38 detainees have been released as a result of this process.
- The right, before the CSRT, to testify, introduce evidence, call witnesses, question those the Government calls, and secure release, if and when appropriate.
- The right to the aid of a personal representative in arranging and presenting their cases before a CSRT.
- Before the D.C. Circuit, the right to employ counsel, challenge the factual record, contest the lower tribunal's legal determinations, ensure compliance with the Constitution and laws, and secure release, if any errors below establish their entitlement to such relief.

In sum, the DTA satisfies the majority's own criteria for assessing adequacy. This statutory scheme provides the combatants held at Guantanamo greater procedural protections than have ever been afforded alleged enemy detainees—whether citizens or aliens—in our national history.

So who has won? Not the detainees. The Court's analysis leaves them with only the prospect of further litigation to determine the content of their new habeas right, followed by further litigation to resolve their particular cases, followed by further litigation before the D.C. Circuit—where they could have started had they invoked the DTA procedure. Not Congress, whose attempt to "determine—through democratic means—how best" to balance the security of the American people with the detainees' liberty interests, has been unceremoniously brushed aside. Not the Great Writ, whose majesty is hardly enhanced by its extension to a jurisdictionally quirky outpost, with no tangible benefit to anyone. Not the rule of law, unless by that is meant the rule of lawyers, who will now arguably have a greater role than military and intelligence officials in shaping policy for alien enemy combatants.

And certainly not the American people, who today lose a bit more control over the conduct of this Nation's foreign policy to unelected, politically unaccountable judges.

I respectfully dissent.

## Bibliography

Gonzales, Alberto R. "Waging War within the Constitution." *Texas Tech Law Review* 42 (2010): 843.

Neuman, Gerald L. "The Extraterritorial Constitution after *Boumediene v. Bush.*" *S. California Law Review* 82 (2009): 259.

Pushaw, Robert J., Jr. "Creating Legal Rights for Suspected Terrorists: Is the Court Being Courageous or Politically Pragmatic?" *Notre Dame Law Review* 84 (2009): 1975.

Scibner, Heather P. "A Fundamental Misconception of Separation of Powers: *Boumediene v. Bush.*" *Texas Review of Law and Politics* 14 (2009).

## *Medellin v. Texas*

**Citation: 552 U.S. 491.**

**Issue: Does the Constitution provide the President with the independent power to ensure that non-self-executing treaties are enforced, absent Congressional authorization?**

**Year of Decision: 2008.**

**Outcome: No. The responsibility for transforming a non-self-executing treaty into domestic law falls to Congress.**

**Author of Opinion: Chief Justice John Roberts.**

**Vote: 6-3.**

Article II, §2 of the Constitution allows the President to negotiate treaties with foreign nations, but requires that they be ratified by a two-thirds vote of the Senate. Treaties are either self-executing, meaning they are automatically binding as law in the United States, or they require enabling legislation before they may be implemented domestically. The President's constitutional authority in the area of implementing treaties was curtailed by the Court in 2008 in the *Medellin* case.

Jose Medellin, a Mexican national, was sentenced to death for participating in the gang rape and murder of two teenage girls. Medellin raised a challenge to his sentence, arguing that the state had violated his rights under the Vienna Convention Treaty, which the United States entered into with several nations, including Mexico. Article 36 of the Treaty gives any foreign national arrested by a foreign country the right to contact his consulate. Medellin argued that his conviction should be reconsidered, relying, in part, on a ruling by the International Court of Justice (ICJ), which held that the United States had violated the Vienna Convention rights of numerous Mexican nationals (including Medellin) by denying them the right to contact their consulate. Medellin also asserted that the President of the United States, George Bush, had instructed state courts to comply with the ICJ's rulings and rehear the cases. Medellin further contended that the Constitution provides the President with broad power to ensure that treaties are enforced, in both federal and state court proceedings.

The Supreme Court ruled that the Vienna Convention Treaty was not self-executing such that Congress must enact it into law before it could be binding upon state courts. Writing for the Court, Chief Justice Roberts characterized the President's action as a violation of Separation-of-Powers: "[The] President has an array of political and diplomatic means available to enforce international obligations, but unilaterally converting a non-self-executing treaty into a self-executing one is not among them. The responsibility for transforming an international obligation arising from a non-self-executing treaty into domestic law falls to Congress." Thus, even where the President's actions involve foreign affairs, where the Chief Executive's power is at its zenith, the Court will continue to scrutinize carefully such actions under the doctrine of Separation of Powers.

### Chief Justice ROBERTS delivered the opinion of the Court.

. . . This Court has long recognized the distinction between treaties that automatically have effect as domestic law, and those that—while they constitute international law commitments—do not by themselves function as binding federal law. The distinction was well explained by Chief Justice Marshall's opinion in *Foster v. Neilson,* which held that a treaty is "equivalent to an act of the legislature," and hence self-executing, when it "operates of itself without the aid of any legislative provision." When, in contrast, "[treaty] stipulations are not self-executing they can only be enforced pursuant to legislation to carry them into effect." In sum, while treaties "may comprise international commitments ... they are not domestic law unless Congress has either enacted implementing statutes or the treaty itself conveys an intention that it be 'self-executing' and is ratified on these terms."

A treaty is, of course, "primarily a compact between independent nations." It ordinarily "depends for the enforcement of its provisions on the interest and the honor of the governments which are parties to it." "If these [interests] fail, its infraction becomes the subject of international negotiations and reclamations .... It is obvious that with all this the judicial courts have nothing to do and can give no redress." *Head Money Cases.* Only "[i]f the treaty contains stipulations which are self-executing, that is, require no legislation to make them operative, [will] they have the force and effect of a legislative enactment." Medellín and his *amici* nonetheless contend that the Optional Protocol, United Nations Charter, and ICJ Statute supply the "relevant obligation" to give the *Avena* judgment binding effect in the domestic courts of the United States. Because none of these treaty sources creates binding federal law in the absence of implementing legislation, and because it is uncontested that no such legislation exists, we conclude that the *Avena* judgment is not automatically binding domestic law.

The interpretation of a treaty, like the interpretation of a statute, begins with its text. Because a treaty ratified by the United States is "an agreement among sovereign powers," we have also considered as "aids to its interpretation" the negotiation and drafting history of the treaty as well as "the postratification understanding" of signatory nations.

As a signatory to the Optional Protocol, the United States agreed to submit disputes arising out of the Vienna Convention to the ICJ. The Protocol provides: "Disputes arising out of the interpretation or application of the [Vienna] Convention shall lie within the compulsory jurisdiction of the International Court of Justice." Of course, submitting to jurisdiction and agreeing to be bound are two different things. A party could, for example, agree to compulsory nonbinding arbitration. Such an agreement would require the party to appear before the arbitral tribunal without obligating the party to treat the tribunal's decision as binding.

The most natural reading of the Optional Protocol is as a bare grant of jurisdiction. It provides only that "[d]isputes arising out of the interpretation or application of the [Vienna] Convention shall lie within the compulsory jurisdiction of the International Court of Justice" and "may accordingly be brought before the [ICJ] ... by any party to the dispute being a Party to the present Protocol." The Protocol says nothing about the effect of an ICJ decision and does not itself commit signatories to comply with an ICJ judgment. The Protocol is similarly silent as to any enforcement mechanism. . . .

Our Framers established a careful set of procedures that must be followed before federal law can be created under the Constitution—vesting that decision in the political branches, subject to checks and balances. U.S. Const., Art. I, § 7. They also recognized that treaties could create federal law, but again through the political branches, with the President making the treaty and the Senate approving it. Art. II, § 2. The dissent's understanding of the treaty route, depending on an ad hoc judgment of the judiciary without looking to the treaty language—the very language negotiated by the President and approved by the Senate—cannot readily be ascribed to those same Framers. . . .

The dissent's approach risks the United States' involvement in international agreements. It is hard to believe that the United States would enter into treaties that are sometimes enforceable and sometimes not. Such a treaty would be the equivalent of writing a blank check to the judiciary. Senators could never be quite sure what the treaties on which they were voting meant. Only a judge could say for sure and only at some future date. This uncertainty could hobble the United States' efforts to negotiate and sign international agreements.

In this case, the dissent—for a grab bag of no less than seven reasons—would tell us that this *particular* ICJ judgment is federal law. That is no sort of guidance. Nor is it any answer to say that the federal courts will diligently police international agreements and enforce the decisions of international tribunals only when they *should be* enforced. The point of a non-self-executing treaty is that it "addresses itself to the political, *not* the judicial department; and the legislature must execute the contract before it can become a rule for the Court." The dissent's contrary approach would assign to the courts—not the political branches—the primary role in deciding when and how international agreements will be enforced. To read a treaty so that it sometimes has the effect of domestic law and sometimes does not is tantamount to vesting with the judiciary the power not only to interpret but also to create the law. . . .

## Justice BREYER, with whom Justice SOUTER and Justice GINSBURG join, dissenting.

. . . The majority's two holdings taken together produce practical anomalies. They unnecessarily complicate the President's foreign affairs task insofar as, for example, they increase the likelihood of Security Council *Avena* enforcement proceedings, of worsening relations with our neighbor Mexico, of precipitating actions by other nations putting at risk American citizens who have the misfortune to be arrested while traveling abroad, or of diminishing our Nation's reputation abroad as a result of our failure to follow the "rule of law" principles that we preach. The holdings also encumber Congress with a task (postratification legislation) that, in respect to many decisions of international tribunals, it may not want and which it may find difficult to execute. At the same time, insofar as today's holdings make it more difficult to enforce the judgments of international tribunals, including technical non-politically-controversial judgments, those holdings weaken that rule of law for which our Constitution stands.

These institutional considerations make it difficult to reconcile the majority's holdings with the workable Constitution that the Founders envisaged. They reinforce the importance, in practice and in principle, of asking Chief Justice Marshall's question: Does a treaty provision address the "Judicial" Branch rather than the "Political Branches" of Government. And they show the wisdom of the well-established precedent that indicates that the answer to the question here is "yes."

In sum, a strong line of precedent, likely reflecting the views of the Founders, indicates that the treaty provisions before us and the judgment of the International Court of Justice address themselves to the Judicial Branch and consequently are self-executing. In reaching a contrary conclusion, the Court has failed to take proper account of that precedent and, as a result, the Nation may well break its word even though the President seeks to live up to that word and Congress has done nothing to suggest the contrary.

For the reasons set forth, I respectfully dissent.

## Bibliography

Hallerman, Mary D. "*Medellin v. Texas*: The Treaties that Bind." *University of Richmond Law Review* 43 (2009): 797.

Quigley, John. "A Tragi-Comedy of Errors Erodes Self-execution of Treaties: *Medellín v. Texas* and Beyond." *Case Western Reserve Journal of International Law* 45 (2012): 403.

Turner, Michael J. "Fade to Black: the Formalization of Jackson's Youngstown Taxonomy by *Hamdan* and *Medellin*." *American University Law Review* 58 (2009): 665.

# Chapter 3

# The Power of Congress

Mistrust of centralized authority was an overarching influence upon the nation's founding and has been a significant factor in the Constitution's evolution. Early constitutional case law focusing upon congressional authority reflects this concern. In *McCulloch v. Maryland* (1819), for instance, the Court addressed the issue of whether congressional power should be limited strictly to what the Constitution specified or allowed for action that enabled Congress to exercise its authority more effectively. In ruling for a broader definition of congressional power, the Court set a principle and tone that favored development of a national identity. Separation of power controversies typically arise from disputes over which branch of government should exercise authority in a particular context. Separation of power concerns are not limited, however, to conflict between branches. As federal powers have expanded over the course of the twentieth century in particular, Congress has initiated efforts to increase the efficacy and efficiency of governmental operations. Its ability to delegate legislative authority to administrative agencies, charged with responsibility to manage increasingly complex social and economic problems and needs within Congress's scope of responsibility, generally has been upheld since the middle of the twentieth century. Other structural efficiencies, such as the legislative veto reviewed in *Immigration and Naturalization Service v. Chadha* (1983), have not survived constitutional scrutiny. Additionally, the Court must interpret statutory language in order to determine the extent of the Congressional power being asserted. In *King v. Burwell* (2015), the Court ruled that certain language in the controversial Affordable Health Care Act, which language appeared on its face to limit tax credits to individuals seeking insurance in *State* run health care exchanges, in fact also allowed tax credits to individuals seeking insurance in *Federal* health care exchanges in cases where a State had declined to establish a health care exchange.

## *Immigration and Naturalization Service v. Chadha*

**Citation: 462 U.S. 919.**

**Issue: Whether Congress may authorize one house to veto administrative regulations.**

**Year: 1983.**

**Outcome: No. The "one-house veto" violates the concept of separation of powers.**
**Author of Opinion: Chief Justice Warren Burger.**
**Vote: 6-3.**

Since the constitutional crisis of the 1930s, which led to a dramatic shift in the United States Supreme Court's approach to federal power, federal administrative power has grown so dramatically that some now refer to the administrative bureaucracy as a "veritable fourth branch of government." Not only has there been a significant increase in the number of administrative agencies, but those agencies now create a large quantity of law in the form of administrative regulations. Although Congress has searched for ways to rein in administrative power, none has proved effective.

*Immigration and Naturalization Service v. Chadha* involves one attempt by Congress to rein in administrative power through the use of the so-called one-house veto. The case arose in a deportation proceeding involving Chadha. Although Chadha conceded that he was deportable because he had overstayed his visa, he applied for a suspension of deportation. An immigration judge agreed to suspend the deportation. Under the governing statute, which allowed either house of Congress to overturn the suspension order, Congress reversed the decision of the immigration judge. Thereupon, Chadha challenged the law on constitutional grounds.

Ultimately, the United States Supreme Court agreed with Chadha. The Court noted that the Constitution requires that all legislation be passed by *both* houses of Congress and that it then be presented to the President for signature or veto. The Court regarded this "presentment" power as extremely important: "The decision to provide the President with a limited and qualified power to nullify proposed legislation by veto was based on the profound conviction of the Framers that the powers conferred on Congress were the powers to be most carefully circumscribed." The presidential function "in the lawmaking process also reflects the Framers' careful efforts to check whatever propensity a particular Congress might have to enact oppressive, improvident, or ill-considered measures."

The Court also rejected the one-house veto under the bicameralism requirement of Art. I, § 1, cl. 7. That clause requires that, in order to pass legislation, it must be passed by both houses of Congress. The Court concluded that the one-house veto was exercised in a "legislative" manner and that it could act only bicamerally: "Neither the House of Representatives nor the Senate contends that, absent the veto provision in § 244(c)(2), either of them, or both of them acting together, could effectively require the Attorney General to deport an alien once the Attorney General, in the exercise of legislatively delegated authority, had determined the alien should remain in the United States." The Court concluded that, when the Constitution authorizes one house of Congress to act unilaterally, it stated that power explicitly. The Court concluded that the Constitution provided for unilateral action in only four situations: "(a) The House of Representatives alone was given the power to initiate impeachments. Art. I, § 2, cl. 6; (b) The Senate alone was given the power to conduct trials following impeachment on charges initiated by the House and to convict following trial. Art. I, § 3, cl. 5; (c) The Senate alone was given final unreviewable power to approve or to disapprove presidential appointments. Art. II, § 2, cl. 2; (d) The Senate alone was given unreviewable power to ratify treaties negotiated by the President. Art. II, § 2, cl. 2." Otherwise, the Court concluded, Congress must act in a bicameral manner and must present the legislation to the President for his signature or veto.

While the Court agreed that the one-house veto provided a "convenient shortcut" by which Congress could assert authority over the Executive branch, and thereby share power with it, the Court held that "the records of the Convention, contemporaneous writings and debates, that the Framers ranked other values higher than efficiency."

Justice Byron White dissented noting that the Court's decision "strikes down in one fell swoop provisions in more laws enacted by Congress than the Court has cumulatively invalidated in its history." He went on to express concern that "it will now be more difficult 'to insure that the fundamental policy decisions in our society will be made not by an appointed official but by the body immediately responsible to the people, . . . I must dissent."

*Chadha* is an extremely important decision because it invalidates Congress's attempt to gain control over the administrative bureaucracy through the mechanism of the one-house veto. After *Chadha,* Congress was forced to search for alternate methods for reining in the growth of administrative lawmaking.

## Chief Justice BURGER delivered the opinion of the Court.

. . . Although not "hermetically" sealed from one another, the powers delegated to the three Branches are functionally identifiable. When any Branch acts, it is presumptively exercising the power the Constitution has delegated to it. When the Executive acts, it presumptively acts in an executive or administrative capacity as defined in Art. II. And when, as here, one House of Congress purports to act, it is presumptively acting within its assigned sphere.

Beginning with this presumption, we must nevertheless establish that the challenged action . . . is of the kind to which the procedural requirements of Art. I, § 7 apply. Not every action taken by either House is subject to the bicameralism and presentment requirements of Art. I. Whether actions taken by either House are, in law and fact, an exercise of legislative power depends not on their form but upon "whether they contain matter which is properly to be regarded as legislative in its character and effect."

Examination of the action taken here by one House . . . reveals that it was essentially legislative in purpose and effect. In purporting to exercise power defined in Art. I, § 8, cl. 4 to "establish an uniform Rule of Naturalization," the House took action that had the purpose and effect of altering the legal rights, duties and relations of persons, including the Attorney General, Executive Branch officials and Chadha, all outside the legislative branch. . . . The one-House veto operated in this case to overrule the Attorney General and mandate Chadha's deportation; absent the House action, Chadha would remain in the United States. Congress has *acted* and its action has altered Chadha's status. . . .

The nature of the decision implemented by the one-House veto in this case further manifests its legislative character. After long experience with the clumsy, time consuming private bill procedure, Congress made a deliberate choice to delegate to the Executive Branch, and specifically to the Attorney General, the authority to allow deportable aliens to remain in this country in certain specified circumstances. It is not disputed that this choice to delegate authority is precisely the kind of decision that can be implemented only in accordance with the procedures set out in Art. I. Disagreement with the Attorney General's decision on Chadha's deportation—that is, Congress' decision to deport Chadha—no less than Congress' original choice to delegate to the Attorney General the authority to make that decision, involves determinations of policy that Congress can implement in only one way; bicameral passage followed by presentment to the President. Congress must abide by its delegation of authority until that delegation is legislatively altered or revoked.

Finally, we see that when the Framers intended to authorize either House of Congress to act alone and outside of its prescribed bicameral legislative role, they narrowly and precisely defined the procedure for such action. . . .

Clearly, when the Draftsmen sought to confer special powers on one House, independent of the other House, or of the President, they did so in explicit, unambiguous terms. These carefully defined exceptions from presentment and bicameralism underscore the difference between the legislative functions of Congress and other unilateral but important and binding one-House acts provided for in the Constitution. These exceptions are narrow, explicit, and separately justified; none of them authorize the action challenged here. . . .

Since it is clear that the action by the House under . . . was not within any of the express constitutional exceptions authorizing one House to act alone, and equally clear that it was an exercise of legislative power, that action was subject to the standards prescribed in Article I. The bicameral requirement, the Presentment Clauses, the President's veto, and Congress' power to override a veto were intended to erect enduring checks on each Branch and to protect the people from the improvident exercise of power by mandating certain prescribed steps. To preserve those checks, and maintain the separation of powers, the carefully defined limits on the power of each Branch must not be eroded. To accomplish what has been attempted by one House of Congress in this case requires action in conformity with the express procedures of the Constitution's prescription for legislative action: passage by a majority of both Houses and presentment to the President.

Justice WHITE, dissenting.

Today the Court not only invalidates § 244(c)(2) of the Immigration and National-ity Act, but also sounds the death knell for nearly 200 other statutory provisions in which Congress has reserved a "legislative veto." For this reason, the Court's decision is of surpassing importance. And it is for this reason that the Court would have been well-advised to decide the case, if possible, on the narrower grounds of separation of powers, leaving for full consideration the constitutionality of other congressional review statutes operating on such varied matters as war powers and agency rulemaking, some of which concern the independent regulatory agencies.

The prominence of the legislative veto mechanism in our contemporary political system and its importance to Congress can hardly be overstated. It has become a central means by which Congress secures the accountability of executive and inde-pendent agencies. Without the legislative veto, Congress is faced with a Hobson's choice: either to refrain from delegating the necessary authority, leaving itself with a hopeless task of writing laws with the requisite specificity to cover endless special circumstances across the entire policy landscape, or in the alternative, to abdicate its law-making function to the executive branch and independent agencies. To choose the former leaves major national problems unresolved; to opt for the latter risks unaccountable policymaking by those not elected to fill that role. Accordingly, over the past five decades, the legislative veto has been placed in nearly 200 stat-utes. The device is known in every field of governmental concern: reorganization, budgets, foreign affairs, war powers, and regulation of trade, safety, energy, the environment and the economy. . . .

## Bibliography

Greene, Abner S. "Checks and Balances in an Era of Presidential Lawmaking." *University of Chicago Law Review* 61 (1994): 123, 126.

Lively, D., P. Haddon, D. Roberts, R. Weaver, and W. Araiza. *Constitutional Law: Cases, His-tory, and Dialogues.* 2nd ed. Cincinnati, OH: Anderson Publishing, 2000, 428.

Wheeler, Darren A. "Actor Pregerence and the Implementation of *INS v. Chadha.*" *BYU Jour-nal of Public Law* 23 (2008): 83.

## *King v. Burwell*

**Citation: 576 U.S. ___.**

**Issue: Whether the Affordable Health Care Act extended tax credits to individuals seeking health care insurance under federal exchanges as well as those created by the states, despite language in the Act that appears to limit the tax credits to those seeking insurance only under state exchanges.**

**Year: 2015.**

**Outcome: Yes. The Affordable Health Care Act extended tax credits to individuals seeking health care insurance under federal exchanges as well as those created by the states.**
**Author of Opinion: Chief Justice John Roberts.**
**Vote: 6-3.**

Congress passed the Affordable Care Act (ACA) by the narrowest of margins in 2010. The ostensible purpose of the ACA was to increase the number of Americans covered by health insurance and decrease the cost of health care. The ACA allowed for tax credits to individuals who purchase health insurance through "an exchange established by the state." Many states, however, elected not to establish "exchanges," including Virginia, the home state of the petitioners in this case. As a result of these states deciding to opt out, the IRS promulgated a rule that tax credits would be available to individuals who purchased health insurance through a *federal* exchange. However, the plain language of the ACA appeared to limit tax credits to only those individuals who purchased insurance through one of the state exchanges. Without the IRS rule, the entire feasibility of the ACA would be called into question.

Virginia declined to establish a state-run exchange and had one operated by the federal government. A group of Virginia residents who, without the tax credits, would be exempt from having to purchase health insurance, sued and argued that the IRS regulation exceeded the agency's statutory authority.

Chief Justice Roberts delivered the opinion for the 6-3 majority. The Court held that reading the language of the statute in the context of Congress's overall intent led to the conclusion that the tax credits were meant to be available through both types of exchanges, even though a reading of the plain language would appear to suggest otherwise. The majority argued that Congress's overall intent in passing the ACA was to cover as many qualified individuals as possible, and that limiting tax credits only to those individuals who accessed state exchanges would run counter to this overall intent.

Justice Antonin Scalia wrote a dissent in which he was joined by Justices Thomas and Alito. Scalia argued that that the plain language of the statute clearly limits the tax credits to state-created exchanges. The majority opinion's attempt to use context to justify a different reading amounts to rewriting the statute. Justice Scalia also argued that interpreting the language to refer to both state-created and federally created exchanges ignores the times when Congress explicitly chose to conflate the two types of exchanges, as opposed to the times it did not. The reading that some parts of the statute refer to both types of exchanges and other parts do not is more consistent with the statute as a whole and gives better effect to Congress's intent in enacting it. The majority opinion's effort to rewrite the ACA in order to save it, Justice Scalia argued, amounts to judicial activism.

## Chief Justice ROBERTS delivered the opinion of the Court.

The Patient Protection and Affordable Care Act adopts a series of interlocking reforms designed to expand coverage in the individual health insurance market. First, the Act bars insurers from taking a person's health into account when deciding whether to sell health insurance or how much to charge. Second, the Act generally requires each person to maintain insurance coverage or make a payment to the Internal Revenue Service. And third, the Act gives tax credits to certain people to make insurance more affordable.

In addition to those reforms, the Act requires the creation of an "Exchange" in each State—basically, a marketplace that allows people to compare and purchase insurance plans. The Act gives each State the opportunity to establish its own Exchange, but provides that the Federal Government will establish the Exchange if the State does not.

This case is about whether the Act's interlocking reforms apply equally in each State no matter who establishes the State's Exchange. Specifically, the question presented is whether the Act's tax credits are available in States that have a Federal Exchange. . . .

In addition to those three reforms, the Act requires the creation of an "Exchange" in each State where people can shop for insurance, usually online. An Exchange may be created in one of two ways. First, the Act provides that "[e]ach State shall . . . establish an American Health Benefit Exchange ... for the State." *Ibid.* Second, if a State nonetheless chooses not to establish its own Exchange, the Act provides that the Secretary of Health and Human Services "shall ... establish and operate such Exchange within the State."

The issue in this case is whether the Act's tax credits are available in States that have a Federal Exchange rather than a State Exchange. The Act initially provides that tax credits "shall be allowed" for any "applicable taxpayer." The Act then provides that the amount of the tax credit depends in part on whether the taxpayer has enrolled in an insurance plan through "an Exchange *established by the State* under section 1311 of the Patient Protection and Affordable Care Act."

The IRS addressed the availability of tax credits by promulgating a rule that made them available on both State and Federal Exchanges. As relevant here, the IRS Rule provides that a taxpayer is eligible for a tax credit if he enrolled in an insurance plan through "an Exchange," which is defined as "an Exchange serving the individual market . . . regardless of whether the Exchange is established and operated by a State . . . or by HHS." At this point, 16 States and the District of Columbia have established their own Exchanges; the other 34 States have elected to have HHS do so. . . .

When analyzing an agency's interpretation of a statute, we often apply [a] two-step framework. . . . Under that framework, we ask whether the statute is ambiguous and, if so, whether the agency's interpretation is reasonable. This approach "is premised on the theory that a statute's ambiguity constitutes an implicit delegation from Congress to the agency to fill in the statutory gaps." . . .

This is one of those cases. The tax credits are among the Act's key reforms, involving billions of dollars in spending each year and affecting the price of health insurance for millions of people. Whether those credits are available on Federal Exchanges is thus a question of deep "economic and political significance" that is central to this statutory scheme; had Congress wished to assign that question to an agency, it surely would have done so expressly. It is especially unlikely that Congress would have delegated this decision to the IRS, which has no expertise in crafting health insurance policy of this sort. This is not a case for the IRS.

It is instead our task to determine the correct reading of Section 36B. If the statutory language is plain, we must enforce it according to its terms. But oftentimes the "meaning—or ambiguity—of certain words or phrases may only become evident when placed in context." So when deciding whether the language is plain, we must read the words "in their context and with a view to their place in the overall statutory scheme."

We begin with the text of Section 36B. As relevant here, Section 36B allows an individual to receive tax credits only if the individual enrolls in an insurance plan through "an Exchange established by the State under [42 U.S.C. § 18031]." In other words, three things must be true: First, the individual must enroll in an insurance plan through "an Exchange." Second, that Exchange must be "established by the State." And third, that Exchange must be established "under [42 U.S.C. § 18031]." We address each requirement in turn. . . .

Given that the text is ambiguous, we must turn to the broader structure of the Act to determine the meaning of Section 36B. "A provision that may seem ambiguous in isolation is often clarified by the remainder of the statutory scheme . . . because only one of the permissible meanings produces a substantive effect that is compatible with the rest of the law." Here, the statutory scheme compels us to reject petitioners' interpretation because it would destabilize the individual insurance market in any State with a Federal Exchange, and likely create the very "death spirals" that Congress designed the Act to avoid.

As discussed above, Congress based the Affordable Care Act on three major reforms: first, the guaranteed issue and community rating requirements; second, a requirement that individuals maintain health insurance coverage or make a payment to the IRS; and third, the tax credits for individuals with household incomes between 100 percent and 400 percent of the federal poverty line. In a State that establishes its own Exchange, these three reforms work together to expand insurance coverage. The guaranteed issue and community rating requirements ensure that anyone can buy insurance; the coverage requirement creates an incentive for people to do so before they get sick; and the tax credits—it is hoped—make insurance more affordable. Together, those reforms "minimize ... adverse selection and broaden the health insurance risk pool to include healthy individuals, which will lower health insurance premiums."

Under petitioners' reading, however, the Act would operate quite differently in a State with a Federal Exchange. As they see it, one of the Act's three major reforms—the tax credits—would not apply. And a second major reform—the coverage requirement—would not apply in a meaningful way. As explained earlier, the coverage requirement applies only when the cost of buying health insurance (minus the amount of the tax credits) is less than eight percent of an individual's income. So without the tax credits, the coverage requirement would apply to fewer individuals. And it would be a *lot* fewer. In 2014, approximately 87 percent of people who bought insurance on a Federal Exchange did so with tax credits, and virtually all of those people would become exempt. If petitioners are right, therefore, only one of the Act's three major reforms would apply in States with a Federal Exchange.

The combination of no tax credits and an ineffective coverage requirement could well push a State's individual insurance market into a death spiral. . . .

It is implausible that Congress meant the Act to operate in this manner. Congress made the guaranteed issue and community rating requirements applicable in every State in the Nation. But those requirements only work when combined with the coverage requirement and the tax credits. So it stands to reason that Congress meant for those provisions to apply in every State as well. . . .

Petitioners' arguments about the plain meaning of Section 36B are strong. But while the meaning of the phrase "an Exchange established by the State under [42 U.S.C. § 18031]" may seem plain "when viewed in isolation," such a reading turns out to be "untenable in light of [the statute] as a whole." In this instance, the context and structure of the Act compel us to depart from what would otherwise be the most natural reading of the pertinent statutory phrase.

Reliance on context and structure in statutory interpretation is a "subtle business, calling for great wariness lest what professes to be mere rendering becomes creation and attempted interpretation of legislation becomes legislation itself." For the reasons we have given, however, such reliance is appropriate in this case, and leads us to conclude that Section 36B allows tax credits for insurance purchased on any Exchange created under the Act. Those credits are necessary for the Federal Exchanges to function like their State Exchange counterparts, and to avoid the type of calamitous result that Congress plainly meant to avoid. . . .

## Justice Scalia, with whom Justice Thomas and Justice Alito join, dissenting.

The Court holds that when the Patient Protection and Affordable Care Act says "Exchange established by the State" it means "Exchange established by the State or the Federal Government." That is of course quite absurd, and the Court's 21 pages of explanation make it no less so.

The Patient Protection and Affordable Care Act makes major reforms to the American health-insurance market. It provides, among other things, that every

State "shall . . . establish an American Health Benefit Exchange"—a marketplace where people can shop for health-insurance plans. And it provides that if a State does not comply with this instruction, the Secretary of Health and Human Services must "establish and operate such Exchange within the State."

A separate part of the Act—housed in § 36B of the Internal Revenue Code—grants "premium tax credits" to subsidize certain purchases of health insurance made on Exchanges. The tax credit consists of "premium assistance amounts" for "coverage months." An individual has a coverage month only when he is covered by an insurance plan "that was enrolled in through an Exchange established by the State under [§ 18031]." § 36B(c)(2)(A). And the law ties the size of the premium assistance amount to the premiums for health plans which cover the individual "and which were enrolled in through an Exchange established by the State under [§ 18031]." § 36B(b)(2)(A). The premium assistance amount further depends on the cost of certain other insurance plans "offered through the same Exchange."

This case requires us to decide whether someone who buys insurance on an Exchange established by the Secretary gets tax credits. You would think the answer would be obvious—so obvious there would hardly be a need for the Supreme Court to hear a case about it. In order to receive any money under § 36B, an individual must enroll in an insurance plan through an "Exchange established by the State." The Secretary of Health and Human Services is not a State. So an Exchange established by the Secretary is not an Exchange established by the State—which means people who buy health insurance through such an Exchange get no money under § 36B.

Words no longer have meaning if an Exchange that is *not* established by a State is "established by the State." It is hard to come up with a clearer way to limit tax credits to state Exchanges than to use the words "established by the State." And it is hard to come up with a reason to include the words "by the State" other than the purpose of limiting credits to state Exchanges. "[T]he plain, obvious, and rational meaning of a statute is always to be preferred to any curious, narrow, hidden sense that nothing but the exigency of a hard case and the ingenuity and study of an acute and powerful intellect would discover." Under all the usual rules of interpretation, in short, the Government should lose this case. But normal rules of interpretation seem always to yield to the overriding principle of the present Court: The Affordable Care Act must be saved. . . .

The Court's decision reflects the philosophy that judges should endure whatever interpretive distortions it takes in order to correct a supposed flaw in the statutory machinery. That philosophy ignores the American people's decision to give *Congress* "[a]ll legislative Powers" enumerated in the Constitution. Art. I, § 1. They made Congress, not this Court, responsible for both making laws and mending them. This Court holds only the judicial power—the power to pronounce the law as Congress has enacted it. We lack the prerogative to repair laws that do not work out in practice, just as the people lack the ability to throw us out of office if they dislike the solutions we concoct. We must always remember, therefore, that "[o]ur task is to apply the text, not to improve upon it."

Trying to make its judge-empowering approach seem respectful of congressional authority, the Court asserts that its decision merely ensures that the Affordable

Care Act operates the way Congress "meant [it] to operate." First of all, what makes the Court so sure that Congress "meant" tax credits to be available everywhere? Our only evidence of what Congress meant comes from the terms of the law, and those terms show beyond all question that tax credits are available only on state Exchanges. More importantly, the Court forgets that ours is a government of laws and not of men. That means we are governed by the terms of our laws, not by the unenacted will of our lawmakers. "If Congress enacted into law something different from what it intended, then it should amend the statute to conform to its intent." In the meantime, this Court "has no roving license ... to disregard clear language simply on the view that . . . Congress 'must have intended' something broader."

Even less defensible, if possible, is the Court's claim that its interpretive approach is justified because this Act "does not reflect the type of care and deliberation that one might expect of such significant legislation." It is not our place to judge the quality of the care and deliberation that went into this or any other law. A law enacted by voice vote with no deliberation whatever is fully as binding upon us as one enacted after years of study, months of committee hearings, and weeks of debate. Much less is it our place to make everything come out right when Congress does not do its job properly. It is up to Congress to design its laws with care, and it is up to the people to hold them to account if they fail to carry out that responsibility.

Rather than rewriting the law under the pretense of interpreting it, the Court should have left it to Congress to decide what to do about the Act's limitation of tax credits to state Exchanges. If Congress values above everything else the Act's applicability across the country, it could make tax credits available in every Exchange. If it prizes state involvement in the Act's implementation, it could continue to limit tax credits to state Exchanges while taking other steps to mitigate the economic consequences predicted by the Court. If Congress wants to accommodate both goals, it could make tax credits available everywhere while offering new incentives for States to set up their own Exchanges. And if Congress thinks that the present design of the Act works well enough, it could do nothing. Congress could also do something else altogether, entirely abandoning the structure of the Affordable Care Act. The Court's insistence on making a choice that should be made by Congress both aggrandizes judicial power and encourages congressional lassitude.

Just ponder the significance of the Court's decision to take matters into its own hands. The Court's revision of the law authorizes the Internal Revenue Service to spend tens of billions of dollars every year in tax credits on federal Exchanges. It affects the price of insurance for millions of Americans. It diminishes the participation of the States in the implementation of the Act. It vastly expands the reach of the Act's individual mandate, whose scope depends in part on the availability of credits. What a parody today's decision makes of Hamilton's assurances to the people of New York: "The legislature not only commands the purse but prescribes the rules by which the duties and rights of every citizen are to be regulated. The judiciary, on the contrary, has no influence over ... the purse; no direction ... of the wealth of society, and can take no active resolution whatever. It may truly be said to have neither force nor will but merely judgment." The Federalist No. 78. . . .

Perhaps the Patient Protection and Affordable Care Act will attain the enduring status of the Social Security Act or the Taft–Hartley Act; perhaps not. But this Court's two decisions on the Act will surely be remembered through the years. The somersaults of statutory interpretation they have performed ("penalty" means tax, "further [Medicaid] payments to the State" means only incremental Medicaid payments to the State, "established by the State" means not established by the State) will be cited by litigants endlessly, to the confusion of honest jurisprudence. And the cases will publish forever the discouraging truth that the Supreme Court of the United States favors some laws over others, and is prepared to do whatever it takes to uphold and assist its favorites.

# Part II
# Power to Regulate or Affect the Economy

The primary driver for the United States Constitution was the need to create a viable economic union. This imperative was a shared concern that had been generated by experience under the Articles of Confederation. The initial postcolonial experience with self-government had broken down pursuant to interstate rivalries and frictions that made the confederation a sum less than its parts. The efforts of states to gain advantage over others, by means of tariffs and other trade barriers, were primary incidents of this syndrome. Framing of the federal constitution reflected a legacy concerned with centralization of power. Lessons learned under the Articles of Confederation, with respect to the essential requirements for a successful economic union, were applied in the framing of the federal constitution. Foremost in this regard was Congress's power to regulate commerce "among the several states." The commerce clause of the Constitution gives the federal government primary authority over interstate commerce. This power at times intersects with state police power to regulate health, safety, and morals, raising questions of state or federal primacy in such instances. When these clashes enter the legal system, the Supreme Court is sometimes called upon to determine whether state or federal powers and interests should prevail.

# Chapter 4

# Federal Power

Federal power to regulate interstate commerce through the early twentieth century was interpreted narrowly. As the nation plunged into a national economic crisis in the form of the Great Depression, however, case law became highly deferential toward federal power to regulate any activity that might affect the national economy. For half a century thereafter, the Court consistently upheld regulatory initiatives that expanded federal power into areas traditionally reserved for state control. Expansion of the federal commerce power slowed in the 1990s, as the Court began to insist on a more demonstrable relationship between federal concern and national economic impact. The Court's decision in *United States v. Lopez* (1995) was a front-wave ruling in this regard.

*Lopez, Raich,* and *Sebelius* together reflect a somewhat ambiguous effort by the Court to reconsider—and rein in—the previous decades of almost complete deference by the Court to Congress's power to regulate under the Commerce Clause. While *Lopez* signaled the Court's new-found insistence on requiring a clear factual demonstration by Congress that the intrastate activity it sought to regulate be truly economic in nature, as well as have a clearly substantial effect on interstate commerce, *Raich* seemed to provide an exception to *Lopez*, since it allowed regulation of any intrastate activity that could be described as part of a comprehensive regulatory scheme (as opposed to a more limited, discrete law targeting local conduct alone). In the case of such large federal regulatory schemes, the Court will once-again defer to Congress's judgment on whether the intrastate activity, even if non-economic in nature, affects interstate commerce. Nevertheless, it is at least clear from the *Sebelius* decision that the Court will not allow Congress to regulate *nonactivity* under the Commerce Clause, regardless of whether the regulation relates to a larger comprehensive regulatory scheme.

## United States v. Lopez

**Citation: 514 U.S. 549.**

**Issue: Whether the federal power to regulate interstate commerce gives Congress the power to regulate gun possession in school zones.**

**Year of Decision: 1995.**

**Outcome: Congress lacks the power to regulate guns in school zones because of an insufficient relationship to interstate commerce.**

**Author of Opinion: Chief Justice William Rehnquist.**

**Vote: 5-4.**

In the Articles of Confederation, the governing document that preceded the United States Constitution, the founders of the United States gave the states broad authority, including the power to regulate commerce. Over time, it became clear that the Articles were fatally flawed. The states used their power over commerce to protect their own economies and to discriminate against interstate trade. As state economies floundered, however, the states ultimately found it necessary to replace the Articles of Confederation with a new governing document, the United States Constitution.

The Constitution gave the federal government the power to control commerce "among the several states," as well as commerce between the United States and foreign countries. However, in addition to providing the new federal government with significantly broader powers than the Articles of Confederation provided, the framers sought to limit those new powers as well by creating a federal government of specific enumerated powers. This arrangement reserved the remaining powers (including some limited power over commerce) to the states or to the people. This balance of powers, between the federal government, on the one hand, and state and local governments, on the other, is known as "federalism," and continues to be a rich source of constitutional debate within the Court.

Until the 1930s, the federal government struggled to define the scope of the federal commerce power and to clarify the dividing line between federal power and state power. In a number of cases, the Court concluded that Congress had exceeded the scope of its power. For example, in *Hammer v. Dagenhart* (1918), the Court struck down a prohibition on the interstate transportation of goods manufactured in violation of child labor laws. In other cases, the Court suggested that Congress did not have the power to regulate such activities as "production," "manufacturing," or "mining." For example, in *United States v. E.C. Knight Co.* (1895), the Court found that "[c]ommerce succeeds to manufacture, and is not part of it." Finally, in *Carter v. Carter Coal Co.* (1936), the Court distinguished between "direct" and "indirect" effects on interstate commerce and concluded that Congress did not have power to control the latter.

The Court's attitude towards federal power changed dramatically in the 1930s. Following the 1929 stock market crash, the country settled into a prolonged period of economic depression. More than 2,000 banks failed, one-fourth of the nation's work force fell into unemployment (with much higher levels of unemployment in some cities), the price of wheat dropped by nearly 90 percent, and industrial output fell by 60 percent.

In 1932 President Franklin Delano Roosevelt was elected on the promise of a "New Deal," and he took office demanding "action, and action now." One of his first acts was to call an extraordinary session of Congress to begin just five days after his inauguration. During his first 100 days, Roosevelt pushed through Congress a host of bills regulating financial markets, creating federal works programs, and regulating prices and wages. Many of these acts were received with suspicion by the federal courts. Decisions like *Panama Refining* and *Schechter,* coupled with the Court's restrictive interpretation of the commerce clause in cases like *Carter Coal Co.,* angered President Roosevelt, who viewed the Court as an obstacle to his New Deal policies.

Following his landslide reelection victory in the 1936 election, President Roosevelt developed his infamous "court packing plan," which would have altered the Court's membership (and, presumably, its decisions) by adding members to the Court. The plan provided that, when a judge or justice of any federal court reached the age of 70 without availing himself of the opportunity to retire, an additional justice could be appointed by the President. At the time, six justices were age 70 or older. If the plan had passed, the Court's membership would have expanded to 15 members, presumably giving Roosevelt a majority of members sympathetic to his policy positions.

Despite the popularity of both President Roosevelt and his New Deal, many opposed the court packing legislation. Even though Congress was constitutionally authorized to control the number of Supreme Court justices, many believed that Roosevelt was trying to manipulate the Court's membership in an obvious effort to control the Court's decisions.

In the midst of the controversy over the court packing plan, the Court decided *NLRB v. Jones and Laughlin Steel Corp.* (1937) and adopted a more deferential attitude towards Congress's commerce clause authority. Many believe that the Court's more deferential approach resulted from the pressure conveyed by the court packing plan. Regardless, *Jones and Laughlin* ushered in a half-century during which the Court upheld essentially every assertion of federal regulatory power under the commerce clause. Basically, as long as Congress has a rational basis for believing that the activity (even if predominantly *intrastate*) affects interstate commerce, then the law will be upheld as constitutional.

Alongside *Jones and Laughlin*, the case of *Wickard v. Filburn* (1942) cemented the new deferential attitude of the Court in commerce clause jurisprudence. Responding to the dramatic rise in wheat prices, Congress had passed the Agricultural Adjustment Act (AAA) in hopes of countering the rise. Under the AAA, quotas were established limiting the amount of wheat farmers could produce. Farmer Filburn grew wheat on his farm and exceeded his quota, even though Filburn primarily used his wheat for home consumption. After he was fined, Filburn sued, claiming this application of the AAA was unconstitutional because it sought to regulate his purely intrastate use of the wheat, thereby lacking the necessary interstate nexus.

The Court rejected Filburn's argument, and established what has come to be known as the 'aggregation principle,' whereby the activity in question can be added to other hypothetical activity of a similar kind, thereby achieving the interstate nexus. As Justice Jackson argued for the Court "[Although Filburn's] own contribution for the demand for wheat may be trivial by itself, [it] is not enough to remove him from the scope of federal regulation where, as here, his contribution, taken together with that of many others similarly situated, is far from trivial."

This post-1937 deferential approach came to an end with the holding in *Lopez*. This case concerned the *Gun-Free School Zones Act of 1990,* in which Congress made it a federal offense "for any individual knowingly to possess a firearm at a place that the individual knows, or has reasonable cause to believe, is a school zone." Lopez, who was then a 12th-grade student, arrived at Edison High School in San Antonio, Texas, carrying a concealed .38 caliber handgun and five bullets. When he was arrested and charged with violating the federal enactment, he defended himself on the basis that Congress had exceeded its power to regulate commerce. The Court agreed and reversed Lopez's conviction.

In deciding the case, the Court reaffirmed the notion the Constitution created a federal government of "enumerated powers." The Court quoted James Madison's statements in the Federalist Papers: "[t]he powers delegated by the proposed Constitution to the federal government are few and defined. Those which are to remain in the State governments are numerous and indefinite." In addition, the Court recognized that decisions like *Jones and Laughlin Steel* had greatly expanded Congress's authority. Then, for the first time in more than half a century, the Court held that Congress's power to regulate interstate commerce is "subject to outer limits." The Court concluded that Congress may regulate commerce in three different situations: it "may regulate the use of the channels of interstate commerce; it may regulate and protect the instrumentalities of interstate commerce, or persons or things in interstate commerce, even though the threat may come only from intrastate activities; & Congress' commerce authority includes the power to regulate those activities having a substantial relation to interstate commerce, i.e., those activities that substantially affect interstate commerce." In *Lopez*, the Court concluded that the latter category requires proof that the regulated activity "substantially affects" interstate commerce.

In striking down the *Gun-Free School Zones Act,* the Court found that the first two categories of authority were absent because the Act did not regulate the channels of interstate commerce and did not prohibit the interstate transportation of a commodity through the channels of commerce. As a result, if the Act was to be upheld, the Court would have to find that it involved regulation of an activity that substantially affects interstate commerce. The difficulty was that the Court found that the law had "nothing to do with 'commerce' or any sort of economic enterprise, however broadly one might define those terms." The Government argued that possession of a firearm in a school zone can "result in violent crime and that violent crime can be expected to affect the functioning of the national economy" because insurance spreads the cost of crime throughout the nation, and because violent crime reduces the willingness of individuals to travel to places that are regarded as unsafe. The Government also argued that the presence of guns in schools presents a substantial threat to the educational process by threatening the learning environment and resulting in "a less productive citizenry" with a consequent impact "on the nation's economic well-being."

The Court refused to accept these arguments, noting that such arguments would allow Congress virtually unfettered authority to regulate the day-to-day lives of the people. Under the government's "costs of crime" rationale, Congress could "regulate not only all violent crime, but all activities that might lead to violent crime, regardless of how tenuously they relate to interstate commerce." Moreover, if the government's "national productivity" reasoning were accepted, Congress could regulate any activity that it found was related to economic productivity including family law in general and issues like marriage, divorce, and child custody in particular. It could also regulate the entire educational process mandating curricula for all schools. The Court rejected these possibilities, noting that the "possession of a gun in a local school zone is in no sense an economic activity that might, even through repetition elsewhere, substantially affect any sort of interstate commerce." The Court emphasized that there was no proof that either Lopez or his weapon had been involved in interstate commerce. "To uphold the Government's contentions here, we would have to pile inference upon inference in a manner that would bid fair to convert congressional authority under the commerce clause to a general police power of the sort retained by the States."

Justice Anthony Kennedy, joined by Justice Sandra Day O'Connor, concurred, arguing the Act "upsets the federal balance to a degree that renders it an unconstitutional assertion of the commerce power." Even though he doubted that any reasonable person would argue students should be allowed to carry guns on school premises, he believed that states should be allowed to experiment and use their expertise "in an area to which States lay claim by right of history and expertise."

Justice Stephen Breyer, joined by three other justices, dissented, arguing Congress could have found that guns in school zones significantly undermine the quality of education in the country, and "that gun-related violence in and around schools is a commercial, as well as a human, problem." He also worried that the Court's holding raised questions regarding the validity of other federal criminal statutes premised on the commerce power. He noted that more than 100 sections of the United States Code are premised on the commerce power, and he wondered whether they would be upheld or struck down.

*Lopez* is an extremely important decision because it ends half a century of judicial deference to congressional assertions of power under the commerce clause. In subsequent decisions, the Court has required a more substantial nexus between a regulated activity and interstate commerce than it had previously required. However, the Court has struggled to find a proper balance between its prior deferential approach to congressional power and *Lopez*'s more rigorous review.

### Chief Justice REHNQUIST delivered the opinion of the Court.

. . . First, we have upheld a wide variety of congressional Acts regulating intrastate economic activity where we have concluded that the activity substantially affected interstate commerce. Examples include the regulation of intrastate coal mining, intrastate extortionate credit transactions, restaurants utilizing substantial interstate supplies, inns and hotels catering to interstate guests, and production and consumption of homegrown wheat. These examples are by no means exhaustive, but the pattern is clear. Where economic activity substantially affects interstate commerce, legislation regulating that activity will be sustained.

Even *Wickard,* which is perhaps the most far reaching example of Commerce Clause authority over intrastate activity, involved economic activity in a way that the possession of a gun in a school zone does not. Roscoe Filburn operated a small farm in Ohio, on which, in the year involved, he raised 23 acres of wheat. It was his practice to sow winter wheat in the fall, and after harvesting it in July to sell a portion of the crop, to feed part of it to poultry and livestock on the farm, to use some in making flour for home consumption, and to keep the remainder for seeding future crops. The Secretary of Agriculture assessed a penalty against him under the Agricultural Adjustment Act of 1938 because he harvested about 12 acres more wheat than his allotment under the Act permitted. The Act was designed to regulate the volume of wheat moving in interstate and foreign commerce in order to avoid surpluses and shortages, and concomitant fluctuation in wheat prices, which had previously obtained. The Court said, in an opinion sustaining the application of the Act to Filburn's activity:

"One of the primary purposes of the Act in question was to increase the market price of wheat and to that end to limit the volume thereof that could affect the market. It can hardly be denied that a factor of such volume and variability as home-consumed wheat would have a substantial influence on price and market conditions. This may arise because being in marketable condition such wheat overhangs the market and, if induced by rising prices, tends to flow into the market and check price increases. But if we assume that it is never marketed, it supplies a need of the man who grew it which would otherwise be reflected by purchases in the open market. Home-grown wheat in this sense competes with wheat in commerce."

[The Gun-Free School Zones Act] is a criminal statute that by its terms has nothing to do with "commerce" or any sort of economic enterprise, however broadly one might define those terms. [It] is not an essential part of a larger regulation of economic activity, in which the regulatory scheme could be undercut unless the intrastate activity were regulated. It cannot, therefore, be sustained under our cases upholding regulations of activities that arise out of or are connected with a commercial transaction, which viewed in the aggregate, substantially affects interstate commerce.

Second, [the Act] contains no jurisdictional element which would ensure, through case-by-case inquiry, that the firearm possession in question affects interstate commerce. . . .

Although as part of our independent evaluation of constitutionality under the Commerce Clause we of course consider legislative findings, and indeed even congressional committee findings, regarding effect on interstate commerce, the Government concedes that "[n]either the statute nor its legislative history contain[s] express congressional findings regarding the effects upon interstate commerce of gun possession in a school zone." We agree with the Government that Congress normally is not required to make formal findings as to the substantial burdens that an activity has on interstate commerce. But to the extent that congressional findings would enable us to evaluate the legislative judgment that the activity in question substantially affected interstate commerce, even though no such substantial effect was visible to the naked eye, they are lacking here. . . .

The Government's essential contention, *in fine,* is that we may determine here that [the Act] is valid because possession of a firearm in a local school zone does indeed substantially affect interstate commerce. The Government argues that possession of a firearm in a school zone may result in violent crime and that violent crime can be expected to affect the functioning of the national economy in two ways. First, the costs of violent crime are substantial, and, through the mechanism of insurance, those costs are spread throughout the population. Second, violent crime reduces the willingness of individuals to travel to areas within the country that are perceived to be unsafe. The Government also argues that the presence of guns in schools poses a substantial threat to the educational process by threatening the learning environment. A handicapped educational process, in turn, will result in a less productive citizenry. That, in turn, would have an adverse effect on the Nation's economic well-being. As a result, the Government argues that Congress could rationally have concluded that [the Act] substantially affects interstate commerce. . . .

Under the theories that the Government presents in support of [the Act], it is difficult to perceive any limitation on federal power, even in areas such as criminal law enforcement or education where States historically have been sovereign. Thus, if we were to accept the Government's arguments, we are hard pressed to posit any activity by an individual that Congress is without power to regulate.

## Justice KENNEDY, with whom Justice O'CONNOR joins, concurring.

The statute before us upsets the federal balance to a degree that renders it an unconstitutional assertion of the commerce power, and our intervention is required. As THE CHIEF JUSTICE explains, unlike the earlier cases to come before the Court here neither the actors nor their conduct has a commercial character, and neither the purposes nor the design of the statute has an evident commercial nexus. The statute makes the simple possession of a gun within 1,000 feet of the grounds of the school a criminal offense. In a sense any conduct in this interdependent world of ours has an ultimate commercial origin or consequence, but we have not yet said the commerce power may reach so far. If Congress attempts that extension, then at the least we must inquire whether the exercise of national power seeks to intrude upon an area of traditional state concern. . . .

The statute now before us forecloses the States from experimenting and exercising their own judgment in an area to which States lay claim by right of history and expertise, and it does so by regulating an activity beyond the realm of commerce in the ordinary and usual sense of that term. The tendency of this statute to displace state regulation in areas of traditional state concern is evident from its territorial operation. There are over 100,000 elementary and secondary schools in the United States. Each of these now has an invisible federal zone extending 1,000 feet beyond the (often irregular) boundaries of the school property. In some communities no doubt it would be difficult to navigate without infringing on those zones. Yet throughout these areas, school officials would find their own programs for the prohibition of guns in danger of displacement by the federal authority unless the State chooses to enact a parallel rule.

## Justice BREYER, with whom Justice STEVENS, Justice SOUTER, and Justice GINSBURG join, dissenting.

. . . To hold this statute constitutional is not to "obliterate" the "distinction between what is national and what is local," nor is it to hold that the Commerce Clause permits the Federal Government to "regulate any activity that it found was related to the economic productivity of individual citizens," to regulate "marriage, divorce, and child custody," or to regulate any and all aspects of education. First, this statute is aimed at curbing a particularly acute threat to the educational process—the possession (and use) of life-threatening firearms in, or near, the classroom. The empirical evidence that I have discussed above unmistakably documents the special way in which guns and education are incompatible. This Court has previously recognized the singularly disruptive potential on interstate commerce that acts of violence may have. Second, the immediacy of the connection between education and the national economic well-being is documented by scholars and accepted by society at large in a way and to a degree that may not hold true for other social institutions. It must surely be the rare case, then, that a statute strikes at conduct that (when considered in the abstract) seems so removed from commerce, but which (practically speaking) has so significant an impact upon commerce.

In sum, a holding that the particular statute before us falls within the commerce power would not expand the scope of that Clause. Rather, it simply would apply preexisting law to changing economic circumstances. It would recognize that, in today's economic world, gun-related violence near the classroom makes a significant difference to our economic, as well as our social, well-being. In accordance with well-accepted precedent, such a holding would permit Congress "to act in terms of economic ... realities," would interpret the commerce power as "an affirmative power commensurate with the national needs," and would acknowledge that the "commerce clause does not operate so as to render the nation powerless to defend itself against economic forces that Congress decrees inimical or destructive of the national economy."

## Bibliography

Frantz, John P. "The Reemergence of the Commerce Clause as a Limit on Federal Power: *United States v. Lopez*." *Harvard Journal of Law and Public Policy* 19 (1995): 161.

Lively, D., P. Haddon, D. Roberts, R. Weaver, and W. Araiza. *Constitutional Law: Cases, History, and Dialogues*. 2nd ed. Cincinnati, OH: Anderson Publishing, 2000, 514–24.

McElvaine, Robert S. *The Great Depression*. New York: Times Books, 1984, 137.

Nelson, Grant S., and Robert J. Pushaw, Jr. "Rethinking the Commerce Clause: Applying First Principles to Uphold Federal Commercial Regulations but Preserve State Control over Social Issues." *Iowa Law Review* 85 (1999): 1.

Nourse, V. F. "Toward a New Constitutional Anatomy." *Stanford Law Review* 56 (2004): 835.

Rossiter, Clinton, ed. *The Federalist No. 45*. New York: New American Library, 1961, 292–93.

## *Gonzales v. Raich*

**Citation: 545 U.S. 1.**

**Issue: Does Congress have the constitutional authority under the commerce clause to regulate the intrastate cultivation and possession of marijuana for medical use?**

**Year of Decision: 2005.**

**Outcome: Yes. Congress does have the authority to prohibit the local cultivation and use of marijuana under the commerce clause, despite state law to the contrary.**

**Author of Opinion: Justice Stevens.**

**Vote: 6-3.**

Ten years after the *Lopez* decision, the Court appeared to have returned to a somewhat more deferential attitude toward Congress's broad power to regulate state activity under the commerce clause. In *Raich*, the Court considered a California law that legalized the cultivation and use of small amounts of marijuana by people like Raich who used the drug for medicinal purposes. The Federal Controlled Substances Act (CSA), however, continued to criminalize such activity.

The Court upheld the federal law as constitutional under the commerce clause, thereby preempting the state law. In part, the Court relied on *Wickard*'s "aggregation principle" surmising that the aggregation of activity by people similarly situated to Raich could have a substantial effect on the interstate drug trade, and thus on interstate commerce. The Court also seemed to expand the definition of what constitutes "economic activity" beyond what was intended in *Lopez*, to include "the production, distribution, and consumption of commodities." Finally, the Court seemed to distinguish discrete, limited laws like the Gun Free School Zones Act in *Lopez*, from what the Court referred to as a "larger regulatory scheme," like the federal Controlled Substances Act in *Raich*. It appears that when dealing with larger regulatory schemes, Congress can regulate far more, including *non-economic*, *intrastate* activity that, when aggregated, Congress has a rational basis for thinking it may substantially affect interstate commerce.

Justice O'Connor, joined by justices Rehnquist and Thomas, dissented, maintaining that the decision was "tantamount to removing meaningful limits on the Commerce Clause. . . ." By singling out larger regulatory schemes for such deference, O'Connor argued, the Court has turned the *Lopez* decision into "nothing more than a drafting guide" by which Congress need only characterize the law as part of the larger regulatory scheme to avoid the limitations set forth in *Lopez*. Moreover, she maintained, "[t]he Court's definition of economic activity is breathtaking. It defines as economic any activity involving the production, distribution, and consumption of commodities."

At least when it comes to laws that are in the nature of comprehensive regulatory schemes, as opposed to limited, focused laws, the Court appears to have returned to a more deferential posture toward congressional use of the commerce clause power, characteristic of pre-*Lopez* case law.

### Justice STEVENS delivered the opinion of the Court.

. . . [T]he activities regulated by the CSA are quintessentially economic. "Economics" refers to "the production, distribution, and consumption of commodities." The CSA is a statute that regulates the production, distribution, and consumption of commodities for which there is an established, and lucrative, interstate market. Prohibiting the intrastate possession or manufacture of an article of commerce is a rational (and commonly utilized) means of regulating commerce in that product. Such prohibitions include specific decisions requiring that a drug be withdrawn from the market as a result of the failure to comply with regulatory requirements as well as decisions excluding Schedule I drugs entirely from the market. . . .

The Court of Appeals was able to conclude otherwise only by isolating a "separate and distinct" class of activities that it held to be beyond the reach of federal power, defined as "the intrastate, noncommercial cultivation, possession and use of marijuana for personal medical purposes on the advice of a physician and in accordance with state law." The court characterized this class as "different in kind from drug trafficking." The differences between the members of a class so defined and the principal traffickers in Schedule I substances might be sufficient to justify a policy decision exempting the narrower class from the coverage of the CSA. The question, however, is whether Congress' contrary policy judgment, *i.e.*, its decision to include this narrower "class of activities" within the larger regulatory scheme, was constitutionally deficient. We have no difficulty concluding that Congress acted rationally in determining that none of the characteristics making up the purported class, whether viewed individually or in the aggregate, compelled an exemption from the CSA; rather, the subdivided class of activities defined by the Court of Appeals was an essential part of the larger regulatory scheme.

First, the fact that marijuana is used "for personal medical purposes on the advice of a physician" cannot itself serve as a distinguishing factor. The CSA designates marijuana as contraband for *any* purpose; in fact, by characterizing marijuana as a Schedule I drug, Congress expressly found that the drug has no acceptable medical uses. Moreover, the CSA is a comprehensive regulatory regime specifically designed to regulate which controlled substances can be utilized for medicinal purposes, and in what manner. Indeed, most of the substances classified in the CSA "have a useful and legitimate medical purpose." Thus, even if respondents are correct that marijuana does have accepted medical uses and thus should be redesignated as a lesser schedule drug, the CSA would still impose controls beyond what is required by California law. . . . Accordingly, the mere fact that marijuana—like virtually every other controlled substance regulated by the CSA—is used for medicinal purposes cannot possibly serve to distinguish it from the core activities regulated by the CSA.

Nor can it serve as an "objective marke[r]" or "objective facto[r]" to arbitrarily narrow the relevant class as the dissenters suggest. More fundamentally, if, as the principal dissent contends, the personal cultivation, possession, and use of marijuana for medicinal purposes is beyond the "'outer limits' of Congress' Commerce Clause authority," it must also be true that such personal use of marijuana (or any other homegrown drug) for recreational purposes is also beyond those "'outer limits,'" whether or not a State elects to authorize or even regulate such use. . .

Respondents . . . contend that their activities were not "an essential part of a larger regulatory scheme" because they had been "isolated by the State of California, and [are] policed by the State of California," and thus remain "entirely separated from the market." The dissenters fall prey to similar reasoning. The notion that California law has surgically excised a discrete activity that is hermetically sealed off from the larger interstate marijuana market is a dubious proposition, and, more importantly, one that Congress could have rationally rejected.

Indeed, that the California exemptions will have a significant impact on both the supply and demand sides of the market for marijuana is not just "plausible" as the principal dissent concedes, it is readily apparent. The exemption for physicians provides them with an economic incentive to grant their patients permission to use the drug. In contrast to most prescriptions for legal drugs, which limit the dosage and duration of the usage, under California law the doctor's permission to recommend marijuana use is open-ended. The authority to grant permission whenever the doctor determines that a patient is afflicted with "any other illness for which marijuana provides relief," is broad enough to allow even the most scrupulous doctor to conclude that some recreational uses would be therapeutic. And our cases have taught us that there are some unscrupulous physicians who over-prescribe when it is sufficiently profitable to do so.

The exemption for cultivation by patients and caregivers can only increase the supply of marijuana in the California market. The likelihood that all such production will promptly terminate when patients recover or will precisely match the patients' medical needs during their convalescence seems remote; whereas the danger that excesses will satisfy some of the admittedly enormous demand for recreational use seems obvious. Moreover, that the national and international narcotics trade has thrived in the face of vigorous criminal enforcement efforts suggests that no small number of unscrupulous people will make use of the California exemptions to serve their commercial ends whenever it is feasible to do so. . . . Congress could have rationally concluded that the aggregate impact on the national market of all the transactions exempted from federal supervision is unquestionably substantial.

So, from the "separate and distinct" class of activities identified by the Court of Appeals (and adopted by the dissenters), we are left with "the intrastate, non-commercial cultivation, possession, and use of marijuana." Thus the case for the exemption comes down to the claim that a locally cultivated product that is used domestically rather than sold on the open market is not subject to federal regulation. Given the findings in the CSA and the undisputed magnitude of the commercial market for marijuana, our decisions in *Wickard v. Filburn* and the later cases endorsing its reasoning foreclose that claim. . . .

### Justice SCALIA, concurring in the judgment.

. . . Today's principal dissent objects that, by permitting Congress to regulate activities necessary to effective interstate regulation, the Court reduces *Lopez* and *Morrison* to little "more than a drafting guide." I think that criticism unjustified. Unlike the power to regulate activities that have a substantial effect on interstate commerce, the power to enact laws enabling effective regulation of interstate commerce can only be exercised in conjunction with congressional regulation of an interstate market, and it extends only to those measures necessary to make the interstate regulation effective. As *Lopez* itself states, and the Court affirms today, Congress may regulate noneconomic intrastate activities only where the failure to do so "could . . . undercut" its regulation of interstate commerce. This is not a power that threatens to obliterate the line between "what is truly national and what is truly local."

*Lopez* and *Morrison* affirm that Congress may not regulate certain "purely local" activity within the States based solely on the attenuated effect that such activity may have in the interstate market. But those decisions do not declare noneconomic intrastate activities to be categorically beyond the reach of the Federal Government. Neither case involved the power of Congress to exert control over intrastate activities in connection with a more comprehensive scheme of regulation; *Lopez* expressly disclaimed that it was such a case, and *Morrison* did not even discuss the possibility that it was. (The Court of Appeals in *Morrison* made clear that it was not.) To dismiss this distinction as "superficial and formalistic," is to misunderstand the nature of the Necessary and Proper Clause, which empowers Congress to enact laws in effectuation of its enumerated powers that are not within its authority to enact in isolation.

And there are other restraints upon the Necessary and Proper Clause authority. As Chief Justice Marshall wrote in *McCulloch v. Maryland,* even when the end is constitutional and legitimate, the means must be "appropriate" and "plainly adapted" to that end. Moreover, they may not be otherwise "prohibited" and must be "consistent with the letter and spirit of the constitution." These phrases are not merely hortatory. . . .

The application of these principles to the case before us is straightforward. In the CSA, Congress has undertaken to extinguish the interstate market in Schedule I controlled substances, including marijuana. The Commerce Clause unquestionably permits this. The power to regulate interstate commerce "extends not only to those regulations which aid, foster and protect the commerce, but embraces those which prohibit it." To effectuate its objective, Congress has prohibited almost all intrastate activities related to Schedule I substances-both economic activities (manufacture, distribution, possession with the intent to distribute) and noneconomic activities (simple possession). That simple possession is a noneconomic activity is immaterial to whether it can be prohibited as a necessary part of a larger regulation. Rather, Congress's authority to enact all of these prohibitions of intrastate controlled-substance activities depends only upon whether they are appropriate means of achieving the legitimate end of eradicating Schedule I substances from interstate commerce.

By this measure, I think the regulation must be sustained. Not only is it impossible to distinguish "controlled substances manufactured and distributed intrastate" from "controlled substances manufactured and distributed interstate," but it hardly makes sense to speak in such terms. Drugs like marijuana are fungible commodities. As the Court explains, marijuana that is grown at home and possessed for personal use is never more than an instant from the interstate market—and this is so whether or not the possession is for medicinal use or lawful use under the laws of a particular State. Congress need not accept on faith that state law will be effective in maintaining a strict division between a lawful market for "medical" marijuana and the more general marijuana market. "To impose on [Congress] the necessity of resorting to means which it cannot control, which another government may furnish or withhold, would render its course precarious, the result of its measures uncertain, and create a dependence on other governments, which might disappoint its most important designs, and is incompatible with the language of the constitution." . . .

Justice O'CONNOR, with whom THE CHIEF JUSTICE and Justice THOMAS join, dissenting.

We enforce the "outer limits" of Congress' Commerce Clause authority not for their own sake, but to protect historic spheres of state sovereignty from excessive federal encroachment and thereby to maintain the distribution of power fundamental to our federalist system of government. One of federalism's chief virtues, of course, is that it promotes innovation by allowing for the possibility that "a single courageous State may, if its citizens choose, serve as a laboratory; and try novel social and economic experiments without risk to the rest of the country."

This case exemplifies the role of States as laboratories. The States' core police powers have always included authority to define criminal law and to protect the health, safety, and welfare of their citizens. Exercising those powers, California (by ballot initiative and then by legislative codification) has come to its own conclusion about the difficult and sensitive question of whether marijuana should be available to relieve severe pain and suffering. Today the Court sanctions an application of the federal Controlled Substances Act that extinguishes that experiment, without any proof that the personal cultivation, possession, and use of marijuana for medicinal purposes, if economic activity in the first place, has a substantial effect on interstate commerce and is therefore an appropriate subject of federal regulation. In so doing, the Court announces a rule that gives Congress a perverse incentive to legislate broadly pursuant to the Commerce Clause—nestling questionable assertions of its authority into comprehensive regulatory schemes—rather than with precision. . . .

What is the relevant conduct subject to Commerce Clause analysis in this case? The Court takes its cues from Congress, applying the above considerations to the activity regulated by the Controlled Substances Act (CSA) in general. The Court's decision rests on two facts about the CSA: (1) Congress chose to enact a single statute providing a comprehensive prohibition on the production, distribution, and possession of all controlled substances, and (2) Congress did not distinguish between various forms of intrastate noncommercial cultivation, possession, and use of marijuana. Today's decision suggests that the federal regulation of local activity is immune to Commerce Clause challenge because Congress chose to act with an ambitious, all-encompassing statute, rather than piecemeal. In my view, allowing Congress to set the terms of the constitutional debate in this way, i.e., by packaging regulation of local activity in broader schemes, is tantamount to removing meaningful limits on the Commerce Clause.

The Court's principal means of distinguishing Lopez from this case is to observe that the Gun-Free School Zones Act of 1990 was a "brief, single-subject statute," whereas the CSA is "a lengthy and detailed statute creating a comprehensive framework for regulating the production, distribution, and possession of five classes of 'controlled substances.'" Thus, according to the Court, it was possible in Lopez to evaluate in isolation the constitutionality of criminalizing local activity (gun possession in school zones), whereas the local activity that the CSA targets (in this case cultivation and possession of marijuana for personal medicinal use) cannot be separated from the general drug control scheme of which it is a part.

Today's decision allows Congress to regulate intrastate activity without check, so long as there is some implication by legislative design that regulating intrastate activity is essential (and the Court appears to equate "essential" with "necessary") to the interstate regulatory scheme. Seizing upon our language in *Lopez* that the statute prohibiting gun possession in school zones was "not an essential part of a larger regulation of economic activity, in which the regulatory scheme could be undercut unless the intrastate activity were regulated," the Court appears to reason that the placement of local activity in a comprehensive scheme confirms that it is essential to that scheme. If the Court is right, then *Lopez* stands for nothing more than a drafting guide: Congress should have described the relevant crime as "transfer or possession of a firearm anywhere in the nation"—thus including commercial and noncommercial activity, and clearly encompassing some activity with assuredly substantial effect on interstate commerce. Had it done so, the majority hints, we would have sustained its authority to regulate possession of firearms in school zones. Furthermore, today's decision suggests we would readily sustain a congressional decision to attach the regulation of intrastate activity to a pre-existing comprehensive (or even not-so-comprehensive) scheme. If so, the Court invites increased federal regulation of local activity even if, as it suggests, Congress would not enact a *new* interstate scheme exclusively for the sake of reaching intrastate activity.

I cannot agree that our decision in *Lopez* contemplated such evasive or over-broad legislative strategies with approval. Until today, such arguments have been made only in dissent. *Lopez* and *Morrison* did not indicate that the constitutionality of federal regulation depends on superficial and formalistic distinctions. Likewise I did not understand our discussion of the role of courts in enforcing outer limits of the Commerce Clause for the sake of maintaining the federalist balance our Constitution requires, as a signal to Congress to enact legislation that is more extensive and more intrusive into the domain of state power. If the Court always defers to Congress as it does today, little may be left to the notion of enumerated powers.

The hard work for courts, then, is to identify objective markers for confining the analysis in Commerce Clause cases. Here, respondents challenge the constitutionality of the CSA as applied to them and those similarly situated. I agree with the Court that we must look beyond respondents' own activities. Otherwise, individual litigants could always exempt themselves from Commerce Clause regulation merely by pointing to the obvious—that their personal activities do not have a substantial effect on interstate commerce. The task is to identify a mode of analysis that allows Congress to regulate more than nothing (by declining to reduce each case to its litigants) and less than everything (by declining to let Congress set the terms of analysis). The analysis may not be the same in every case, for it depends on the regulatory scheme at issue and the federalism concerns implicated.

A number of objective markers are available to confine the scope of constitutional review here. Both federal and state legislation—including the CSA itself, the California Compassionate Use Act, and other state medical marijuana legislation—recognize that medical and nonmedical (*i.e.,* recreational) uses of drugs are realistically distinct and can be segregated, and regulate them differently. Respondents challenge only the application of the CSA to medicinal use of marijuana. Moreover, because fundamental structural concerns about dual sovereignty animate our Commerce Clause cases, it is relevant that this case involves the interplay of federal and state regulation in areas of criminal law and social policy, where "States lay claim by right of history and expertise." California, like other States, has drawn on its reserved powers to distinguish the regulation of medicinal marijuana. To ascertain whether Congress' encroachment is constitutionally justified in this case, then, I would focus here on the personal cultivation, possession, and use of marijuana for medicinal purposes. . . .

### Bibliography

Crowell, David M. "*Gonzales v. Raich* and the Development of Commerce Clause Jurisprudence: is the Necessary and Proper Clause the Perfect Drug?" *Rutgers Law Journal* 38 (2006): 251.

Ghoshray, Saby. "From Wheat to Marijuana: Revisiting the Federalism Debate Post-*Gonzales v. Raich*." *Wayne Law Review* 58 (2012): 63.

## *National Federation of Independent Businesses v. Sebelius*

> **Citation: 132 S.Ct. 2566.**
>
> **Issue: Does Congress have power under the Commerce Clause to require most Americans to purchase health insurance?**
>
> **Year of Decision: 2012.**
>
> **Outcome: No.**
>
> **Author of Opinion: Chief Justice Roberts.**
>
> **Vote: 5-4.**

In the face of a House of Representatives and Senate deeply divided along partisan political lines, Congress passed the Patient Protection and Affordable Care Act (ACA). The ACA became effective in 2010. The ACA sought to affect a massive overhaul of the health care system in the United States. Among its voluminous provisions, the ACA contained an individual mandate requiring nonexempt individuals to purchase and maintain a minimum level of health insurance or face a yearly financial penalty for failure to do so.

In a 5-4 decision, the Court ultimately upheld the individual mandate provision under the Taxing and Spending Clause of the Constitution. However, the Court rejected the constitutionality of the individual mandate as a valid exercise of the Commerce Clause. The Court ruled that "[u]pholding the Affordable Care Act under the Commerce Clause would give Congress the same license to regulate what people do not do. The Framers knew the difference between doing something and doing nothing. They gave Congress the power to regulate commerce, not to compel it. Ignoring that distinction would undermine the principle that the Federal Government is a government of limited and enumerated powers." As part of a jointly written dissenting opinion, Justices Antonin Scalia, Anthony Kennedy, Clarence Thomas, and Samuel Alito disagreed with the majority's finding that the mandate was a tax, arguing that because Congress characterized the payment as a *penalty*, to instead characterize it as a tax would amount to rewriting the Act.

**Chief Justice ROBERTS announced the judgment of the Court and delivered the opinion of the Court with respect to its principal parts.**

. . . Given its expansive scope, it is no surprise that Congress has employed the commerce power in a wide variety of ways to address the pressing needs of the time. But Congress has never attempted to rely on that power to compel individuals not engaged in commerce to purchase an unwanted product. . .

The Constitution grants Congress the power to "*regulate* Commerce." Art. 1, § 8, cl. 3. The power to *regulate* commerce presupposes the existence of commercial activity to be regulated. If the power to "regulate" something included the power to create it, many of the provisions in the Constitution would be superfluous. For example, the Constitution gives Congress the power to "coin Money," in addition to the power to "regulate the Value thereof." And it gives Congress the power to "raise and support Armies" and to "provide and maintain a Navy," in addition to the power to "make Rules for the Government and Regulation of the land and naval Forces." If the power to regulate the armed forces or the value of money included the power to bring the subject of the regulation into existence, the specific grant of such powers would have been unnecessary. The language of the Constitution reflects the natural understanding that the power to regulate assumes there is already something to be regulated. . . .

The individual mandate, however, does not regulate existing commercial activity. It instead compels individuals to *become* active in commerce by purchasing a product, on the ground that their failure to do so affects interstate commerce. Construing the Commerce Clause to permit Congress to regulate individuals precisely *because* they are doing nothing would open a new and potentially vast domain to congressional authority. Every day individuals do not do an infinite number of things. In some cases they decide not to do something; in others they simply fail to do it. Allowing Congress to justify federal regulation by pointing to the effect of inaction on commerce would bring countless decisions an individual could *potentially* make within the scope of federal regulation, and—under the Government's theory—empower Congress to make those decisions for him. . . .

People, for reasons of their own, often fail to do things that would be good for them or good for society. Those failures—joined with the similar failures of others—can readily have a substantial effect on interstate commerce. Under the Government's logic, that authorizes Congress to use its commerce power to compel citizens to act as the Government would have them act.

That is not the country the Framers of our Constitution envisioned. James Madison explained that the Commerce Clause was "an addition which few oppose and from which no apprehensions are entertained." The Federalist No. 45. While Congress's authority under the Commerce Clause has of course expanded with the growth of the national economy, our cases have "always recognized that the power to regulate commerce, though broad indeed, has limits." The Government's theory would erode those limits, permitting Congress to reach beyond the natural extent of its authority, "everywhere extending the sphere of its activity and drawing all power into its impetuous vortex." The Federalist No. 48. Congress already enjoys vast power to regulate much of what we do. Accepting the Government's theory would give Congress the same license to regulate what we do not do, fundamentally changing the relation between the citizen and the Federal Government.

**Justice GINSBURG, with whom Justice SOTOMAYOR joins, and with whom Justice BREYER and Justice KAGAN join as to Parts I, II, III, and IV, concurring in part, concurring in the judgment in part, and dissenting in part.**

. . . Consistent with the Framers' intent, we have repeatedly emphasized that Congress' authority under the Commerce Clause is dependent upon "practical" considerations, including "actual experience." We afford Congress the leeway "to undertake to solve national problems directly and realistically."

Until today, this Court's pragmatic approach to judging whether Congress validly exercised its commerce power was guided by two familiar principles. First, Congress has the power to regulate economic activities "that substantially affect interstate commerce." *Gonzales v. Raich.* This capacious power extends even to local activities that, viewed in the aggregate, have a substantial impact on interstate commerce.

Second, we owe a large measure of respect to Congress when it frames and enacts economic and social legislation. When appraising such legislation, we ask only (1) whether Congress had a "rational basis" for concluding that the regulated activity substantially affects interstate commerce, and (2) whether there is a "reasonable connection between the regulatory means selected and the asserted ends." In answering these questions, we presume the statute under review is constitutional and may strike it down only on a "plain showing" that Congress acted irrationally.

Straightforward application of these principles would require the Court to hold that the minimum coverage provision is proper Commerce Clause legislation. Beyond dispute, Congress had a rational basis for concluding that the uninsured, as a class, substantially affect interstate commerce. Those without insurance consume billions of dollars of health-care products and services each year. Those goods are produced, sold, and delivered largely by national and regional companies who routinely transact business across state lines. The uninsured also cross state lines to receive care. Some have medical emergencies while away from home. Others, when sick, go to a neighboring State that provides better care for those who have not prepaid for care.

Not only do those without insurance consume a large amount of health care each year; critically, as earlier explained, their inability to pay for a significant portion of that consumption drives up market prices, foists costs on other consumers, and reduces market efficiency and stability. Given these far-reaching effects on interstate commerce, the decision to forgo insurance is hardly inconsequential or equivalent to "doing nothing." [I]t is, instead, an economic decision Congress has the authority to address under the Commerce Clause.

The minimum coverage provision, furthermore, bears a "reasonable connection" to Congress' goal of protecting the health-care market from the disruption caused by individuals who fail to obtain insurance. By requiring those who do not carry insurance to pay a toll, the minimum coverage provision gives individuals a strong incentive to insure. This incentive, Congress had good reason to believe, would reduce the number of uninsured and, correspondingly, mitigate the adverse impact the uninsured have on the national health-care market.

Congress also acted reasonably in requiring uninsured individuals, whether sick or healthy, either to obtain insurance or to pay the specified penalty. As earlier observed, because every person is at risk of needing care at any moment, all those who lack insurance, regardless of their current health status, adversely affect the price of health care and health insurance. Moreover, an insurance-purchase requirement limited to those in need of immediate care simply could not work. Insurance companies would either charge these individuals prohibitively expensive premiums, or, if community-rating regulations were in place, close up shop. "[W]here we find that the legislators ... have a rational basis for finding a chosen regulatory scheme necessary to the protection of commerce, our investigation is at an end." Congress' enactment of the minimum coverage provision, which addresses a specific interstate problem in a practical, experience-informed manner, easily meets this criterion. . . .

## Bibliography

Adler, Jonathan H. "The Conflict of Visions in *NFIB v. Sebelius*." *Drake Law Review* 62 (2014).

Graetz, Michael J., and Jerry L. Mashaw. "Constitutional Uncertainty and the Design of Social Insurance: Reflections on the Obamacare Case." *Harvard Law and Policy Review* 7 (2013): 343.

# Chapter 5

# State Power

Although the commerce clause vests the federal government with exclusive authority over the national economy, the states retain an interest in regulating matters of health, safety, and public welfare. A state law that prohibits smoking in restaurants, for instance, accounts for public health but also affects interstate commerce. Regulation of this nature is allowable, however, so long as it does not unduly burden federal interests in efficient interstate commerce. Dormant commerce clause issues are not contingent upon congressional enactment of a conflicting regulation, and this absence of federal law is the reason these issues are referred to as "dormant" commerce clause issues. Such controversies are resolved pursuant to the supremacy clause and associated preemption principles, discussed later in *Pacific Gas and Electric Co. v. State Energy Resources Conservation and Development Commission* (1983). The seminal dormant commerce clause case arose in the mid-nineteenth century when, in *Cooley v. Board of Wardens* (1851), the Court upheld a state law requiring ships to use local pilots for navigation to and from the port of Philadelphia. This outcome correlates with modern standards providing that, absent protectionist methods or an undue burden upon interstate commerce, state regulation is permissible. The Court's ruling, in *Philadelphia v. New Jersey* (1978), exemplifies the Court's intolerance for state regulation that would secure an economic advantage and undermine the premises of a national economic union.

The Court has ruled, however, that states may have the power to sue an agency of the federal government in order to force that agency to comply with what the state considers its obligations—for instance, to deal with climate change—under federal law. In *Massachusstts v. Environmental Protection Agency*, the Court ruled that Massachusetts could sue to challenge the EPA's failure to set forth rules dealing with greenhouse gas emissions.

## *City of Philadelphia v. New Jersey*

**Citation: 437 U.S. 617.**

**Issue: Whether the State of New Jersey violated the constitutional ban on discrimination against interstate commerce when it banned the importation of out-of-state landfill waste.**

**Year of Decision: 1978.**

**Outcome: A city may not discriminate against interstate commerce by prohibiting the importation of out-of-state garbage.**

**Author of Opinion: Justice Potter Stewart.**

**Vote: 7-2.**

Following the American Revolution, the 13 colonies adopted the Articles of Confederation and retained for themselves the authority to regulate commerce. Under the Articles, the economy did not function well as the individual states established trade barriers and imposed protectionist measures, and it eventually became clear that the Articles must be amended (or some other action taken) to provide the federal government with greater power over commerce. Ultimately, a decision was made to replace the Articles with the United States Constitution and to vest control over interstate commerce in the federal government. Under the Constitution, the states retained the "police power," which gave them the right to promote health, safety, and welfare issues. However, the Court placed limits on the states' power to discriminate against, or impose burdens on, interstate commerce.

*City of Philadelphia v. New Jersey* involves the ongoing conflict between Congress's power to regulate interstate commerce and the state's police powers. *City of Philadelphia* involved a New Jersey law that prohibited the importation of most "solid or liquid waste which originated or was collected outside the territorial limits of the State.. . ." The law was challenged by private New Jersey landfills, as well as by cities in other states that had contracts with the landfills, on the basis that the law involved an unconstitutional discrimination against interstate commerce. The New Jersey Supreme Court upheld the law on the basis that it advanced "vital health and environmental objectives" and imposed no economic discrimination against, and with little burden upon, interstate commerce.

In reversing, the United States Supreme Court recognized that many aspects of commerce escape congressional attention "because of their local character and their number and diversity" and that the states may retain authority to regulate these subjects. When a state seeks to advance legitimate health and safety interests, and there is no attempt to discriminate against interstate commerce, the Court suggested that it would evaluate the restriction under a less restrictive level of review. However, the Court held that its prior decisions generally prohibited state and local governments from imposing "economic isolation" and protectionism and that "a virtually *per se* rule of invalidity has been erected" against isolationist measures.

In evaluating the New Jersey law, the Court quickly concluded that it was a "protectionist" measure. Although the state was concerned about the environmental effects of waste, the state sought to preserve its landfill sites exclusively for New

Jersey citizens. The state thus determined that the best way to extend the life of its landfill sites was by excluding out-of-state waste. The Court concluded that, "whatever New Jersey's ultimate purpose, it may not be accomplished by discriminating against articles of commerce coming from outside the State unless there is some reason, apart from their origin, to treat them differently. Both on its face and in its plain effect, ch. 363 violates this principle of nondiscrimination."

Justice William Rehnquist, joined by Chief Justice Warren Burger, dissented, arguing that problems with the sanitary treatment and disposal of solid waste is growing and that "landfills present significant health risks because they produce noxious liquids and pollute ground and surface water." He disagreed with the Court's conclusion that New Jersey could not prohibit out-of-state waste from being deposited in New Jersey landfills and pointed out that New Jersey was free to prohibit the importation of items "which, on account of their existing condition, would bring in and spread disease, pestilence, and death, such as rags or other substances infected with the germs of yellow fever or the virus of small-pox, or cattle or meat or other provisions that are diseased or decayed or otherwise, from their condition and quality, unfit for human use or consumption." On the same basis, he concluded that "New Jersey should be free to prohibit the importation of solid waste because of the health and safety problems that such waste poses to its citizens. The fact that New Jersey continues to, and indeed must continue to, dispose of its own solid waste does not mean that New Jersey may not prohibit the importation of even more solid waste into the State."

*City of Philadelphia* is an important decision because it reaffirms the long-standing principle that the states may not enact protectionist measures and may not discriminate against interstate commerce. Even when the "commerce" involves sanitary waste, which presents potential safety and health risks to a state's citizens, the state has no power to discriminate.

## Mr. Justice STEWART delivered the opinion of the Court.

. . . The New Jersey law at issue in this case falls squarely within the area that the Commerce Clause puts off limits to state regulation. On its face, it imposes on out-of-state commercial interests the full burden of conserving the State's remaining landfill space. It is true that in our previous cases the scarce natural resource was itself the article of commerce, whereas here the scarce resource and the article of commerce are distinct. But that difference is without consequence. In both instances, the State has overtly moved to slow or freeze the flow of commerce for protectionist reasons. It does not matter that the State has shut the article of commerce inside the State in one case and outside the State in the other. What is crucial is the attempt by one State to isolate itself from a problem common to many by erecting a barrier against the movement of interstate trade.

The appellees argue that not all laws which facially discriminate against out-of-state commerce are forbidden protectionist regulations. In particular, they point to quarantine laws, which this Court has repeatedly upheld even though they appear to single out interstate commerce for special treatment. In the appellees' view, [the law] is analogous to such health-protective measures, since it reduces the exposure of New Jersey residents to the allegedly harmful effects of landfill sites.

It is true that certain quarantine laws have not been considered forbidden protectionist measures, even though they were directed against out-of-state commerce. But those quarantine laws banned the importation of articles such as diseased livestock that required destruction as soon as possible because their very movement risked contagion and other evils. Those laws thus did not discriminate against interstate commerce as such, but simply prevented traffic in noxious articles, whatever their origin.

The New Jersey statute is not such a quarantine law. There has been no claim here that the very movement of waste into or through New Jersey endangers health, or that waste must be disposed of as soon and as close to its point of generation as possible. The harms caused by waste are said to arise after its disposal in landfill sites, and at that point, as New Jersey concedes, there is no basis to distinguish out-of-state waste from domestic waste. If one is inherently harmful, so is the other. Yet New Jersey has banned the former while leaving its landfill sites open to the latter. The New Jersey law blocks the importation of waste in an obvious effort to saddle those outside the State with the entire burden of slowing the flow of refuse into New Jersey's remaining landfill sites. That legislative effort is clearly impermissible under the Commerce Clause of the Constitution.

Today, cities in Pennsylvania and New York find it expedient or necessary to send their waste into New Jersey for disposal, and New Jersey claims the right to close its borders to such traffic. Tomorrow, cities in New Jersey may find it expedient or necessary to send their waste into Pennsylvania or New York for disposal, and those States might then claim the right to close their borders. The Commerce Clause will protect New Jersey in the future, just as it protects her neighbors now, from efforts by one State to isolate itself in the stream of interstate commerce from a problem shared by all. . . .

## Mr. Justice REHNQUIST, with whom CHIEF JUSTICE BURGER joins, dissenting.

. . . The question presented in this case is whether New Jersey must also continue to receive and dispose of solid waste from neighboring States, even though these will inexorably increase the health problems discussed above. The Court answers this question in the affirmative. New Jersey must either prohibit *all* landfill operations, leaving itself to cast about for a presently nonexistent solution to the serious problem of disposing of the waste generated within its own borders, or it must accept waste from every portion of the United States, thereby multiplying the health and safety problems which would result if it dealt only with such wastes generated within the State. Because past precedents establish that the Commerce Clause does not present appellees with such a Hobson's choice, I dissent. . . .

## Bibliography

Adler, Jonathon A. "Waste and the Dormant Commerce Clause—A Reply." *Green Bag* 3 (2000): 353.

Kirsten Engel, "Reconsidering the National Market in Solid Waste: Trade-Offs in Equity, Efficiency, Environmental Protection and State Autonomy," 73 *North Carolina Law Review* 1481 (1995).

Epstein, Richard A. "Waste and the Dormant Commerce Clause." *Green Bag* 3 (1999): 29.

Verchic, Robert R. M. "The Commerce Clause, Environmental Justice, and the Interstate Garbage Wars." *S. California Law Review* 70 (1997): 1239.

## *Massachusetts v. Environmental Protection Agency*

**Citation: 549 U.S. 497.**

**Issue: Whether a state has the legally authority to challenge a federal agency's failure to regulate matters affecting the economy, such as global emission.**

**Year of Decision: 2007.**

**Outcome: Yes.**

**Author of Opinion: Justice John Paul Stevens.**

**Vote: 5-4.**

The State of Massachusetts sued the Environmental Protection Agency, claiming the agency had failed to promulgate rules to deal with climate change that the State maintained was adversely affecting its shoreline. In a five to four decision divided along conservative / liberal lines, the Court ruled that Massachusetts could sue, despite the considerable scientific uncertainty concerning the degree to which such rules would decrease the problem of global warming in general, and the State's shoreline erosion in particular. In an opinion authored by Justice Stevens, the Court cited "the enormity of the potential consequences associated with manmade climate change" in deciding to rule as it did despite the uncertainty involved.

Writing for Justices Scalia, Thomas and Alito, Chief Justice Roberts maintained that a party has standing to sue only when it can demonstrate that its claimed injury is likely to be redressed by a favorable ruling. With respect to Massachusetts's claim, Justice Roberts argued that "[t]he realities make it pure conjecture to suppose that EPA regulation of new automobile emissions will likely prevent the loss of Massachusetts coastal land."

## Justice STEVENS delivered the opinion of the Court.

... A well-documented rise in global temperatures has coincided with a significant increase in the concentration of carbon dioxide in the atmosphere. Respected scientists believe the two trends are related. For when carbon dioxide is released into the atmosphere, it acts like the ceiling of a greenhouse, trapping solar energy and retarding the escape of reflected heat. It is therefore a species—the most important species—of a "greenhouse gas."

Calling global warming "the most pressing environmental challenge of our time," a group of States, local governments, and private organizations alleged in a petition for certiorari that the Environmental Protection Agency (EPA) has abdicated its responsibility under the Clean Air Act to regulate the emissions of four greenhouse gases, including carbon dioxide. Specifically, petitioners asked us to answer two questions concerning the meaning of § 202(a)(1) of the Act: whether EPA has the statutory authority to regulate greenhouse gas emissions from new motor vehicles; and if so, whether its stated reasons for refusing to do so are consistent with the statute.

In response, EPA, supported by 10 intervening States and six trade associations, correctly argued that we may not address those two questions unless at least one petitioner has standing to invoke our jurisdiction under Article III of the Constitution. Notwithstanding the serious character of that jurisdictional argument and the absence of any conflicting decisions construing § 202(a)(1), the unusual importance of the underlying issue persuaded us to grant the writ. ...

While it may be true that regulating motor-vehicle emissions will not by itself *reverse* global warming, it by no means follows that we lack jurisdiction to decide whether EPA has a duty to take steps to *slow* or *reduce* it. Because of the enormity of the potential consequences associated with manmade climate change, the fact that the effectiveness of a remedy might be delayed during the (relatively short) time it takes for a new motor-vehicle fleet to replace an older one is essentially irrelevant. Nor is it dispositive that developing countries such as China and India are poised to increase greenhouse gas emissions substantially over the next century: A reduction in domestic emissions would slow the pace of global emissions increases, no matter what happens elsewhere.

We moreover attach considerable significance to EPA's "agree[ment] with the President that 'we must address the issue of global climate change,'" and to EPA's ardent support for various voluntary emission-reduction programs. ...

In sum—at least according to petitioners' uncontested affidavits—the rise in sea levels associated with global warming has already harmed and will continue to harm Massachusetts. The risk of catastrophic harm, though remote, is nevertheless real. That risk would be reduced to some extent if petitioners received the relief they seek. We therefore hold that petitioners have standing to challenge EPA's denial of their rulemaking petition. . . .

EPA has refused to comply with this clear statutory command. Instead, it has offered a laundry list of reasons not to regulate. For example, EPA said that a number of voluntary Executive Branch programs already provide an effective response to the threat of global warming, regulating greenhouse gases might impair the President's ability to negotiate with "key developing nations" to reduce emissions, and that curtailing motor-vehicle emissions would reflect "an inefficient, piecemeal approach to address the climate change issue".

Although we have neither the expertise nor the authority to evaluate these policy judgments, it is evident they have nothing to do with whether greenhouse gas emissions contribute to climate change. Still less do they amount to a reasoned justification for declining to form a scientific judgment. In particular, while the President has broad authority in foreign affairs, that authority does not extend to the refusal to execute domestic laws. In the Global Climate Protection Act of 1987, Congress authorized the State Department—not EPA—to formulate United States foreign policy with reference to environmental matters relating to climate. EPA has made no showing that it issued the ruling in question here after consultation with the State Department. Congress did direct EPA to consult with other agencies in the formulation of its policies and rules, but the State Department is absent from that list.

Nor can EPA avoid its statutory obligation by noting the uncertainty surrounding various features of climate change and concluding that it would therefore be better not to regulate at this time. If the scientific uncertainty is so profound that it precludes EPA from making a reasoned judgment as to whether greenhouse gases contribute to global warming, EPA must say so. That EPA would prefer not to regulate greenhouse gases because of some residual uncertainty—which, contrary to Justice SCALIA's apparent belief, is in fact all that it said—is irrelevant. The statutory question is whether sufficient information exists to make an endangerment finding.

In short, EPA has offered no reasoned explanation for its refusal to decide whether greenhouse gases cause or contribute to climate change. Its action was therefore "arbitrary, capricious, ... or otherwise not in accordance with law." We need not and do not reach the question whether on remand EPA must make an endangerment finding, or whether policy concerns can inform EPA's actions in the event that it makes such a finding. We hold only that EPA must ground its reasons for action or inaction in the statute. . . .

### Chief Justice ROBERTS, with whom Justice SCALIA, Justice THOMAS, and Justice ALITO join, dissenting.

Global warming may be a "crisis," even "the most pressing environmental problem of our time." Indeed, it may ultimately affect nearly everyone on the planet in some potentially adverse way, and it may be that governments have done too little to address it. It is not a problem, however, that has escaped the attention of policymakers in the Executive and Legislative Branches of our Government, who continue to consider regulatory, legislative, and treaty-based means of addressing global climate change.

Apparently dissatisfied with the pace of progress on this issue in the elected branches, petitioners have come to the courts claiming broad-ranging injury, and attempting to tie that injury to the Government's alleged failure to comply with a rather narrow statutory provision. I would reject these challenges as nonjusticiable. Such a conclusion involves no judgment on whether global warming exists, what causes it, or the extent of the problem. Nor does it render petitioners without recourse. This Court's standing jurisprudence simply recognizes that redress of grievances of the sort at issue here "is the function of Congress and the Chief Executive," not the federal courts. I would vacate the judgment below and remand for dismissal of the petitions for review. . . .

Petitioners' difficulty in demonstrating causation and redressability is not surprising given the evident mismatch between the source of their alleged injury—catastrophic global warming—and the narrow subject matter of the Clean Air Act provision at issue in this suit. The mismatch suggests that petitioners' true goal for this litigation may be more symbolic than anything else. The constitutional role of the courts, however, is to decide concrete cases—not to serve as a convenient forum for policy debates. When dealing with legal doctrine phrased in terms of what is "fairly" traceable or "likely" to be redressed, it is perhaps not surprising that the matter is subject to some debate. But in considering how loosely or rigorously to define those adverbs, it is vital to keep in mind the purpose of the inquiry. The limitation of the judicial power to cases and controversies "is crucial in maintaining the tripartite allocation of power set forth in the Constitution." In my view, the Court today—addressing Article III's "core component of standing,"—fails to take this limitation seriously.

To be fair, it is not the first time the Court has done so. Today's decision recalls the previous high-water mark of diluted standing requirements, *United States v. Students Challenging Regulatory Agency Procedures (SCRAP)* (1973). *SCRAP* involved "[p]robably the most attenuated injury conferring Art. III standing" and "surely went to the very outer limit of the law"—until today. In *SCRAP*, the Court based an environmental group's standing to challenge a railroad freight rate surcharge on the group's allegation that increases in railroad rates would cause an increase in the use of nonrecyclable goods, resulting in the increased need for natural resources to produce such goods. According to the group, some of these resources might be taken from the Washington area, resulting in increased refuse that might find its way into area parks, harming the group's members.

Over time, *SCRAP* became emblematic not of the looseness of Article III standing requirements, but of how utterly manipulable they are if not taken seriously as a matter of judicial self-restraint. *SCRAP* made standing seem a lawyer's game, rather than a fundamental limitation ensuring that courts function as courts and not intrude on the politically accountable branches. Today's decision is *SCRAP* for a new generation.

Perhaps the Court recognizes as much. How else to explain its need to devise a new doctrine of state standing to support its result? The good news is that the Court's "special solicitude" for Massachusetts limits the future applicability of the diluted standing requirements applied in this case. The bad news is that the Court's self-professed relaxation of those Article III requirements has caused us to transgress "the proper—and properly limited—role of the courts in a democratic society." . . .

## Bibliography

DeShazo, J. R., and Jody Freeman. "Timing and Form of Federal Regulation: The Case of Climate Change." *University of Pennsylvania Law Review* 155 (2007): 1499.

Taylor, Tiffany L. "From *Georgia v. Tennessee Copper Co.* to *Massachusetts v. EPA*: An Overview of America's History of Air Pollution Regulation and Its Effect on Future Remedies to Climate Change." *University of Memphis Law Review* 28 (2008): 763.

# Chapter 6

# Federal Preemption of State Power

Wariness of a strong central government was a central theme of the federal Constitution's framing and ratification. Although the national government was conceived as a government of limited power, the Constitution's supremacy clause provides that laws enacted "under the Authority of the United States, shall be the supreme Law of the Land." Determining whether a conflict exists is not always easy. Congress, moreover, often does not indicate whether its enactments intend to preempt state regulation. The Supreme Court, however, has developed standards for determining whether a conflict between federal and state law exists and, if so, how to resolve it. In *Pacific Gas and Electric Co. v. State Energy Resources Conservation and Development Commission* (1983), the Court applied these principles to the issue of whether a state moratorium on nuclear power plant development preempted the federal government's interest in regulating the economics of atomic energy. More recently, in *Arizona v. United States*, (2012), preemption issues arose in the context of a state, Arizona, attempting to deal with immigration problems it faced although Congress had already passed laws in the immigration area in question.

## *Pacific Gas and Electric Co. v. State Energy Resources Conservation and Development Commission*

**Citation: 461 U.S. 190.**

**Issue: Whether Congress's regulation of nuclear power plant safety preempted a state moratorium on nuclear power plant certification.**

**Year of Decision: 1983.**

**Outcome: Federal regulation did not preempt the state's ability to regulate the economics of the nuclear power industry.**

**Author of Opinion: Justice Byron White.**

**Vote: 9-0.**

The supremacy clause of the Constitution, set forth in Article VI, Section 2, establishes federal law as "the supreme Law of the Land." This provision is implicated when a state enacts legislation that conflicts with a federal law. It is reminiscent of the commerce clause, which is a barrier to state laws that unduly burden or discriminate against interstate commerce. Unlike the commerce clause, however, the supremacy clause operates only when Congress has enacted a law and an actual conflict is identified. A threshold issue in all preemption cases thus is whether, in fact, a conflict exists between federal and state law. Because congressional intent to preempt is not always manifested by explicit terminology, the Supreme Court has developed criteria for determining whether it can be identified.

Numerous activities and conditions are subject to both federal and state regulation. In many instances, dual regulation may be complementary rather than conflicting. Within the framework of dual sovereignty, case law establishes a preference for accommodation rather than preemption. Inquiry under the supremacy clause thus begins with a presumption that the state law is valid. This orientation is reflected in the Court's analysis, in *Pacific Gas and Electric Co. v. State Energy Resources Conservation and Development Commission* (1983), of California's imposed moratorium on certifying nuclear power plants. The reason for the moratorium was expressed in economic rather than safety terms. As the state of California explained it, the lack of effective technology eventually might force closure of nuclear power plants. This condition, if it were to arise, would have a profoundly negative impact upon the cost and availability of electricity.

The issue of preemption turned upon the *Atomic Energy Act of 1954*. Pursuant to this enactment, Congress created the Atomic Energy Commission (now the Nuclear Regulatory Commission) (NRC) and gave it authority over the safety of nuclear power plant construction and operation. The Commission's charge included responsibility for licensing nuclear power plants and regulating the disposal of radioactive waste. Despite the argument that the moratorium violated the supremacy clause, the Court found no conflict between federal and state law.

Justice Byron White, speaking for the majority, drew a distinction between the federal concern with the safety of nuclear power plants and their economic viability. In this regard, he noted that the federal enactment did not take away from states their traditional authority to regulate the economics of the power industry. If a state determined that nuclear power did not make economic sense, moreover, the federal government could not force a contrary decision. Absent competing or conflicting impositions, therefore, the Court found no basis for preemption. A different result would have been achieved if the state had acted upon safety grounds.

Justice Harry Blackmun, in a concurring opinion, contended that the moratorium was allowable even if it was grounded in concern with the safety of nuclear power. The *Atomic Energy Act,* as Justice Blackmun understood it, intended to diversify the nation's sources of electricity. From his perspective, there was no reason to deny states a parallel interest in accounting for safety. Justice Blackmun's position that the moratorium should be upheld regardless of the state's purpose reflects awareness that an effort to identify motive typically is a futile undertaking. The challenge of identifying a true motive is heightened in the legislative context, where outcomes typically reflect negotiation and trade-offs. The majority opinion indicates that a state regulation will not be preempted when the federal and state interests and objectives are distinct. This emphasis upon separate federal and state concerns actually might invite lawmakers, whose real concern is with safety, to adopt a false front.

Either way, the majority opinion effectively illuminates the key principles of preemption doctrine. Regardless of the case, review commences with a presumption that the state law is valid. Barring explicit congressional language announcing the intent to preempt state law, a court must assess whether there are indications to this effect. Within this context, three possibilities for preemption arise. First, an intent to preempt may be found when the "scheme of federal regulation [is] so pervasive as to make reasonable the inference that Congress left no room to supplement it." Because responsibility for electric power generation was shared by federal and state government, a pervasive national interest could not be identified. A second possibility for preemption arises when "the federal interest is so dominant that the federal system will be assumed to preclude enforcement of state laws on the same subject." Given the states' power and interest with respect to the generation of electricity, the federal interest was not dominant to the point of precluding state regulatory action. Preemption also is appropriate when state law imposes requirements that are at odds with federal law. This third basis for preemption also was inapplicable. The federal law was based upon safety concerns and did not mandate the use of nuclear power. The moratorium thus did not impose any demands that competed with federal law.

Regardless of whether the majority or Justice Blackmun provides the better model of analysis, the decision reflects the importance that the Court assigns to the imperatives of federalism. This principle of accommodation is key to balancing individual state interests and actions within the framework of a national union. Viewed in this light, the Court's decision connects closely with a premise that was central to the republic's founding and critical to the maintenance of a system governed by dual sovereigns.

## Justice WHITE delivered the opinion of the Court.

. . . There is little doubt that a primary purpose of the Atomic Energy Act was, and continues to be, the promotion of nuclear power. The Act itself states that it is a program "to encourage widespread participation in the development and utilization of atomic energy for peaceful purposes to the maximum extent consistent with the common defense and security and with the health and safety of the public." The House and Senate Reports confirmed that it was "a major policy goal of the United States" that the involvement of private industry would "speed the further development of the peaceful uses of atomic energy." The same purpose is manifest in the passage of the Price-Anderson Act, which limits private liability from a nuclear accident. The Act was passed "in order to protect the public and to encourage the development of the atomic energy industry..."

The Court of Appeals' suggestion that legislation since 1974 has indicated a "change in congressional outlook" is unconvincing. The court observed that Congress reorganized the Atomic Energy Commission in 1974 dividing the promotional and safety responsibilities of the AEC, giving the former to the Energy Research and Development Administration (ERDA) and the latter to the NRC. Energy Reorganization Act of 1974. The evident desire of Congress to prevent safety from being compromised by promotional concerns does not translate into an abandonment of the objective of promoting nuclear power. The legislation was carefully drafted, in fact, to avoid any anti-nuclear sentiment. . . . It is true, of course, that Congress has sought to simultaneously promote the development of alternative energy sources, but we do not view these steps as an indication that Congress has retreated from its oft-expressed commitment to further development of nuclear power for electricity generation.

The Court of Appeals is right, however, that the promotion of nuclear power is not to be accomplished "at all costs." The elaborate licensing and safety provisions and the continued preservation of state regulation in traditional areas belie that. Moreover, Congress has allowed the States to determine—as a matter of economics—whether a nuclear plant vis-a-vis a fossil fuel plant should be built. The decision of California to exercise that authority does not, in itself, constitute a basis for preemption. Therefore, while the argument of petitioners and the United States has considerable force, the legal reality remains that Congress has left sufficient authority in the states to allow the development of nuclear power to be slowed or even stopped for economic reasons. Given this statutory scheme, it is for Congress to rethink the division of regulatory authority in light of its possible exercise by the states to undercut a federal objective. The courts should not assume the role which our system assigns to Congress. . . .

### Justice BLACKMUN, with whom Justice STEVENS joins, concurring in part and concurring in the judgment.

. . . I join the Court's opinion, except to the extent it suggests that a State may not prohibit the construction of nuclear power plants if the State is motivated by concerns about the safety of such plants. Since the Court finds that California was not so motivated, this suggestion is unnecessary to the Court's holding. More important, I believe the Court's dictum is wrong in several respects.

The Court takes the position that a State's safety-motivated decision to prohibit construction of nuclear power plants would be pre-empted for three distinct reasons. First, the Court states that "the Federal Government has occupied the entire field of nuclear safety concerns, except the limited powers expressly ceded to the States." Second, the Court indicates that "a state judgment that nuclear power is not safe enough to be further developed would conflict squarely with the countervailing judgment of the NRC ... that nuclear construction may proceed notwithstanding

extant uncertainties as to waste disposal." Third, the Court believes that a prohibition on construction of new nuclear plants would "be in the teeth of the Atomic
Energy Act's objective to insure that nuclear technology be safe enough for widespread development and use." For reasons summarized below, I cannot agree that
a State's nuclear moratorium, even if motivated by safety concerns, would be pre-
empted on any of these grounds. . . .

In sum, Congress has not required States to "go nuclear," in whole or in part.
The Atomic Energy Act's twin goals were to promote the development of a technology and to ensure the safety of that technology. Although that Act reserves
to the NRC decisions about how to build and operate nuclear plants, the Court
reads too much into the Act in suggesting that it also limits the States' traditional power to decide what types of electric power to utilize. Congress simply
has made the nuclear option available, and a State may decline that option for
any reason. Rather than rest on the elusive test of legislative motive, therefore, I
would conclude that the decision whether to build nuclear plants remains with
the States. In my view, a ban on construction of nuclear power plants would
be valid even if its authors were motivated by fear of a core meltdown or other
nuclear catastrophe.

## Bibliography

Hoke, S. Candice. "Preemption Pathologies and Civic Republican Virtues." *Boston University Law Review* 71 (1991): 685.

Rotunda, Ronald D. "The Doctrine of the Inner Political Check, The Dormant Commerce
Clause, and Federal Preemption." *Transportation Practitioners Journal* 53 (1986): 263.

## *Arizona v. United States*

Citation: 132 S.Ct 2492.

Issue: Do the federal immigration laws preempt Arizona's efforts at
cooperative law enforcement?

Year of Decision: 2012.

Outcome: Yes. Federal laws do preempt three of the four Arizona
immigration laws being challenged.

Author of Opinion: Justice Anthony Kennedy.

Vote: 5-3.

In April 2010 Arizona passed S.B. 1070, a far-reaching and immensely controversial anti-illegal immigration measure. Later that year, the United States challenged
the law as unconstitutional. The district court enjoined four provisions of the law.
Arizona appealed the district court's decision to the Ninth Circuit Court of Appeals.
The Ninth Circuit affirmed the district court's decision, holding that the United

States had shown that federal law likely preempted the following four provisions of Arizona's law: (1) Arizona's criminalizing violations of federal registration laws, (2) Arizona's criminalizing work by unauthorized aliens, (3) Arizona's requirement that the citizenship of all detained persons be verified, and (4) Arizona's provision that a state officer, "without a warrant, may arrest a person if the officer has probable cause to believe . . . [the person] has committed any public offense that makes [him] removable from the United States."

As a general matter of principle, the Supreme Court held that "[t]he National Government has significant power to regulate immigration. With power comes responsibility, and the sound exercise of national power over immigration depends on the Nation's meeting its responsibility to base its laws on a political will informed by searching, thoughtful, rational civic discourse. Arizona may have understandable frustrations with the problems caused by illegal immigration while that process continues, but the State may not pursue policies that undermine federal law."

More specifically, the Court held that the first of the above-noted provisions is preempted because it conflicts with federal law's registration requirements and enforcement provisions. The second provision is preempted because "the correct instruction to draw from the text, structure, and history of [the Federal law] is that Congress decided it would be inappropriate to impose criminal penalties on aliens who seek or engage in unauthorized employment. It follows that a state law to the contrary is an obstacle to the regulatory system Congress chose." The Court found the third provision preempted because Congress had put in place a system in which state law enforcement could not make warrantless arrests of aliens based on possible removability except in limited circumstances. By authorizing state officers to engage in these enforcement activities as a general matter, Arizona created an obstacle to the full objectives of Congress.

However, the Court upheld the fourth provision as constitutional on its face. This provision merely allows state law enforcement officials to communicate with the federal Immigrations and Customs Enforcement office during lawful arrests. Nothing on the face of the law showed that it conflicted with federal law. Justice Kennedy did note, however, that the Court's decision did not foreclose future constitutional challenges to the law on an as applied basis.

### Justice KENNEDY delivered the opinion of the Court.

. . . The Government of the United States has broad, undoubted power over the subject of immigration and the status of aliens. This authority rests, in part, on the National Government's constitutional power to "establish an uniform Rule of Naturalization," U.S. Const., Art. I, § 8, cl. 4, and its inherent power as sovereign to control and conduct relations with foreign nations. The federal power to determine immigration policy is well settled. Immigration policy can affect trade, investment, tourism, and diplomatic relations for the entire Nation, as well as the perceptions and expectations of aliens in this country who seek the full protection of its laws. . . .

It is fundamental that foreign countries concerned about the status, safety, and security of their nationals in the United States must be able to confer and communicate on this subject with one national sovereign, not the 50 separate States. This Court has reaffirmed that "[o]ne of the most important and delicate of all international relationships ... has to do with the protection of the just rights of a country's own nationals when those nationals are in another country."

Federal governance of immigration and alien status is extensive and complex. Congress has specified categories of aliens who may not be admitted to the United States. Unlawful entry and unlawful reentry into the country are federal offenses. Once here, aliens are required to register with the Federal Government and to carry proof of status on their person. Failure to do so is a federal misdemeanor. Federal law also authorizes States to deny noncitizens a range of public benefits, and it imposes sanctions on employers who hire unauthorized workers. . . .

The pervasiveness of federal regulation does not diminish the importance of immigration policy to the States. Arizona bears many of the consequences of unlawful immigration. Hundreds of thousands of deportable aliens are apprehended in Arizona each year. Unauthorized aliens who remain in the State comprise, by one estimate, almost six percent of the population. And in the State's most populous county, these aliens are reported to be responsible for a disproportionate share of serious crime.

Statistics alone do not capture the full extent of Arizona's concerns. Accounts in the record suggest there is an "epidemic of crime, safety risks, serious property damage, and environmental problems" associated with the influx of illegal migration across private land near the Mexican border. Phoenix is a major city of the United States, yet signs along an interstate highway 30 miles to the south warn the public to stay away. One reads, "DANGER—PUBLIC WARNING—TRAVEL NOT RECOMMENDED/Active Drug and Human Smuggling Area/Visitors May Encounter Armed Criminals and Smuggling Vehicles Traveling at High Rates of Speed." The problems posed to the State by illegal immigration must not be underestimated.

These concerns are the background for the formal legal analysis that follows. The issue is whether, under preemption principles, federal law permits Arizona to implement the state-law provisions in dispute. . . .

However the law is interpreted, if [Arizona's fourth provision] only requires state officers to conduct a status check during the course of an authorized, lawful detention or after a detainee has been released, the provision likely would survive preemption—at least absent some showing that it has other consequences that are adverse to federal law and its objectives. There is no need in this case to address whether reasonable suspicion of illegal entry or another immigration crime would be a legitimate basis for prolonging a detention, or whether this too would be preempted by federal law.

The nature and timing of this case counsel caution in evaluating the validity of [Arizona's fourth provision]. The Federal Government has brought suit against a sovereign State to challenge the provision even before the law has gone into effect. There is a basic uncertainty about what the law means and how it will be enforced. At this stage, without the benefit of a definitive interpretation from the state courts, it would be inappropriate to assume [Arizona's fourth provision] will be construed in a way that creates a conflict with federal law. This opinion does not foreclose other preemption and constitutional challenges to the law as interpreted and applied after it goes into effect. . . .

## Justice THOMAS, concurring in part and dissenting in part.

I agree with Justice SCALIA that federal immigration law does not pre-empt any of the challenged provisions of S.B. 1070. I reach that conclusion, however, for the simple reason that there is no conflict between the "ordinary meanin[g]" of the relevant federal laws and that of the four provisions of Arizona law at issue here.

Section 2(B) of S.B. 1070 provides that, when Arizona law enforcement officers reasonably suspect that a person they have lawfully stopped, detained, or arrested is unlawfully present, "a reasonable attempt shall be made, when practicable, to determine the immigration status of the person" pursuant to the verification procedure established by Congress in 8 U.S.C. § 1373(c). Nothing in the text of that or any other federal statute prohibits Arizona from directing its officers to make immigration-related inquiries in these situations. To the contrary, federal law expressly states that "no State or local government entity may be prohibited, or in any way restricted, from sending to or receiving from" federal officials "information regarding the immigration status" of an alien. And, federal law imposes an affirmative obligation on federal officials to respond to a State's immigration-related inquiries.

Section 6 of S.B. 1070 authorizes Arizona law enforcement officers to make warrantless arrests when there is probable cause to believe that an arrestee has committed a public offense that renders him removable under federal immigration law. States, as sovereigns, have inherent authority to conduct arrests for violations of federal law, unless and until Congress removes that authority. Federal law does limit the authority of *federal* officials to arrest removable aliens, but those statutes do not apply to *state* officers. And, federal law expressly recognizes that state officers may "cooperate with the Attorney General" in the "apprehension" and "detention" of "aliens not lawfully present in the United States." Nothing in that statute indicates that such cooperation requires a prior "request, approval, or other instruction from the Federal Government."

Section 3 of S.B. 1070 makes it a crime under Arizona law for an unlawfully present alien to willfully fail to complete or carry an alien registration document in violation of 8 U.S.C. § 1304(e) and § 1306(a). Section 3 simply incorporates federal registration standards. Unlike the Court, I would not hold that Congress pre-empted the field of enforcing those standards. "[O]ur recent cases have frequently rejected field pre-emption in the absence of statutory language expressly requiring it." Here, nothing in the text of the relevant federal statutes indicates that

Congress intended enforcement of its registration requirements to be exclusively the province of the Federal Government. That Congress created a "full set of standards governing alien registration," merely indicates that it intended the scheme to be capable of working on its own, not that it wanted to preclude the States from enforcing the federal standards. . . . But here, Arizona is merely seeking to enforce the very registration requirements that Congress created.

Section 5(C) of S.B. 1070 prohibits unlawfully present aliens from knowingly applying for, soliciting, or performing work in Arizona. Section 5(C) operates only on individuals whom Congress has already declared ineligible to work in the United States. Nothing in the text of the federal immigration laws prohibits States from imposing their own criminal penalties on such individuals. Federal law expressly pre-empts States from "imposing civil or criminal sanctions (other than through licensing and similar laws) upon *those who employ,* or recruit or refer for a fee for employment, unauthorized aliens." But it leaves States free to impose criminal sanctions on the employees themselves.

Despite the lack of any conflict between the ordinary meaning of the Arizona law and that of the federal laws at issue here, the Court holds that various provisions of the Arizona law are pre-empted because they "stan[d] as an obstacle to the accomplishment and execution of the full purposes and objectives of Congress." I have explained that the "purposes and objectives" theory of implied pre-emption is inconsistent with the Constitution because it invites courts to engage in freewheeling speculation about congressional purpose that roams well beyond statutory text. Under the Supremacy Clause, pre-emptive effect is to be given to congressionally enacted laws, not to judicially divined legislative purposes. Thus, even assuming the existence of some tension between Arizona's law and the supposed "purposes and objectives" of Congress, I would not hold that any of the provisions of the Arizona law at issue here are pre-empted on that basis.

## Bibliography

Abrams, Kerry. "Plenary Power Preemption." *Virginia Law Review* 99 (2013).

Chacón, Jennifer M. "Policing Immigration after *Arizona.*" *Wake Forest Journal of Law and Policy* 3(2013): 2.

# Chapter 7

# Privileges and Immunities

The privileges and immunities clause of Article IV, Section 2, has a common history with the commerce clause. Both of these provisions reflect the framers' concern with state protectionism that undermines the viability of a national economic union. Cases under the privileges and immunities clause typically concern state efforts to manage public resources or opportunities (such as public employment). The Court's decision, in *Baldwin v. Fish and Game Commission of Montana* (1978), exemplifies the use of the privileges and immunities clause as a barrier to protectionist resource management.

## *Baldwin v. Fish and Game Commission of Montana*

**Citation: 436 U.S. 371.**

**Issue: Whether higher license fees for out-of-state hunters violated the privileges and immunities clause.**

**Year of Decision: 1978.**

**Outcome: The fee differential did not abridge the privileges and immunities clause.**

**Author of Opinion: Justice Harry Blackmun.**

**Vote: 6-3.**

As noted, both the privileges and immunities clause and commerce clause originated from concern with states using their police power to secure parochial advantage at the expense of a national economic union. Dormant commerce clause analysis requires the Supreme Court to measure a state law against the federal interest in efficient interstate commerce. The privileges and immunities clause also guards against state policies that would secure economic advantage at the cost of interstate functionality. In these cases, the Court must determine whether a state law imposes economic burdens or disadvantages upon citizens of other states.

Inclusion of the commerce power in the Constitution established a mechanism to ensure that states did not pursue self-interested economic policies that undermined the interests of a viable economic union. Dormant commerce clause analysis, however, does not account for state actions that do not necessarily undermine federal interests but do negatively impact other states' interests. This need is accounted for by Article IV, Section II, of the Constitution, which provides that "[t]he Citizens of each State shall be entitled to all Privileges and Immunities of Citizens in the several States." Put somewhat more simply, the privileges and immunities clause establishes a rule that states generally must not discriminate against citizens of other states merely because of their citizenship. Like other constitutional guarantees, the clause is not an absolute. Consequently, states can treat nonresidents differently under certain circumstances. Interpretation of the privileges and immunities clause thus has presented two primary challenges. The first is identifying interests that are protected under the clause. The second is determining the extent to which states may discriminate among persons on the basis of state citizenship.

There are two privileges and immunities clauses in the Constitution—one that is set forth in the Fourteenth Amendment and another that is enshrined by Article IV, Section II. The Fourteenth Amendment privileges and immunities clause secures the privileges and immunities of federal citizenship against state abridgment. As interpreted in the *Slaughter-House Cases* (1873), these privileges and immunities include:

> the right of the citizen . . . to come to the seat of government to assert any claim he may have upon that government, to transact any business he may have with it, to seek its protection, to share its offices, to engage in administering its functions, . . . [to] free access to [the nation's] seaports, . . . to the subtreasuries, land offices, and courts of justices of the several States, . . . to demand the care and protection of the Federal government over his life, liberty, and property when on the high seas or within the jurisdiction of a foreign government, . . . [t]he right to peaceably assemble and petition for redress of grievances, the privilege of the writ of *habeas corpus,* . . . [t]he right to use the navigable waters of the United States, . . . all rights secured to our citizens by treaties with foreign nations, . . .

The Article IV, Section II, privileges and immunities clause concerns itself with relationships and interactions among the states, particularly policies that favor local citizens over citizens of other states. In *Corfield v. Coryell* (1823), Justice Bushrod Washington characterized the privileges and immunities of state citizenship as including:

> those privileges and immunities which are *fundamental;* which belong of right to the citizens of all free governments, and which have at all times been enjoyed by the citizens of the several States which compose this Union.. . . What these fundamental principles are, it would be more tedious than difficult to enumerate. They may all, however, be comprehended under the following general heads: protection by the government, with the right to acquire and possess property of every kind, and to pursue and obtain happiness and safety, . . . the right of a citizen to pass through, or to reside in any other state, for purposes of trade, agriculture, professional pursuits, or otherwise; to claim the benefit of the writ of habeas corpus; to institute and maintain actions of any kind in the courts of the state; to take, hold and dispose of property, either real or personal; and an exemption from higher

taxes than are paid by other citizens of the state; [and] the elective franchise, as regulated and established by the law or constitution of the state in which it is to be exercised.

Although this itemization was set forth in a federal appeals court decision, the Supreme Court has cited it frequently and approvingly. The privileges and immunities clause was central to the Court's review, in *Baldwin v. Fish and Game Commission of Montana*, of a state policy that imposed higher hunting license fees upon out-of-state residents. Under the fee system, Montana residents could hunt elk for $9 a year. Out-of-state hunters, however, were required to pay $225 for the same privilege. The state justified the differential on grounds it evenly distributed the cost of managing the state's elk herd.

Out-of-state hunters maintained that the license fee disparity violated the privileges and immunities clause. The Court, however, sided with the state. In so doing, it stated that the privileges and immunities clause does not prohibit all burdens or distinctions correlated to state citizenship or residency. In support of this proposition, the Court cited the right to vote. The Court pointed out that "[n]o one would suggest that the Privileges and Immunities Clause requires a state to open its polls to a 'nonresident.'" Appropriate distinctions between residents and nonresidents, as the Court observed, "reflect the fact that this is a Nation composed of individual states." The privileges and immunities clause, from the Court's perspective, is offended only by those "distinctions" that "hinder the formation, the purpose or the development of a single Union of [all] States.. . . Only with respect to those 'privileges' and 'immunities' bearing upon the vitality of the Nation as a single entity must the State treat all citizens, resident and non-resident, equally."

Against this backdrop, the critical factor in support of the state's regulatory scheme was whether it burdened a basic right. Because elk hunting is a recreational pursuit that is the province of a small demographic, the Court found that it "did not rise to a level of national economic importance implicating the Privileges and Immunities Clause." A different outcome might have been reached if nonresidents had been denied their livelihood as a consequence of the policy. The bottom line in the Court's view was that elk hunting was not so significant as to be "basic to the maintenance of well-being of the Union."

Justice William Brennan, in a dissenting opinion joined by Justices Byron White and Thurgood Marshall, criticized the Court's focus upon whether elk hunting was a "fundamental" interest. In this regard, he argued that the significance of the interest should not drive the inquiry. Rather, as Justice Brennan saw it, the concern should be with the state's reason for its discrimination. Differentiation on the basis of citizenship should be permissible, he maintained, only when a problem is attributable to nonresidents and the state's regulatory response "bears a substantial relation to the problem they present." Out-of-state hunters made up only 12 percent of Montana's hunting population. In light of these numbers, Justice Brennan argued that they posed no special danger to the elk population or the state's management of it. From his perspective, no "substantial relationship" existed between the discrimination against out-of-state hunters and the problem identified by the state. To the extent the state's discriminatory licensing system responded to this concern, it represented an overreaction.

The Court's inquiry into whether an interest is "fundamental" raises issues akin to those generated when the Court identifies and develops rights that are not enumerated by constitutional text. Judicial creation of fundamental rights, in interpreting the Due Process Clause of the Fifth and Fourteenth Amendments, elicits objection on grounds the Court is overreaching its boundaries and performing a legislative function. A determination that a law violates the Due Process Clause, however, restricts the legislative branch's ability to act. When the Court determines that an interest is fundamental for privileges and immunities clause analysis, however, it expands the ambit of opportunity for states to legislate. Either way, the focus upon relative degree of importance invites criticism that analysis is more subjective than it should be.

### Mr. Justice BLACKMUN delivered the opinion of the Court.

. . . Does the distinction made by Montana between residents and nonresidents in establishing access to elk hunting threaten a basic right in a way that offends the Privileges and Immunities Clause? Merely to ask the question seems to provide the answer. We repeat much of what already has been said above: Elk hunting by nonresidents in Montana is a recreation and a sport. In itself—wholly apart from license fees—it is costly and obviously available only to the wealthy nonresident or to the one so taken with the sport that he sacrifices other values in order to indulge in it and to enjoy what it offers. It is not a means to the nonresident's livelihood. The mastery of the animal and the trophy are the ends that are sought; appellants are not totally excluded from these. The elk supply, which has been entrusted to the care of the State by the people of Montana, is finite and must be carefully tended in order to be preserved.

Appellants' interest in sharing this limited resource on more equal terms with Montana residents simply does not fall within the purview of the Privileges and Immunities Clause. Equality in access to Montana elk is not basic to the maintenance or well-being of the Union. Appellants do not—and cannot—contend that they are deprived of a means of a livelihood by the system or of access to any part of the State to which they may seek to travel. We do not decide the full range of activities that are sufficiently basic to the livelihood of the Nation that the States may not interfere with a nonresident's participation therein without similarly interfering with a resident's participation. Whatever rights or activities may be "fundamental" under the Privileges and Immunities Clause, we are persuaded, and hold, that elk hunting by nonresidents in Montana is not one of them.

**Mr. Justice BRENNAN, with whom Mr. Justice WHITE and Mr. Justice MARSHALL join, dissenting.**

. . . I think the time has come to confirm explicitly that which has been implicit in our modern privileges and immunities decisions, namely that an inquiry into whether a given right is "fundamental" has no place in our analysis of whether a State's discrimination against nonresidents—who "are not represented in the [discriminating] State's legislative halls,"—violates the Clause. Rather, our primary concern is the State's justification for its discrimination. Drawing from the principles announced in *Toomer* and *Mullaney*, a State's discrimination against nonresidents is permissible where (1) the presence or activity of nonresidents is the source or cause of the problem or effect with which the State seeks to deal, and (2) the discrimination practiced against nonresidents bears a substantial relation to the problem they present. Although a State has no burden to prove that its laws are not violative of the Privileges and Immunities Clause, its mere assertion that the discrimination practiced against nonresidents is justified by the peculiar problem nonresidents present will not prevail in the face of a prima facie showing that the discrimination is not supportable on the asserted grounds. This requirement that a State's unequal treatment of nonresidents be reasoned and suitably tailored furthers the federal interest in ensuring that "a norm of comity," prevails throughout the Nation while simultaneously guaranteeing to the States the needed leeway to draw viable distinctions between their citizens and those of other States.

It is clear that under a proper privileges and immunities analysis Montana's discriminatory treatment of nonresident big-game hunters in this case must fall. Putting aside the validity of the requirement that nonresident hunters desiring to hunt elk must purchase a combination license that resident elk hunters need not buy, there are three possible justifications for charging nonresident elk hunters an amount at least 7.5 times the fee imposed on resident big-game hunters. The first is conservation. The State did not attempt to assert this as a justification for its discriminatory licensing scheme in the District Court, and apparently does not do so here. Indeed, it is difficult to see how it could consistently with the first prong of a modern privileges and immunities analysis. First, there is nothing in the record to indicate that the influx of nonresident hunters created a special danger to Montana's elk or to any of its other wildlife species. Second, if Montana's discriminatorily high big-game license fee is an outgrowth of general conservation policy to discourage elk hunting, this too fails as a basis for the licensing scheme. Montana makes no effort similarly to inhibit its own residents.

The second possible justification for the fee differential Montana imposes on nonresident elk hunters—the one presented in the District Court and principally relied upon here—is a cost justification. Appellants have never contended that the Privileges and Immunities Clause requires that identical fees be assessed residents and nonresidents . . . . Their position throughout this litigation has been that the higher fee extracted from nonresident elk hunters is not a valid effort by Montana to recoup state expenditures on their behalf, but a price gouged from those who can satisfactorily pursue their avocation in no other State in the Union. The licensing scheme, appellants contend, is simply an attempt by Montana to shift the costs of its conservation efforts, however commendable they may be, onto the shoulders of nonresidents who are powerless to help themselves at the ballot box. The District Court agreed, finding that "[o]n a consideration of [the] evidence . . . and with due regard to the presumption of constitutionality . . . the ratio of 7.5 to 1 cannot be justified on any basis of cost allocation." Montana's attempt to cost-justify its discriminatory licensing practices thus fails under the second prong of a correct privileges and immunities analysis—that which requires the discrimination a State visits upon nonresidents to bear a substantial relation to the problem or burden they pose.

The third possible justification for Montana's licensing scheme is actually no justification at all, but simply an assertion that a State "owns" the wildlife within its borders in trust for its citizens and may therefore do with it what it pleases.

In unjustifiably discriminating against nonresident elk hunters, Montana has not "exercised its police power in conformity with the . . . Constitution." The State's police power interest in its wildlife cannot override the appellants' constitutionally protected privileges and immunities right. I respectfully dissent and would reverse.

## Bibliography

Broyles, D. Scott. "Doubting Thomas: Justice Clarence Thomas' Effort to Resurrect the Privileges or Immunities Clause." *Indiana Law Review,* Vol. 46, No. 2 (2013).

Nowak, John E., and Ronald D. Rotunda. *Constitutional Law.* St. Paul, MN: West, 1995.

Tribe, Laurence H. *American Constitutional Law.* Mineola, NY: Foundation Press, 1988.

Wiecek, William. *The Sources of Antislavery Constitutionalism in America, 1760–1848.* Ithaca, NY: Cornell University Press, 1977.

# Part III
# Equality Concepts

The guarantee of equal protection was not set forth in the Constitution as originally framed and ratified. Although the premise that "[a]ll men are created equal" was central to the Declaration of Independence, equal protection as a constitutional concept was an incident of Reconstruction following the Civil War. The Equal Protection Clause of the Fourteenth Amendment responded primarily to the nation's experience with slavery and represented a fundamental statement with respect to each individual's common relationship to the law and the legal system. As written into the Fourteenth Amendment, the Equal Protection Clause provides that no state shall "deny to any person within its jurisdiction the equal protection of the laws."

In its first significant interpretation of the Equal Protection Clause, the Supreme Court in *Strauder v. West Virginia* (1879) announced that it was intended to secure for persons of African descent "all the civil rights that the superior race may enjoy." The Court further observed that the provision implied "a positive immunity, or right, most valuable to the colored race—the right to exemption from unfriendly legislation against them distinctively as colored, exemption from legal discrimination, implying inferiority in civil society . . . and discriminations which are steps toward reducing them to the condition of a subject race." Despite this antidiscrimination interpretation, the equal protection guarantee for many decades was not a significant barrier to the official systems of segregation that managed much of racial reality. The separate but equal doctrine, which the Court announced in *Plessy v. Ferguson* (1896), was the dominant reference point for racially significant law and policy until it eventually was invalidated in *Brown v. Board of Education* (1954). The general significance of the equal protection guarantee until then was best captured by Justice Oliver Wendell Holmes, Jr., who, in *Buck v. Bell* (1927), described it as "the last resort of constitutional argument."

The determination in *Brown v. Board of Education* that officially segregated schools were "inherently unequal" transformed the Equal Protection Clause into a significant force against laws that discriminated on the basis of race. Over the next two decades, the Court expanded the guarantee's scope to account for discrimination on the basis of gender, alienage, and illegitimacy. The expanded reach of the Equal Protection Clause contrasts with original interpretation reflected in the *Slaughter-House Cases* (1873), when the Court "doubt[ed] very much whether any action of a State not directed against the Negroes as a class, or on account of their race, will ever be held to come within the purview of this provision." Subsequent history disproved this prophesy. Although the slavery experience and its aftermath of racial inequality were primary sources of inspiration for the equal protection guarantee, the status and experience of other disadvantaged groups have been found to be sufficiently comparable to merit protected status. Equal protection also became a basis for striking down laws that selectively deny a right or liberty regardless of a person's group status. Decisions in this part of the book concern the desegregation experience, application of the equal protection guarantee to gender discrimination, principles that limit the provision's operation, and affirmative action.

# Chapter 8

# Race

The equal protection guarantee emerged as a significant constitutional force when it was used to dismantle official segregation. Following the decision in *Brown v. Board of Education* (1954), the Court confronted widespread resistance to implementing its mandate to desegregate public schools. Over the course of nearly two decades following *Brown*, the Court consistently pressed for compliance. Despite an initially limited impact, passage of the Civil Rights Act of 1964 enabled the federal government to use its power and litigation resources to advance the process of desegregation. As the case for desegregation expanded beyond the South, and into Northern and Western communities where racial separation often was a result of factors less traceable to government action, the Court pondered the equal protection guarantee's limits. In *Keyes v. School District No. 1* (1973), the Court narrowed desegregation obligations to circumstances where racial segregation had been compelled by the state. One year later, in *Milliken v. Bradley* (1974), the Court announced that interdistrict busing was impermissible when a district had not caused segregation in the other district. Taking this principle beyond just the desegregation process, the Court in *Washington v. Davis* (1976) determined that any equal protection claim was dependent upon proof of an actual intent to discriminate. This standard is readily satisfied in cases where a racial preference or disadvantage is manifest by the terms of the law itself. Racial preferences, aimed at accounting for past discrimination or to achieve the benefits of diversity, became a primary focal point of equal protection jurisprudence in the final quarter of the twentieth century and the first decade of the twenty-first century. They became the basis for significant decisions in *Regents of the University of California v. Bakke* (1978), *City of Richmond v. J.A. Croson Co.* (1989), *Adarand Constructors, Inc. v. Pena* (1995), *Grutter v. Bollinger* (2003), and *Gratz v. Bollinger* (2003).

In more recent decisions, the Court appears to have become somewhat less accommodating toward race-based affirmative action programs. In *Schuette v. Coalition to Defend Affirmative Action* (2014), Michigan voters adopted Proposal 2 of the State Constitution, which prohibits the use of race-based preferences as part of the admissions process for state universities. Justice Kennedy argued on behalf of the three-person plurality that protecting interests based on race risked allowing the government to classify people based on race, and that this risks perpetuating the kind of racism the affirmative action policies were meant to counter. In upholding the Michigan referendum to outlaw affirmative action, the court stated that voters have the right to determine that some race-based preferences are helpful, as well as the right to deny the voters their democratic rights to make such choices. In *Fisher v. University of Texas* (2013), Amy Fisher challenged University of Texas's affirmative action program. The Court held that such programs must be held to the demanding review required by strict scrutiny, and remanded the case for reconsideration because the lower court had failed to do so. Specifically, the Court cautioned that "the reviewing court must ultimately be satisfied that no workable race-neutral alternatives would produce the educational benefits of diversity." Accordingly, state schools of higher education must be increasingly mindful that they can meet *Fisher's* high bar of strict scrutiny, and that the court will no longer be as willing to defer to such schools' claims that they have considered race-neutral alternatives.

## Keyes v. School District No. 1, Denver, Colorado

**Citation: 413 U.S. 189.**

**Issue: Whether segregation of public schools is unconstitutional only if required by law.**

**Year of Decision: 1973.**

**Outcome: De jure but not de facto segregation violates the Constitution.**

**Author of Opinion: Justice William Brennan.**

**Vote: 5-4.**

The Supreme Court's determination in *Brown v. Board of Education* (1954) that racially segregated schools were unconstitutional did not end segregation. The Court's command in *Brown* for desegregation "with all deliberate speed" generally was met with resistance of and challenge to its authority. The Arkansas legislature even enacted a law that purportedly freed its citizens from compliance and asserted its own authority to review "in every Constitutional manner the Unconstitutional desegregation decisions . . . of the United States Supreme Court."

In *Cooper v. Aaron* (1958), however, the Court reaffirmed that its word on the onstitution was final and binding. President Dwight Eisenhower backed the Court by dispatching federal troops to Arkansas to enforce implementation of desegregation.

Desegregation accomplishments overall in the decade after *Brown* were minimal. So limited was progress during this time that the Court eventually shifted from the "with all deliberate speed standard" to insistence upon remedies "that promise[ ] realistically to work now."

Even as the Court held firm in its demand to abolish racially segregated schools, public attitude toward desegregation became an increasingly significant factor in the process. The busing of students to achieve desegregation became a major issue in the 1968 presidential election. It was a concern not just in the South but in the

North and West, where racially segregated schools also were a common phenomenon. Outside the South, segregated public schools were less a consequence of legal mandate than of residential demographics. In *Keyes v. School District No. 1,* the Court was called upon to decide whether this type of segregation also violated the Constitution.

At issue in this case were decisions by the Denver, Colorado, school board with respect to the location of public schools, drawing of district lines, and placement of students. The Court found that the school board had developed policies and made implementations in these areas for the purpose of maintaining racial segregation. Whether legislated or otherwise, the Court determined that officially prescribed segregation conflicted with the equal protection guarantee. More significantly, it decided that proof of government's intent to segregate was a prerequisite for establishing a constitutional violation. The other side of this premise was that if segregation was not the result of intentional state action, it was not constitutionally significant.

The *Keyes* Court thus drew a line between what it characterized as *de jure* segregation and *de facto* segregation. The key aspect of *de jure* segregation, and the basis for its unconstitutionality, is official segregative intent. As the Court put it, "the differentiating factor between *de jure* segregation and so-called *de facto* segregation . . . is *purpose* or *intent* to segregate." Pursuant to its determination that racial segregation in Denver public schools was purposeful, the Court ordered their desegregation. Absent the finding of segregative intent, racial segregation would have been characterized as *de facto* and thus constitutionally inconsequential.

Significant as the difference between *de jure* and *de facto* segregation may be, the line between these two conditions is not necessarily precise. Residential segregation outside the South typically has been viewed as the result of private choice in choosing where to live. Racially identifiable neighborhoods in the North and West, however, often were facilitated and maintained by official policy. Until they were found unconstitutional in *Shelley v. Kraemer* (1948), restrictive covenants were used to create and preserve segregated neighborhoods. Such agreements are negotiated and executed as a private transaction, but their viability is dependent upon judicial enforcement. Government involvement in this manner was the basis for the Court's eventual finding that restrictive covenants were unconstitutional. Their segregative consequences, however, lasted long beyond the determination that they were invalid.

Federal home loan policies contributed further to racially segregated neighborhoods and derivatively to racially segregated public schools. The Federal Housing Administration denied loans for home purchases that would undermine the racial identity of a neighborhood. Residential segregation was fortified further by government policies regarding the siting of public schools and public housing distribution of urban renewal funds. These linkages, as Justice William Douglas observed, established a clear line between government action and racial segregation. The

Court, however, was not persuaded that these connections moved it from a *de facto* to a *de jure* condition.

Justice Lewis Powell, like Justice Douglas, was unable to differentiate segregation in the way that the Court did. He viewed it as unfair that desegregation obligations should be the work of only one region. The primary evil he perceived in racial segregation related less to official intent and more to its effect on educational opportunity. In an opinion that concurred in part with and dissented in part from the majority, Justice Powell thus advocated an outcome that would eliminate any distinction between *de jure* and *de facto* segregation.

The bottom line of *Keyes v. School District No. 1* was that the constitutional duty to desegregate hinged upon proof of official segregative intent. Making such a case was not difficult insofar as segregation was a clear and open mandate of the law, as it was during the separate but equal era. With segregation prohibited, a purpose to segregate typically did not manifest itself openly. Justice Powell noted the difficulty of identifying such a motive and that it could be disguised. Within the public school context, he mentioned how segregation could be achieved and maintained through a variety of methods that could hide the real purpose. Among these ways were the location and size of new schools, the configuration of attendance zones, faculty recruiting and assignment, curriculum, and tracking of students into academic or vocational programs.

In his dissenting opinion, Justice Thurgood Marshall expressed dissatisfaction with the distinction between *de jure* and *de facto* segregation. In Justice Marshall's view, racially segregated schools were a source of stigma regardless of causation or intent. He maintained that constitutional rights should not turn upon whether a child was "born into a *de facto* society." From his perspective, racially segregated schools under any circumstance created a sense of inferiority among students, impaired their educational opportunity, and undermined their development.

Despite the contrary views of Justices Douglas, Powell, and Marshall, the distinction between *de jure* and *de facto* segregation has become a settled boundary. The practical result has been a narrowed reach of the desegregation mandate and an impact primarily upon the South. Exceptions to this norm arose in the North and West to the extent school boards had established racially segregated schools and had not dismantled them consistent with the dictate of *Brown v. Board of Education.* In *Columbus Board of Education v. Penick* (1979), for example, the Court found segregation in Columbus, Ohio, schools attributable to knowing acts of omissions by the school board. As in *Keyes v. School District No. 1,* it thus also found a constitutional violation. The Court thus rejected arguments that segregated schooling was unconstitutional even if not commanded by state law as in the South. Noting that segregation was the direct result of cognitive acts or omissions by the school board that resulted in an enclave of separate, black schools, the Court found a constitutional violation.

By requiring proof of official segregative purpose, the Court established a significant limiting principle. Despite criticism that the distinction between *de jure* and *de facto* segregation is artificial, it is a dividing line between constitutional and unconstitutional. The result in *Keyes v. School District No. 1* did not break a two decade tradition of forceful application of the desegregation mandate. The segregative intent standard, however, made proof of a constitutional violation much more difficult. This consequence has become evident in the declining number of instances in which racially segregated schools, although still a widespread phenomenon, presented a constitutional issue.

### Mr. Justice BRENNAN delivered the opinion of the Court.

. . . Plainly, a finding of intentional segregation as to a portion of a school system is not devoid of probative value in assessing the school authorities' intent with respect to other parts of the same school system. On the contrary where, as here, the case involves one school board, a finding of intentional segregation on its part in one portion of a school system is highly relevant to the issue of the board's intent with respect to the other segregated schools in the system. This is merely an application of the well-settled evidentiary principle that 'the prior doing of other similar acts, whether clearly a part of a scheme or not, is useful as reducing the possibility that the act in question was done with innocent intent.' Similarly, a finding of illicit intent as to a meaningful portion of the item under consideration has substantial probative value on the question of illicit intent as to the remainder.

Applying these principles in the special context of school desegregation cases, we hold that a finding of intentionally segregative school board actions in a meaningful portion of a school system, as in this case, creates a presumption that other segregated schooling within the system is not adventitious. It establishes, in other words, a prima facie case of unlawful segregative design on the part of school authorities, and shifts to those authorities the burden of proving that other segregated schools within the system are not also the result of intentionally segregative actions. This is true even if it is determined that different areas of the school district should be viewed independently of each other because, even in that situation, there is high probability that where school authorities have effectuated an intentionally segregative policy in a meaningful portion of the school system, similar impermissible considerations have motivated their actions in other areas of the system. We emphasize that the differentiating factor between de jure segregation and so-called de facto segregation to which we referred in *Swann* is purpose or intent to segregate. Where school authorities have been found to have practiced purposeful segregation in part of a school system, they may be expected to oppose system-wide desegregation, as did the respondents in this case, on the ground that their purposefully segregative actions were isolated and individual events, thus leaving plaintiffs with the burden of proving otherwise. . .

This burden-shifting principle is not new or novel. There are no hard-and-fast standards governing the allocation of the burden of proof in every situation. . . In the context of racial segregation in public education, the courts, including this Court, have recognized a variety of situations in which "fairness" and "policy" require state authorities to bear the burden of explaining actions or conditions which appear to be racially motivated.

In discharging that burden, it is not enough, of course, that the school authorities rely upon some allegedly logical, racially neutral explanation for their actions. Their burden is to adduce proof sufficient to support a finding that segregative intent was not among the factors that motivated their actions. The courts below attributed much significance to the fact that many of the Board's actions in the core city area antedated our decision in Brown. . . .

This is not to say, however, that the prima facie case may not be met by evidence supporting a finding that a lesser degree of segregated schooling in the core city area would not have resulted even if the Board had not acted as it did. . . Thus, if respondent School Board cannot disprove segregative intent, it can rebut the prima facie case only by showing that its past segregative acts did not create or contribute to the current segregated condition of the core city schools.

The respondent School Board invoked at trial its "neighborhood school policy" as explaining racial and ethnic concentrations within the core city schools, arguing that since the core city area population had long been Negro and Hispano, the concentrations were necessarily the result of residential patterns and not of purposefully segregative policies. We have no occasion to consider in this case whether a "neighborhood school policy" of itself will justify racial or ethnic concentrations in the absence of a finding that school authorities have committed acts constituting de jure segregation. It is enough that we hold that the mere assertion of such a policy is not dispositive where, as in this case, the school authorities have been found to have practiced de jure segregation in a meaningful portion of the school system by techniques that indicate that the "neighborhood school" concept has not been maintained free of manipulation. . . .

In summary, the District Court on remand, first, will afford respondent School Board the opportunity to prove its contention that the Park Hill area is a separate, identifiable and unrelated section of the school district that should be treated as isolated from the rest of the district. If respondent School Board fails to prove that contention, the District Court, second, will determine whether respondent School Board's conduct over almost a decade after 1960 in carrying out a policy of deliberate racial segregation in the Park Hill schools constitutes the entire school system a dual school system. If the District Court determines that the Denver school system is a dual school system, respondent School Board has the affirmative duty to desegregate the entire system 'root and branch.' If the District Court determines, however, that the Denver school system is not a dual school system by reason of the Board's actions in Park Hill, the court, third, will afford respondent School Board the opportunity to rebut petitioners' prima facie case of intentional segregation in the core city schools raised by the finding of intentional segregation in the Park Hill schools. There, the Board's burden is to show that its policies and practices with respect to schoolsite location, school size, school renovations and additions, student-attendance zones, student assignment and transfer options, mobile classroom units, transportation of students, assignment of faculty and staff, etc., considered together and premised on the Board's so-called 'neighborhood school' concept, either were not taken in effectuation of a policy to create or maintain segregation in the core city schools, or, if unsuccessful in that effort, were not factors in causing the existing condition of segregation in these schools. Considerations of 'fairness' and 'policy' demand no less in light of the Board's intentionally segregative actions. If respondent Board fails to rebut petitioners' prima facie case, the District Court must, as in the case of Park Hill, decree all-out desegregation of the core city schools.

## Mr. Justice POWELL concurring in part and dissenting in part.

. . . There is thus no reason as a matter of constitutional principle to adhere to the de jure/de facto distinction in school desegregation cases. In addition, there are reasons of policy and prudent judicial administration which point strongly toward the adoption of a uniform national rule. The litigation heretofore centered in the South already is surfacing in other regions. The decision of the Court today, emphasizing as it does the elusive element of segregative intent, will invite numerous desegregation suits in which there can be little hope of uniformity of result.

The issue in these cases will not be whether regregated education exists. This will be conceded in most of them. The litigation will focus as a consequence of the Court's decision on whether segregation has resulted in any "meaningful or significant" portion of a school system from a school board's "segregative intent." The intractable problems involved in litigating this issue are obvious to any lawyer. The results of litigation—often arrived at subjectively by a court endeavoring to ascertain the subjective intent of school authorities with respect to action taken or not taken over many years—will be fortuitous, unpredictable and even capricious.

The Denver situation is illustrative of the problem. The court below found evidence of de jure violations with respect to the Park Hill schools and an absence of such violations with respect to the core city schools, despite the fact that actions taken by the school board with regard to those two sections were not dissimilar. It is, for example, quite possible to contend that both the construction of Manual High School in the core city area and Barrett Elementary School in the Park Hill area operated to serve their surrounding Negro communities and, in effect, to merge school attendance zones with segregated residential patterns. Yet findings even on such similar acts will, under the de jure/de facto distinction, continue to differ, especially since the Court has never made clear what suffices to establish the requisite "segregative intent" for an initial constitutional violation. Even if it were possible to clarify this question, wide and unpredictable differences of opinion among judges would be inevitable when dealing with an issue as slippery as "intent" or "purpose," especially when related to hundreds of decisions made by school authorities under varying conditions over many years.

This Court has recognized repeatedly that it is "extremely difficult for a court to ascertain the motivation, or collection of different motivations, that lie behind a legislative enactment," Whatever difficulties exist with regard to a single statute will be compounded in a judicial review of years of administration of a large and complex school system. Every act of a school board and school administration, and indeed every failure to act where affirmative action is indicated, must now be subject to scrutiny. The most routine decisions with respect to the operation of schools, made almost daily, can affect in varying degrees the extent to which schools are initially segregated, remain in that condition, are desegregated, or—for the long term future—are likely to be one or the other. These decisions include action or nonaction with respect to school building construction and location; the timing of building new schools and their size; the closing and consolidation of schools; the drawing or gerrymandering of student attendance zones; the extent to which a neighborhood policy is enforced; the recruitment, promotion and assignment of faculty and supervisory personnel; policies with respect to transfers from one school to another; whether, and to what extent, special schools will be provided, where they will be located, and who will qualify to attend them; the determination of curriculum, including whether there will be "tracks" that lead primarily to college or to vocational training, and the routing of students into these tracks; and even decisions as to social, recreational, and athletic policies.

In *Swann* the Court did not have to probe into segregative intent and proximate cause with respect to each of these "endless" factors. The basis for its de jure finding there was rooted primarily in the prior history of the desegregation suit. But in a case of the present type, where no such history exists, a judicial examination of these factors will be required under today's decision. This will lead inevitably to uneven and unpredictable results, to protracted and inconclusive litigation, to added burdens on the federal courts, and to serious disruption of individual school systems. In the absence of national and objective standards, school boards and administrators will remain in a state of uncertainty and disarray, speculating as to what is required and when litigation will strike.

Rather than continue to prop up a distinction no longer grounded in principle, and contributing to the consequences indicated above, we should acknowledge that whenever public school segregation exists to a substantial degree there is prima facie evidence of a constitutional violation by the responsible school board. It is true, of course, that segregated schools—wherever located—are not solely the product of the action or inaction of public school authorities. Indeed, as indicated earlier, there can be little doubt that principal causes of the pervasive school segregation found in the major urban areas of this country, whether in the North, West, or South, are the socio-economic influences which have concentrated our minority citizens in the inner cities while the more mobile white majority disperse to the suburbs. But it is also true that public school boards have continuing, detailed responsibility for the public school system within their district and, as Judge John Minor Wisdom has noted, "(w)hen the figures (showing segregation in the schools) speak so eloquently, a prima facie case of discrimination is established." Moreover, as foreshadowed in *Swann* and as implicitly held today, school boards have a duty to minimize and ameliorate segregated conditions by pursuing an affirmative policy of desegregation. It is this policy which must be applied consistently on a national basis without regard to a doctrinal distinction which has outlived its time. . . .

## Bibliography

Barnes, Craig. "A Personal Memoir of Plaintiffs' Co-Counsel in *Keyes v. School District No. 1*." *Denver University Law Review* 90 (2013): 1059.

Goodman, Frank I. "De Facto Segregation: A Constitutional and Empirical Analysis." *California Law Review* 60 (1972): 275.

Karst, Kenneth L. "Not One Law at Rome and Another at Athens: The Fourteenth Amendment in Nationwide Application." *Washington University Law Quarterly* 3 (1972).

Tuttle, William, Jr. *Race Riot: Chicago in the Red Summer of 1919*. New York: Atheneum, 1971.

## *Milliken v. Bradley*

**Citation: 418 U.S. 717.**

**Issue: Whether suburban schools could be included in a plan to desegregate schools in a major city.**

**Year of Decision: 1974.**

**Outcome: An interdistrict desegregation plan was permissible only if segregation in one district was the result of purposeful segregative action by officials in the other district.**

**Author of Opinion: Chief Justice Warren Burger.**

**Vote: 5-4.**

Racial segregation outside the South is grounded in processes that were less formal and comprehensive but nonetheless effective in achieving separation of the races. During the early twentieth century, many African Americans moved northward in search of economic opportunity and to escape the harsh racial realities of the South. This migration coincided with industrial expansion and demand for labor in the North's large cities. It was spurred further by World War II and its demands for increased factory productivity.

Although a source of economic opportunity, the North was not a haven from racial prejudice. Northern states did not have the comprehensive systems of racial management that typified the South. African Americans who relocated there, however, were routed into separate neighborhoods by legal and extralegal processes. Segregated housing was established and maintained pursuant to restrictive covenants. These private agreements barred a homeowner from selling his or her dwelling to persons of a different race. Federal lending policies prohibited loans to home buyers whose purchase would undermine racially identifiable neighborhoods. Neighborhood schools in the North thus reflected residential demographics and thus became segregated on the basis of race. School district boundaries, pupil placement policies, and faculty recruiting and assignments further reflected these realities.

The duty to desegregate racially segregated public schools, set forth in *Brown v. Board of Education* (1954), arose in the context of other significant changes. The advent of the automobile and emergence of suburban communities reflected an increasingly mobile society. The movement of families to new middle class and upper class communities near but apart from traditional urban centers resulted in school systems that did not even exist when *Brown v. Board of Education* (1954) was decided. These communities, although composed of persons who might have supported or facilitated segregation in their previous environment, had no history of segregation themselves. Minus this legacy, there was no record of the segregative intent that the Court had identified as the key prerequisite for an equal protection violation. As Justice Lewis Powell put it, "[t]he type of state-enforced segregation that *Brown* condemned no longer exists in this country." Despite this change, public schools in major cities reflected the historical realities of racial discrimination. Coupled with the accelerated exodus of white families to suburban communities, urban schools increasingly became racially identifiable. In cities like Baltimore, Detroit, New York, and Washington, D.C., African American students ranged from 70 percent to more than 90 percent of total enrollments. Even in the event of a constitutional violation in such circumstances, a desegregation order could not alter racial makeup of the system if it did not cross district lines.

In *Milliken v. Bradley* (1974), the Court considered the permissibility of interdistrict remedies as a means of achieving desegregation in function as well as in form. At issue was a federal district court order requiring desegregation of public schools in the Detroit metropolitan area. The order was based upon detailed findings that segregation was the result of purposeful action by the city and state. In particular, the lower court found that segregated schools were attributable in part to the school board's attendance, transportation, and school siting policies. The trial court found that the state also had caused segregated schools by nullifying a voluntary desegregation plan, using transportation to maintain segregation, and signing off on pupil assignment plans that created racially identifiable schools.

The Supreme Court, although conceding that segregation in Detroit was the result of purposeful government action, refused to uphold the interdistrict remedy. Chief Justice Warren Burger, writing for a 5-4 majority, found that responsibility for the segregated schools extended no further than the city itself. Unless the state or suburbs had engaged in actions that purposefully contributed to the segregated conditions, the Court determined that they had no obligation to participate in the desegregation process. The Court thus concluded that the scope of the district court's remedy exceeded that of the violation. This understanding left open the possibility of interdistrict relief in theory, but limited it to the rare instance in which purposeful action to cause segregation in another community could be demonstrated.

The basic principle of *Milliken v. Bradley*, that the relief must not exceed the scope of the constitutional violation, has been criticized on grounds that the Court understated the state's role in causing segregation. The result nonetheless was a significant barrier to desegregation plans that would achieve racial mixing. For practical purposes, it also demonstrated that desegregation did not necessarily require integration. Even if caused by intentional government action, segregation could be addressed only with the obvious constraint of demographic limitations. Desegregation under such circumstances thus meant ridding the system of factors that caused racially identifiable schools but did not require the elimination of racial segregation conditions themselves.

Justice Byron White, in a dissenting opinion, contended that the Court effectively had denied a needed and justifiable remedy. Justice White pointed out that the actions and policies of state public school officials over many years were a primary cause of segregated schools in Detroit, so remedial responsibility extended beyond the city limits. The state's role, although a basis for the district court's order, was minimized by the majority. Reversal of the district court represented a significant turnabout from the Supreme Court's interaction with lower courts during the first two decades of school desegregation. After years of dissatisfaction with the failure of lower courts to press the desegregation mandate, the Court in *Milliken v. Bradley* expressed displeasure with the district court pushing too hard. As Justice Thurgood Marshall saw it, the outcome provided "no remedy at all . . . guaranteeing that Negro children . . . will receive the same separately and inherently unequal education in the future as they have in the past."

The Court's ruling defined the outer limits of the desegregation principle with respect to geography and prefaced a similar restriction with respect to time. Two years later, in *Pasadena City Board of Education v. Spangler* (1976), the Court determined that school districts that had achieved desegregation were not obligated to maintain an integrated condition. To the extent that white flight or other factors may cause resegregation, and unless official action recreates a dual school system based upon race, no constitutional duty exists to preserve the fruits of desegregation. From Justice William Rehnquist's perspective, demographic change that unsettled the results of desegregation were attributable to the quite normal pattern of human migration. Dissenting as he did in *Milliken*, Justice Marshall argued that a state that created a system where whites and Negroes were intentionally kept apart so that they could not become accustomed to learning together is responsible for the fact that many whites will react to the dismantling of that segregated system by attempting to flee to the suburbs.

The curtailment of desegregation demands during the 1970s reflected a growing attitude that conditions addressed in 1954 either had been accounted for or had changed. As Justice Powell saw it, segregated schools had become a function of familiar segregated housing patterns . . . caused by social, economic, and demographic forces for which no school board is responsible. Despite the Court's initial resolve to have its orders implemented, the marking of desegregation boundaries two decades after *Brown* indicated a growing sense of limits to the judiciary's own influence. Consistent with this perspective, Justice Rehnquist observed that even if the Constitution required it, and it were possible for federal courts to do it, no equitable decree can fashion an Emerald City where all races, ethnic groups, and persons of various income levels live side by side. By the century's final decade, the Court itself had downscaled not just the principle but the rhetoric of desegregation. No longer would school systems be required to eliminate all vestiges of racial discrimination root and branch. Rather, as pointed out in *Board of Education of Oklahoma City Public Schools v. Dowell* (1991), good faith compliance with desegregation requirements was to be measured by whether those vestiges had been eradicated to the extent practicable.

### Mr. Chief Justice BURGER delivered the opinion of the Court.

. . . The controlling principle consistently expounded in our holdings is that the scope of the remedy is determined by the nature and extent of the constitutional violation. Before the boundaries of separate and autonomous school districts may be set aside by consolidating the separate units for remedial purposes or by imposing a cross-district remedy, it must first be shown that there has been a constitutional violation within one district that produces a significant segregative effect in another district. Specifically, it must be shown that racially discriminatory acts of the state or local school districts, or of a single school district have been a substantial cause of interdistrict segregation. Thus an interdistrict remedy might be in order where the racially discriminatory acts of one or more school districts caused racial segregation in an adjacent district, or where district lines have been deliberately drawn on the basis of race. In such circumstances an interdistrict remedy would be appropriate to eliminate the interdistrict segregation directly caused by the constitutional violation. Conversely, without an interdistrict violation and interdistrict effect, there is no constitutional wrong calling for an interdistrict remedy.

The record before us, voluminous as it is, contains evidence of de jure segregated conditions only in the Detroit schools; indeed, that was the theory on which the litigation was initially based and on which the District Court took evidence. With no showing of significant violation by the 53 outlying school districts and no evidence of any interdistrict violation or effect, the court went beyond the original theory of the case as framed by the pleadings and mandated a metropolitan area remedy. To approve the remedy ordered by the court would impose on the outlying districts, not shown to have committed any constitutional violation, a wholly impermissible remedy based on a standard not hinted at in *Brown I* and *II* or any holding of this Court. . . .

Petitioners have urged that they were denied due process by the manner in which the District Court limited their participation after intervention was allowed, thus precluding adequate opportunity to present evidence that they had committed no acts having a segregative effect in Detroit. In light of our holding that, absent an interdistrict violation, there is no basis for an interdistrict remedy, we need not reach these claims. It is clear, however, that the District Court, with the approval of the Court of Appeals, has provided an interdistrict remedy in the face of a record which shows no constitutional violations that would call for equitable relief except within the city of Detroit. In these circumstances there was no occasion for the parties to address, or for the District Court to consider whether there were racially discriminatory acts for which any of the 53 outlying districts were responsible and which had direct and significant segregative effect on schools of more than one district.

We conclude that the relief ordered by the District Court and affirmed by the Court of Appeals was based upon an erroneous standard and was unsupported by record evidence that acts of the outlying districts effected the discrimination found to exist in the schools of Detroit. Accordingly, the judgment of the Court of Appeals is reversed and the case is remanded for further proceedings consistent with this opinion leading to prompt formulation of a decree directed to eliminating the segregation found to exist in Detroit city schools, a remedy which has been delayed since 1970.

### Mr. Justice MARSHALL, with whom Mr. Justice DOUGLAS, Mr. Justice BRENNAN, and Mr. Justice WHITE join, dissenting.

In *Brown v. Board of Education,* this Court held that segregation of children in public schools on the basis of race deprives minority group children of equal educational opportunities and therefore denies them the equal protection of the laws under the Fourteenth Amendment. This Court recognized then that remedying decades of segregation in public education would not be an easy task. Subsequent events, unfortunately, have seen that prediction bear bitter fruit. But however imbedded old ways, however ingrained old prejudices, this Court has not been diverted from its appointed task of making "a living truth" of our constitutional ideal of equal justice under law.

After 20 years of small, often difficult steps toward that great end, the Court today takes a giant step backwards. Notwithstanding a record showing widespread and pervasive racial segregation in the educational system provided by the State of Michigan for children in Detroit, this Court holds that the District Court was powerless to require the State to remedy its constitutional violation in any meaningful fashion. Ironically purporting to base its result on the principle that the scope of the remedy in a desegregation case should be determined by the nature and the extent of the constitutional violation, the Court's answer is to provide no remedy at all for the violation proved in this case, thereby guaranteeing that Negro children in Detroit will receive the same separate and inherently unequal education in the future as they have been unconstitutionally afforded in the past.

I cannot subscribe to this emasculation of our constitutional guarantee of equal protection of the laws and must respectfully dissent. Our precedents, in my view, firmly establish that where, as here, state-imposed segregation has been demonstrated, it becomes the duty of the State to eliminate root and branch all vestiges of racial discrimination and to achieve the greatest possible degree of actual desegregation. I agree with both the District Court and the Court of Appeals that, under the facts of this case, this duty cannot be fulfilled unless the State of Michigan involves outlying metropolitan area school districts in its desegregation remedy. Furthermore, I perceive no basis either in law or in the practicalities of the situation justifying the State's interposition of school district boundaries as absolute barriers to the implementation of an effective desegregation remedy. Under established and frequently used Michigan procedures, school district lines are both flexible and permeable for a wide variety of purposes, and there is no reason why they must now stand in the way of meaningful desegregation relief.

The rights at issue in this case are too fundamental to be abridged on grounds as superficial as those relied on by the majority today. We deal here with the right of all of our children, whatever their race, to an equal start in life and to an equal opportunity to reach their full potential as citizens. Those children who have been denied that right in the past deserve better than to see fences thrown up to deny them that right in the future. Our Nation, I fear, will be ill served by the Court's refusal to remedy separate and unequal education, for unless our children begin to learn together, there is little hope that our people will ever learn to live together. . . .

## Bibliography

Drake, St. Clair, and Horace R. Clayton. *Black Metropolis*. New York: Harcourt, Brace and Co., 1945.

Jones, Nathaniel R. "*Brown v. Board of Education* and Its Legacy: A Tribute to Justice Thurgood Marshall." *Fordham Law Review* 61 (1992): 49.

## *Washington v. Davis*

**Citation: 426 U.S. 229.**

**Issue: Whether a test to screen police officer candidates was unconstitutional because a disproportionate number of African Americans failed it.**

**Year of Decision: 1976.**

**Outcome: Proof of discriminatory motive is an essential prerequisite for an equal protection violation.**

**Author of Opinion: Justice Byron White.**

**Vote: 5-4.**

The equal protection guarantee during the final half of the twentieth century established itself as the primary constitutional barrier against racial discrimination. Determining what constitutes discrimination, however, was not a simple task. Government action or policy may have a disproportionate impact upon individuals based, among other things, upon their group status. Placement of a solid waste disposal site near a poor neighborhood, for instance, may impose a disparate burden upon members of a historically disadvantaged racial minority. Whether this action constitutes racial discrimination, however, depends upon how the term is defined.

In the context of school desegregation, the Court differentiated between *de jure* and *de facto* segregation. *De jure* segregation, which reflects an official segregative purpose, is constitutionally prohibited. *De facto* segregation, which is a consequence of private choice, has no constitutional implications. This distinction, made in *Keyes v. School District No. 1* (1973), narrowed the reach of desegregation to circumstances where an actual purpose to segregate could be demonstrated. Put another way, the equal protection guarantee's concern was with segregative intent rather than segregative effect.

Whether discrimination should be understood in terms of purpose or effect is a question that extended beyond segregated schools. In *Washington v. Davis* (1976), the issue arose with respect to an employment test administered by the Washington, D.C., police department to all officer candidates. The examination, which assessed verbal ability, vocabulary, and reading, yielded racially disparate results. The number of African Americans failing the test was four times greater than for whites. Despite these disproportionate results, the trial court found that the examination was reasonably related to police training and performance. It also determined that the examination was not designed or utilized in a manner that discriminated on the basis of race. The trial court's ruling was reversed by the Court of Appeals, which concluded that the disproportionate impact by itself established an equal protection violation. As the Court of Appeals viewed it, the constitutional offense was not dependent upon a showing of discriminatory purpose.

The Supreme Court sided with the trial court and reversed the Court of Appeals ruling. It thus determined that the unconstitutionality of government action cannot rest solely on the basis of a racially disproportionate impact. Rather, there must be proof that it was motivated by a discriminatory purpose. In finding that disproportionate effect by itself did not establish a constitutional violation, the Court noted too that disparity was not entirely irrelevant. Discrimination is not always self-evident, particularly when potential violators know that it is illegal and thus are motivated to disguise the true nature of their actions. Laws that may be racially neutral on their face also may be applied in a discriminatory manner. In this regard, the Court referenced *Yick Wo v. Hopkins* (1886). This case concerned a city ordinance prohibiting the operation of laundries in wood frame buildings. Although racially neutral on its face, this law was struck down because it was applied only to persons of Chinese descent.

Identifying a discriminatory purpose is uncomplicated when the law speaks openly with respect to its intent. Discerning a discriminatory purpose was easy, for instance, when enactments typical of the separate but equal era were challenged. Once segregation and discrimination were declared unconstitutional, however, overt indications of purposeful wrongdoing became harder to pinpoint. Against this backdrop, the Court indicated that discriminatory purpose might be inferred from a variety of factors including disproportionate impact. It also might be identified in circumstances where disproportionality is difficult to explain on nonracial grounds.

When discriminatory purpose is identified, the Court intensifies its review to the level of "strict scrutiny." Pursuant to this standard, a state must demonstrate that its action is justified by compelling reasons and is narrowly tailored to achieve the result desired. Disproportionate effect alone does not trigger this high level of review. When present without a showing of discriminatory purpose, the question is whether the action or regulation reflects a legitimate state interest and is reasonably related to its goal. Viewing the police candidate test itself as a legitimate method for determining critical skills, the Court found that it was racially neutral and reasonably related to its objective.

The Court's refusal to give greater weight to disproportionate effect reflected concern with making any difference the basis for a constitutional controversy. Such an orientation, the Court feared, would "rais[e] serious questions about and possibly invalidat[e] a whole range of tax, welfare, public service, regulatory and licensing statutes." These laws by their nature have disparate consequences, but they generally are not motivated by a purpose to discriminate.

In narrowing the range of the equal protection guarantee's concern, the decision in *Washington v. Davis* set the scene for controversy over how purposeful discrimination is demonstrated. In *Arlington Heights v. Metropolitan Housing Development Corp.* (1977), one year later, the Court reviewed a local zoning ordinance that limited land use to single family dwellings. Because the village denied an application to construct racially integrated housing, the zoning decision was challenged on grounds it discriminated on the basis of race. The Court acknowledged that "[t]he impact of the Village's decision does arguably bear more heavily on racial minorities." It found no evidence of discriminatory purpose, however, and restated the proposition that disproportionate effect by itself does not establish a constitutional violation or basis for strict scrutiny.

The Court indicated its awareness that proof of discriminatory purpose may be more challenging when a racial motive is not stated or otherwise manifest. It thus suggested ways in which discriminatory purpose may be inferred from relevant circumstances. Toward this end, it noted relevant factors such as "the historical background of a decision including any indications of invidious purposes, departures from normal procedures, changes in standards for decision-making, and legislative or administrative history including contemporaneous remarks by officials."

Collectively, these factors signaled that history is particularly relevant as a means of drawing inferences of discriminatory purpose. A decade later, in *McCleskey v. Kemp* (1987), the Court heard arguments against the Georgia death penalty that referenced the history of a dual system of criminal justice. The Court also was presented with a report that showed major disparities in the administration of capital punishment. Evidence showed that prosecutors pursued the death penalty in 70 percent of the cases involving black defendants and white victims, 32 percent of the cases involving white defendants and black victims, 15 percent of the cases involving black defendants and black victims, and 19 percent of the cases involving white defendants and black victims. The death penalty was applied in 22 percent of the cases involving black defendants and white victims, 1 percent of the cases involving black defendants and black victims, and 3 percent of the cases involving white defendants and black victims. The Court, in reviewing this evidence, reaffirmed the premise that disproportionality by itself does not establish an equal protection violation or basis for strict scrutiny. It also described the disparate results as a "discrepancy that appears to correlate with race . . . [and] an inevitable part of our criminal justice system."

Justice William Brennan authored a dissenting opinion that was joined by three other justices. Justice Brennan maintained that the Court had ignored historical reality and thus the factor that it had declared relevant. On this point, he cited a long tradition in Georgia of operating a dual system of criminal justice system. Of particular consequence, given this history, was the practical consequence for counsel when having to advise defendants in capital cases on whether to accept a plea bargain. In his view, an attorney in this context could not ignore the potential for outcomes that differed on the basis of race. As Justice Brennan put it, "[a]t some point in this case, [the defendant] doubtless asked his lawyer whether a jury was likely to sentence him to die. A candid assessment by the attorney invariably would include the information that cases involving black defendants and white victims are more likely to result in a death sentence than cases featuring any other racial combination of defendant and victim."

Although a settled premise of the law, the discriminatory purpose standard still is a magnet for criticism. Among its detractors is the noted constitutional scholar Laurence Tribe, who contends that equal protection is not just about "stamp[ing] out impure thoughts." Rather, it should factor "government action which in the light of history, context, source, and effect are likely to perpetuate subordination of or reflect hostility, blindness or indifference toward a group that traditionally has been subjugated." Other critics, such as Charles Lawrence III, argue that motive-based inquiry is obsolete and unproductive because it overlooks or cannot detect subtle discrimination and unconscious racism.

Chief Justice William Rehnquist, who joined the majority in *Village of Arlington Heights v. Metropolitan Housing Authority,* also has expressed concern with motive-based inquiry in other constitutional contexts. In a commerce clause case that raised the question of whether a state transportation regulation discriminated against out-of-state highway users, Chief Justice Rehnquist dissented from an inquiry into actual intent. His concern, in *Kassel v. Consolidated Freightways Corp.* (1981), was that legislative intent generally was indeterminable.

Justice Antonin Scalia, although signing on to discriminatory motive inquiry for equal protection purposes, also has described it as a usually impossible task. In *Edwards v. Aguillard* (1987), Justice Scalia identified a multiplicity of reasons why a legislator might vote for a particular outcome. As he put it, a legislator might vote in a particular manner based not only on the merits of the legislation but whether it would provide jobs for his district, might enable him or her to make amends with a previously alienated political faction, was sponsored by a close friend, presented an opportunity to repay a favor to another politician, earned him appreciation from influential colleagues or wealthy contributors, represented the strong will of his or her constituency, was a way of getting even with a political nemesis or even a spouse that had made him or her mad, or whether it was voted on while he or she was intoxicated and [thus] utterly *un*motivated.

Consistent with his understanding that a legislated outcome may reflect any combination of these and other motivations, Justice Scalia maintained that "looking for *the sole purpose* of even a single legislator is probably to look for something that does not exist."

Consistent with the difficulty of establishing discriminatory motive, when this factor is not manifest, the success rate of equal protection claims over the past few decades has diminished. The most notable equal protection victories in contemporary times concern cases challenging racial preferences in employment and education. Like official segregation, and although differing with respect to utility and objective, these programs have a manifest racial orientation. Based upon these decisions, equal protection review responds primarily to formality and has yet to develop the capacity to factor more subtle or disguised variants of discrimination.

## Mr. Justice WHITE delivered the opinion of the Court.

. . . The central purpose of the Equal Protection Clause of the Fourteenth Amendment is the prevention of official conduct discriminating on the basis of race. It is also true that the Due Process Clause of the Fifth Amendment contains an equal protection component prohibiting the United States from invidiously discriminating between individuals or groups. But our cases have not embraced the proposition that a law or other official act, without regard to whether it reflects a racially discriminatory purpose, is unconstitutional solely because it has a racially disproportionate impact. . . .

The school desegregation cases have also adhered to the basic equal protection principle that the invidious quality of a law claimed to be racially discriminatory must ultimately be traced to a racially discriminatory purpose. That there are both predominantly black and predominantly white schools in a community is not alone violative of the Equal Protection Clause. The essential element of De jure segregation is "a current condition of segregation resulting from intentional state action. The Court has also recently rejected allegations of racial discrimination based solely on the statistically disproportionate racial impact of various provisions of the Social Security Act because "(t)he acceptance of appellants' constitutional theory would render suspect each difference in treatment among the grant classes, however lacking in racial motivation and however otherwise rational the treatment might be."

This is not to say that the necessary discriminatory racial purpose must be express or appear on the face of the statute, or that a law's disproportionate impact is irrelevant in cases involving Constitution-based claims of racial discrimination. A statute, otherwise neutral on its face, must not be applied so as invidiously to discriminate on the basis of race. . . With a prima facie case made out, "the burden of proof shifts to the State to rebut the presumption of unconstitutional action by showing that permissible racially neutral selection criteria and procedures have produced the monochromatic result."

Necessarily, an invidious discriminatory purpose may often be inferred from the totality of the relevant facts, including the fact, if it is true, that the law bears more heavily on one race than another. It is also not infrequently true that the discriminatory impact in the jury cases for example, the total or seriously disproportionate exclusion of Negroes from jury venires may for all practical purposes demonstrate unconstitutionality because in various circumstances the discrimination is very difficult to explain on nonracial grounds. Nevertheless, we have not held that a law, neutral on its face and serving ends otherwise within the power of government to pursue, is invalid under the Equal Protection Clause simply because it may affect a greater proportion of one race than of another. Disproportionate impact is not irrelevant, but it is not the sole touchstone of an invidious racial discrimination forbidden by the Constitution. Standing alone, it does not trigger the rule. . . .

As an initial matter, we have difficulty understanding how a law establishing a racially neutral qualification for employment is nevertheless racially discriminatory and denies "any person . . . equal protection of the laws" simply because a greater proportion of Negroes fail to qualify than members of other racial or ethnic groups. Had respondents, along with all others who had failed Test 21, whether white or black, brought an action claiming that the test denied each of them equal protection of the laws as compared with those who had passed with high enough scores to qualify them as police recruits, it is most unlikely that their challenge would have been sustained. Test 21, which is administered generally to prospective Government employees, concededly seeks to ascertain whether those who take it have acquired a particular level of verbal skill; and it is untenable that the Constitution prevents the Government from seeking modestly to upgrade the communicative abilities of its employees rather than to be satisfied with some lower level of competence, particularly where the job requires special ability to communicate orally and in writing. Respondents, as Negroes, could no more successfully claim that the test denied them equal protection than could white applicants who also failed. . . .

## Bibliography

Brest, Paul. "*Palmer v. Thompson:* An Approach to the Problem of Unconstitutional Legislative Motive." *Supreme Court Review* 95 (1971).

Haney-López, Ian. "Intentional Blindness." *New York University Law Review* 87 (2012): 1779.

Lawrence III, Charles R. "The Id, the Ego, and Equal Protection: Reckoning with Unconscious Racism." *Stanford Law Review* 39 (1987): 317.

Ortiz, Daniel R. "The Myth of Intent in Equal Protection." *Stanford Law Review* 41 (1989): 1105.

Straus, David A. "Discriminatory Intent and the Taming of Brown." *University of Chicago Law Review* 56 (1989): 935.

## *Regents of the University of California v. Bakke*

**Citation: 438 U.S. 265.**

**Issue: Whether a public university medical school's admissions policy, which reserved some seats for designated minorities, violated the equal protection guarantee.**

**Year of Decision: 1978.**

**Outcome: Race cannot be an exclusive factor in the admissions process, but it may be used as one of several factors in achieving a diverse student body.**

**Author of Opinion: No majority opinion.**

**Vote: 4-4-1.**

The vision of a color-blind society represents an ideal that society has struggled to achieve. An initial understanding of the Constitution as "color-blind" was advanced by Justice John Harlan. Dissenting from the majority's embrace of the separate but equal doctrine, in *Plessy v. Ferguson* (1896), he maintained that "the Constitution permits no caste system." Justice Harlan's observation was coupled with a sense that, although the Constitution was color-blind, the white race still would dominate because of its superiority. Several decades later in *Brown v. Board of Education* (1954), when it struck down official segregation in public schools, the Supreme Court made no specific mention of constitutional color-blindness. It is an underlying premise of modern equal protection understanding, however, which assumes that any official classification on the basis of race is "suspect."

Prohibition of racial segregation and other forms of discrimination did not erase a history of disadvantage based upon group status. During the final decades of the twentieth century, this legacy became the basis for government initiatives designed to account for and overcome it. These efforts typically consisted of programs or policies that tried to offset historical disadvantage by establishing preferences for designated minorities in employment and education. The use of racial classifications in this manner, commonly referred to as affirmative action, ultimately became the basis for a new chapter of equal protection controversy.

The use of race to remedy the effects of prejudice and discrimination was not a foreign concept. Desegregation of public schools, for instance, necessarily factored race in redistributing students from single race schools to mixed race schools. The term "affirmative action" first made its way into government policy when President John F. Kennedy issued an executive order that mandated the hiring of federal contractors without regard to race. His successor, President Lyndon Johnson, established the Office of Federal Contract Compliance and charged it with developing federal antidiscrimination guidelines in contracting. Guidelines announced by the Office in 1968 included goals and timetables for implementing equal employment opportunity. These incidents were followed in subsequent years by policies that focused upon achievement of specific results. Paralleling government's activity in this regard were private sector programs that aimed to increase minority participation in business and education.

As these race-conscious plans took root, they were challenged by persons who saw the opposite side of an advantage to minorities as a disadvantage to members of other racial groups. Those opposing affirmative action also contended that race-conscious government actions work to undermine the principle that it ultimately is *the individual*, not members of groups, which the law protects. The first of these cases to reach the Supreme Court, *DeFunis v. Odegaard* (1974), concerned the racially preferential admissions policy of the University of Washington School of Law. The plaintiff, a white male, argued that the policy resulted in his being denied admission on the basis of his race. The Court did not reach the merits of the dispute. Because the plaintiff had enrolled pursuant to a lower court decision, the university had not dismissed him, and he would graduate soon, the Court dismissed the case as moot. Four dissenting justices objected to the dismissal and maintained that the Court was avoiding an important issue.

Four years later, in *Regents of the University of California v. Bakke* (1978), the Court revisited preferential admission policies in the context of university professional schools. At issue was a program at the University of California–Davis medical school that allocated a certain number of seats in each entering class to members of designated minority groups. The plaintiff claimed that, but for the preferential admissions policy, he would have been admitted. Agreeing with his argument, the California Supreme Court declared the program unconstitutional. The United States Supreme Court affirmed this ruling, but did so without establishing a majority position. Rather, the Court fragmented into two opposing groups and a single justice whose opinion in this context had particular significance. The first bloc of four justices viewed that admissions policy as a violation of Title VI of the *Civil Rights Act of 1964*. Given a statutory basis for resolving the controversy, this group refused to address the constitutional question. Four other justices found that the program violated neither the equal protection guarantee nor Title VI. Writing only for himself, Justice Lewis Powell maintained that the policy was inconsistent with the Equal Protection Clause and the federal statute. Justice Powell indicated, however, that race could be factored to a limited extent in the admissions process. Coupling his position with that of the four justices who found no constitutional violation, a majority of the Court expressed support at least for taking race into account as a means of achieving a diverse student body—provided that it was not a decisive factor in the admissions policy or process.

Because of its critical role in defining the permissible use of race in the case, Justice Powell's opinion generally has been viewed as the most significant of those presented. The initial question confronting the Court in *Bakke* was what standard of review it should use. The traditional standard of review for racial classifications was established in *Korematsu v. United States* (1944). In that case, the Court determined that any racial classification should be the subject of searching judicial review. This model of review, also referred to as "strict scrutiny," became the basis for striking down laws that discriminated against racial minorities. Proponents of affirmative action maintained that, given their remedial aim, they should be evaluated pursuant to a more relaxed standard. Justice Powell rejected this proposed differentiation and concluded that any racial classification, regardless of whom it benefits or burdens, should be the subject of searching judicial review.

Having embraced the most rigorous model of judicial review, Justice Powell applied it to the four justifications that the medical school had offered in support of its preferential admissions policy. The school's first argument was that the setting aside of seats for minorities was an appropriate means to diversify the student body. Justice Powell found this methodology of racial quotas or goals to be invalid on its face. The school's second argument was that its preferential admissions policy was a means of eliminating the consequences of historic discrimination. Justice Powell determined that the prerequisite for such remedial action was findings of prior discrimination by the school itself. Evidence to this effect was not presented, and Justice Powell maintained that the school could not respond merely to the general reality of societal discrimination. The institution's third argument was that its admissions policy would increase minority graduates and thus result in improved health care in disadvantaged communities. Justice Powell determined that this premise assumed too much and that it did not necessarily follow that minority graduates would practice in disadvantaged communities. The school's final contention was that the interest in a diverse student body by itself was compelling. Justice Powell agreed with this premise, but stressed that diversification objectives could not be limited to race or ethnicity alone. As he put it, "students with a particular background whether it be ethnic, geographic, culturally advantaged, or disadvantaged may bring to a professional school of medicine experiences, outlooks and ideas that enrich the training of its student body and better equip its graduates to render with understanding their vital service to humanity."

In an opinion joined by three of his colleagues, Justice John Paul Stevens maintained that the Constitution was color-blind for all purposes. From this perspective, racial classifications were impermissible regardless of their purpose or whom they helped or hurt.

Justice William Brennan, joined by three other colleagues, contended that racial classifications designed to benefit members of traditionally disadvantaged groups should not be assessed in the same manner as those that burdened them. Because strict scrutiny tends to limit legislative initiative, Justice Brennan would not have applied it to policy making that creatively tries to account for the nation's legacy of racial discrimination. From his perspective, affirmative action plans should be assessed on the basis of whether they reflect or perpetuate harmful racial stereotypes. He did not view the school's set-aside plan as a function of such stereotyping. Justice Brennan also believed that the interest in overcoming the consequences of societal discrimination outweighed any burden imposed upon persons of the majority race.

Justices Thurgood Marshall and Harry Blackmun, in separate opinions, referred to the nation's history of racial discrimination as a justification for race-conscious remedial efforts. As Justice Blackmun put it, "[i]n order to get beyond racism, we must first take account of race."

Significant as the decision was, the divided nature of the Court's thinking left the future of affirmative action in an uncertain state. One year later, in *Fullilove v. Klutznick* (1980), the Court upheld a federal program setting aside 10 percent of public projects works for minority contractors. The Court again was badly divided, and it was impossible to identify a clear trend in its analysis. Movement toward a more unified position was evidenced in *Wygant v. Jackson Board of Education* (1986). In this case, the Court invalidated a preferential layoff program provided for by the collective bargaining agreement reached between public school teachers and the school board. In an opinion authored by Justice Powell, four justices found that an interest in "alleviat[ing] the effects of societal discrimination" was not sufficiently compelling to withstand strict scrutiny.

Despite indications of evolution toward a restrictive view of affirmative action, the Court still had not achieved a majority position. In a case concerning a well-documented history of discrimination in hiring and promotion, the Court in *United States v. Paradise* (1987) actually implemented a quota system to remedy a state agency's employment practices. Still eluding the Court, however, was a standard of review that a majority of the Court would embrace. Persisting division among the justices, a decade after the *Bakke* decision, confirmed the accuracy of observations made when the Court first confronted the issue of affirmative action. As Justice Brennan put it in *DeFunis v. Odegaard,* and history has demonstrated, "few constitutional questions in recent history have stirred as much debate." Nor have many generated as much discord within the Court itself.

### Mr. Justice POWELL announced the judgment of the Court.

. . . Petitioner urges us to adopt for the first time a more restrictive view of the Equal Protection Clause and hold that discrimination against members of the white "majority" cannot be suspect if its purpose can be characterized as "benign." The clock of our liberties, however, cannot be turned back to 1868. It is far too late to argue that the guarantee of equal protection to *all* persons permits the recognition of special wards entitled to a degree of protection greater than that accorded others. "The Fourteenth Amendment is not directed solely against discrimination due to a 'two-class theory'—that is, based upon differences between 'white' and Negro."

Once the artificial line of a "two-class theory" of the Fourteenth Amendment is put aside, the difficulties entailed in varying the level of judicial review according to a perceived "preferred" status of a particular racial or ethnic minority are intractable. The concepts of "majority" and "minority" necessarily reflect temporary arrangements and political judgments. As observed above, the white "majority" itself is composed of various minority groups, most of which can lay claim to a history of prior discrimination at the hands of the State and private individuals. Not all of these groups can receive preferential treatment and corresponding judicial tolerance of distinctions drawn in terms of race and nationality, for then the only "majority" left would be a new minority of white Anglo-Saxon Protestants. There is no principled basis for deciding which groups would merit "heightened judicial solicitude" and which would not. Courts would be asked to evaluate the extent of the prejudice and consequent harm suffered by various minority groups. Those whose societal injury is thought to exceed some arbitrary level of tolerability then would be entitled to preferential classifications at the expense of individuals belonging to other groups. Those classifications would be free from exacting judicial scrutiny. As these preferences began to have their desired effect, and the consequences of past discrimination were undone, new judicial rankings would be necessary. The kind of variable sociological and political analysis necessary to produce such rankings simply does not lie within the judicial competence—even if they otherwise were politically feasible and socially desirable.

Moreover, there are serious problems of justice connected with the idea of preference itself. First, it may not always be clear that a so-called preference is in fact benign. Courts may be asked to validate burdens imposed upon individual members of a particular group in order to advance the group's general interest. Nothing in the Constitution supports the notion that individuals may be asked to suffer otherwise impermissible burdens in order to enhance the societal standing of their ethnic groups. Second, preferential programs may only reinforce common stereotypes holding that certain groups are unable to achieve success without special protection based on a factor having no relationship to individual worth. . . .

By hitching the meaning of the Equal Protection Clause to these transitory considerations, we would be holding, as a constitutional principle, that judicial scrutiny of classifications touching on racial and ethnic background may vary with the ebb and flow of political forces. Disparate constitutional tolerance of such classifications well may serve to exacerbate racial and ethnic antagonisms rather than alleviate them. . . . If it is the individual who is entitled to judicial protection against classifications based upon his racial or ethnic background because such distinctions impinge upon personal rights, rather than the individual only because of his membership in a particular group, then constitutional standards may be applied consistently. Political judgments regarding the necessity for the particular classification may be weighed in the constitutional balance, but the standard of justification will remain constant. This is as it should be, since those political judgments are the product of rough compromise struck by contending groups within the democratic process. When they touch upon an individual's race or ethnic background, he is entitled to a judicial determination that the burden he is asked to bear on that basis is precisely tailored to serve a compelling governmental interest. The Constitution guarantees that right to every person regardless of his background. . . .

We have never approved a classification that aids persons perceived as members of relatively victimized groups at the expense of other innocent individuals in the absence of judicial, legislative, or administrative findings of constitutional or statutory violations. . . .

Petitioner does not purport to have made, and is in no position to make, such findings. Its broad mission is education, not the formulation of any legislative policy or the adjudication of particular claims of illegality. For reasons similar to those stated in Part III of this opinion, isolated segments of our vast governmental structures are not competent to make those decisions, at least in the absence of legislative mandates and legislatively determined criteria. . . .

The fourth goal asserted by petitioner is the attainment of a diverse student body. This clearly is a constitutionally permissible goal for an institution of higher education. Academic freedom, though not a specifically enumerated constitutional right, long has been viewed as a special concern of the First Amendment. The freedom of a university to make its own judgments as to education includes the selection of its student body. Mr. Justice Frankfurter summarized the "four essential freedoms" that constitute academic freedom:

"It is the business of a university to provide that atmosphere which is most conducive to speculation, experiment and creation. It is an atmosphere in which there prevail "the four essential freedoms" of a university—to determine for itself on academic grounds who may teach, what may be taught, how it shall be taught, and who may be admitted to study."

Thus, in arguing that its universities must be accorded the right to select those students who will contribute the most to the "robust exchange of ideas," petitioner invokes a countervailing constitutional interest, that of the First Amendment. In this light, petitioner must be viewed as seeking to achieve a goal that is of paramount importance in the fulfillment of its mission. . . .

Ethnic diversity, however, is only one element in a range of factors a university properly may consider in attaining the goal of a heterogeneous student body. Although a university must have wide discretion in making the sensitive judgments as to who should be admitted, constitutional limitations protecting individual rights may not be disregarded. Respondent urges—and the courts below have held—that petitioner's dual admissions program is a racial classification that impermissibly infringes his rights under the Fourteenth Amendment. As the interest of diversity is compelling in the context of a university's admissions program, the question remains whether the program's racial classification is necessary to promote this interest.

It may be assumed that the reservation of a specified number of seats in each class for individuals from the preferred ethnic groups would contribute to the attainment of considerable ethnic diversity in the student body. But petitioner's argument that this is the only effective means of serving the interest of diversity is seriously flawed. In a most fundamental sense the argument misconceives the nature of the state interest that would justify consideration of race or ethnic background. It is not an interest in simple ethnic diversity, in which a specified percentage of the student body is in effect guaranteed to be members of selected ethnic groups, with the remaining percentage an undifferentiated aggregation of students. The diversity that furthers a compelling state interest encompasses a far broader array of qualifications and characteristics of which racial or ethnic origin is but a single though important element. Petitioner's special admissions program, focused *solely* on ethnic diversity, would hinder rather than further attainment of genuine diversity.

### Bibliography

Ely, John Hart. "The Constitutionality of Reverse Discrimination." *University of Chicago Law Review* 41 (1974): 723.

Moran, Rachel F. "Of Doubt and Diversity: the Future of Affirmative Action in Higher Education." *Ohio State Law Journal* 67 (2006): 201.

Posner, Richard. "The DeFunis case and the Constitutionality of Preferential Treatment of Racial Minorities." *Supreme Court Review* 1 (1974).

Sowell, Thomas. *Race and Culture*. New York: Basic Books, 1994.

Taylor, Jared. *Paved with Good Intentions*. New York: Carroll & Graf, 1992.

## City of Richmond v. J.A. Croson Co.

**Citation: 488 U.S. 469.**

**Issue: Whether a city's set-aside plan for minority contractors, designed to remedy societal discrimination, violated the equal protection guarantee.**

**Year of Decision: 1989.**

**Outcome: Racial preferences are subject to strict scrutiny regardless of their purpose.**

**Author of Opinion: Justice Sandra Day O'Connor.**

**Vote: 5-4.**

Affirmative action was one of the most divisive issues that the Court confronted over the final decades of the twentieth century. When the matter first was reviewed in *Regents of the University of California v. Bakke* (1978), Justice Harry Blackmun expressed support for affirmative action as a means to get beyond racism. In his view, racially preferential programs would not be necessary on a permanent basis. Slightly more than a decade later, the need for affirmative action continued to be debated. Constitutional uncertainty persisted, moreover, as the Court had yet to establish a majority position on a standard of review.

A significant step toward clarity was taken, however, in *City of Richmond v. J.A. Croson Co.* (1989). At issue in this case was a set-aside program approved by the Richmond, Virginia, City Council. The program was modeled upon a federal set-aside program that the Supreme Court had upheld, albeit without any majority opinion, in *Fullilove v. Klutznick* (1980). Like the federal prototype, the city reserved at least 10 percent of municipal building contracts for minority business enter-prises. Architects of the plan cited the same evidence used by Congress to dem-onstrate a history of racial discrimination in the construction. Offered too was a study showing that minority businesses received less than 1 percent of city building contracts, even though African Americans constituted half of Richmond's popula-tion. Enactment of the set-aside plan thus represented an effort to address historical discrimination and create opportunity in a field where minorities traditionally had not been able to compete.

Even though the set-aside program paralleled the federal model and had a remedial purpose, the Court found that it was unconstitutional. This decision was significant not just with respect to the outcome, but because a majority embraced strict scrutiny of all racial classifications regardless of their purpose. Any racial classification, even if well-intended, thus must be justified by a compelling reason. It also must account for that purpose effectively and be demonstrated that racially neutral methods are inadequate. Justice Sandra Day O'Connor, joined by three of her colleagues, asserted that "searching judicial inquiry was an essential tool for purposes of determining what classifications are 'benign' or 'remedial' and what classifications are in fact motivated by illegitimate notions of racial inferiority or simple racial politics." The plurality of four justices thus viewed strict scrutiny as an essential tool for detecting illegitimate uses of race by assuring that government "is pursuing a goal important enough to warrant use of a highly suspect tool."

Adoption of a strict scrutiny standard of review reflected the plurality's sense that distinctions between benign and harmful racial classifications were conceptu-ally difficult to make. As the plurality viewed them, racial classifications regardless of their purpose are suspect. Although they may be well-intended, race-conscious programs designed to remedy the past may "promote notions of racial inferiority and lead to a politics of racial hostility." Given this risk, the plurality maintained that they should be reserved only as a remedy for proven instances of racial discrimina-tion. Adding to its concern in this case, the plurality noted that African Americans constituted half of Richmond's population and controlled the city council. In this context, the plurality expressed concern that set-asides may be nothing more than a political entitlement. From its perspective, searching judicial review would mini-mize this danger and the risk that "race will always be relevant in America."

The plurality acknowledged what it characterized as "the nation's sorry history of both private and public discrimination." This historical reality by itself, however, was not sufficient to support race-conscious policies as a means to overcome it. Such methods may be permissible when a specific instance of discrimination has been proved. Minus such a showing, the plurality was concerned that there would be no ending point for policies that redistributed opportunity on the basis of race. The use of race in any remedial context, except when a specific instance of discrim-ination was proven, thus was barred. This outcome reflected the plurality's sense of what was necessary to ensure "[t]he dream of a Nation of equal citizens in a society where race is irrelevant to personal opportunity." If race was to be the basis for managing opportunity, the plurality feared, "achievement would be lost in a mosaic of shifting preferences based on inherently unmeasurable claims of past wrongs."

By itself, the plurality opinion did not reflect a majority position. The concurring opinion of Justice Antonin Scalia established a majority, however, in support of the strict scrutiny standard of review. Justice Scalia advocated an even more rigorous version of strict scrutiny that would deny reference to race under most any circumstance. From his perspective, the challenge was not so much overcoming the effects of discrimination but eliminating "the tendency, fatal to a nation such as ours to classify and judge men on the basis of their country of origin or the color of their skin." Policies that accounted for racial discrimination in a race-conscious manner, at least for Justice Scalia, were "no solution at all." In his opinion, race could be a factor only when necessary to undo a segregated school system or "in a social emergency rising to the level of imminent danger of life and limb." Outside these contexts, Justice Scalia contended that "[w]here injustice is the game . . . turn-about is not fair play."

The emergence of a majority in favor of strict scrutiny for all racial classifications drew a long and pointed dissent by Justice Thurgood Marshall. He was joined by Justices William Brennan and Harry Blackmun in arguing that the Court had moved in the wrong direction. Justice Marshall thought it was ironic that the Court would "second-guess the judgment" (the city council's judgment). Richmond, he pointed out, is "the former capital of the Confederacy . . . [and] knows what racial discrimination is." In his view, the Court had taken "a deliberate and giant step backward." Justice Marshall would have upheld the program on grounds that it served a useful and important purpose. As he saw it, the set-aside policy not only addressed the consequences of racial discrimination but ensured that city spending did not reinforce and perpetuate that legacy. Justice Marshall also contested the notion that the city had not produced sufficient evidence of specific acts of discrimination. In this regard, he cited federal and local studies and the absence of any dispute with respect to Richmond's discriminatory history. The analysis and outcome, in his view, reflected an inability to grasp why the contracting industry had such limited minority participation.

Justice Marshall found the strict scrutiny standard objectionable too because of what he perceived to be "[a] profound difference separat[ing] governmental actions that themselves are racist, and governmental actions that seek to remedy the effects of prior racism or to prevent governmental activity from perpetuating the effects of such racism." He criticized the Court for ignoring "the tragic and indelible fact that [racial] discrimination . . . has pervaded our Nation's history and continues to scar our society." Justice Marshall thus expressed dismay with the "signals that [the Court] regards racial discrimination as largely a phenomenon of the past, and that government bodies need no longer preoccupy themselves with rectifying racial injustice."

Justice Marshall's sense that the Court had foreclosed remedial initiatives altogether proved to be somewhat premature. In *Metro Broadcasting, Inc. v. Federal*

*Communications Commission,* 497 U.S. 547 (1990), the Court upheld a federal regulation that established a preference for designated minorities in the licensing of radio and television broadcasters. This turnabout was short-lived, as the Court overturned this ruling in *Adarand Constructors, Inc. v. Pena* (1995). The *Croson* decision established that any racial classification would be subject to searching judicial review, at least to the extent it was established by a state. Left to be resolved were two primary questions. The first was whether the same standard would operate with respect to federal policy. The second was the extent to which the Court would find reasons for racial classifications to be sufficiently compelling. These issues eventually would be addressed in the final decade of the twentieth century and first decade of the twenty-first century.

### Justice O'CONNOR announced the judgment of the Court and delivered the opinion of the Court with respect to the principal parts of the decision.

. . . The Equal Protection Clause of the Fourteenth Amendment provides that "[n]o State shall . . . deny to *any person* within its jurisdiction the equal protection of the laws." (Emphasis added.) As this Court has noted in the past, the "rights created by the first section of the Fourteenth Amendment are, by its terms, guaranteed to the individual. The rights established are personal rights." The Richmond Plan denies certain citizens the opportunity to compete for a fixed percentage of public contracts based solely upon their race. To whatever racial group these citizens belong, their "personal rights" to be treated with equal dignity and respect are implicated by a rigid rule erecting race as the sole criterion in an aspect of public decisionmaking.

Absent searching judicial inquiry into the justification for such race-based measures, there is simply no way of determining what classifications are "benign" or "remedial" and what classifications are in fact motivated by illegitimate notions of racial inferiority or simple racial politics. Indeed, the purpose of strict scrutiny is to "smoke out" illegitimate uses of race by assuring that the legislative body is pursuing a goal important enough to warrant use of a highly suspect tool. The test also ensures that the means chosen "fit" this compelling goal so closely that there is little or no possibility that the motive for the classification was illegitimate racial prejudice or stereotype.

Classifications based on race carry a danger of stigmatic harm. Unless they are strictly reserved for remedial settings, they may in fact promote notions of racial inferiority and lead to a politics of racial hostility. We thus reaffirm the view expressed by the plurality in *Wygant* that the standard of review under the Equal Protection Clause is not dependent on the race of those burdened or benefited by a particular classification. . . .

Even were we to accept a reading of the guarantee of equal protection under which the level of scrutiny varies according to the ability of different groups to defend their interests in the representative process, heightened scrutiny would still be appropriate in the circumstances of this case. One of the central arguments for applying a less exacting standard to "benign" racial classifications is that such measures essentially involve a choice made by dominant racial groups to disadvantage themselves. If one aspect of the judiciary's role under the Equal Protection Clause is to protect "discrete and insular minorities" from majoritarian prejudice or indifference, some maintain that these concerns are not implicated when the "white majority" places burdens upon itself. . . .

We think it clear that the factual predicate offered in support of the Richmond Plan suffers from the same two defects identified as fatal in *Wygant*. The District Court found the city council's "findings sufficient to ensure that, in adopting the Plan, it was remedying the present effects of past discrimination in the *construction industry*." Like the "role model" theory employed in *Wygant*, a generalized assertion that there has been past discrimination in an entire industry provides no guidance for a legislative body to determine the precise scope of the injury it seeks to remedy. It "has no logical stopping point." "Relief" for such an ill-defined wrong could extend until the percentage of public contracts awarded to MBE's in Richmond mirrored the percentage of minorities in the population as a whole. . . .

It is sheer speculation how many minority firms there would be in Richmond absent past societal discrimination, just as it was sheer speculation how many minority medical students would have been admitted to the medical school at Davis absent past discrimination in educational opportunities. Defining these sorts of injuries as "identified discrimination" would give local governments license to create a patchwork of racial preferences based on statistical generalizations about any particular field of endeavor.

These defects are readily apparent in this case. The 30% quota cannot in any realistic sense be tied to any injury suffered by anyone. . . .

The District Court accorded great weight to the fact that the city council designated the Plan as "remedial." But the mere recitation of a "benign" or legitimate purpose for a racial classification is entitled to little or no weight. Racial classifications are suspect, and that means that simple legislative assurances of good intention cannot suffice. . . .

Nothing we say today precludes a state or local entity from taking action to rectify the effects of identified discrimination within its jurisdiction. If the city of Richmond had evidence before it that nonminority contractors were systematically excluding minority businesses from subcontracting opportunities it could take action to end the discriminatory exclusion. Where there is a significant statistical disparity between the number of qualified minority contractors willing and able to perform a particular service and the number of such contractors actually engaged by the locality or the locality's prime contractors, an inference of discriminatory exclusion could arise. Under such circumstances, the city could act to dismantle the closed business system by taking appropriate measures against those who discriminate on the basis of race or other illegitimate criteria. In the extreme case, some form of narrowly tailored racial preference might be necessary to break down patterns of deliberate exclusion.

Nor is local government powerless to deal with individual instances of racially motivated refusals to employ minority contractors. Where such discrimination occurs, a city would be justified in penalizing the discriminator and providing appropriate relief to the victim of such discrimination. Moreover, evidence of a pattern of individual discriminatory acts can, if supported by appropriate statistical proof, lend support to a local government's determination that broader remedial relief is justified.

Even in the absence of evidence of discrimination, the city has at its disposal a whole array of race-neutral devices to increase the accessibility of city contracting opportunities to small entrepreneurs of all races. Simplification of bidding procedures, relaxation of bonding requirements, and training and financial aid for disadvantaged entrepreneurs of all races would open the public contracting market to all those who have suffered the effects of past societal discrimination or neglect. Many of the formal barriers to new entrants may be the product of bureaucratic inertia more than actual necessity, and may have a disproportionate effect on the opportunities open to new minority firms. Their elimination or modification would have little detrimental effect on the city's interests and would serve to increase the opportunities available to minority business without classifying individuals on the basis of race. The city may also act to prohibit discrimination in the provision of credit or bonding by local suppliers and banks. Business as usual should not mean business pursuant to the unthinking exclusion of certain members of our society from its rewards.

In the case at hand, the city has not ascertained how many minority enterprises are present in the local construction market nor the level of their participation in city construction projects. The city points to no evidence that qualified minority contractors have been passed over for city contracts or subcontracts, either as a group or in any individual case. Under such circumstances, it is simply impossible to say that the city has demonstrated "a strong basis in evidence for its conclusion that remedial action was necessary."

Proper findings in this regard are necessary to define both the scope of the injury and the extent of the remedy necessary to cure its effects. Such findings also serve to assure all citizens that the deviation from the norm of equal treatment of all racial and ethnic groups is a temporary matter, a measure taken in the service of the goal of equality itself. Absent such findings, there is a danger that a racial classification is merely the product of unthinking stereotypes or a form of racial politics. "[I]f there is no duty to attempt either to measure the recovery by the wrong or to distribute that recovery within the injured class in an evenhanded way, our history will adequately support a legislative preference for almost any ethnic, religious, or racial group with the political strength to negotiate 'a piece of the action' for its members." Because the city of Richmond has failed to identify the need for remedial action in the awarding of its public construction contracts, its treatment of its citizens on a racial basis violates the dictates of the Equal Protection Clause. Accordingly, the judgment of the Court of Appeals for the Fourth Circuit is *Affirmed*.

## Justice MARSHALL, with whom Justice BRENNAN and Justice BLACKMUN join, dissenting.

. . . I would ordinarily end my analysis at this point and conclude that Richmond's ordinance satisfies both the governmental interest and substantial relationship prongs of our Equal Protection Clause analysis. However, I am compelled to add more, for the majority has gone beyond the facts of this case to announce a set of principles which unnecessarily restricts the power of governmental entities to take race-conscious measures to redress the effects of prior discrimination.

Today, for the first time, a majority of this Court has adopted strict scrutiny as its standard of Equal Protection Clause review of race-conscious remedial measures. This is an unwelcome development. A profound difference separates governmental actions that themselves are racist, and governmental actions that seek to remedy the effects of prior racism or to prevent neutral governmental activity from perpetuating the effects of such racism.

Racial classifications "drawn on the presumption that one race is inferior to another or because they put the weight of government behind racial hatred and separatism" warrant the strictest judicial scrutiny because of the very irrelevance of these rationales. By contrast, racial classifications drawn for the purpose of remedying the effects of discrimination that itself was race based have a highly pertinent basis: the tragic and indelible fact that discrimination against blacks and other racial minorities in this Nation has pervaded our Nation's history and continues to scar our society. As I stated in *Fullilove:* "Because the consideration of race is relevant to remedying the continuing effects of past racial discrimination, and because governmental programs employing racial classifications for remedial purposes can be crafted to avoid stigmatization, ... such programs should not be subjected to conventional 'strict scrutiny'—scrutiny that is strict in theory, but fatal in fact."

In concluding that remedial classifications warrant no different standard of review under the Constitution than the most brutal and repugnant forms of state-sponsored racism, a majority of this Court signals that it regards racial discrimination as largely a phenomenon of the past, and that government bodies need no longer preoccupy themselves with rectifying racial injustice. I, however, do not believe this Nation is anywhere close to eradicating racial discrimination or its vestiges. In constitutionalizing its wishful thinking, the majority today does a grave disservice not only to those victims of past and present racial discrimination in this Nation whom government has sought to assist, but also to this Court's long tradition of approaching issues of race with the utmost sensitivity.

## Bibliography

Carter, Stephen L. *Reflections of an Affirmative Action Baby.* New York: Basic Books, 1991.

Kennedy, Randall. "Persuasion and Distrust: A Comment on the Affirmative Action Debate."
    *Harvard Law Review* 99 (1986): 1327.
Steele, Shelby. *The Content of Our Character*. New York: St. Martin's Press, 1990.

## *Adarand Constructors, Inc. v. Pena*

**Citation: 515 U.S. 200.**

**Issue: Whether a federal program incentivizing general contractors to hire minority subcontractors should be strictly scrutinized.**

**Year of Decision: 1995.**

**Outcome: Race-conscious policies, whether federal or state and regardless of their purpose, are subject to strict scrutiny.**

**Author of Opinion: Justice Sandra Day O'Connor.**

**Vote: 5-4.**

The American political system is grounded in two independent sovereigns—the federal and state governments. These two powers have separate functions and responsibilities but sometimes overlapping interests. The federal government, for instance, regulates the national economy on the basis of its constitutional power to govern commerce. Through their police power, states often enact laws that also operate as economic policy. Civil rights is another area of dual responsibility. Both federal and state governments have enacted laws concerning discrimination. Through the mid-twentieth century, many states not only permitted racial discrimination but prescribed it. After segregation was declared unconstitutional, and Congress passed the *Civil Rights Act of 1964,* both the federal government and states developed affirmative action policies that aimed to remedy past discrimination.

In *City of Richmond v. J.A. Croson Co.* (1989), the Supreme Court announced that racial preferences of any kind could not survive strict constitutional review unless they were narrowly tailored to remedy a specific instance of discrimination. Notwithstanding this determination, the Court in the following year upheld a federal program establishing racial preferences in the licensing of broadcasters. The basis for differentiation, set forth in *Metro Broadcasting, Inc. v. Federal Communications Commission* (1990), was Congress's aggregation of powers including the authority to regulate the national economy and enforce the Fourteenth Amendment by appropriate legislation. Given the Constitution's specific charge of power to Congress, the Court concluded that federal preferences for minorities should be subject to a less rigorous standard of review than those created by the states.

The *Metro Broadcasting* decision drew upon prior case law that gives deference to Congress in its Fourteenth Amendment enforcement role. Despite initial indications, however, the Court did not create a lasting safe harbor for minority preferences under federal law. In *Adarand Constructors, Inc. v. Pena* (1995), the Court overruled the *Metro Broadcasting* decision and made federal and state preferences for minorities subject to the same standard of review. At issue in *Adarand Constructors* was a Department of Transportation program that, through financial incentives, encouraged government contractors to hire subcontractors owned by persons with "socially and economically disadvantaged" backgrounds. This program was established pursuant to a federal law that established a minimum goal of five percent minority participation on all primary contracting and subcontracting awards. It also created a presumption that members of certain minority groups were disadvantaged for purposes of the law. The law was challenged by a nonminority subcontractor which, although it submitted the lowest bid, lost the contract to a minority-owned business.

By a 5-4 margin, and in an opinion authored by Justice Sandra Day O'Connor, the Court held that federal affirmative action programs should be subject to strict scrutiny. In so doing, it identified three reasons why the use of racial or ethnic preferences should be subject to a rigorous level of review. First, the Court referenced the importance of "skepticism" in evaluating any racial classification. Attention to this factor reflected not only historical experience with racial discrimination, but also emphasis upon skepticism was grounded in an understanding that discrimination sometimes may be subtle rather than overt. Thus, it is essential to take a hard look at any racially preferential program or policy. Minus strict scrutiny, the Court concluded, there was no way to sort out benign or beneficial classifications from wrongly motivated ones. Strict scrutiny, as the Court put it, enables the judiciary to "smoke out" illegitimate uses and ensure that the classification was not a reflection of racial prejudice or stereotype.

The Court identified "consistency" as its second consideration in support of strict scrutiny. In this regard, the Court stressed that the standard of review for equal protection does not vary according to the race that is burdened or benefited. The third factor was the interest of "congruence." Whether an equal protection claim arises against the federal government under the Fifth Amendment or a state government under the Fourteenth Amendment, the Court's position was that the same standard of review applies. As the Court observed, these propositions "derive from the basic proposition that the Fifth and Fourteenth Amendments to the Constitution protect persons, not groups." Taken collectively, they supported "the conclusion that any person, of whatever race, has the right to demand that any governmental actor subject to the Constitution justify any racial classification subjecting that person to unequal treatment under the strictest scrutiny." Consistent with this premise, the Court held that "all racial classifications, imposed by whatever federal, state, or local governmental actor, must be analyzed by a reviewing court under strict scrutiny. In other words, such classifications are constitutional only if they are narrowly tailored measures that further compelling governmental interests."

In a part of the opinion that did not command majority support, Justice O'Connor challenged any understanding that "strict scrutiny is 'strict in theory, but fatal in fact.'" Noting that the practice and effects of racial discrimination against minorities were a persisting reality, Justice O'Connor asserted that government was not disabled from responding to it. Although acknowledging that persons wronged by racial discrimination should have a remedy, Justice Antonin Scalia in a concurring opinion countered that "under our Constitution there can be no such thing as either a creditor or debtor race." For Justice Scalia, even well-intended "concept[s] of racial entitlement" reinforced and preserved for future mischief the ways of thinking that generated racially based slavery, privilege, and hatred. From his perspective, he considered "unlikely, if not impossible, that the challenged program would survive this understanding of strict scrutiny." This sentiment was echoed by Justice Clarence Thomas, who perceived the preferential program as an exercise in "paternalism" that was "at war with the principle of inherent equality that underlies and infuses our Constitution."

Justice John Paul Stevens, in a dissenting opinion joined by Justice Ruth Bader Ginsburg, challenged the majority's use of the terms "skepticism," "consistency," and "congruence." With respect to skepticism, Justice Stevens agreed that courts should be wary of racial classifications because race seldom provides a relevant basis for treating persons differently. On the point of consistency, Justice Stevens maintained that there are differences between a majority's decision to burden a racial minority and one to benefit it despite the incidental impact upon the majority itself.

From his perspective, there was neither a moral nor a constitutional equivalence between a policy that supports a caste system and enactments designed to eliminate racial subordination. Put simply, in Justice Stevens's view, the majority ignored the difference "between oppression and assistance." With respect to congruence, Justice Stevens also found untenable the premise that there is no meaningful difference between a congressional and state decision to adopt an affirmative action program. He referenced prior case law that had identified Congress's "special 'institutional competence'" and the need for deference toward the national legislature when it was acting under specific powers to provide for the "'general Welfare of the United States' and 'enforce . . . the equal protection guarantee of the Fourteenth Amendment.'"

Justice David Souter, joined by Justices Ruth Bader Ginsburg and Stephen Breyer, authored a separate dissent. So did Justice Ginsburg, who was joined by Justice Souter. These opinions attempted to soften the impact of the majority opinion. Together, they stressed that the Court had not foreclosed the possibility that some racial classifications might survive strict scrutiny. In her opinion, Justice O'Connor had noted the permissibility of race-conscious methods remedies the effects of discrimination. The extent to which other interests might be found compelling, however, was reserved for future review.

Justice O'CONNOR announced the judgment of the Court and delivered an opinion with respect to the principal parts of the decision.

. . . Our action today makes explicit what Justice Powell thought implicit in the *Fullilove* lead opinion: Federal racial classifications, like those of a State, must serve a compelling governmental interest, and must be narrowly tailored to further that interest. Of course, it follows that to the extent (if any) that *Fullilove* held federal racial classifications to be subject to a less rigorous standard, it is no longer controlling. But we need not decide today whether the program upheld in *Fullilove* would survive strict scrutiny as our more recent cases have defined it.

Some have questioned the importance of debating the proper standard of review of race-based legislation. But we agree with Justice STEVENS that, "[b]ecause racial characteristics so seldom provide a relevant basis for disparate treatment, and because classifications based on race are potentially so harmful to the entire body politic, it is especially important that the reasons for any such classification be clearly identified and unquestionably legitimate," and that "[r]acial classifications are simply too pernicious to permit any but the most exact connection between justification and classification." We think that requiring strict scrutiny is the best way to ensure that courts will consistently give racial classifications that kind of detailed examination, both as to ends and as to means.

Finally, we wish to dispel the notion that strict scrutiny is "strict in theory, but fatal in fact." The unhappy persistence of both the practice and the lingering effects of racial discrimination against minority groups in this country is an unfortunate reality, and government is not disqualified from acting in response to it. As recently as 1987, for example, every Justice of this Court agreed that the Alabama Department of Public Safety's "pervasive, systematic, and obstinate discriminatory conduct" justified a narrowly tailored race-based remedy. When race-based action is necessary to further a compelling interest, such action is within constitutional constraints if it satisfies the "narrow tailoring" test this Court has set out in previous cases.

## Bibliography

Barrett, Paul M. "*Successful,* Affluent but Still 'Disadvantaged,'" *Wall Street Journal,* June 13, 1995.

Days, Drew. *Fullilove. Yale Law Journal* 96 (1987): 453.

## Grutter v. Bollinger

> **Citation: 539 U.S. 306.**
>
> **Issue: Whether a public university law school's admissions policy that factored race as a nonexclusive consideration in creating a diverse student body violated the Equal Protection Clause.**
>
> **Year of Decision: 2003.**
>
> **Outcome: The use of race as a nonexclusive factor to achieve a diverse law school student body does not offend the equal protection guarantee.**
>
> **Author of Opinion: Justice Sandra Day O'Connor.**
>
> **Vote: 5-4.**

Case law by the end of the twentieth century had curbed substantially the potential operation of affirmative action. Although acknowledging that racial discrimination and its consequences were not mere historical relics, the Court embraced an exacting standard of review for any policy or program designed to remedy racial discrimination. Whether any government initiative other than narrowly tailored remediation might be sufficient to satisfy the demands of strict scrutiny, however, was a question that spilled over into the twenty-first century. In its first reckoning with affirmative action, in *Regents of the University of California v. Bakke* (1978), the Court wrestled with the issue of whether diversity in the academic world was sufficiently important to justify a preferential admissions policy. Although the Court was closely divided and no majority opinion was rendered, five justices agreed that race or ethnicity could be a factor in the admissions process. Justice Lewis Powell, in an influential concurring opinion, stressed that race could not be a decisive factor in the decision to admit students. He noted, however, that the university had a compelling interest in a diverse student body.

A quarter of a century later, *Grutter v. Bollinger* (2003) revisited this issue. It did so against the backdrop of *Hopwood v. Texas* (5th Cir. 1996), a court of appeals decision which held that diversity could not be a compelling interest. The *Hopwood* ruling invalidated a University of Texas policy that factored diversity into the law school admissions process. At issue in *Grutter* was the University of Michigan Law School admissions policy that too was grounded in the interest of a diverse student body. Under this policy, each applicant's file was reviewed individually by an admissions officer. An assessment was made not only of traditional academic quality indicators but also personal statements, letters of recommendation, and "an essay describing ways in which the applicant will contribute to the life and diversity of the Law School." Although the policy did not define diversity exclusively in terms of race or ethnicity, or restrict the scope of eligible diversity contributions, it reaffirmed the institution's particular interest in "groups which have been historically discriminated against, like African-Americans." The policy also provided that no applicant should be admitted without the school's expectation that he or she would be academically successful.

The policy was challenged by an applicant, who claimed that her rejection owed to the school's use of race as a "'predominant' factor" in the admissions process. Her argument was that, for practical purposes, the policy improved the admission prospects of certain minorities and thus created favored and disfavored racial groups. Drawing upon case law that requires strict scrutiny of any racial classification, she maintained that the program was unsupported by any compelling interest. The Supreme Court, in a majority opinion authored by Justice Sandra Day O'Connor, disagreed and held that "student body diversity is a compelling state interest that can justify the use of race in university admissions."

As a starting point for its analysis, the Court reaffirmed the proposition that all racial classifications are subject to strict scrutiny. The purpose of such rigorous review is to "'smoke out' illegitimate uses of race by assuring that [government] is pursuing a goal important enough to warrant use of a highly suspect tool." The Court made it clear that strict scrutiny is not necessarily fatal, however, and race-based action may be permissible provided it is narrowly tailored to achieve a compelling governmental interest. The strict scrutiny framework thus represents "a framework for carefully examining the importance and the sincerity of the reasons advanced by the governmental decisionmaker for the use of race" in a specific context.

Until *Grutter,* the Court had found no compelling interest in affirmative action beyond the remedying of past discrimination. It deferred to the school's judgment, however, that "diversity [was] essential to its educational mission." A basic premise of the policy was that, to achieve an "exceptionally academically qualified and broadly diverse" class, "a 'critical mass' of minority students" was essential. Such an aim, as the Court saw it, was different for constitutional purposes than seeking a specified percentage of a racial or ethnic group. Among the specific educational benefits that the Court attributed to a diverse student body were "cross-racial understanding," the breaking down of racial stereotypes, and enhanced classroom discussion. The Court noted that the learning experience helps incubate skills that are demanded "in today's increasingly global marketplace." Because law schools are a primary source of the nation's future leaders, the Court thought it particularly important that they "be inclusive of talented and qualified individuals of every race and ethnicity."

Having identified diversity as a compelling governmental interest, the Court turned its attention to whether the admissions policy was narrowly tailored. Stressing first that a racial quota system is impermissible, the Court observed that it must be flexible enough "to consider all pertinent elements of diversity in light of the particular qualifications of each applicant, and to place them on the same footing for consideration, although not necessarily according them the same weight." For race or ethnicity to be taken into account as a factor, therefore, the key element of an admissions process was "individualized consideration." Evaluating the program in these terms, the Court found that the goal of achieving a "critical mass" did not create a quota. This conclusion by itself did not satisfy the "individualized consideration" requirement. The Court, however, found that the school's "highly individualized, holistic review of each applicant's file" met the standard. It also determined that there were no viable race-neutral alternatives for achieving the school's goals and the policy did not impose undue burdens on persons outside the favored group.

In closing, the Court stressed that any race-conscious admissions policy "must be limited in time." This premise aims to ensure that temporary methods for getting beyond discrimination do not become perpetual preserves or entitlements. Although the law school had no sunset provision, the Court accepted its promise to terminate the program as soon as possible. The Court noted, however, that "[w]e expect that 25 years from now, the use of racial preferences will no longer be necessary to further the interest approved today." Justice Ruth Bader Ginsburg, joined by Justice Stephen Breyer, authored a concurring opinion endorsing the proposition "that race-conscious programs 'must have a logical end point.'" Justice Ginsburg intimated, however, that the challenge of overcoming racial discrimination may require more time.

Chief Justice William Rehnquist, in a dissenting opinion joined by Justices Antonin Scalia, Anthony Kennedy, and Clarence Thomas, disputed the Court's finding that the admissions policy was narrowly tailored. Chief Justice Rehnquist saw the "critical mass" premise as a "veil . . . [for] a naked effort to achieve racial balancing." Because African American admissions were dramatically higher than for other minority groups, his view was that the extreme disproportionality among underrepresented groups undermined achievement of a real "critical mass." Chief Justice Rehnquist also pointed to evidence that virtually every applicant from the targeted minority groups was admitted. From his perspective, this correlation "must result from careful race based planning by the Law School." In addition to finding such "racial balancing . . . 'patently unconstitutional,'" Chief Justice Rehnquist also faulted the program for having no precise time limit on its duration.

Justice Kennedy, in a separate dissent, maintained that the school failed to prove its compliance with the individualized consideration requirement. He noted that up to 85 percent of the seats in an entering class were awarded on the basis of grade point averages and standardized admission tests. Race and ethnicity, Justice Kennedy observed, became a factor only with respect to the remaining seats that were filled late in the process. Given the school's interest in a diverse student body and tightness of competition for a small number of spots, he saw "the real potential to compromise individual review." Consistency of minority enrollment percentages over the years also led Justice Kennedy to infer "that the Law School subverted individual determination."

Justice Scalia, joined by Justice Thomas, also added a separate dissent. He described the school's "'critical mass' justification" as a challenge even for "the most gullible mind." Justice Scalia also challenged the "educational benefits" that the institution attributed to a diverse student body. As he described it, factors like "cross-racial understanding" and preparing students "for an increasingly diverse workforce and society" represented "lessons in life" that were not unique to a law school or necessarily teachable. Based upon the Court's ruling, Justice Scalia predicted an increased volume of litigation that would need to sort out issues of whether educational institutions had provided individualized consideration, created actual or *de facto* quotas, realized tangible educational benefits, or were committed to diversity in a *bona fide* sense. His proposed solution was a reading of the Constitution that "proscribes government discrimination on the basis of race, and [makes] state-provided education . . . no exception."

In his separate opinion concurring in part and dissenting in part, and joined for the most part by Justice Scalia, Justice Thomas maintained that the success of all students regardless of their color would be facilitated best "without the meddling of university administrators." Insofar as a law school such as the University of Michigan maintains an "elitist admissions policy," Justice Thomas observed, "racially disproportionate results" knowingly will follow. He added, however, that "[r]acial discrimination is not a permissible solution to the[se] self-inflicted wounds."

Asserting that a public university law school is not a pressing public necessity, Justice Thomas challenged the Court's finding of a compelling interest. Even if a diversified student body provided educational benefits, Justice Thomas could find no basis for a race-conscious admissions policy absent a compelling interest in the school's existence. He also contended that the school's interest in maintaining its elite status was not compelling, and that this concern with academic ranking was the only barrier to the racially neutral alternative of relaxed admission standards. As Justice Thomas saw it, "the Law School should be forced to choose between its classroom aesthetic and its exclusionary admissions system." By accepting all students who met a minimum qualifications standard, the school could achieve a racially diverse "student body without the use of racial discrimination."

Justice Thomas contested the Court's deference to the law school's judgment, noting that the interest in "educational autonomy" does not confer a license to ignore the Equal Protection Clause. He also questioned the premise that educational benefits will flow from diversity. In this regard, Justice Thomas referenced social science data indicating that "heterogeneity actually impairs learning among black students." It thus was conceivable, from Justice Thomas's perspective, that a historically black college or university could justify a racially exclusionary admissions policy. Against this backdrop, he characterized the Court's opinion as "the seed of a new constitutional justification for . . . racial segregation."

In his dissent, Justice Thomas also criticized the school for ignoring the diversity successes of other elite state law schools that did not factor race into their admissions process. He also chastised it for relying heavily upon flawed standard-ized admission tests that then create the need for the race-conscious policy. Fur-ther, Justice Thomas faulted the school for building a "facade" that "looks right" but essentially admitting "overmatched students" who are unable to succeed in the competitive environment of an elite institution. Asserting that most "blacks are admitted to Law School because of discrimination," Justice Thomas complained that "all are tarred as undeserving" and thus "stigmatized."

Despite the strong urging of the dissenting justices, *Grutter* rejected the proposi-tion that racial classifications are impermissible under any circumstance. Key to the viability of any race-conscious admissions policy is whether it is perceived as operat-ing on the basis of quotas or more flexible and individualized review. The importance of this factor is highlighted not only by the *Grutter* decision but by the outcome of the companion case of *Gratz v. Bollinger* (2003). In *Gratz,* the Court held that a Uni-versity of Michigan undergraduate admissions policy violated the Equal Protection Clause. The program was structured on a basis that enabled an applicant to receive a total of 150 points. Admission was guaranteed with 100 points, and 20 points were awarded automatically to any applicant who was the member of an under-represented minority. Because "virtually any minimally qualified minority applicant" was admitted under this program, the Court saw it as a "practical quota." A critical missing link differentiating the undergraduate model from the law school system, from the Court's perspective, was the absence of individualized consideration.

### Justice O'CONNOR delivered the opinion of the Court.

. . . We have long recognized that, given the important purpose of public education and the expansive freedoms of speech and thought associated with the university environment, universities occupy a special niche in our constitutional tradition. . . . Our conclusion that the Law School has a compelling interest in a diverse student body is informed by our view that attaining a diverse student body is at the heart of the Law School's proper institutional mission, and that "good faith" on the part of a university is "presumed" absent "a showing to the contrary."

As part of its goal of "assembling a class that is both exceptionally academically qualified and broadly diverse," the Law School seeks to "enroll a 'critical mass' of minority students." The Law School's interest is not simply "to assure within its stu-dent body some specified percentage of a particular group merely because of its race or ethnic origin." That would amount to outright racial balancing, which is patently unconstitutional. Rather, the Law School's concept of critical mass is defined by reference to the educational benefits that diversity is designed to produce.

The Law School's claim of a compelling interest is further bolstered by its *amici,* who point to the educational benefits that flow from student body diversity. In addition to the expert studies and reports entered into evidence at trial, numerous studies show that student body diversity promotes learning outcomes, and "better prepares students for an increasingly diverse workforce and society, and better prepares them as professionals.". . .

Even in the limited circumstance when drawing racial distinctions is permissible to further a compelling state interest, government is still "constrained in how it may pursue that end: [T]he means chosen to accomplish the [government's] asserted purpose must be specifically and narrowly framed to accomplish that purpose. The purpose of the narrow tailoring requirement is to ensure that "the means chosen 'fit' th[e] compelling goal so closely that there is little or no possibility that the motive for the classification was illegitimate racial prejudice or stereotype.". . .

To be narrowly tailored, a race-conscious admissions program cannot use a quota system—it cannot "insulat[e] each category of applicants with certain desired qualifications from competition with all other applicants." Instead, a university may consider race or ethnicity only as a "'plus' in a particular applicant's file," without "insulat[ing] the individual from comparison with all other candidates for the available seats." In other words, an admissions program must be "flexible enough to consider all pertinent elements of diversity in light of the particular qualifications of each applicant, and to place them on the same footing for consideration, although not necessarily according them the same weight."

We find that the Law School's admissions program bears the hallmarks of a narrowly tailored plan. As Justice Powell made clear in *Bakke,* truly individualized consideration demands that race be used in a flexible, nonmechanical way. It follows from this mandate that universities cannot establish quotas for members of certain racial groups or put members of those groups on separate admissions tracks. Nor can universities insulate applicants who belong to certain racial or ethnic groups from the competition for admission. Universities can, however, consider race or ethnicity more flexibly as a "plus" factor in the context of individualized consideration of each and every applicant.

The Law School's goal of attaining a critical mass of underrepresented minority students does not transform its program into a quota. As the Harvard plan described by Justice Powell recognized, there is of course "some relationship between numbers and achieving the benefits to be derived from a diverse student body, and between numbers and providing a reasonable environment for those students admitted." Nor, as Justice KENNEDY posits, does the Law School's consultation of the "daily reports," which keep track of the racial and ethnic composition of the class (as well as of residency and gender), "sugges[t] there was no further attempt at individual review save for race itself" during the final stages of the admissions process. To the contrary, the Law School's admissions officers testified without contradiction that they never gave race any more or less weight based on the information contained in these reports. . . .

That a race-conscious admissions program does not operate as a quota does not, by itself, satisfy the requirement of individualized consideration. When using race as a "plus" factor in university admissions, a university's admissions program must remain flexible enough to ensure that each applicant is evaluated as an individual and not in a way that makes an applicant's race or ethnicity the defining feature of his or her application. The importance of this individualized consideration in the context of a race-conscious admissions program is paramount. . . .

What is more, the Law School actually gives substantial weight to diversity factors besides race. The Law School frequently accepts nonminority applicants with grades and test scores lower than underrepresented minority applicants (and other nonminority applicants) who are rejected. This shows that the Law School seriously weighs many other diversity factors besides race that can make a real and dispositive difference for nonminority applicants as well. By this flexible approach, the Law School sufficiently takes into account, in practice as well as in theory, a wide variety of characteristics besides race and ethnicity that contribute to a diverse student body. . . .

### Justice THOMAS, with whom Justice SCALIA joins as to Parts I–VII, concurring in part and dissenting in part.

Frederick Douglass, speaking to a group of abolitionists almost 140 years ago, delivered a message lost on today's majority:

"[I]n regard to the colored people, there is always more that is benevolent, I perceive, than just, manifested towards us. What I ask for the negro is not benevolence, not pity, not sympathy, but simply *justice*. The American people have always been anxious to know what they shall do with us. . . . I have had but one answer from the beginning. Do nothing with us! Your doing with us has already played the mischief with us. Do nothing with us! If the apples will not remain on the tree of their own strength, if they are worm-eaten at the core, if they are early ripe and disposed to fall, let them fall! ... And if the negro cannot stand on his own legs, let him fall also. All I ask is, give him a chance to stand on his own legs! Let him alone! . . . [Y]our interference is doing him positive injury." What the Black Man Wants: An Address Delivered in Boston, Massachusetts, on 26 January 1865, reprinted in 4 The Frederick Douglass Papers 59, 68 (J. Blassingame and J. McKivigan eds.1991) (emphasis in original).

Like Douglass, I believe blacks can achieve in every avenue of American life without the meddling of university administrators. Because I wish to see all students succeed whatever their color, I share, in some respect, the sympathies of those who sponsor the type of discrimination advanced by the University of Michigan Law School (Law School). The Constitution does not, however, tolerate institutional devotion to the status quo in admissions policies when such devotion ripens into racial discrimination. Nor does the Constitution countenance the unprecedented deference the Court gives to the Law School, an approach inconsistent with the very concept of "strict scrutiny."

No one would argue that a university could set up a lower general admissions standard and then impose heightened requirements only on black applicants. Similarly, a university may not maintain a high admissions standard and grant exemptions to favored races. The Law School, of its own choosing, and for its own purposes, maintains an exclusionary admissions system that it knows produces racially disproportionate results. Racial discrimination is not a permissible solution to the self-inflicted wounds of this elitist admissions policy.

The majority upholds the Law School's racial discrimination not by interpreting the people's Constitution, but by responding to a faddish slogan of the cognoscenti. . . .

The Constitution abhors classifications based on race, not only because those classifications can harm favored races or are based on illegitimate motives, but also because every time the government places citizens on racial registers and makes race relevant to the provision of burdens or benefits, it demeans us all. "Purchased at the price of immeasurable human suffering, the equal protection principle reflects our Nation's understanding that such classifications ultimately have a destructive impact on the individual and our society.". . .

## Justice KENNEDY, dissenting.

. . . The Law School has the burden of proving, in conformance with the standard of strict scrutiny, that it did not utilize race in an unconstitutional way. At the very least, the constancy of admitted minority students and the close correlation between the racial breakdown of admitted minorities and the composition of the applicant pool, require the Law School either to produce a convincing explanation or to show it has taken adequate steps to ensure individual assessment. The Law School does neither.

The obvious tension between the pursuit of critical mass and the requirement of individual review increased by the end of the admissions season. Most of the decisions where race may decide the outcome are made during this period. . . .

The consultation of daily reports during the last stages in the admissions process suggests there was no further attempt at individual review save for race itself. The admissions officers could use the reports to recalibrate the plus factor given to race depending on how close they were to achieving the Law School's goal of critical mass. The bonus factor of race would then become divorced from individual review; it would be premised instead on the numerical objective set by the Law School.

The Law School made no effort to guard against this danger. It provided no guidelines to its admissions personnel on how to reconcile individual assessment with the directive to admit a critical mass of minority students. The admissions program could have been structured to eliminate at least some of the risk that the promise of individual evaluation was not being kept. The daily consideration of racial breakdown of admitted students is not a feature of affirmative-action programs used by other institutions of higher learning. The Little Ivy League colleges, for instance, do not keep ongoing tallies of racial or ethnic composition of their entering students.

To be constitutional, a university's compelling interest in a diverse student body must be achieved by a system where individual assessment is safeguarded through the entire process. There is no constitutional objection to the goal of considering race as one modest factor among many others to achieve diversity, but an educational institution must ensure, through sufficient procedures, that each applicant receives individual consideration and that race does not become a predominant factor in the admissions decisionmaking. The Law School failed to comply with this requirement, and by no means has it carried its burden to show otherwise by the test of strict scrutiny.

### Bibliography

Williams, Patricia J. *Metro Broadcasting, Inc. v. Federal Communications Commission, Harvard Law Review* 104 (1990): 525.

## *Gratz v. Bollinger*

**Citation: 539 U.S. 249.**

**Issue: Whether a public university's admissions policy that factored race in creating a diverse student body violated the Equal Protection Clause.**

**Year of Decision: 2003.**

**Outcome: Yes. The university's policy, which automatically distributed 20 points, or one-fifth of the points needed to guarantee admission, to every single "underrepresented minority" applicant solely because of race violated the Equal Protection Clause.**

**Author of Opinion: Chief Justice William Rehnquist.**

**Vote: 5-4.**

In *Grutter v. Bollinger* (2003), a closely divided Supreme Court held that a public university law school admissions policy that factored race as a *nonexclusive* consideration in creating a diverse student body was not a violation of the Equal Protection Clause. In a companion case to *Grutter* known as *Gratz v. Bollinger* (2003), however, the Court held in a narrow 5-4 decision that a University of Michigan undergraduate admissions policy violated the Equal Protection Clause. The program was structured on a basis that enabled an applicant to receive a total of 150 points. Admission was guaranteed with 100 points, and 20 points were awarded automatically to any applicant who was the member of an underrepresented minority. Because "virtually any minimally qualified minority applicant" was admitted under this program, the Court saw it as a "practical quota." A critical missing link differentiating the undergraduate model from the law school system, from the Court's perspective, was the absence of individualized consideration.

**Justice REHNQUIST, C.J. delivered the opinion of the Court, in which O'CONNOR, SCALIA, KENNEDY, and THOMAS, JJ., joined.**

. . . Petitioners Jennifer Gratz and Patrick Hamacher both applied for admission to the University of Michigan's (University) College of Literature, Science, and the Arts (LSA) as residents of the State of Michigan. Both petitioners are Caucasian.

Gratz, who applied for admission for the fall of 1995, was notified in January of that year that a final decision regarding her admission had been delayed until April. This delay was based upon the University's determination that, although Gratz was "well qualified," she was "less competitive than the students who ha[d] been admitted on first review." Gratz was notified in April that the LSA was unable to offer her admission. . . .

Petitioners argue, first and foremost, that the University's use of race in undergraduate admissions violates the Fourteenth Amendment. Specifically, they contend that this Court has only sanctioned the use of racial classifications to remedy identified discrimination, a justification on which respondents have never relied. Brief for Petitioners 15–16. Petitioners further argue that "diversity as a basis for employing racial preferences is simply too open-ended, ill-defined, and indefinite to constitute a compelling interest capable of supporting narrowly-tailored means." But for the reasons set forth today in *Grutter v. Bollinger,* the Court has rejected these arguments of petitioners.

Petitioners alternatively argue that even if the University's interest in diversity can constitute a compelling state interest, the District Court erroneously concluded that the University's use of race in its current freshman admissions policy is narrowly tailored to achieve such an interest. Petitioners argue that the guidelines the University began using in 1999 do not "remotely resemble the kind of consideration of race and ethnicity that Justice Powell endorsed in *Bakke*." . . .

It is by now well established that "all racial classifications reviewable under the Equal Protection Clause must be strictly scrutinized." . . . Thus, "any person, of whatever race, has the right to demand that any governmental actor subject to the Constitution justify any racial classification subjecting that person to unequal treatment under the strictest of judicial scrutiny."

To withstand our strict scrutiny analysis, respondents must demonstrate that the University's use of race in its current admissions program employs "narrowly tailored measures that further compelling governmental interests." . . . We find that the University's policy, which automatically distributes 20 points, or one-fifth of the points needed to guarantee admission, to every single "underrepresented minority" applicant solely because of race, is not narrowly tailored to achieve the interest in educational diversity that respondents claim justifies their program. . . .

Justice Powell's opinion in *Bakke* emphasized the importance of considering each particular applicant as an individual, assessing all of the qualities that individual possesses, and in turn, evaluating that individual's ability to contribute to the unique setting of higher education. The admissions program Justice Powell described, however, did not contemplate that any single characteristic automatically ensured a specific and identifiable contribution to a university's diversity. Instead, under the approach Justice Powell described, each characteristic of a particular applicant was to be considered in assessing the applicant's entire application.

The current LSA policy does not provide such individualized consideration. The LSA's policy automatically distributes 20 points to every single applicant from an "underrepresented minority" group, as defined by the University. The only consideration that accompanies this distribution of points is a factual review of an application to determine whether an individual is a member of one of these minority groups. Moreover, unlike Justice Powell's example, where the race of a "particular black applicant" could be considered without being decisive, the LSA's automatic distribution of 20 points has the effect of making "the factor of race . . . decisive" for virtually every minimally qualified underrepresented minority applicant. . . .

Respondents contend that "[t]he volume of applications and the presentation of applicant information make it impractical for [the University] to use the . . . admissions system" upheld by the Court today in *Grutter*. But the fact that the implementation of a program capable of providing individualized consideration might present administrative challenges does not render constitutional an otherwise problematic system. We conclude, therefore, that because the University's use of race in its current freshman admissions policy is not narrowly tailored to achieve respondents' asserted compelling interest in diversity, the admissions policy violates the Equal Protection Clause of the Fourteenth Amendment.

## Justice THOMAS, concurring.

I join the Court's opinion because I believe it correctly applies our precedents, including today's decision in *Grutter v. Bollinger*. For similar reasons to those given in my separate opinion in that case, however, I would hold that a State's use of racial discrimination in higher education admissions is categorically prohibited by the Equal Protection Clause. . . .

## Justice GINSBURG, with whom Justice SOUTER joins, dissenting.

Educational institutions, the Court acknowledges, are not barred from any and all consideration of race when making admissions decisions. But the Court once again maintains that the same standard of review controls judicial inspection of all official race classifications. This insistence on "consistency," would be fitting were our Nation free of the vestiges of rank discrimination long reinforced by law. But we are not far distant from an overtly discriminatory past, and the effects of centuries of law-sanctioned inequality remain painfully evident in our communities and schools.

In the wake "of a system of racial caste only recently ended," large disparities endure. Unemployment, poverty, and access to health care, vary disproportionately by race. Neighborhoods and schools remain racially divided. African American and Hispanic children are all too often educated in poverty-stricken and underperforming institutions. Adult African Americans and Hispanics generally earn less than whites with equivalent levels of education. Equally credentialed job applicants receive different receptions depending on their race. Irrational prejudice is still encountered in real estate markets and consumer transactions. "Bias both conscious and unconscious, reflecting traditional and unexamined habits of thought, keeps up barriers that must come down if equal opportunity and nondiscrimination are ever genuinely to become this country's law and practice."

The Constitution instructs all who act for the government that they may not "deny to any person . . . the equal protection of the laws." In implementing this equality instruction, as I see it, government decisionmakers may properly distinguish between policies of exclusion and inclusion. Actions designed to burden groups long denied full citizenship stature are not sensibly ranked with measures taken to hasten the day when entrenched discrimination and its aftereffects have been extirpated.

Our jurisprudence ranks race a "suspect" category, "not because [race] is inevitably an impermissible classification, but because it is one which usually, to our national shame, has been drawn for the purpose of maintaining racial inequality." But where race is considered "for the purpose of achieving equality," no automatic proscription is in order. For, as insightfully explained: "The Constitution is both color blind and color conscious. To avoid conflict with the Equal Protection Clause, a classification that denies a benefit, causes harm, or imposes a burden must not be based on race. In that sense, the Constitution is color blind. But the Constitution is color conscious to prevent discrimination being perpetuated and to undo the effects of past discrimination." Contemporary human rights documents draw just this line; they distinguish between policies of oppression and measures designed to accelerate *de facto* equality.

The mere assertion of a laudable governmental purpose, of course, should not immunize a race-conscious measure from careful judicial inspection. Close review is needed "to ferret out classifications in reality malign, but masquerading as benign," and to "ensure that preferences are not so large as to trammel unduly upon the opportunities of others or interfere too harshly with legitimate expectations of persons in once-preferred groups." . . .

## Bibliography

Harpalani, Vinay. "Diversity Within Racial Groups and the Constitutionality of Race-Conscious Admissions." *University of Pennsylvania Journal of Constitutional Law* 15 (2012) 463.

## *Fisher v. University of Texas*

**Citation: 570 U.S. ___, 133 S. Ct. 2411.**

**Issue: What level of judicial review of an affirmative action plan is required under strict Scrutiny?**

**Year of Decision: 2013.**

**Outcome: Strict scrutiny means that affirmative action programs must be closely scrutinized and the University must demonstrate that there were no race-neutral alternatives available to achieve its goal of a diverse student body.**

**Author of Opinion: Justice Anthony Kennedy.**

**Vote: 7-1.**

In 1997, Texas passed a law requiring the University of Texas to admit all in-state high school seniors who finished in the top ten percent of their high school classes. The University decided to modify its race-neutral admissions policy, however, after finding that the racial and ethnic makeup of the university's undergraduate population differed from the state's population overall. The University continued to admit all in-state students who graduated in the top ten percent of their high school classes. The new policy, however, now considered race as a factor in admission for the remainder of the in-state freshman class who did finish in the top ten percent of their classes.

Abigail N. Fisher, a white female, applied for admission to the University of Texas in 2008. Because she was not in the top ten percent of her high school class, she competed for admission with other applicants who had also not finished in the top ten percent of their classes. The University denied Fisher's application for admission. She alleged that the University's consideration of race in admissions violated the Equal Protection Clause.

The Court confronted the question of whether it should be deferential towards the University's claim that it had acted in good faith in choosing the best means by which to accomplish its goal of achieving a diverse student body. Since affirmative action programs are race-conscious and so require strict scrutiny, the Court ruled that no such deference should be shown and that it is the University's burden to demonstrate that it had considered all race-neutral means to achieve its goal of diversity. In the Court's words, "the University must prove that the means it chose to attain . . . diversity are narrowly tailored to its goal. On this point, the University receives no deference. [cite] It is at all times the University's obligation to demonstrate, and the Judiciary's obligation to determine, that admissions processes 'ensure that each applicant is evaluated as an individual and not in a way that makes an applicant's race or ethnicity the defining feature of his or her application.'" In effect, the *Fisher* Court adopted the reasoning in Justice Kennedy's dissent in *Grutter*, to the effect that the Court must faithfully apply the requirement of strict scrutiny, and place the burden on the University (or law school) to prove that it had truly considered all possible race-neutral means to achieve a diverse student body.

Justices Scalia and Thomas concurred in the judgment, but offered their separate opinions to the effect that government's use of race in higher education admissions decisions is categorically prohibited by the Equal Protection Clause. Justice Thomas went further, describing the goal of diversity using racial categorizations as comparable to the claims segregationists made about the beneficial uses of racial considerations on behalf of their programs before they were overturned by the decision in *Brown v. Board of Education*. Justice Thomas, like Justice Scalia, advances the argument that the Constitution is strictly color-blind.

KENNEDY, J., delivered the opinion of the Court, in which ROBERTS, C.J., and SCALIA, THOMAS, BREYER, ALITO, and SOTOMAYOR, JJ., joined.

. . . Once the University has established that its goal of diversity is consistent with strict scrutiny, however, there must still be a further judicial determination that the admissions process meets strict scrutiny in its implementation. The University must prove that the means chosen by the University to attain diversity are narrowly tailored to that goal. On this point, the University receives no deference. True, a court can take account of a university's experience and expertise in adopting or rejecting certain admissions processes. But, as the Court said in *Grutter*, it remains at all times the University's obligation to demonstrate, and the Judiciary's obligation to determine, that admissions processes "ensure that each applicant is evaluated as an individual and not in a way that makes an applicant's race or ethnicity the defining feature of his or her application."

Narrow tailoring also requires that the reviewing court verify that it is "necessary" for a university to use race to achieve the educational benefits of diversity. This involves a careful judicial inquiry into whether a university could achieve sufficient diversity without using racial classifications. Although "[n]arrow tailoring does not require exhaustion of every *conceivable* race-neutral alternative," strict scrutiny does require a court to examine with care, and not defer to, a university's "serious, good faith consideration of workable race-neutral alternatives." Consideration by the university is of course necessary, but it is not sufficient to satisfy strict scrutiny: The reviewing court must ultimately be satisfied that no workable race-neutral alternatives would produce the educational benefits of diversity. If a nonracial approach . . . could promote the substantial interest about as well and at tolerable administrative expense, then the university may not consider race. A plaintiff, of course, bears the burden of placing the validity of a university's adoption of an affirmative action plan in issue. But strict scrutiny imposes on the university the ultimate burden of demonstrating, before turning to racial classifications, that available, workable race-neutral alternatives do not suffice.

Rather than perform this searching examination, however, the Court of Appeals held petitioner could challenge only "whether [the University's] decision to reintroduce race as a factor in admissions was made in good faith." And in considering such a challenge, the court would "presume the University acted in good faith" and place on petitioner the burden of rebutting that presumption. The Court of Appeals held that to "second-guess the merits" of this aspect of the University's decision was a task it was "ill-equipped to perform" and that it would attempt only to "ensure that [the University's] decision to adopt a race-conscious admissions policy followed from [a process of] good faith consideration." The Court of Appeals thus concluded that "the narrow-tailoring inquiry—like the compelling-interest inquiry—is undertaken with a degree of deference to the Universit[y]." Because "the efforts of the University have been studied, serious, and of high purpose," the Court of Appeals held that the use of race in the admissions program fell within "a constitutionally protected zone of discretion."

These expressions of the controlling standard are at odds with *Grutter's* command that "all racial classifications imposed by government 'must be analyzed by a reviewing court under strict scrutiny.'" In *Grutter,* the Court approved the plan at issue upon concluding that it was not a quota, was sufficiently flexible, was limited in time, and followed "serious, good faith consideration of workable race-neutral alternatives." *Grutter* did not hold that good faith would forgive an impermissible consideration of race. It must be remembered that "the mere recitation of a 'benign' or legitimate purpose for a racial classification is entitled to little or no weight." Strict scrutiny does not permit a court to accept a school's assertion that its admissions process uses race in a permissible way without a court giving close analysis to the evidence of how the process works in practice.

The higher education dynamic does not change the narrow tailoring analysis of strict scrutiny applicable in other contexts. "[T]he analysis and level of scrutiny applied to determine the validity of [a racial] classification do not vary simply because the objective appears acceptable. . . . While the validity and importance of the objective may affect the outcome of the analysis, the analysis itself does not change."

The District Court and Court of Appeals confined the strict scrutiny inquiry in too narrow a way by deferring to the University's good faith in its use of racial classifications and affirming the grant of summary judgment on that basis. The Court vacates that judgment, but fairness to the litigants and the courts that heard the case requires that it be remanded so that the admissions process can be considered and judged under a correct analysis. Unlike *Grutter,* which was decided after trial, this case arises from cross-motions for summary judgment. In this case, as in similar cases, in determining whether summary judgment in favor of the University would be appropriate, the Court of Appeals must assess whether the University has offered sufficient evidence that would prove that its admissions program is narrowly tailored to obtain the educational benefits of diversity. Whether this record— and not "simple . . . assurances of good intention,"—is sufficient is a question for the Court of Appeals in the first instance.

Strict scrutiny must not be "strict in theory, but fatal in fact." But the opposite is also true. Strict scrutiny must not be strict in theory but feeble in fact. In order for judicial review to be meaningful, a university must make a showing that its plan is narrowly tailored to achieve the only interest that this Court has approved in this context: the benefits of a student body diversity that "encompasses a . . . broa[d] array of qualifications and characteristics of which racial or ethnic origin is but a single though important element." The judgment of the Court of Appeals is vacated, and the case is remanded for further proceedings consistent with this opinion.

## Justice THOMAS, concurring.

I join the Court's opinion because I agree that the Court of Appeals did not apply strict scrutiny to the University of Texas at Austin's (University) use of racial discrimination in admissions decisions. I write separately to explain that I would overrule *Grutter v. Bollinger,* and hold that a State's use of race in higher education admissions decisions is categorically prohibited by the Equal Protection Clause.

The Fourteenth Amendment provides that no State shall "deny to any person . . . the equal protection of the laws." The Equal Protection Clause guarantees every person the right to be treated equally by the State, without regard to race. "At the heart of this [guarantee] lies the principle that the government must treat citizens as individuals, and not as members of racial, ethnic, or religious groups."

Under strict scrutiny, all racial classifications are categorically prohibited unless they are "'necessary to further a compelling governmental interest'" and "narrowly tailored to that end." This most exacting standard "has proven automatically fatal" in almost every case. And rightly so. "Purchased at the price of immeasurable human suffering, the equal protection principle reflects our Nation's understanding that [racial] classifications ultimately have a destructive impact on the individual and our society." "The Constitution abhors classifications based on race" because "every time the government places citizens on racial registers and makes race relevant to the provision of burdens or benefits, it demeans us all." *Grutter.*

## Justice GINSBURG, dissenting.

The University of Texas at Austin (University) is candid about what it is endeavoring to do: It seeks to achieve student-body diversity through an admissions policy patterned after the Harvard plan referenced as exemplary in Justice Powell's opinion in *Bakke*. The University has steered clear of a quota system like the one struck down in *Bakke*, which excluded all nonminority candidates from competition for a fixed number of seats. And, like so many educational institutions across the Nation, the University has taken care to follow the model approved by the Court in *Grutter.*

Petitioner urges that Texas' Top Ten Percent Law and race-blind holistic review of each application achieve significant diversity, so the University must be content with those alternatives. I have said before and reiterate here that only an ostrich could regard the supposedly neutral alternatives as race unconscious. As Justice Souter observed, the vaunted alternatives suffer from "the disadvantage of deliberate obfuscation."

Texas' percentage plan was adopted with racially segregated neighborhoods and schools front and center stage. It is race consciousness, not blindness to race, that drives such plans. As for holistic review, if universities cannot explicitly include race as a factor, many may "resort to camouflage" to "maintain their minority enrollment."

I have several times explained why government actors, including state universities, need not be blind to the lingering effects of "an overtly discriminatory past," the legacy of "centuries of law-sanctioned inequality." Among constitutionally permissible options, I remain convinced, "those that candidly disclose their consideration of race [are] preferable to those that conceal it."

Accordingly, I would not return this case for a second look. As the thorough opinions below show, the University's admissions policy flexibly considers race only as a "factor of a factor of a factor of a factor" in the calculus, followed a yearlong review through which the University reached the reasonable, good-faith judgment that supposedly race-neutral initiatives were insufficient to achieve, in appropriate measure, the educational benefits of student-body diversity, and is subject to periodic review to ensure that the consideration of race remains necessary and proper to achieve the University's educational objectives. Justice Powell's opinion in *Bakke* and the Court's decision in *Grutter* require no further determinations.

The Court rightly declines to cast off the equal protection framework settled in *Grutter*. Yet it stops short of reaching the conclusion that framework warrants. Instead, the Court vacates the Court of Appeals' judgment and remands for the Court of Appeals to "assess whether the University has offered sufficient evidence [to] prove that its admissions program is narrowly tailored to obtain the educational benefits of diversity." As I see it, the Court of Appeals has already completed that inquiry, and its judgment, trained on this Court's *Bakke* and *Grutter* pathmarkers, merits our approbation. . . .

## Bibliography

Blumstein, James F. "*Grutter* and *Fisher*: a Reassessment and a Preview." *Vanderbilt Law Review En Banc* 65 (2012): 57.

Pacelli, Kimberly A. "*Fisher v. University of Texas at Austin*: Navigating the Narrows Between *Grutter* and Parents Involved." *Maine Law Review* 63 (2011): 569.

## *Schuette v. Coalition to Defend Affirmative Action*

**Citation: 572 U. S. ___, 134 S.Ct. 1623 (2014).**

**Issue: May the judiciary set aside Michigan laws that commit to the voters the decision whether racial preferences may be considered in governmental decisions, in particular with respect to school admissions?**

**Year of Decision: 2014.**

**Outcome: No.**

**Author of Opinion: Justice Anthony Kennedy.**

**Vote: 6-2.**

After the Court issued its opinions in *Grutter* and *Gratz*, Michigan voters adopted Proposal 2 of the State Constitution, which prohibits the use of race-based preferences as part of the admissions process for state universities.

The Court framed the issue as follows: "the question here is not how to address or prevent injury caused on account of race but whether voters may determine whether a policy of race-based preferences should be continued. By approving Proposal 2 . . . ," Michigan voters exercised their privilege to enact laws as a basic exercise of their democratic power, bypassing public officials they considered unresponsive to their concerns about a policy of granting race-based preferences.

Writing for the three-justice plurality, Justice Kennedy argued that protecting interests based on race risked allowing the government to classify people based on race. Such classifications perpetuate the kind of racism the affirmative-action policies were meant to counter. Voters have the right to determine that some race-based preferences are helpful. Voters also have the right to decide otherwise, and the courts do not have the right to deny the voters their democratic rights to make such choices.

Chief Justice Roberts wrote a concurring opinion contending that the use of racial preferences would likely add to racial attitudes. In a concurring opinion, Justice Scalia wrote that judges should not be in the position of dividing the country into racial groups and determining what policies are in each group's interests. Moreover, because the Michigan amendment prohibits the use of racial preferences, it clearly secures equal protection under the law as intended by the Fourteenth Amendment. Justice Breyer wrote a separate opinion concurring in the judgment, arguing that "the Constitution allows local, state, and national communities to adopt narrowly tailored race-conscious programs designed to bring about greater inclusion and diversity. But the Constitution foresees the ballot box, not the courts, as the normal instrument for resolving differences and debates about the merits of these programs."

Justice Sonia Sotomayor wrote a dissenting opinion in which she argued that the democratic process is not adequate to protect against the oppression of minority groups. The constitution, Justice Sotomayor contended, protects against the implementation of laws such as Michigan's that would oppress certain groups on the basis of race.

### Justice KENNEDY announced the judgment of the Court and delivered an opinion, in which CHIEF JUSTICE ROBERTS and Justice ALITO join.

. . . The Court in this case must determine whether an amendment to the Constitution of the State of Michigan, approved and enacted by its voters, is invalid under the Equal Protection Clause of the Fourteenth Amendment to the Constitution of the United States.

In 2003 the Court reviewed the constitutionality of two admissions systems at the University of Michigan, one for its undergraduate class and one for its law school. The undergraduate admissions plan was addressed in *Gratz v. Bollinger.* The law school admission plan was addressed in *Grutter v. Bollinger.* Each admissions process permitted the explicit consideration of an applicant's race. In *Gratz,* the Court invalidated the undergraduate plan as a violation of the Equal Protection Clause. In *Grutter,* the Court found no constitutional flaw in the law school admission plan's more limited use of race-based preferences.

In response to the Court's decision in *Gratz,* the university revised its undergraduate admissions process, but the revision still allowed limited use of race-based preferences. After a statewide debate on the question of racial preferences in the context of governmental decisionmaking, the voters, in 2006, adopted an amendment to the State Constitution prohibiting state and other governmental entities in Michigan from granting certain preferences, including race-based preferences, in a wide range of actions and decisions. Under the terms of the amendment, race-based preferences cannot be part of the admissions process for state universities. That particular prohibition is central to the instant case.

The ballot proposal was called Proposal 2 and, after it passed by a margin of 58 percent to 42 percent, the resulting enactment became Article I, § 26, of the Michigan Constitution. . . .

Before the Court addresses the question presented, it is important to note what this case is not about. It is not about the constitutionality, or the merits, of race-conscious admissions policies in higher education. The consideration of race in admissions presents complex questions, in part addressed last Term in *Fisher v. University of Texas at Austin.* In *Fisher,* the Court did not disturb the principle that the consideration of race in admissions is permissible, provided that certain conditions are met. In this case, as in *Fisher,* that principle is not challenged. The question here concerns not the permissibility of race-conscious admissions policies under the Constitution but whether, and in what manner, voters in the States may choose to prohibit the consideration of racial preferences in governmental decisions, in particular with respect to school admissions. . . .

In cautioning against "impermissible racial stereotypes," this Court has rejected the assumption that "members of the same racial group—regardless of their age, education, economic status, or the community in which they live—think alike, share the same political interests, and will prefer the same candidates at the polls." It cannot be entertained as a serious proposition that all individuals of the same race think alike. . . . And if it were deemed necessary to probe how some races define their own interest in political matters, still another beginning point would be to define individuals according to race. But in a society in which those lines are becoming more blurred, the attempt to define race-based categories also raises serious questions of its own. Government action that classifies individuals on the basis of race is inherently suspect and carries the danger of perpetuating the very racial divisions the polity seeks to transcend. Were courts to embark upon this venture not only would it be undertaken with no clear legal standards or accepted sources to guide judicial decision but also it would result in, or at least impose a high risk of, inquiries and categories dependent upon demeaning stereotypes, classifications of questionable constitutionality on their own terms. . . .

Perhaps, when enacting policies as an exercise of democratic self-government, voters will determine that race-based preferences should be adopted. The constitutional validity of some of those choices regarding racial preferences is not at issue here. The holding in the instant case is simply that the courts may not disempower the voters from choosing which path to follow. In the realm of policy discussions the regular give-and-take of debate ought to be a context in which rancor or discord based on race are avoided, not invited. And if these factors are to be interjected, surely it ought not to be at the invitation or insistence of the courts. . . .

By approving Proposal 2 and thereby adding § 26 to their State Constitution, the Michigan voters exercised their privilege to enact laws as a basic exercise of their democratic power. In the federal system States "respond, through the enactment of positive law, to the initiative of those who seek a voice in shaping the destiny of their own times." Michigan voters used the initiative system to bypass public officials who were deemed not responsive to the concerns of a majority of the voters with respect to a policy of granting race-based preferences that raises difficult and delicate issues.

The freedom secured by the Constitution consists, in one of its essential dimensions, of the right of the individual not to be injured by the unlawful exercise of governmental power. . . . Yet freedom does not stop with individual rights. Our constitutional system embraces, too, the right of citizens to debate so they can learn and decide and then, through the political process, act in concert to try to shape the course of their own times and the course of a nation that must strive always to make freedom ever greater and more secure. Here Michigan voters acted in concert and statewide to seek consensus and adopt a policy on a difficult subject against a historical background of race in America that has been a source of tragedy and persisting injustice. That history demands that we continue to learn, to listen, and to remain open to new approaches if we are to aspire always to a constitutional order in which all persons are treated with fairness and equal dignity. Were the Court to rule that the question addressed by Michigan voters is too sensitive or complex to be within the grasp of the electorate; or that the policies at issue remain too delicate to be resolved save by university officials or faculties, acting at some remove from immediate public scrutiny and control; or that these matters are so arcane that the electorate's power must be limited because the people cannot prudently exercise that power even after a full debate, that holding would be an unprecedented restriction on the exercise of a fundamental right held not just by one person but by all in common. It is the right to speak and debate and learn and then, as a matter of political will, to act through a lawful electoral process.

### Justice SCALIA, with whom Justice THOMAS joins, concurring in the judgment.

It has come to this. Called upon to explore the jurisprudential twilight zone between two errant lines of precedent, we confront a frighteningly bizarre question: Does the Equal Protection Clause of the Fourteenth Amendment *forbid* what its text plainly *requires*? Needless to say (except that this case obliges us to say it), the question answers itself. "The Constitution proscribes government discrimination on the basis of race, and state-provided education is no exception." It is precisely this understanding—the correct understanding—of the federal Equal Protection Clause that the people of the State of Michigan have adopted for their own fundamental law. By adopting it, they did not simultaneously *offend* it.

Even taking this Court's sorry line of race-based-admissions cases as a given, I find the question presented only slightly less strange: Does the Equal Protection Clause forbid a State from banning a practice that the Clause barely—and only provisionally—permits? Reacting to those race-based-admissions decisions, some States—whether deterred by the prospect of costly litigation; aware that *Grutter*'s bell may soon toll, or simply opposed in principle to the notion of "benign" racial discrimination—have gotten out of the racial-preferences business altogether. And with our express encouragement: "Universities in California, Florida, and Washington State, where racial preferences in admissions are prohibited by state law, are currently engaging in experimenting with a wide variety of alternative approaches. Universities in other States can *and should* draw on the most promising aspects of these race-neutral alternatives as they develop." Respondents seem to think this admonition was merely in jest. The experiment, they maintain, is not only over; it never rightly began. Neither the people of the States nor their legislatures ever had the option of directing subordinate public-university officials to cease considering the race of applicants, since that would deny members of those minority groups the option of enacting a policy designed to further their interest, thus denying them the equal protection of the laws. Never mind that it is hotly disputed whether the practice of race-based admissions is *ever* in a racial minority's interest. And never mind that, were a public university to stake its defense of a race-based-admissions policy on the ground that it was *designed* to benefit primarily minorities (as opposed to all students, regardless of color, by enhancing diversity), *we would hold the policy unconstitutional.* . . .

### Justice SOTOMAYOR, with whom Justice GINSBURG joins, dissenting.

. . . We are fortunate to live in a democratic society. But without checks, democratically approved legislation can oppress minority groups. For that reason, our Constitution places limits on what a majority of the people may do. This case implicates one such limit: the guarantee of equal protection of the laws. Although that guarantee is traditionally understood to prohibit intentional discrimination under existing laws, equal protection does not end there. Another fundamental strand of our equal protection jurisprudence focuses on process, securing to all citizens the right to participate meaningfully and equally in self-government. That right is the bedrock of our democracy, for it preserves all other rights. . . .

This case involves this last chapter of discrimination: A majority of the Michigan electorate changed the basic rules of the political process in that State in a manner that uniquely disadvantaged racial minorities. Prior to the enactment of the constitutional initiative at issue here, all of the admissions policies of Michigan's public colleges and universities—including race-sensitive admissions policies—were in the hands of each institution's governing board. The members of those boards are nominated by political parties and elected by the citizenry in statewide elections. After over a century of being shut out of Michigan's institutions of higher education, racial minorities in Michigan had succeeded in persuading the elected board representatives to adopt admissions policies that took into account the benefits of racial diversity. . . .

### Bibliography

D'Alessio, Christopher E. "A Bridge Too Far: the Limits of the Political Process Doctrine in *Schuette v. Coalition to Defend Affirmative Action.*" *Duke Journal of Constitutional Law and Public Policy-Sidebar* 9 (2013): 103.

# Chapter 9

# Gender

As originally framed and ratified, the Constitution reflected the input and interests of white males. The Reconstruction Amendments factored racial reality into the constitutional framework. Gender remained beyond the pale of constitutional concern, however, until the twentieth century. Until then, constitutional challenges to laws restricting freedom of or opportunities for women were unsuccessful. Typifying the Supreme Court's early thinking was its decision in *Bradwell v. Illinois* (1873), upholding a state law that barred women from practicing law. In support of this result, the Court observed that "[t]he paramount destiny of and mission of woman are to fulfill the noble and benign offices of wife and mother. This is the law of the Creator. And the rules of civil society must be adapted to the general constitution of things."

Original pronouncements on the meaning of the Equal Protection Clause made it clear, at least at the time, that it had nothing to do with gender. This understanding was evident in the Supreme Court's first decision concerning the equal protection guarantee. In the *Slaughter-House Cases* (1873), the Court "doubt[ed] very much whether any action of a State not directed by way of discrimination against the Negroes as a class, or on account of their race, will ever be held to come within the purview of this provision." This point was made even more directly with respect to gender during the same term the Court upheld a state law denying women the opportunity to practice law. This determination, in *Bradwell v. Illinois* (1873), was coupled with the observation that "[i]n the nature of things it is not every citizen of every age, sex and condition that is qualified for every calling and position."

The Court's rulings through the middle of the twentieth century reflected a sense that the legislature could account for traditional differences associated with men and women. Underlying this orientation was an understanding, referenced in *Bradwell v. Illinois,* that "the family institution is repugnant to the idea of a woman adopting a distinct and independent career from that of her husband."

In 1920 the Nineteenth Amendment established that the right "to vote shall not be denied or abridged . . . on account of sex." For another half century, however, the Court resisted interpreting the equal protection guarantee as a means of accounting for gender inequality. In the early 1970s, the Court gave indications that laws discriminating on the basis of gender might implicate the Equal Protection Clause. This possibility became a reality in *Craig v. Boren* (1976), when the Court announced that it would take a harder look at gender classifications.

This decision, and case law that followed it, established the Equal Protection Clause as a barrier to traditional distinctions on the basis of gender. Representative of these decisions was *United States v. Virginia* (1996), which emphasized the importance of not basing public policy on the basis of dated stereotypes.

## Craig v. Boren

**Citation: 429 U.S. 190.**

**Issue: Whether a law prohibiting the sale and consumption of beer to males between the ages of 18 and 21, but not to females in the same age category, violated the Equal Protection Clause.**

**Year of Decision: 1976.**

**Outcome: The gender-based discrimination violated the equal protection guarantee.**

**Author of Opinion: Justice William Brennan.**

**Vote: 6-2.**

Even as the social and legal standing of women changed over the decades, the Court was slow to change its thinking with respect to the Equal Protection Clause. In *Goesart v. Cleary* (1949), it thus upheld a state law barring women from working as bartenders unless related to the owner. As the Court put it, "[t]he fact that women may now have achieved the virtues that men have long practiced, does not preclude the States from drawing a sharp line between the sexes."

Over the course of the twentieth century, significant changes took place with respect to the status of women. The Twenty-first Amendment prohibited gender-based abridgment of the right to vote. The Civil Rights Act of 1964 barred discrimination in employment not merely on the basis of race but also on the basis of gender. This progress represented the work of the political process, rather than any changed understanding of the Constitution. Evolution in this regard began to manifest itself, however, in the early 1970s.

An early indication of impending change was the Court's decision in *Reed v. Reed* (1971). In this case, the Court invalidated an Idaho law that favored the use of men to administer estates in probate. Although it announced no new standard of review in *Reed v. Reed,* the Court drove a result that indicated a change in orientation. Two years later, in *Frontiero v. Richardson* (1973), the Court reviewed a federal benefits law presuming that a military serviceman's spouse was dependent upon him. The regulation required a servicewoman, however, to prove the dependency of her spouse. Although no majority opinion was announced, Justice William Brennan and three other justices maintained that gender classifications were no different than racial classifications under the Equal Protection Clause. Accordingly, they concluded that such classifications are suspect and should be subject to searching judicial review. In a concurring opinion, Justice Lewis Powell agreed with the outcome but refused to adopt strict scrutiny as the appropriate model of review. He also noted that an equal rights amendment to the Constitution was pending possible ratification. Justice Powell thus favored withholding a determination with respect to a standard of review so as not to preempt the political process.

Although the equal rights amendment eventually failed the ratification process, the Court announced a standard of review that would subject gender classifications to heightened scrutiny. The key decision in this regard was *Craig v. Boren* (1976), when the Court indicated that it no longer would defer to legislative judgment on matters of gender. The issue in this case was an Oklahoma law that banned the sale of 3.2 percent beer to and by males under the age of 21. Sale to females between the ages of 18 and 21 was not similarly prohibited. In support of this gender-based classification, the state argued that males in the relevant age group presented a higher risk of driving while intoxicated and to highway safety. Actual data evidenced that men between the ages of 18 and 21 accounted for 2 percent of the state's driving while intoxicated arrests. Females in the age group made up .18 percent of the state's arrests.

If the law had been evaluated on the basis of traditional standards of review, it would have survived. Barring a classification such as race that merits searching judicial review, the Court typically asks only whether the state has a rational basis for its action and its regulatory means are reasonably related to the regulatory objective. The Court announced, however, that classifications on the basis of gender are subject to a higher level of scrutiny under the Equal Protection Clause. It thus implemented a standard of review requiring the state to demonstrate that a gender classification serves an important governmental objective and is substantially related to achieving this goal.

Judged by this standard, the Oklahoma law was found wanting. The Court accepted that the state's interest in safe highways was important. It determined that this interest was not substantially advanced, however, by gender-specific regulation. The major deficiency of the male-only prohibition was its failure to account for the state's regulatory interest. In this regard, the Court noted that the relationship between the gender-based restriction and traffic safety was minimal. Undermining the enactment's efficacy too was the fact that the measure did not prohibit consumption of beer purchased by a third party. The state also failed to demonstrate that the sale of 3.2 percent beer presented a greater risk to highway safety than other forms of liquor. Statistical evidence was seen as weak in documenting risk differentials on the basis of age and gender. Despite acknowledging the legitimacy and importance of the state's interest, the Court determined that the state's use of a gender classification conflicted with the Equal Protection Clause.

Justice William Rehnquist opposed the equal protection guarantee's extension to gender. In a dissenting opinion, he argued for an interpretation consistent with original understanding that confines the Equal Protection Clause to matters of racial discrimination. Justice Rehnquist also was mystified why the Court had decided to use a heightened standard of review when men were the target of gender-based regulation. As he saw it, the status of men was unlike that associated with the condition of historically disadvantaged groups. For Justice Rehnquist, they were the last group needing protection from the political process.

The Court's ruling represented a significant expansion of the equal protection guarantee's boundaries. Despite a century of resistance to this extension, the result is consistent with the history of any principle that operates to equalize some condition or status. Various constitutional authorities have noted that, when an equality principle is introduced on behalf of one group, it invariably is pushed to account for the interests of other groups. Charles Fairman, who wrote extensively on the Fourteenth Amendment, observed that "equal protection as it spreads out tends to lift all to the level of the most favored." Consistent with this phenomenon, the determination that racial classifications warranted heightened judicial review represented a starting point rather than an ending point for the evolution of equal protection doctrine. Its application to gender reflects an acquired sense of commonality in racial and gender experiences based upon exclusion from the political process, historical disadvantage based upon group status, and immutable characteristics.

Because women have full access to the political process, some critics maintain that gender should not be an object of special judicial attention. The Court largely has rejected this argument. Although its standards for reviewing gender classifications are not as intense as those used for assessing racial classifications, the Court nonetheless continues to be alert to classifications that reflect outdated stereotypes with respect to the role of women.

### Mr. Justice BRENNAN delivered the opinion of the Court.

. . . Analysis may appropriately begin with the reminder that *Reed* [an earlier Supreme Court case] emphasized that statutory classifications that distinguish between males and females are "subject to scrutiny under the Equal Protection Clause." To withstand constitutional challenge, previous cases establish that classifications by gender must serve important governmental objectives and must be substantially related to achievement of those objectives. Thus, in Reed, the objectives of "reducing the workload on probate courts," and "avoiding intrafamily controversy," were deemed of insufficient importance to sustain use of an overt gender criterion in the appointment of administrators of intestate decedents" estates. . . .

*Reed* has also provided the underpinning for decisions that have invalidated statutes employing gender as an inaccurate proxy for other, more germane bases of classification. Hence, "archaic and overbroad" generalizations, concerning the financial position of servicewomen, and working women, could not justify use of a gender line in determining eligibility for certain governmental entitlements. Similarly, increasingly outdated misconceptions concerning the role of females in the home rather than in the "marketplace and world of ideas" were rejected as loose-fitting characterizations incapable of supporting state statutory schemes that were premised upon their accuracy. In light of the weak congruence between gender and the characteristic or trait that gender purported to represent, it was necessary that the legislatures choose either to realign their substantive laws in a gender-neutral fashion, or to adopt procedures for identifying those instances where the sex-centered generalization actually comported with fact.

 . . . We turn then to the question whether, under *Reed*, the difference between males and females with respect to the purchase of 3.2% beer warrants the differential in age drawn by the Oklahoma statute. We conclude that it does not. . . .

We accept for purposes of discussion the District Court's identification of the objective underlying [Oklahoma's law] as the enhancement of traffic safety. Clearly, the protection of public health and safety represents an important function of state and local governments. However, appellees' statistics in our view cannot support the conclusion that the gender-based distinction closely serves to achieve that objective and therefore the distinction cannot under Reed withstand equal protection challenge.

The appellees introduced a variety of statistical surveys. First, an analysis of arrest statistics for 1973 demonstrated that 18-20-year-old male arrests for "driving under the influence" and "drunkenness" substantially exceeded female arrests for that same age period. Similarly, youths aged 17-21 were found to be over-represented among those killed or injured in traffic accidents, with males again numerically exceeding females in this regard. Third, a random roadside survey in Oklahoma City revealed that young males were more inclined to drive and drink beer than were their female counterparts. Fourth, Federal Bureau of Investigation nationwide statistics exhibited a notable increase in arrests for "driving under the influence." Finally, statistical evidence gathered in other jurisdictions, particularly Minnesota and Michigan, was offered to corroborate Oklahoma's experience by indicating the pervasiveness of youthful participation in motor vehicle accidents following the imbibing of alcohol. Conceding that "the case is not free from doubt," the District Court nonetheless concluded that this statistical showing substantiated "a rational basis for the legislative judgment underlying the challenged classification."

Even were this statistical evidence accepted as accurate, it nevertheless offers only a weak answer to the equal protection question presented here. The most focused and relevant of the statistical surveys, arrests of 18-20-year-olds for alcohol-related driving offenses, exemplifies the ultimate unpersuasiveness of this evidentiary record. Viewed in terms of the correlation between sex and the actual activity that Oklahoma seeks to regulate driving while under the influence of alcohol the statistics broadly establish that .18% of females and 2% of males in that age group were arrested for that offense. While such a disparity is not trivial in a statistical sense, it hardly can form the basis for employment of a gender line as a classifying device. Certainly if maleness is to serve as a proxy for drinking and driving, a correlation of 2% must be considered an unduly tenuous "fit." Indeed, prior cases have consistently rejected the use of sex as a decisionmaking factor even though the statutes in question certainly rested on far more predictive empirical relationships than this. . . .

There is no reason to belabor this line of analysis. It is unrealistic to expect either members of the judiciary or state officials to be well versed in the rigors of experimental or statistical technique. But this merely illustrates that proving broad sociological propositions by statistics is a dubious business, and one that inevitably is in tension with the normative philosophy that underlies the Equal Protection Clause. Suffice to say that the showing offered by the appellees does not satisfy us that sex represents a legitimate, accurate proxy for the regulation of drinking and driving. In fact, when it is further recognized that Oklahoma's statute prohibits only the selling of 3.2% beer to young males and not their drinking the beverage once acquired (even after purchase by their 18-20-year-old female companions), the relationship between gender and traffic safety becomes far too tenuous to satisfy Reed's requirement that the gender-based difference be substantially related to achievement of the statutory objective.

We hold, therefore, that under Reed, Oklahoma's 3.2% beer statute invidiously discriminates against males 18-20 years of age.

## Mr. Justice REHNQUIST, dissenting.

The Court's disposition of this case is objectionable on two grounds. First is its conclusion that men challenging a gender-based statute which treats them less favorably than women may invoke a more stringent standard of judicial review than pertains to most other types of classifications. Second is the Court's enunciation of this standard, without citation to any source, as being that "classifications by gender must serve important governmental objectives and must be substantially related to achievement of those objectives." The only redeeming feature of the Court's opinion, to my mind, is that it apparently signals a retreat by those who joined the plurality opinion in *Frontiero v. Richardson*, from their view that sex is a "suspect" classification for purposes of equal protection analysis. I think the Oklahoma statute challenged here need pass only the "rational basis" equal protection analysis expounded in cases such as [cites], and I believe that it is constitutional under that analysis.

In *Frontiero v. Richardson,* supra, the opinion for the plurality sets forth the reasons of four Justices for concluding that sex should be regarded as a suspect classification for purposes of equal protection analysis. These reasons center on our Nation's "long and unfortunate history of sex discrimination," which has been reflected in a whole range of restrictions on the legal rights of women, not the least of which have concerned the ownership of property and participation in the electoral process. Noting that the pervasive and persistent nature of the discrimination experienced by women is in part the result of their ready identifiability, the plurality rested its invocation of strict scrutiny largely upon the fact that "statutory distinctions between the sexes often have the effect of invidiously relegating the entire class of females to inferior legal status without regard to the actual capabilities of its individual members."

Subsequent to *Frontiero*, the Court has declined to hold that sex is a suspect class, and no such holding is imported by the Court's resolution of this case. However, the Court's application here of an elevated or "intermediate" level scrutiny, like that invoked in cases dealing with discrimination against females, raises the question of why the statute here should be treated any differently from countless legislative classifications unrelated to sex which have been upheld under a minimum rationality standard.

Most obviously unavailable to support any kind of special scrutiny in this case, is a history or pattern of past discrimination, such as was relied on by the plurality in Frontiero to support its invocation of strict scrutiny. There is no suggestion in the Court's opinion that males in this age group are in any way peculiarly disadvantaged, subject to systematic discriminatory treatment, or otherwise in need of special solicitude from the courts.

The Court does not discuss the nature of the right involved, and there is no reason to believe that it sees the purchase of 3.2% beer as implicating any important interest, let alone one that is "fundamental" in the constitutional sense of invoking strict scrutiny. Indeed, the Court's accurate observation that the statute affects the selling but not the drinking of 3.2% beer, further emphasizes the limited effect that it has on even those persons in the age group involved. There is, in sum, nothing about the statutory classification involved here to suggest that it affects an interest, or works against a group, which can claim under the Equal Protection Clause that it is entitled to special judicial protection.

It is true that a number of our opinions contain broadly phrased dicta implying that the same test should be applied to all classifications based on sex, whether affecting females or males. However, before today, no decision of this Court has applied an elevated level of scrutiny to invalidate a statutory discrimination harmful to males, except where the statute impaired an important personal interest protected by the Constitution. There being no such interest here, and there being no plausible argument that this is a discrimination against females, the Court's reliance on our previous sex-discrimination cases is ill-founded. It treats gender classification as a talisman which without regard to the rights involved or the persons affected calls into effect a heavier burden of judicial review.

The Court's conclusion that a law which treats males less favorably than females "must serve important governmental objectives and must be substantially related to achievement of those objectives" apparently comes out of thin air. The Equal Protection Clause contains no such language, and none of our previous cases adopt that standard. I would think we have had enough difficulty with the two standards of review which our cases have recognized the norm of "rational basis," and the "compelling state interest" required where a "suspect classification" is involved so as to counsel weightily against the insertion of still another "standard" between those two. How is this Court to divine what objectives are important? How is it to determine whether a particular law is "substantially" related to the achievement of such objective, rather than related in some other way to its achievement? Both of the phrases used are so diaphanous and elastic as to invite subjective judicial preferences or prejudices relating to particular types of legislation, masquerading as judgments whether such legislation is directed at "important" objectives or, whether the relationship to those objectives is "substantial" enough.

I would have thought that if this Court were to leave anything to decision by the popularly elected branches of the Government, where no constitutional claim other than that of equal protection is invoked, it would be the decision as to what governmental objectives to be achieved by law are "important," and which are not. As for the second part of the Court's new test, the Judicial Branch is probably in no worse position than the Legislative or Executive Branches to determine if there is any rational relationship between a classification and the purpose which it might be thought to serve. But the introduction of the adverb "substantially" requires courts to make subjective judgments as to operational effects, for which neither their expertise nor their access to data fits them. And even if we manage to avoid both confusion and the mirroring of our own preferences in the development of this new doctrine, the thousands of judges in other courts who must interpret the Equal Protection Clause may not be so fortunate.

## Bibliography

Colker, Ruth. "Anti-Subordination Above All: Sex, Race and Equal Protection." *New York University Law Review* 61 (1986): 1003.

Law, Sylvia. "Rethinking Sex and the Constitution." *University of Pennsylvania Law Review* 132 (1984): 955.

MacKinnon, Catharine A. *Toward a Feminist Theory of the State*. Cambridge, MA: Harvard University Press, 1991.

## *United States v. Virginia*

**Citation: 518 U.S. 515.**

**Issue: Whether a state military college's male-only admission policy violated the Equal Protection Clause.**

**Year of Decision: 1996.**

**Outcome: The gender exclusive policy violated the equal protection guarantee.**

**Author of Opinion: Justice Ruth Bader Ginsburg.**

**Vote: 7-1.**

Race is a factor that the law cannot take into account unless the state has a compelling reason and cannot achieve its purpose in a racially neutral manner. Regardless of whether racial classifications are intended to burden or benefit historically disadvantaged groups, as the Court put it in *Adarand Constructors, Inc. v. Pena* (1995), they are subject to the same "searching review." Although gender classifications are subject to a heightened standard of review, scrutiny of them is not as intense as it is for race.

The operative standard, as described by the Court in *Craig v. Boren* (1976), is whether they "serve important [rather than compelling] government interests and are substantially [rather than necessarily] related to achievement of those objectives." Also, unlike distinctions on the basis of race, some gender classifications are considered altogether unworrisome. The state thus may treat men and women separately in instances where there are legitimate differences between them. When gender classifications are assessed, therefore, a preliminary question is whether men and women are "similarly situated." The underlying premise is that there are characteristics or interests unique to men and women that require or deserve a gender-based accounting.

In *Rostker v. Goldberg* (1981), for instance, the Court determined that Congress could authorize registration of men only for the military draft. The reason for this result was that, because women were restricted from combat, they were not similarly situated with men. In determining whether men and women are similarly situated, the central question is whether a gender-based distinction reflects an outdated stereotype or speaks to a real concern. An easy case for gender differentiation would arise in the context of separate public restrooms. Segregation on the basis of race, at least since the mid-twentieth century, is constitutionally unthinkable. Given well-established and uncontested conventions with respect to propriety, it is hard to imagine separate restrooms for men and women becoming a constitutional issue. Cases and controversies are more likely to arise when perspectives on gender are in competition rather than the basis for consensus.

This reality, and an associated standard of review that probes for outdated stereotypes, was evidenced in *Mississippi University for Women v. Hogan* (1982). In this case, the Court determined that a state university's single-sex admission policy violated the Equal Protection Clause. The state argued that the policy aimed to compensate women for discrimination. Because women were not underrepresented in the field of nursing, the Court found that exclusion of males from the school "perpetuated the stereotyped view of nursing as an exclusively women's job."

The question of same-sex education arose in *United States v. Virginia* (1996), when the Court reviewed the male-only admission policy of Virginia Military Institute (VMI). Writing for the majority, Justice Ruth Bader Ginsburg determined that the policy failed the traditional standard of review for gender classifications. The state identified two justifications for the exclusionary policy. These rationales were that single-sex education at VMI (1) facilitated "diversity in educational approaches," and (2) enabled a unique "adversative" model of "character development and leadership training" that would have to be modified if women were admitted. Although acknowledging that diverse models of education may be laudable, the Court was not convinced that the state's interest in this regard was real. It noted, for instance, the absence of any single-sex educational program for women. The Court also disagreed that VMI would have to alter its "adversative" methods if women were admitted. In this regard, it noted that "many men would not want to be educated in such an environment."

The Court thus saw the issue as being "not whether women or men should be forced to attend VMI," but whether the state can deny women who have "the will and capacity, the training and opportunity that VMI uniquely affords." On this matter, the Court determined that the state had failed to prove the admission of women "downgrade[s] VMI's stature, destroy[s] the adversative system, and, with it, even the school." It equated these concerns to "other 'self-fulfilling prophecies' once routinely used to deny rights or opportunities" to enter fields such as law and medicine. Consistent with its sensitivity to gender-based stereotypes, the Court stressed that "[s]tate actors controlling gates to opportunity cannot exclude qualified individuals based on 'fixed notions' concerning the roles and abilities of males and females." It also found that a proposed remedy, which would have created a parallel women's institute, also reflected inappropriate stereotypes.

The single-sex policy failed because it lacked a substantial relationship to an important government interest. Compared with prior decisions on gender, however, the Court's analysis suggested a more rigorous standard of review. Typically, as noted previously, the inquiry is into whether the state has shown that a challenged classification "serves important governmental objectives and that the discriminatory means employed are substantially related to those objectives." In *United States v. Virginia*, the Court described its role further as having to "determine whether the proffered justification is exceedingly persuasive." It further noted that the state's "justification must be genuine, not hypothesized or invented *post hoc* in response to litigation. And it must not rely on overbroad generalizations about the different talents, capabilities, or preferences of males and females."

In a concurring opinion, Chief Justice William Rehnquist agreed that the single-sex policy was at odds with the equal protection guarantee. He advocated, however, a more forthright application of traditional standards of review relating to gender. In this regard, Chief Justice Rehnquist expressed his sense that the "exceedingly persuasive justification" criterion had heightened the standard for reviewing gender classifications.

Justice Antonin Scalia perceived in the Court's terminology and orientation a new standard of review for gender classifications. As Justice Scalia put it in his dissenting opinion, the Court had "drastically revise[d] our established standards for reviewing sex-based classifications." His understanding is shared by other observers who view the "exceedingly persuasive justification" terminology as being more akin to the strict scrutiny hallmark of a "compelling justification." Justice Scalia also maintained that the Court improvidently had removed a matter of education and social policy from the political process where it properly belonged. In his view, the Court merely had substituted its own debatable policy preferences as a basis for "displac[ing] longstanding national traditions as the primary determinant of what the Constitution means." He thus saw the Court "bemoaning . . . 'fixed notions'" and making "smug assurances" regarding women and substituting its own "notions so fixedly that it is willing to write them into the" Constitution. From Justice Scalia's perspective, "[t]his is not the interpretation of a Constitution, but the creation of one."

The decision in *United States v. Virginia* marks a significant evolution from the original understanding of the equal protection doctrine as it relates to gender. Over the course of its first century, the Fourteenth Amendment provided no recourse for arguments that it was a proper basis for addressing gender-based discrimination. Modern case law indicates that review of gender classification is not as intense as the strict scrutiny that applies to race but more rigorous than the assessment of garden-variety social and economic classifications. This "intermediate" standard of review has enabled the Court to strike down laws that it perceives to be the function of dated stereotypes.

At the same time, as the Court explained in *United States v. Virginia,* the standard respects "inherent differences between men and women [that] are enduring." Although "inherent differences" are unacceptable grounds for differentiation in the context of race, "the two sexes are not fungible." Consistent with this premise, the Court's focus upon gender classifications has become increasingly sharpened. Notwithstanding legitimate differences that may be identified, review of gender-based classifications aims to ensure that they are not used "for denigration of the members of either sex or for artificial constraints on an individual's opportunity."

## Justice GINSBURG delivered the opinion of the Court.

Virginia's public institutions of higher learning include an incomparable military college, Virginia Military Institute (VMI). The United States maintains that the Constitution's equal protection guarantee precludes Virginia from reserving exclusively to men the unique educational opportunities VMI affords. We agree. . . .

The heightened review standard our precedent establishes does not make sex a proscribed classification. Supposed "inherent differences" are no longer accepted as a ground for race or national origin classifications. Physical differences between men and women, however, are enduring: "[T]he two sexes are not fungible; a community made up exclusively of one [sex] is different from a community composed of both."

"Inherent differences" between men and women, we have come to appreciate, remain cause for celebration, but not for denigration of the members of either sex or for artificial constraints on an individual's opportunity. Sex classifications may be used to compensate women "for particular economic disabilities [they have] suffered," to "promot[e] equal employment opportunity," [or] to advance full development of the talent and capacities of our Nation's people. But such classifications may not be used, as they once were, to create or perpetuate the legal, social, and economic inferiority of women.

Measuring the record in this case against the review standard just described, we conclude that Virginia has shown no "exceedingly persuasive justification" for excluding all women from the citizen-soldier training afforded by VMI. We therefore affirm the Fourth Circuit's initial judgment, which held that Virginia had violated the Fourteenth Amendment's Equal Protection Clause. Because the remedy proffered by Virginia—the Mary Baldwin VWIL program—does not cure the constitutional violation, i.e., it does not provide equal opportunity, we reverse the Fourth Circuit's final judgment in this case. . . .

Single-sex education affords pedagogical benefits to at least some students, Virginia emphasizes, and that reality is uncontested in this litigation. Similarly, it is not disputed that diversity among public educational institutions can serve the public good. But Virginia has not shown that VMI was established, or has been maintained, with a view to diversifying, by its categorical exclusion of women, educational opportunities within the Commonwealth. In cases of this genre, our precedent instructs that "benign" justifications proffered in defense of categorical exclusions will not be accepted automatically; a tenable justification must describe actual state purposes, not rationalizations for actions in fact differently grounded. . . .

Neither recent nor distant history bears out Virginia's alleged pursuit of diversity through single-sex educational options. In 1839, when the Commonwealth established VMI, a range of educational opportunities for men and women was scarcely contemplated. Higher education at the time was considered dangerous for women; reflecting widely held views about women's proper place, the Nation's first universities and colleges—for example, Harvard in Massachusetts, William and Mary in Virginia—admitted only men. . . .

In sum, we find no persuasive evidence in this record that VMI's male-only admission policy "is in furtherance of a state policy of 'diversity.' " No such policy, the Fourth Circuit observed, can be discerned from the movement of all other public colleges and universities in Virginia away from single-sex education. See *ibid.* That court also questioned "how one institution with autonomy, but with no authority over any other state institution, can give effect to a state policy of diversity among institutions." A purpose genuinely to advance an array of educational options, as the Court of Appeals recognized, is not served by VMI's historic and constant plan—a plan to "affor[d] a unique educational benefit only to males." However "liberally" this plan serves the Commonwealth's sons, it makes no provision whatever for her daughters. That is not *equal* protection.

## Justice SCALIA, dissenting.

Today the Court shuts down an institution that has served the people of the Commonwealth of Virginia with pride and distinction for over a century and a half.

To achieve that desired result, it rejects (contrary to our established practice) the factual findings of two courts below, sweeps aside the precedents of this Court, and ignores the history of our people. As to facts: It explicitly rejects the finding that there exist "gender-based developmental differences" supporting Virginia's restriction of the "adversative" method to only a men's institution, and the finding that the all-male composition of the Virginia Military Institute (VMI) is essential to that institution's character. As to precedent: It drastically revises our established standards for reviewing sex-based classifications. And as to history: It counts for nothing the long tradition, enduring down to the present, of men's military colleges supported by both States and the Federal Government.

Much of the Court's opinion is devoted to deprecating the closed-mindedness of our forebears with regard to women's education, and even with regard to the treatment of women in areas that have nothing to do with education. Closed-minded they were—as every age is, including our own, with regard to matters it cannot guess, because it simply does not consider them debatable. The virtue of a democratic system with a First Amendment is that it readily enables the people, over time, to be persuaded that what they took for granted is not so, and to change their laws accordingly. That system is destroyed if the smug assurances of each age are removed from the democratic process and written into the Constitution. So to counterbalance the Court's criticism of our ancestors, let me say a word in their praise: They left us free to change. The same cannot be said of this most illiberal Court, which has embarked on a course of inscribing one after another of the current preferences of the society (and in some cases only the counter-majoritarian preferences of the society's law-trained elite) into our Basic Law. Today it enshrines the notion that no substantial educational value is to be served by an all-men's military academy—so that the decision by the people of Virginia to maintain such an institution denies equal protection to women who cannot attend that institution but can attend others. Since it is entirely clear that the Constitution of the United States—the old one—takes no sides in this educational debate, I dissent.

## Bibliography

Gilligan, Carol. *In a Different Voice: Psychological Theory and Women's Development*. Cambridge, MA: Harvard University Press, 1982.

Gurney, Tod Christopher. "The Aftermath of the Virginia Military Institute Decision: Will Single-gender Education Survive?" *Santa Clara Law Review* 38 (1998): 1183.

Posner, Richard. *Sex and Reason*. Cambridge, MA: Harvard University Press, 1992.

Wright, Robert. *The Moral Animal: Why We Are the Way We Are*. New York: Pantheon Books, 1994.

Chapter 10

# Fundamental Rights

The primary concern of the Equal Protection Clause over the course of its history has been with racial classifications. Grounds for an equal protection claim expanded during the final decades of the twentieth century, as the Supreme Court recognized gender, alienage, and illegitimacy as classifications that merited heightened judicial review. In cases concerning persons in these categories, group status by itself is sufficient to establish an equal protection interest.

Group status, although the dominant basis for equal protection concern, is not an exclusive prerequisite. Since the 1960s, the Court has evolved another dimension of equal protection doctrine that is implicated whenever a fundamental right is denied selectively. If a state allowed Democrats but not Republicans to use a public park for political rallies, for instance, the Republicans would have a claim that their freedom of speech was abridged. They also would have an equal protection claim based not on their group status but on the fact that a fundamental right had been denied in a selective manner.

## EDUCATION

The federal constitution by its specific terms provides no right to an education. When the Court determined that racially segregated public schools were unconstitutional in *Brown v. Board of Education* (1954), however, it described public education as "perhaps the most important function of state and local governments." This observation reflected the Court's "recognition of the importance of education to our democratic society." Two decades later, in *San Antonio Independent School District v. Rodriguez* (1973), the Court reviewed a public school financing plan that resulted in significant funding disparities among school districts. Notwithstanding the close relationship between education and constitutionally protected interests such as voting and expression, the Court rejected the notion that the Constitution implied a right to education.

### *San Antonio Independent School District v. Rodriguez*

**Citation: 411 U.S. 1.**

**Issue: Whether a state funding plan for public education, resulting in financial disparities among school districts violated the Equal Protection Clause.**

**Year of Decision: 1973.**

**Outcome: The funding plan did not violate the Equal Protection Clause, because it neither created a suspect classification nor burdened a fundamental right.**

**Author of Opinion: Justice Lewis Powell.**

**Vote: 5-4.**

Public education over the course of the twentieth century came to be recognized as one of the most significant functions of state and local government. This role contrasted with conditions after the Civil War when the Fourteenth Amendment was framed and ratified. At that time, taxpayer supported education had not taken hold in the South and was unevenly developed in the North. Given these circumstances, as the Supreme Court noted in *Brown v. Board of Education* (1954), it was not surprising that debates over the Fourteenth Amendment made slight reference to public education.

The evolution of public education by 1954 had reached a point that the Court in *Brown* was constrained to assess it "in the light of its full development and its present place in American life throughout the nation."

By then, public education was universally provided, and mandatory attendance through high school was the norm. In *Brown*, the Court described "education [a]s perhaps the most significant function of state and local governments and noted its importance . . . to our democratic society." The Court further characterized it as "the very foundation of good citizenship, a principal instrument in awakening the child to cultural values, in preparing for later professional training, and in helping him to adjust normally to his environment." So central had education become to personal development that the Court was "doubtful that any child may reasonably be expected to succeed in life if he is denied the opportunity of an education." It thus observed that "where the state has undertaken to provide it, it is a right that must be made available to all on equal terms."

The notion of public education as a right that had special significance was restated in *Bolling v. Sharpe* (1954). This decision reached the same result with respect to the federal government that the *Brown* ruling obtained with respect to the states. The *Brown* decision rested on the Equal Protection Clause of the Fourteenth Amendment, which operates against the states. No comparable provision applies to the federal government so, in *Bolling v. Sharpe*, the Court inferred an equal protection guarantee from the Due Process Clause of the Fifth Amendment. In thus striking down segregation of public schools in Washington, D.C., the Court determined that segregation was not reasonably related to any legitimate purpose. It thus imposed "a burden that constitutes an artificial deprivation of liberty in violation of the Due Process Clause."

For nearly two decades after the *Brown* and *Bolling* decisions, the Court persisted in its demand for desegregation at first "with all deliberate speed" and eventually with remedies "that promise realistically to work now." By the early 1970s, however, it had limited the reach of the desegregation mandate. This result was achieved by rulings that conditioned the duty to desegregate upon proof of segregative intent, *Keyes v. School District No. 1* (1973); limited the use of interdistrict remedies even when they were the only practical means for achieving racially mixed schools, *Milliken v. Bradley* (1974); and permitted resegregation of public schools to the extent this condition was not intentionally induced by the state, *Pasadena City Board of Education v. Spangler* (1976).

Taken together, these decisions indicated that desegregation would be limited to circumstances where purposeful segregation was provable and would reach no farther or extend no longer than the scope of the violation itself. Desegregation's primary concern was with the impact of officially separated schools upon educational opportunity. It did not address broader issues of equality in education. Inequality of funding, for instance, was a widespread phenomenon during the separate but equal era. Public spending on education in segregated states typically reflected extreme disparities based on race. In declaring segregated public schools unconstitutional, the *Brown* Court relied upon desegregation as the means to address inequality. Unlike its rulings in the two decades preceding Brown, the Court made no demand for equalization of spending.

Notwithstanding the desegregation process, issues with respect to public school funding disparities eventually resurfaced. In *San Antonio Independent School District v. Rodriguez* (1974), the Court reviewed a Texas plan for financing public education on the basis of state funding allocations and local property taxes. Given variations among communities with respect to their wealth, funding disparities statewide and even in a particular municipality were significant. Expenditures in San Antonio's wealthiest district were $594 per student. In the poorest district, spending was $356 per student. These funding disparities became the basis for arguments that the Texas plan violated the Equal Protection Clause of the Fourteenth Amendment.

Justice Lewis Powell, writing the majority opinion for the Court, commenced his analysis by whether the funding system discriminated against poor persons and, if so, whether indigence was a suspect classification. On this matter, the Court determined that wealth discrimination was a constitutional concern only if a person was unable to pay for a particular benefit and thus was precluded altogether from accessing it. For an example of when wealth discrimination counts, the Court cited *Griffin v. Illinois* (1956). In this case, the Court invalidated a state law that denied indigent defendants access to trial transcripts necessary for appeal. Absent a showing that the Texas system presented a unique disadvantage to the poor, and because education was not deprived altogether, the Court found no basis for finding that the economic disadvantage was suspect in the same manner as race.

Reminded of the significance that the *Brown* Court placed on education, the Court acknowledged its value both for the individual and for society. It noted, however, that "the importance of a service performed by the State does not determine whether it must be regarded as fundamental for purposes of examination under the Equal Protection Clause." This determination reflected an unease on the part of the Court that manifests itself periodically when it is asked to identify a right as fundamental. It thus echoed the sentiments expressed of Justice John Harlan, Jr., in *Shapiro v. Thompson* (1969). Dissenting from the Court's recognition of a right to travel, which became the basis for striking down a state's waiting period for collecting welfare payment, Justice Harlan observed that "[v]irtually every state statute affects important rights." Consistent with this perspective, Justice Powell warned that the Court would become a "super-legislature" if it were to render decisions based upon its own sense of importance.

With these concerns in mind, the Court determined that it had no authority or basis for declaring education a fundamental right. As the Court put it, "the key to discovering whether education is 'fundamental'" did not lie in comparing its relative importance to other interests. Rather, "the answer lies in assessing whether there is a right to education explicitly or implicitly guaranteed by the Constitution. Education is not among the rights explicitly protected by the Constitution."

The argument that education is a fundamental right draws upon the close relationship that the *Brown* Court perceived between it and "other rights and liberties accorded protection under the Constitution." The majority acknowledged this connection between education and freedom of expression and voting. Although these interests are constitutionally protected, the Court observed that it had no authority to guarantee "the most *effective* speech or the most *informed* choice" (emphasis in original). Insofar as the quality of speech or electoral decision making was to be improved, the Court maintained that the responsibility belonged to the legislature rather than the judiciary.

The Court thus rejected the proposition that education was a fundamental right implied by the Constitution. Having reached this conclusion, it reserved the possibility "that some identifiable quantum of education is a constitutionally protected prerequisite to the meaningful exercise of either right." Such a case, at least from the majority's perspective, was not presented by the Texas funding plan. Without a suspect classification (such as race) or a fundamental right, the Court would not engage in searching review. Although the plan might be imperfect, the Court found it rationally related to a legitimate state purpose of facilitating local control of education.

Less than a decade after its decision in *San Antonio Independent School District v. Rodriguez* (1974), the Court reviewed another Texas funding plan that denied state funds to educate children of illegal aliens. At issue, in *Plyler v. Doe* (1982), was whether the state had denied a "quantum of education" sufficient to trigger constitutional concern. The Court reaffirmed the premise that education is not a right secured by the Constitution. It also observed that education was not a garden-variety benefit. Emphasizing education's importance to the individual and "our basic institutions," the Court reasoned that it could not "ignore the significant social costs borne by our Nation when select groups are denied the means to absorb the values and skills upon which our social order rests." Unlike a case of disparate funding, the total and categorical denial of education, as the Court saw it, was an irrational and unconstitutional deprivation. Having previously reserved the possibility that some identifiable quantum of education might be constitutionally significant, the Court determined that a state could not deny basic public education on a categorical basis.

Since the Court's ruling in *San Antonio Independent School District v. Rodriguez*, numerous challenges of public school funding disparities have been made under state constitutions. Included among these was a state court case brought under the Texas Constitution, which establishes a state duty to establish, support, and maintain "an efficient system of public free schools." The state also is required to facilitate a "general diffusion of knowledge" that is "essential to the preservation of the liberties and rights of the people." The Texas Supreme Court, in *Edgewood Independent School District v. Kirby* (1989), found that spending on a student's schooling "has a real and substantial impact on the educational opportunity offered that student." Measuring the plan against this standard, the Texas Supreme Court determined that the funding system was efficient neither on financial grounds nor in promoting the general diffusion of knowledge.

The Texas high court ruling paralleled outcomes in several other states that had reached the same outcome in reviewing similar plans. As the ultimate authority on the law of its state, the Texas Supreme Court was not subject to review by the United States Supreme Court. Based upon the Texas Supreme Court ruling, students in Texas have educational rights that are broader than what the Court has recognized under the federal Constitution. This outcome reflects the nature of a system of dual sovereigns and the capacity for differentiation in the availability and scope of rights within the union.

## Mr. Justice POWELL delivered the opinion of the Court.

. . . However described, it is clear that appellees' suit asks this Court to extend its most exacting scrutiny to review a system that allegedly discriminates against a large, diverse, and amorphous class, unified only by the common factor of residence in districts that happen to have less taxable wealth than other districts. The system of alleged discrimination and the class it defines have none of the traditional indicia of suspectness: the class is not saddled with such disabilities, or subjected to such a history of purposeful unequal treatment, or relegated to such a position of political powerlessness as to command extraordinary protection from the majoritarian political process.

We thus conclude that the Texas system does not operate to the peculiar disadvantage of any suspect class. But in recognition of the fact that this Court has never heretofore held that wealth discrimination alone provides an adequate basis for invoking strict scrutiny, appellees have not relied solely on this contention. They also assert that the State's system impermissibly interferes with the exercise of a 'fundamental' right and that accordingly the prior decisions of this Court require the application of the strict standard of judicial review. It is this question—whether education is a fundamental right, in the sense that it is among the rights and liberties protected by the Constitution—which has so consumed the attention of courts and commentators in recent years. . . .

Nothing this Court holds today in any way detracts from our historic dedication to public education. We are in complete agreement with the conclusion of the three-judge panel below that 'the grave significance of education both to the individual and to our society' cannot be doubted. But the importance of a service performed by the State does not determine whether it must be regarded as fundamental for purposes of examination under the Equal Protection Clause. Mr. Justice Harlan, dissenting from the Court's application of strict scrutiny to a law impinging upon the right of interstate travel, admonished that "(v)irtually every state statute affects important rights." In his view, if the degree of judicial scrutiny of state legislation fluctuated, depending on a majority's view of the importance of the interest affected, we would have gone "far toward making this Court a 'super-legislature.'" We would, indeed, then be assuming a legislative role and one for which the Court lacks both authority and competence. . . .

The lesson of these cases in addressing the question now before the Court is plain. It is not the province of this Court to create substantive constitutional rights in the name of guaranteeing equal protection of the laws. Thus, the key to discovering whether education is 'fundamental' is not to be found in comparisons of the relative societal significance of education as opposed to subsistence or housing. Nor is it to be found by weighing whether education is as important as the right to travel. Rather, the answer lies in assessing whether there is a right to education explicitly or implicitly guaranteed by the Constitution.

Education, of course, is not among the rights afforded explicit protection under our Federal Constitution. Nor do we find any basis for saying it is implicitly so protected. As we have said, the undisputed importance of education will not alone cause this Court to depart from the usual standard for reviewing a State's social and economic legislation. It is appellees' contention, however, that education is distinguishable from other services and benefits provided by the State because it bears a peculiarly close relationship to other rights and liberties accorded protection under the Constitution. Specifically, they insist that education is itself a fundamental personal right because it is essential to the effective exercise of First Amendment freedoms and to intelligent utilization of the right to vote. In asserting a nexus between speech and education, appellees urge that the right to speak is meaningless unless the speaker is capable of articulating his thoughts intelligently and persuasively. The 'marketplace of ideas' is an empty forum for those lacking basic communicative tools. Likewise, they argue that the corollary right to receive information becomes little more than a hollow privilege when the recipient has not been taught to read, assimilate, and utilize available knowledge. . . .

### Mr. Justice BRENNAN, dissenting.

Although I agree with my Brother WHITE that the Texas statutory scheme is devoid of any rational basis, and for that reason is violative of the Equal Protection Clause, I also record my disagreement with the Court's rather distressing assertion that a right may be deemed 'fundamental' for the purposes of equal protection analysis only if it is 'explicitly or implicitly guaranteed by the Constitution.' As my Brother MARSHALL convincingly demonstrates, our prior cases stand for the proposition that 'fundamentality' is, in large measure, a function of the right's importance in terms of the effectuation of those rights which are in fact constitutionally guaranteed. Thus, '(a)s the nexus between the specific constitutional guarantee and the nonconstitutional interest draws closer, the nonconstitutional interest becomes more fundamental and the degree of judicial scrutiny applied when the interest is infringed on a discriminatory basis must be adjusted accordingly.'

Here, there can be no doubt that education is inextricably linked to the right to participate in the electoral process and to the rights of free speech and association guaranteed by the First Amendment. This being so, any classification affecting education must be subjected to strict judicial scrutiny, and since even the State concedes that the statutory scheme now before us cannot pass constitutional muster under this stricter standard of review, I can only conclude that the Texas school-financing scheme is constitutionally invalid.

### Mr. Justice MARSHALL, with whom Mr. Justice DOUGLAS concurs, dissenting.

. . . In conclusion, it is essential to recognize that an end to the wide variations in taxable district property wealth inherent in the Texas financing scheme would entail none of the untoward consequences suggested by the Court or by the appellants.

First, affirmance of the District Court's decisions would hardly sound the death knell for local control of education. It would mean neither centralized decision-making nor federal court intervention in the operation of public schools. Clearly, this suit has nothing to do with local decisionmaking with respect to educational policy or even educational spending. It involves only a narrow aspect of local control—namely, local control over the raising of educational funds. In fact, in striking down interdistrict disparities in taxable local wealth, the District Court took the course which is most likely to make true local control over educational decision-making a reality for all Texas school districts.

Nor does the District Court's decision even necessarily eliminate local control of educational funding. The District Court struck down nothing more than the continued interdistrict wealth discrimination inherent in the present property tax. Both centralized and decentralized plans for educational funding not involving such interdistrict discrimination have been put forward. The choice among these or other alternatives would remain with the State, not with the federal courts. In this regard, it should be evident that the degree of federal intervention in matters of local concern would be substantially less in this context than in previous decisions in which we have been asked effectively to impose a particular scheme upon the States under the guise of the Equal Protection Clause.

Still, we are told that this case requires us 'to condemn the State's judgment in conferring on political subdivisions the power to tax local property to supply revenues for local interests.' Yet no one in the course of this entire litigation has ever questioned the constitutionality of the local property tax as a device for raising educational funds. The District Court's decision, at most, restricts the power of the State to make educational funding dependent exclusively upon local property taxation so long as there exists interdistrict disparities in taxable property wealth. But it hardly eliminates the local property tax as a source of educational funding or as a means of providing local fiscal control.

The Court seeks solace for its action today in the possibility of legislative reform. The Court's suggestions of legislative redress and experimentation will doubtless be of great comfort to the schoolchildren of Texas' disadvantaged districts, but considering the vested interests of wealthy school districts in the preservation of the status quo, they are worth little more. The possibility of legislative action is, in all events, no answer to this Court's duty under the Constitution to eliminate unjustified state discrimination. In this case we have been presented with an instance of such discrimination, in a particularly invidious form, against an individual interest of large constitutional and practical importance. To support the demonstrated discrimination in the provision of educational opportunity the State has offered a justification which, on analysis, takes on at best an ephemeral character. Thus, I believe that the wide disparities in taxable district property wealth inherent in the local property tax element of the Texas financing scheme render that scheme violative of the Equal Protection Clause. . . .

## Bibliography

Brennan, William, Jr. "State Constitutions and the Protection of Individual Rights." *Harvard Law Review* 90 (1977): 489.

Coons, John, William Clune, and Stephen Sugarman. *Private Wealth and Public Education.* Cambridge, MA: Belknap Press of Harvard University Press, 1970.

Kurland, Philip. "Equal Educational Opportunity: The Limits of Constitutional Jurisprudence." *University of Chicago Law Review* 35 (1968): 583.

Sutton, Jeffrey S. "*San Antonio Independent School District v. Rodriguez* and Its Aftermath." *Virginia Law Review* 94 (2008): 1963.

# VOTING

The right to vote is not enumerated by the Constitution. Given its centrality to a system of representative governance, however, the Court has had no difficulty inferring its existence. In *Reynolds v. Sims* (1964), the Court established the principle that the apportionment of state legislatures must reflect the principle of "one person–one vote." The Court thus secured the right to vote against processes that would dilute its weight for some. The relationship between equal protection and voting rights resurfaced as an issue in *Bush v. Gore* (2000), when the Court extended the antidilution principle to vote recounts.

## *Bush v. Gore*

> **Citation: 531 U.S. 98.**
>
> **Issue: Did a selective recount of ballots cast in Florida in a presidential election violate the Equal Protection Clause.**
>
> **Year of Decision: 2000.**
>
> **Outcome: The selective recount of ballots diluted the right to vote and thus violated the Equal Protection Clause.**
>
> **Author of Opinion: Per Curiam.**
>
> **Vote: 5-4.**

The right to vote is not enumerated specifically by the Constitution. It is a guarantee that has been inferred, however, from the political system that the Constitution has established.

As the Court put it in *Reynolds v. Sims* (1964), "[t]he right to vote freely for the candidate of one's choice is of the essence of a democratic society, and any restrictions on that right strike at the heart of representative governance." Supreme Court decisions concerning suffrage generally are grounded in the Equal Protection Clause and mostly have concerned efforts to deny the right to vote on the basis of race or dilute it through processes of apportionment. In either circumstance, the issue typically has related to a policy or strategy consciously designed to advantage one group or interest at the expense of another.

The process of allocating the franchise, however, is not the only means by which the right to vote can be debased or diluted. Voting integrity also can be compromised by methods of counting or recounting. In *Bush v. Gore* (2000), the Supreme Court confronted this issue in the context of a closely contested presidential election. Based upon the initial machine count of approximately six million ballots in Florida, George W. Bush had a 1,700-vote edge over his rival Al Gore. This narrow margin automatically triggered a machine recount which, when completed, reduced Bush's margin to several hundred votes. Gore, who actually won the national popular vote, then demanded manual recounts in four counties. When the Florida Secretary of State refused to extend the deadline for canvassing boards to submit their returns, Gore succeeded in having the Florida Supreme Court overturn her decision. The Court later ordered a statewide manual recount of ballots for purposes of identifying votes that the machines had not been able to detect. These "undervotes" typically were the result of punch cards that had not been completely perforated and thus bore only an indent or a hanging "chad." Pursuant to its understanding that the Florida legislature intended the state's electors to be determined by December 12, so that it would be in accord with federal law requiring any electoral controversy to be resolved by then, the United States Supreme Court stayed the state supreme court's judgment on December 9 and reversed it on December 11. The Court's decision effectively resolved the outcome of the election.

The Court's ruling was supported by a *per curiam* opinion representing the views of Chief Justice William Rehnquist and Justices Sandra Day O'Connor, Antonin Scalia, Anthony Kennedy, and Clarence Thomas. It led with the observation that no citizen has the right to vote for President, unless the state chooses an election as the means for implementing its constitutional power to appoint members of the Electoral College. To the extent that a state gives the people this right to vote, however, it is fundamental. A critical incident of its fundamental nature, the Court observed, "lies in the equal weight accorded to each vote and the equal dignity owed to each voter."

The Court noted that equal protection applies to both the allocation of the franchise and its exercise, and the state may not "value one person's vote over that of another." Pursuant to this premise, the Court had no objection "as an abstract proposition and starting principle" with the Florida Supreme Court's order to discern voter intent from the undercounted ballots. Its concern, however, was with "an absence of specific standards to ensure its equal application." From the Court's perspective, it was problematic that "standards for accepting or rejecting contested ballots might vary from county to county [and even] within a single county from one recount team to another." Citing instances in which standards for defining a legal vote varied and even changed in midstream, the Court concluded that "[t]his is not a process with sufficient guarantees of equal treatment."

Several other factors contributed to the Court's conclusion that the manual recount process was standardless and constitutionally flawed. Concerns included the State Court's exclusion of "overvotes" from the recount process. Overvotes consist of ballots that contained more than one punched hole. Also troublesome to the Court was its readiness to accept partial recounts when the certification deadline was reached and lack of direction with respect to whom should count ballots. Against this backdrop of perceived procedural shortcomings, the Court concluded that "[t]he recount process . . . is inconsistent with the minimum procedures necessary to protect the fundamental right of each voter in the special instance of a statewide recount under the authority of a single state judicial officer."

Having put an end to the manual recount process on constitutional grounds, the Court then limited the scope of its decision. It stressed that the issue was not one of whether local entities can implement different election systems. Rather the point was that, when ordering a statewide remedy, a court must provide "at least some assurance that the rudimentary requirements of equal treatment and fundamental fairness are satisfied." Chief Justice William Rehnquist, in a concurring opinion joined by Justices Antonin Scalia and Clarence Thomas, identified further grounds for reversing the Florida Court. As Chief Justice Rehnquist saw it, the Florida Court had deviated so far from state law concerning the appointment of electors that it violated Article II, Section 1, of the Constitution. This section relates to the qualifications of electors in each state.

Justice John Paul Stevens authored a dissenting opinion that was joined by Justices Ruth Bader Ginsburg and Stephen Breyer. Justice Stevens maintained that the lack of specific detail for discerning voter intent did not "rise to the level of a constitutional violation." Although recognizing that different standards from county to county might raise serious concerns, these problems could be alleviated by the use of a single judge to adjudicate all objections that might arise. Justice Stevens also argued for a remand of the case for development of more specific procedures. His sense was that time existed for more processes, because the December 12 deadline was relevant only in the event there were conflicting slates of electors. Justice Stevens saw no barrier to "counting what the majority concedes to be legal votes until a *bona fide* winner is determined."

Justice David Souter, in a dissent joined by Justices Stephen Breyer, John Paul Stevens, and Ruth Bader Ginsburg, objected on grounds that the Court effectively usurped the state's ability to proceed under the opinions of its own court. He would have remanded the case with instructions to implement uniform standards. Justice Souter also regarded the December 12 deadline as artificial. In her dissent, joined by Justice Stevens, Justice Ginsburg maintained that even a flawed recount would be no less fair than the count that had been certified. Justice Breyer, joined by Justices Stevens, Souter, and Ginsburg, contended that the Court should not have taken the case, should not have entered the stay, and "should now vacate that stay and permit the Florida Supreme Court to decide whether the recount should resume."

The Court's decision was as highly controversial as the presidential election had been hotly contested. Critics maintain that the conservative majority, for result-oriented reasons, departed from its usual aversion to intruding into state matters. They charge that the majority ruled as it did simply to stop a recount that would have provided Gore with the necessary electoral votes for the presidency. Allies of the majority maintain that the Court was right to intervene because the Florida Court had strayed so far from constitutional markings. Although some detractors of the decision in *Bush v. Gore* predicted that the ruling would increase the likelihood of a one-term presidency, the 2004 election, which occurred at a time of relatively high public support for American military action in Iraq after 9/11, yielded President Bush's reelection and even stronger Republican majorities in the House and Senate.

## PER CURIAM.

. . . The right to vote is protected in more than the initial allocation of the franchise. Equal protection applies as well to the manner of its exercise. Having once granted the right to vote on equal terms, the State may not, by later arbitrary and disparate treatment, value one person's vote over that of another. It must be remembered that "the right of suffrage can be denied by a debasement or dilution of the weight of a citizen's vote just as effectively as by wholly prohibiting the free exercise of the franchise."

There is no difference between the two sides of the present controversy on these basic propositions. Respondents say that the very purpose of vindicating the right to vote justifies the recount procedures now at issue. The question before us, however, is whether the recount procedures the Florida Supreme Court has adopted are consistent with its obligation to avoid arbitrary and disparate treatment of the members of its electorate.

Much of the controversy seems to revolve around ballot cards designed to be perforated by a stylus but which, either through error or deliberate omission, have not been perforated with sufficient precision for a machine to register the perforations. In some cases a piece of the card—a chad—is hanging, say, by two corners. In other cases there is no separation at all, just an indentation.

The Florida Supreme Court has ordered that the intent of the voter be discerned from such ballots. For purposes of resolving the equal protection challenge, it is not necessary to decide whether the Florida Supreme Court had the authority under the legislative scheme for resolving election disputes to define what a legal vote is and to mandate a manual recount implementing that definition. The recount mechanisms implemented in response to the decisions of the Florida Supreme Court do not satisfy the minimum requirement for nonarbitrary treatment of voters necessary to secure the fundamental right. Florida's basic command for the count of legally cast votes is to consider the "intent of the voter." This is unobjectionable as an abstract proposition and a starting principle. The problem inheres in the absence of specific standards to ensure its equal application. The formulation of uniform rules to determine intent based on these recurring circumstances is practicable and, we conclude, necessary.

The law does not refrain from searching for the intent of the actor in a multitude of circumstances; and in some cases the general command to ascertain intent is not susceptible to much further refinement. In this instance, however, the question is not whether to believe a witness but how to interpret the marks or holes or scratches on an inanimate object, a piece of cardboard or paper which, it is said, might not have registered as a vote during the machine count. The factfinder confronts a thing, not a person. The search for intent can be confined by specific rules designed to ensure uniform treatment.

The want of those rules here has led to unequal evaluation of ballots in various respects. As seems to have been acknowledged at oral argument, the standards for accepting or rejecting contested ballots might vary not only from county to county but indeed within a single county from one recount team to another. . . .

The question before the Court is not whether local entities, in the exercise of their expertise, may develop different systems for implementing elections. Instead, we are presented with a situation where a state court with the power to assure uniformity has ordered a statewide recount with minimal procedural safeguards. . . .

Upon due consideration of the difficulties identified to this point, it is obvious that the recount cannot be conducted in compliance with the requirements of equal protection and due process without substantial additional work. It would require not only the adoption (after opportunity for argument) of adequate statewide standards for determining what is a legal vote, and practicable procedures to implement them, but also orderly judicial review of any disputed matters that might arise. In addition, the Secretary has advised that the recount of only a portion of the ballots requires that the vote tabulation equipment be used to screen out undervotes, a function for which the machines were not designed. If a recount of overvotes were also required, perhaps even a second screening would be necessary. Use of the equipment for this purpose, and any new software developed for it, would have to be evaluated for accuracy by the Secretary.

The Supreme Court of Florida has said that the legislature intended the State's electors to "participat[e] fully in the federal electoral process," . . . as provided in [the Florida statute in question]. That statute, in turn, requires that any controversy or contest that is designed to lead to a conclusive selection of electors be completed by December 12. That date is upon us, and there is no recount procedure in place under the State Supreme Court's order that comports with minimal constitutional standards. Because it is evident that any recount seeking to meet the December 12 date will be unconstitutional for the reasons we have discussed, we reverse the judgment of the Supreme Court of Florida ordering a recount to proceed. . . .

None are more conscious of the vital limits on judicial authority than are the Members of this Court, and none stand more in admiration of the Constitution's design to leave the selection of the President to the people, through their legislatures, and to the political sphere. When contending parties invoke the process of the courts, however, it becomes our unsought responsibility to resolve the federal and constitutional issues the judicial system has been forced to confront.

The judgment of the Supreme Court of Florida is reversed, and the case is remanded for further proceedings not inconsistent with this opinion.

Justice BREYER, with whom Justice STEVENS and Justice GINSBURG join except as to Part I–A–1, and with whom Justice SOUTER joins as to Part I, dissenting.

The Court was wrong to take this case. It was wrong to grant a stay. It should now vacate that stay and permit the Florida Supreme Court to decide whether the recount should resume. . . .

Despite the reminder that this case involves "an election for the President of the United States," no preeminent legal concern, or practical concern related to legal questions, required this Court to hear this case, let alone to issue a stay that stopped Florida's recount process in its tracks. With one exception, petitioners' claims do not ask us to vindicate a constitutional provision designed to protect a basic human right. Petitioners invoke fundamental fairness, namely, the need for procedural fairness, including finality. But with the one "equal protection" exception, they rely upon law that focuses, not upon that basic need, but upon the constitutional allocation of power. Respondents invoke a competing fundamental consideration—the need to determine the voter's true intent. But they look to state law, not to federal constitutional law, to protect that interest. Neither side claims electoral fraud, dishonesty, or the like. And the more fundamental equal protection claim might have been left to the state court to resolve if and when it was discovered to have mattered. It could still be resolved through a remand conditioned upon issuance of a uniform standard; it does not require reversing the Florida Supreme Court.

Of course, the selection of the President is of fundamental national importance. But that importance is political, not legal. And this Court should resist the temptation unnecessarily to resolve tangential legal disputes, where doing so threatens to determine the outcome of the election.

The Constitution and federal statutes themselves make clear that restraint is appropriate. They set forth a road-map of how to resolve disputes about electors, even after an election as close as this one. That road-map foresees resolution of electoral disputes by *state* courts. But it nowhere provides for involvement by the United States Supreme Court.

To the contrary, the Twelfth Amendment commits to Congress the authority and responsibility to count electoral votes. A federal statute, the Electoral Count Act, enacted after the close 1876 Hayes–Tilden Presidential election, specifies that, after States have tried to resolve disputes (through "judicial" or other means), Congress is the body primarily authorized to resolve remaining disputes. . . .

"Under the Constitution who else could decide? Who is nearer to the State in determining a question of vital importance to the whole union of States than the constituent body upon whom the Constitution has devolved the duty to count the vote?"

The Act goes on to set out rules for the congressional determination of disputes about those votes. If, for example, a State submits a single slate of electors, Congress must count those votes unless both Houses agree that the votes "have not been . . . regularly given." 3 U.S.C. § 15. If, as occurred in 1876, a State submits two slates of electors, then Congress must determine whether a slate has entered the safe harbor of § 5, in which case its votes will have "conclusive" effect. If, as also occurred in 1876, there is controversy about "which of two or more of such State authorities . . . is the lawful tribunal" authorized to appoint electors, then each House shall determine separately which votes are "supported by the decision of such State so authorized by its law." *Ibid.* If the two Houses of Congress agree, the votes they have approved will be counted. If they disagree, then "the votes of the electors whose appointment shall have been certified by the executive of the State, under the seal thereof, shall be counted."

Given this detailed, comprehensive scheme for counting electoral votes, there is no reason to believe that federal law either foresees or requires resolution of such a political issue by this Court. Nor, for that matter, is there any reason to think that the Constitution's Framers would have reached a different conclusion. Madison, at least, believed that allowing the judiciary to choose the Presidential electors "was out of the question." Madison, July 25, 1787 (reprinted in 5 Elliot's Debates on the Federal Constitution 363 (2d ed. 1876)).

The decision by both the Constitution's Framers and the 1886 Congress to minimize this Court's role in resolving close federal Presidential elections is as wise as it is clear. However awkward or difficult it may be for Congress to resolve difficult electoral disputes, Congress, being a political body, expresses the people's will far more accurately than does an unelected Court. And the people's will is what elections are about.

Moreover, Congress was fully aware of the danger that would arise should it ask judges, unarmed with appropriate legal standards, to resolve a hotly contested Presidential election contest. Just after the 1876 Presidential election, Florida, South Carolina, and Louisiana each sent two slates of electors to Washington. Without these States, Tilden, the Democrat, had 184 electoral votes, one short of the number required to win the Presidency. With those States, Hayes, his Republican opponent, would have had 185. In order to choose between the two slates of electors, Congress decided to appoint an electoral commission composed of five Senators, five Representatives, and five Supreme Court Justices. Initially the Commission was to be evenly divided between Republicans and Democrats, with Justice David Davis, an Independent, to possess the decisive vote. However, when at the last minute the Illinois Legislature elected Justice Davis to the United States Senate, the final position on the Commission was filled by Supreme Court Justice Joseph P. Bradley.

The Commission divided along partisan lines, and the responsibility to cast the deciding vote fell to Justice Bradley. He decided to accept the votes by the Republican electors, and thereby awarded the Presidency to Hayes.

Justice Bradley immediately became the subject of vociferous attacks. Bradley was accused of accepting bribes, of being captured by railroad interests, and of an eleventh-hour change in position after a night in which his house "was surrounded by the carriages" of Republican partisans and railroad officials. Many years later, Professor Bickel concluded that Bradley was honest and impartial. He thought that "'the great question' for Bradley was, in fact, whether Congress was entitled to go behind election returns or had to accept them as certified by state authorities," an "issue of principle." Nonetheless, Bickel points out, the legal question upon which

Justice Bradley's decision turned was not very important in the contemporaneous political context. He says that "in the circumstances the issue of principle was trivial, it was overwhelmed by all that hung in the balance, and it should not have been decisive."

For present purposes, the relevance of this history lies in the fact that the participation in the work of the electoral commission by five Justices, including Justice Bradley, did not lend that process legitimacy. Nor did it assure the public that the process had worked fairly, guided by the law. Rather, it simply embroiled Members of the Court in partisan conflict, thereby undermining respect for the judicial process. And the Congress that later enacted the Electoral Count Act knew it.

This history may help to explain why I think it not only legally wrong, but also most unfortunate, for the Court simply to have terminated the Florida recount. Those who caution judicial restraint in resolving political disputes have described the quintessential case for that restraint as a case marked, among other things, by the "strangeness of the issue," its "intractability to principled resolution," its "sheer momentousness, . . . which tends to unbalance judicial judgment," and "the inner vulnerability, the self-doubt of an institution which is electorally irresponsible and has no earth to draw strength from." Those characteristics mark this case.

At the same time, as I have said, the Court is not acting to vindicate a fundamental constitutional principle, such as the need to protect a basic human liberty. No other strong reason to act is present. Congressional statutes tend to obviate the need. And, above all, in this highly politicized matter, the appearance of a split decision runs the risk of undermining the public's confidence in the Court itself. That confidence is a public treasure. It has been built slowly over many years, some of which were marked by a Civil War and the tragedy of segregation. It is a vitally necessary ingredient of any successful effort to protect basic liberty and, indeed, the rule of law itself. We run no risk of returning to the days when a President (responding to this Court's efforts to protect the Cherokee Indians) might have said, "John Marshall has made his decision; now let him enforce it!" But we do risk a self-inflicted wound—a wound that may harm not just the Court, but the Nation.

I fear that in order to bring this agonizingly long election process to a definitive conclusion, we have not adequately attended to that necessary "check upon our own exercise of power," "our own sense of self-restraint." Justice Brandeis once said of the Court, "The most important thing we do is not doing." What it does today, the Court should have left undone. I would repair the damage done as best we now can, by permitting the Florida recount to continue under uniform standards.

I respectfully dissent.

## Bibliography

Foley, Edward B. "The Future of *Bush v. Gore?*" *Ohio State Law Journal* 68 (2007): 925.

Posner, Richard. *Breaking the Deadlock: The 2000 Election, the Constitution, and the Courts.* Princeton, NJ: Princeton University Press, 2001.

Sunstein, Cass, and Richard Epstein, eds. *The Vote: Bush, Gore, and the Supreme Court.* Chicago: University of Chicago Press, 2001.

# Part IV
# Individual Rights and Liberties

The motivation for framing the United States Constitution was to establish a structure of governance. As the original states debated whether to ratify the Constitution, a key concern was with the dangers perceived in a centralized national government. Fear that concentrated power would imperil individual rights and freedoms generated a movement for a specification of rights and liberties that the federal government could not abridge. Although many of the framers and supporters of the Constitution believed that such an itemization was unnecessary, and that the political process itself would safeguard personal liberty, support for a Bill of Rights grew pursuant either to a sense of necessary or as a concession to secure ratification.

Although initially conceived as a check against federal power, the Bill of Rights in many instances has been made applicable to the states. This result has been achieved by the judiciary's determination that most provisions of the Bill of Rights are incorporated into the Fourteenth Amendment. In addition to being a vehicle for extending the reach of constitutionally enumerated rights and liberties, the Fourteenth Amendment has emerged as an independent source of fundamental rights. Constitutional review in the early twentieth century thus established economic liberty as a basic freedom that often defeated governmental efforts to regulate conditions in the workplace. Over the past few decades, the right of privacy has emerged as the basis for several protected interests including the freedom to procreate, elect an abortion, live as an extended family, marry, and decline medical treatment. It also has become a source of protection for sexual orientation.

Part IV commences with an examination of decisions concerning what many regard as the most fundamental liberty. Freedom of speech and freedom of the press traditionally have been regarded as the foundation of self-government. Without it, citizens would be impaired in their ability to make informed judgments and thus performance of their function as the ultimate power in a representative democracy. The First Amendment operates not only to guarantee expressive liberty but also to secure associational and religious freedom. The First Amendment cases are followed by a series of decisions related to the criminal justice system. These rulings implicate, respectively, the Fourth, Fifth, and Sixth Amendments. The final category of cases concerns fundamental rights that, although not specifically enumerated by the Constitution, nonetheless have been established as an incident of due process and judicial review.

# Chapter 11

# First Amendment: Freedom of Speech (Content Regulation)

Freedom of speech has been referred to as the most essential liberty. As the Court put it in *Palko v. Connecticut* (1937), expressive liberty is "the matrix, the indispensable condition of nearly every other form of freedom." This observation is consistent with a jurisprudential tradition that views freedom of speech as essential to informed self-government. The nation's first century included some significant abridgments of expressive freedom. Congress and the Adams administration in the late eighteenth century, for instance, enacted the Sedition Act, which essentially criminalized criticism of the president and legislature. This law was targeted at Jeffersonian critics who, upon being elected to power, turned the law against its architects. Antislavery literature generally was banned from the South prior to the Civil War. Despite this suppression, it was not until the twentieth century that the freedom of speech clause was reviewed by the Supreme Court.

The meaning of freedom of speech, like other constitutional guarantees, has evolved from debate over theory, values, and applications. Among the most eloquent statements with respect to the value of expressive freedom, and the need to tolerate and protect speech challenging the very foundations of the political system, is the concurring opinion of Justices Louis Brandeis and Oliver Wendell Holmes, Jr., in *Whitney v. California* (1927). As they wrote, the framers "believed that freedom to think as you will and to speak as you think are means indispensable to the discovery and spread of political truth. . . . If there be time to expose through discussion the falsehood and fallacies, to avert the evil by the processes of education, the remedy to be applied is more speech, not enforced silence." In trumpeting the virtues of the marketplace of ideas, and the need for government to allow free competition among political views, ideologies, and programs, their views shaped a long-term meaning of expressive freedom in favor of individual rather than authoritative selection.

Perhaps the most straightforward theory was propounded by Justice Hugo Black, who described freedom of speech as an "absolute." Justice Black's understanding of the First Amendment was never embraced by the Court. Rather, it has adopted a more complex model of review that conditions freedom upon content, context, or regulatory purpose. Within the resulting hierarchy of expressive freedom, speech essential to informed self-government is the most protected. Less protected are commercial expression and certain types of defamatory speech. Some expression, such as obscenity, intentional incitement of unlawful activity ("Clear and Present Danger"), true threats and fighting words, is categorically excluded from the First Amendment's protective ambit.

# TORTS

State law historically has established grounds for civil liability activity that constitutes a tort. Although most tort law does not implicate the Constitution, actions for defamation, invasion of privacy, and intentional infliction of emotional distress may operate at cross-purposes with freedom of speech. Libelous or slanderous expression, referred to collectively as defamation, traditionally has been viewed as valueless and thus unworthy of First Amendment protection. Early English law actually made criticism of the king or queen a capital offense. Even in colonial America, truth was an aggravating rather than mitigating factor. A key influence upon the eventual nature of defamation law was the civil rights movement during the middle of the twentieth century. In *New York Times Co. v. Sullivan* (1964), the Supreme Court reviewed an Alabama jury's award of damages to state officials who had been criticized in an editorial advertisement published in the *New York Times*. Realizing that politically motivated defamation actions could chill speech essential to informed self-government, the Court carved out a category of defamation for First Amendment protection. It thus adopted an "actual malice" standard that requires public officials to prove that an allegedly defamatory statement about them was made with knowledge of the falsehood or reckless disregard of the truth. The Court, in *Curtis Publishing Co. v. Butts* (1968), extended the actual malice standard to public figures, but only with respect to the recovery of punitive damages. In *Gertz v. Robert Welch, Inc.* (1974), the Court determined that this criterion should be extended to private persons. It also adopted the actual malice standard, in *Hustler Magazine v. Falwell* (1988), to a public figure's claim of intentional infliction of emotional distress. More recently, the Court took an even more speech protective stance. In *Snyder v. Phelps* (2011), the Court ruled that there can be no recovery at all for intentional infliction of emotional distress when the speech in question amounts to an opinion about matters of "public concern."

## *Gertz v. Robert Welch, Inc.*

**Citation: 418 U.S. 323.**

**Issue: Whether the actual malice standard in a defamation action extends beyond public officials and public figures to private persons.**

**Year of Decision: 1974.**

**Outcome: Private persons, unlike public officials and public figures, are not required to establish that a defamatory statement was made with actual malice.**

**Author of Opinion: Justice Lewis Powell.**

**Vote: 5-4.**

Defamation is a form of expression that provides the basis for a claim on grounds it causes harm to reputation. Historically, it has been viewed as speech with slight social value and thus beyond the protective range of the First Amendment. Even libelous or slanderous speech, however, may add value to political discourse that advances informed self-governance. This understanding was embraced in *New York Times Co. v. Sullivan* (1964), when the Supreme Court established a higher standard of proof for public officials who brought defamation actions. The Court reached this outcome "against the background of a profound national commitment to the principle that debate on public issues should be uninhibited, robust, and wide-open and that it may well include vehement, caustic, and sometimes unpleasantly sharp attacks on government and public officials."

The actual malice standard, which requires public officials to prove that a defamatory statement was made with knowledge of the falsehood or reckless disregard of the truth, provides breathing space for freedom of speech that previously did not exist. The higher standard of proof for public officials was supported by a logic that had the potential to expand with respect to other persons or contexts. Soon after its decision in *New York Times Co. v. Sullivan,* the Court extended the actual malice standard to public figures. It characterized public figures, in *Curtis Publishing Co. v. Butts* (1968), as persons who are "intimately involved in the resolution of important public questions or [who], by reason of their fame, shape events in areas of concern to society at large." The rationale for equating public figures with public officials was that each had special relevance to the information marketplace and processes of informed self-governance.

The focus upon public officials and public figures established protection on the basis of an individual's status. To the extent the aim is to protect speech essential to informed self-government, there is a logical argument that expression should be protected on the basis of subject matter rather than personal function. In *Rosenbloom v. Metromedia, Inc.* (1971), four justices embraced this premise and extended the actual malice standard to "statements concerning matter[s] of general or public interest." Justice Hugo Black advocated an even stronger principle that freedom of speech was absolute, and thus defamation laws were barred entirely by the First Amendment. This position effectively prevented the public interest standard from becoming established as a governing principle. It did not end the process, however, of determining the outer boundaries of the actual malice standard. In *Gertz v. Robert Welch, Inc.* (1974), the Court revisited the scope of the actual malice standard and reverted to a focus upon the status of the person rather than the nature of the speech.

At issue was a defamation claim by an attorney (Elmer Gertz), who had brought a wrongful death action on behalf of a family whose son had been shot by a Chicago policeman. A periodical described Gertz as the "architect [of a] Communist frame-up" who also had an extensive police file. Key to the outcome of the case was whether Gertz was a public figure or whether the actual malice standard extended to public issues or private persons. Justice Lewis Powell, in a majority opinion, determined that the actual malice standard governed only public officials and public figures. Noting an inevitable tension between the interest of "vigorous and uninhibited" expression and the need to remedy reputational harm, the Court reaffirmed the importance of some "strategic protection" for defamatory speech. It could identify no basis, however, for correlating the actual malice standard to public interest or extending it to private persons. Its limits thus reached no further than public officials and those persons "who by reason of the notoriety of their achievements or the vigor and success with which they seek the public's attention are properly classified as public figures."

Requiring persons to prove that a statement was made with knowledge that it was false, or with reckless disregard of the truth, represented what the Court described as a "powerful antidote" to self-censorship. It also, as the Court put it, imposed "a correspondingly high price from the victims of defamatory falsehood." This increased burden was warranted, however, on grounds that public and nonpublic defamation plaintiffs are not similarly situated for First Amendment purposes. A key difference, for instance, is the relatively greater power of public persons to command the media's attention and tell his or her side of the story. Because public persons have greater access to the media than nonpublic persons, the Court believed that they "have a more realistic opportunity to counteract false statements than private individuals normally enjoy."

Significant too, in the Court's view, was the sense that public officials and figures by seeking government office or high-profile positions assume the risk of public scrutiny. Whether as a political candidate or having achieved "especial prominence in the affairs of society," public persons "invite attention and comment." Although exceptions to these norms may exist, the Court reasoned that the "media are entitled to act on the assumption that public officials and public figures have voluntarily exposed themselves to increased risk of injury from defamatory falsehood concerning them." The same determination could not be made, at least from the Court's perspective, with respect to private individuals. Because they did not aspire to be in the public eye, by seeking public office or stature, they ceded no interest in their "good name." Being more vulnerable to reputational harm, as the Court saw it, private persons were more deserving of protection.

Separating public figures and private persons is not always an easy task. As the Court observed, public figures break down into three categories. The first is what the Court characterized as "involuntary public figures." Persons in this group are public figures through no intentional effort of their own. The involuntary public figure, as the Court described it, is an "exceedingly rare" category. The second category of public figures are persons who "occupy positions of such pervasive power and influence that they are deemed public figures for all purposes." The third category comprises those who "have thrust themselves to the forefront of particular public controversies in order to influence the resolution of the issues involved." The Court noted that this group represents the most common type of public figure. With these three possibilities for public figure status, the key question for the Court was whether Gertz fit into any of the categories.

Although Gertz had served on various government commissions and as an attorney was an officer of the Court, the Court found that he did not qualify as a public official for purposes of the action. Despite the official nature of Gertz's positions, the defamatory statements did not pertain to his government service. The Court also was reluctant to subject attorneys as a class to the actual malice standard. Nor did it view him as a public figure. In this regard, the Court specifically determined that he had not attained public figure status involuntarily, on the basis of pervasive power or influence, or by thrusting himself into a public controversy. Rather, the Court saw him as a private person whose claim accordingly was not governed by the actual malice standard. The bottom line was a rule that limits the actual malice standard to public officials and public figures, but allows states the latitude to establish liability for defamation of private persons—so long as it is not imposed "without fault."

Justice Byron White, in a concurring opinion, criticized the Court for having struck what he viewed as an improvident balance. From his perspective, the media were powerful enough to assume liability for reputational harm to a private person whether or not a showing of fault had been made. Justice William Brennan dissented on grounds that the decision underserved First Amendment interests. Justice Brennan voiced concern with the risk of self-censorship when issues of public importance did not implicate public persons.

Case law in the aftermath of Gertz has construed the public figure concept narrowly. The Court, in *Time, Inc. v. Firestone* (1976), determined that a high-profile Palm Beach socialite was not a public figure in the context of a divorce proceeding. At issue in this case was an article stating that her divorce had been granted on grounds of extreme cruelty and adultery. Despite the public process and the plaintiff's regular news conference, the Court determined that she was not an all-purpose public figure and had not voluntarily injected herself into "the forefront of any particular public controversy in order to influence the resolution of the issues involved in it." In *Wolston v. Reader's Digest Association* (1979), the Court determined that a public figure had become a private person over the course of time. In *Dun and Bradstreet,*

*Inc. v. Greenmoss Builders, Inc.* (1985), the Court determined that the type of damages recoverable may turn upon whether the defamation touches upon a matter of public concern. In a concurring opinion, Justice White urged reconsideration of the actual malice standard. Central to his argument was a sense that constitutional protection of falsehood actually undermined First Amendment interests by distorting the information marketplace. At least in the context of public officials and public figures, the Court has continued to favor a free flow of information even if this stream carries some pollutants. In 2011, the Court reaffirmed its protection of speech dealing with matters of "public concern" in *Snyder v. Phelps* (2011). Even hateful, seriously offensive speech is protected if it can be found to be sufficiently related to matters of "public concern." The test for speech that is entitled to special protection because it is a matter of "public concern," is when it can be fairly considered as relating to any matter of political, social, or other concern to the community, or when it is a subject of legitimate news interest.

### Mr. Justice POWELL delivered the opinion of the Court.

. . . This Court has struggled for nearly a decade to define the proper accommodation between the law of defamation and the freedoms of speech and press protected by the First Amendment. With this decision we return to that effort. We granted certiorari to reconsider the extent of a publisher's constitutional privilege against liability for defamation of a private citizen. . . .

We begin with the common ground. Under the First Amendment there is no such thing as a false idea. However pernicious an opinion may seem, we depend for its correction not on the conscience of judges and juries but on the competition of other ideas. But there is no constitutional value in false statements of fact. Neither the intentional lie nor the careless error materially advances society's interest in 'uninhibited, robust, and wide-open' debate on public issues. They belong to that category of utterances which 'are no essential part of any exposition of ideas, and are of such slight social value as a step to truth that any benefit that may be derived from them is clearly outweighed by the social interest in order and morality.'

Although the erroneous statement of fact is not worthy of constitutional protection, it is nevertheless inevitable in free debate. As James Madison pointed out in the Report on the Virginia Resolutions of 1798: "Some degree of abuse is inseparable from the proper use of every thing; and in no instance is this more true than in that of the press." And punishment of error runs the risk of inducing a cautious and restrictive exercise of the constitutionally guaranteed freedoms of speech and press. . . .

The legitimate state interest underlying the law of libel is the compensation of individuals for the harm inflicted on them by defamatory falsehood. We would not lightly require the State to abandon this purpose, for, as Mr. Justice Stewart has reminded us, the individual's right to the protection of his own good name 'reflects no more than our basic concept of the essential dignity and worth of every human being—a concept at the root of any decent system of ordered liberty. The protection of private personality, like the protection of life itself, is left primarily to the individual States under the Ninth and Tenth Amendments. But this does not mean that the right is entitled to any less recognition by this Court as a basic of our constitutional system.' . . .

The *New York Times* standard defines the level of constitutional protection appropriate to the context of defamation of a public person. Those who, by reason of the notoriety of their achievements or the vigor and success with which they seek the public's attention, are properly classed as public figures and those who hold governmental office may recover for injury to reputation only on clear and convincing proof that the defamatory falsehood was made with knowledge of its falsity or with reckless disregard for the truth. . . .

For these reasons we conclude that the States should retain substantial latitude in their efforts to enforce a legal remedy for defamatory falsehood injurious to the reputation of a private individual. The extension of the *New York Times* test proposed by the Rosenbloom plurality would abridge this legitimate state interest to a degree that we find unacceptable. And it would occasion the additional difficulty of forcing state and federal judges to decide on an ad hoc basis which publications address issues of 'general or public interest' and which do not—to determine, in the words of Mr. Justice Marshall, "what information is relevant to self-government." We doubt the wisdom of committing this task to the conscience of judges. Nor does the Constitution require us to draw so thin a line between the drastic alternatives of the *New York Times* privilege and the common law of strict liability for defamatory error. The 'public or general interest' test for determining the applicability of the *New York Times* standard to private defamation actions inadequately serves both of the competing values at stake. On the one hand, a private individual whose reputation is injured by defamatory falsehood that does concern an issue of public or general interest has no recourse unless he can meet the rigorous requirements of New York Times. . . .

We hold that, so long as they do not impose liability without fault, the States may define for themselves the appropriate standard of liability for a publisher or broadcaster of defamatory falsehood injurious to a private individual. . . .

Respondent's characterization of petitioner as a public figure raises a different question. That designation may rest on either of two alternative bases. In some instances an individual may achieve such pervasive fame or notoriety that he becomes a public figure for all purposes and in all contexts. More commonly, an individual voluntarily injects himself or is drawn into a particular public controversy and thereby becomes a public figure for a limited range of issues. In either case such persons assume special prominence in the resolution of public questions.

Petitioner has long been active in community and professional affairs. He has served as an officer of local civic groups and of various professional organizations, and he has published several books and articles on legal subjects. . . . Absent clear evidence of general fame or notoriety in the community, and pervasive involvement in the affairs of society, an individual should not be deemed a public personality for all aspects of his life. It is preferable to reduce the public-figure question to a more meaningful context by looking to the nature and extent of an individual's participation in the particular controversy giving rise to the defamation.

In this context it is plain that petitioner was not a public figure. He played a minimal role at the coroner's inquest, and his participation related solely to his representation of a private client. He took no part in the criminal prosecution of Officer Nuccio. Moreover, he never discussed either the criminal or civil litigation with the press and was never quoted as having done so. He plainly did not thrust himself into the vortex of this public issue, nor did he engage the public's attention in an attempt to influence its outcome. We are persuaded that the trial court did not err in refusing to characterize petitioner as a public figure for the purpose of this litigation.

We therefore conclude that the *New York Times* standard is inapplicable to this case and that the trial court erred in entering judgment for respondent. Because the jury was allowed to impose liability without fault and was permitted to presume damages without proof of injury, a new trial is necessary. We reverse and remand for further proceedings in accord with this opinion.

## Mr. Justice DOUGLAS, dissenting.

The Court describes this case as a return to the struggle of 'defin(ing) the proper accommodation between the law of defamation and the freedoms of speech and press protected by the First Amendment.' It is indeed a struggle, once described by Mr. Justice Black as 'the same quagmire' in which the Court 'is now helplessly struggling in the field of obscenity.' I would suggest that the struggle is a quite hopeless one, for, in light of the command of the First Amendment, no 'accommodation' of its freedoms can be 'proper' except those made by the Framers themselves.

Unlike the right of privacy which, by the terms of the Fourth Amendment, must be accommodated with reasonable searches and seizures and warrants issued by magistrates, the rights of free speech and of a free press were protected by the Framers in verbiage whose prescription seems clear. I have stated before my view that the First Amendment would bar Congress from passing any libel law. This was the view held by Thomas Jefferson and it is one Congress has never challenged through enactment of a civil libel statute. The sole congressional attempt at this variety of First Amendment muzzle was in the Sedition Act of 1798—a criminal libel act never tested in this Court and one which expired by its terms three years after enactment. As President, Thomas Jefferson pardoned those who were convicted under the Act, and fines levied in its prosecution were repaid by Act of Congress. The general consensus was that the Act constituted a regrettable legislative exercise plainly in violation of the First Amendment.

With the First Amendment made applicable to the States through the Fourteenth, I do not see how States have any more ability to 'accommodate' freedoms of speech or of the press than does Congress. This is true whether the form of the accommodation is civil or criminal since '(w)hat a State may not constitutionally bring about by means of a criminal statute is likewise beyond the reach of its civil law of libel.' Like Congress, States are without power 'to use a civil libel law or any other law to impose damages for merely discussing public affairs.'

Continued recognition of the possibility of state libel suits for public discussion of public issues leaves the freedom of speech honored by the Fourteenth Amendment a diluted version of First Amendment protection. This view is only possible if one accepts the position that the First Amendment is applicable to the States only through the Due Process Clause of the Fourteenth, due process freedom of speech being only that freedom which this Court might deem to be 'implicit in the concept of ordered liberty.' But the Court frequently has rested state free speech and free press decisions on the Fourteenth Amendment generally rather than on the Due Process Clause alone. The Fourteenth Amendment speaks not only of due process but also of 'privileges and immunities' of United States citizenship. I can conceive of no privilege or immunity with a higher claim to recognition against state abridgment than the freedoms of speech and of the press. In our federal system we are all subject to two governmental regimes, and freedoms of speech and of the press protected against the infringement of only one are quite illusory. The identity of the oppressor is, I would think, a matter of relative indifference to the oppressed.

There can be no doubt that a State impinges upon free and open discussion when it sanctions the imposition of damages for such discussion through its civil libel laws. Discussion of public affairs is often marked by highly charged emotions, and jurymen, not unlike us all, are subject to those emotions. It is indeed this very type of speech which is the reason for the First Amendment since speech which arouses little emotion is little in need of protection. The vehicle for publication in this case was the American Opinion, a most controversial periodical which disseminates the views of the John Birch Society, an organization which many deem to be quite offensive. The subject matter involved 'Communist plots,' 'conspiracies against law enforcement agencies,' and the killing of a private citizen by the police. With any such amalgam of controversial elements pressing upon the jury, a jury determination, unpredictable in the most neutral circumstances, becomes for those who venture to discuss heated issues, a virtual roll of the dice separating them from liability for often massive claims of damage.

It is only the hardy publisher who will engage in discussion in the face of such risk, and the Court's preoccupation with proliferating standards in the area of libel increases the risks. It matters little whether the standard be articulated as 'malice' or 'reckless disregard of the truth' or 'negligence,' for jury determinations by any of those criteria are virtually unreviewable. This Court, in its continuing delineation of variegated mantles of First Amendment protection, is, like the potential publisher, left with only speculation on how jury findings were influenced by the effect the subject matter of the publication had upon the minds and viscera of the jury. The standard announced today leaves the States free to 'define for themselves the appropriate standard of liability for a publisher or broadcaster' in the circumstances of this case. This of course leaves the simple negligence standard as an option, with the jury free to impose damages upon a finding that the publisher failed to act as 'a reasonable man.' With such continued erosion of First Amendment protection, I fear that it may well be the reasonable man who refrains from speaking.

Since in my view the First and Fourteenth Amendments prohibit the imposition of damages upon respondent for this discussion of public affairs, I would affirm the judgment below.

### Bibliography

Epstein, Richard. "Was *New York Times v. Sullivan* Wrong?" *University of Chicago Law Review* 53 (1986): 782.

Kalven, Harry. "The New York Times Case: A Report on "The Central Meaning of the First Amendment." *Supreme Court Review* 191 (1964).

## Hustler Magazine v. Falwell

**Citation: 485 U.S. 46.**

**Issue: Whether a "public figure" can recover damages for intentional infliction of mental and emotional distress when he suffers an outrageous parody (suggesting that he engaged in an incestuous relationship with his mother) in a pornographically oriented magazine.**

**Year of Decision: 1988.**

**Outcome: Parodies and satire are speech, within the meaning of the First Amendment, and no recovery is permitted unless the parody involves a false assertion of fact that the parodist knew was untrue or acted in reckless disregard for whether it was true or false.**

**Author of Opinion: Chief Justice William Rehnquist.**

**Vote: 9-0.**

Political satire has been a part of American political dialogue since the nation's founding. However, satire can sometimes be brutal and can inflict emotional distress on the subject. In such cases, there is a natural tension between the tort interest in providing compensation for mental and emotional distress and the constitutional right to freedom of speech.

*Hustler Magazine v. Falwell* presents this tension in dramatic relief. The Reverend Jerry Falwell was a nationally prominent minister who was "active as a commentator on politics and public affairs." He was the host of a nationally syndicated television show and the founder and president of a political group known as the "Moral Majority." He was also the founder of Liberty University in Lynchburg, Virginia, and he authored a number of books and publications. *Hustler Magazine,* Falwell's antagonist, was a pornographic magazine that frequently published graphic and base material.

In 1983, *Hustler Magazine* decided to parody Falwell using a Campari Liqueur advertisement. The actual Campari ads portrayed interviews with various celebrities about their "first times." Although the advertisements actually focused on the first time that the celebrities had sampled Campari, the ads played on the double entendre of the first time that the interviewees had engaged in sex. *Hustler Magazine* mimicked the Campari format and created a fictional interview with Falwell in which he stated that his "first time" was during a drunken incestuous rendezvous with his mother in an outhouse. The Hustler parody was written in such a way as to suggest that Falwell is "a hypocrite who preaches only when he is drunk."

Falwell could not sue Hustler for defamation because that cause of action requires a false assertion of fact, and the magazine had not represented the ad parody as "fact." Indeed, at the bottom of the page, in small print, the ad contained the following disclaimer: "ad parody—not to be taken seriously." In addition, the magazine's table of contents flatly stated: "Fiction; Ad and Personality Parody." Because of the disclaimer and the table of contents, it was clear that the parody was false and therefore that there was no false assertion of fact.

Unable to bring a defamation suit, Falwell sued Hustler for intentional infliction of mental distress. A jury awarded Falwell compensatory damages of $100,000 and punitive damages of $50,000. The case eventually made its way to the United States Supreme Court where, in an opinion written by Chief Justice William Rehnquist, the Court reversed.

The Court phrased the issue as whether "a public figure may recover damages for emotional harm caused by the publication of an ad parody offensive to him, and doubtless gross and repugnant in the eyes of most." In answering that question in the negative, the Court emphasized that the First Amendment emphasizes the "fundamental importance" of allowing people to express themselves "on matters of public interest and concern." The Court also recognized that "robust political debate" is likely to result in speech that is critical of public officials and public figures who are "intimately involved in the resolution of important public questions or, by reason of their fame, shape events in areas of concern to society at large." Moreover, those who comment on public affairs are generally protected against liability. For example, when defamation is involved, the Court's landmark decision in *New York Times Co. v. Sullivan,* 376 U.S. 254 (1964), provided that public officials and public figures may not recover unless they can satisfy the actual malice standard. In other words, they must show that the statement was made "with knowledge that it was false or with reckless disregard of whether it was false or not."

Falwell argued that, in emotional distress cases, the courts should impose liability when speech subjects an individual to "severe emotional distress," and the "utterance was intended to inflict emotional distress, was outrageous, and did in fact inflict serious emotional distress." In such circumstances, in Falwell's view, courts should impose liability without regard to "whether the statement was a fact or an opinion, or whether it was true or false." In other words, the defendant's intent to cause injury is critical, and "the State's interest in preventing emotional harm simply outweighs whatever interest a speaker may have in speech of this type."

While the Court agreed that utterances designed to inflict emotional distress should not "receive much solicitude," the Court disagreed with Falwell. The Court noted that "many things done with motives that are less than admirable are protected by the First Amendment." Relying on its prior decision in *Garrison v. Louisiana,* 379 U.S. 64 (1964), the Court noted that, even when a speaker or writer is motivated by hatred or ill-will, his expression may be protected by the First Amendment. Otherwise, there might be a chilling effect on speech. The Court held that these principles apply with particular force to political cartoonists and satirists, recognizing that cartoons and satires have consistently played a significant role in political discussion since the very beginning of the country, and such cartoons were rarely fair and reasoned. For example, early cartoonists had portrayed George Washington as an ass. Moreover, cartoons are "often based on exploitation of unfortunate physical traits or politically embarrassing events—an exploitation often calculated to injure the feelings of the subject of the portrayal" and attempt to bring "scorn and ridicule and satire" on the recipient. In the Court's view, such representations are "usually as welcome as a bee sting." But the Court emphasized the political importance of such satire noting Thomas Nast's sustained "graphic vendetta against William M. 'Boss' Tweed and his corrupt associates in New York City's 'Tweed Ring.'"

Falwell also argued that, even if political satire were generally acceptable, *Hustler's* caricature of him was so "outrageous" as to "distinguish it from more traditional political cartoons" and should be subject to liability. While the Court expressed distaste for *Hustler's* parody of Falwell, the Court doubted that it was possible to clearly differentiate between traditional political cartoons and more outrageous endeavors. In the Court's view, "outrageousness" in "the area of political and social discourse has an inherent subjectiveness about it which would allow a jury to impose liability on the basis of the jurors' tastes or views, or perhaps on the basis of their dislike of a particular expression." The Court expressed concern that damages would, therefore, be awarded simply "because the speech in question may have an adverse emotional impact on the audience."

As a result, the Court concluded that Falwell (and other public figures and public officials) may not recover for intentional infliction of emotional distress unless they can show that the publication contains a false statement of fact which was made with "actual malice," i.e., with knowledge that the statement was false or with reckless disregard as to whether or not it was true. However, since satire and cartoons almost always suggest that they are portraying fiction, this standard can almost never be met. The Court expressed concern that a lesser standard would not provide adequate "breathing space" for "the freedoms protected by the First Amendment." Since the ad parody did not involve assertions of actual facts, Falwell could not, consistently with the First Amendment, recover damages for *Hustler's* ad parody.

*Falwell* is an important decision for free speech in this country. It continues the Court's well-established tradition of providing a high level of protection for those who comment on public affairs, and makes it extremely difficult for politicians and public figures to recover against those who comment on their actions. It also provides protection for the long-established practice of political satire.

## Chief Justice REHNQUIST delivered the opinion of the Court.

. . . At the heart of the First Amendment is the recognition of the fundamental importance of the free flow of ideas and opinions on matters of public interest and concern. "[T]he freedom to speak one's mind is not only an aspect of individual liberty—and thus a good unto itself—but also is essential to the common quest for truth and the vitality of society as a whole." We have therefore been particularly vigilant to ensure that individual expressions of ideas remain free from governmentally imposed sanctions. The First Amendment recognizes no such thing as a "false" idea. . . .

The sort of robust political debate encouraged by the First Amendment is bound to produce speech that is critical of those who hold public office or those public figures who are "intimately involved in the resolution of important public questions or, by reason of their fame, shape events in areas of concern to society at large." . . .

Of course, this does not mean that *any* speech about a public figure is immune from sanction in the form of damages. Since *New York Times Co. v. Sullivan*, we have consistently ruled that a public figure may hold a speaker liable for the damage to reputation caused by publication of a defamatory falsehood, but only if the statement was made "with knowledge that it was false or with reckless disregard of whether it was false or not." False statements of fact are particularly valueless; they interfere with the truth-seeking function of the marketplace of ideas, and they cause damage to an individual's reputation that cannot easily be repaired by counterspeech, however persuasive or effective. But even though falsehoods have little value in and of themselves, they are "nevertheless inevitable in free debate," and a rule that would impose strict liability on a publisher for false factual assertions would have an undoubted "chilling" effect on speech relating to public figures that does have constitutional value. . . .

Generally speaking the law does not regard the intent to inflict emotional distress as one which should receive much solicitude, and it is quite understandable that most if not all jurisdictions have chosen to make it civilly culpable where the conduct in question is sufficiently "outrageous." But in the world of debate about public affairs, many things done with motives that are less than admirable are protected by the First Amendment. In *Garrison v. Louisiana*, we held that even when a speaker or writer is motivated by hatred or ill will his expression was protected by the First Amendment:

"Debate on public issues will not be uninhibited if the speaker must run the risk that it will be proved in court that he spoke out of hatred; even if he did speak out of hatred, utterances honestly believed contribute to the free interchange of ideas and the ascertainment of truth." . . .

Despite their sometimes caustic nature, from the early cartoon portraying George Washington as an ass down to the present day, graphic depictions and satirical cartoons have played a prominent role in public and political debate. Nast's castigation of the Tweed Ring, Walt McDougall's characterization of Presidential candidate James G. Blaine's banquet with the millionaires at Delmonico's as "The Royal Feast of Belshazzar," and numerous other efforts have undoubtedly had an effect on the course and outcome of contemporaneous debate. Lincoln's tall, gangling posture, Teddy Roosevelt's glasses and teeth, and Franklin D. Roosevelt's jutting jaw and cigarette holder have been memorialized by political cartoons with an effect that could not have been obtained by the photographer or the portrait artist. From the viewpoint of history it is clear that our political discourse would have been considerably poorer without them. . . .

We conclude that public figures and public officials may not recover for the tort of intentional infliction of emotional distress by reason of publications such as the one here at issue without showing in addition that the publication contains a false statement of fact which was made with "actual malice," *i.e.,* with knowledge that the statement was false or with reckless disregard as to whether or not it was true. This is not merely a "blind application" of the *New York Times* standard, it reflects our considered judgment that such a standard is necessary to give adequate "breathing space" to the freedoms protected by the First Amendment.

Here it is clear that respondent Falwell is a "public figure" for purposes of First Amendment law. The jury found against respondent on his libel claim when it decided that the Hustler ad parody could not "reasonably be understood as describing actual facts about [respondent] or actual events in which [he] participated." The Court of Appeals interpreted the jury's finding to be that the ad parody "was not reasonably believable," and in accordance with our custom we accept this finding. Respondent is thus relegated to his claim for damages awarded by the jury for the intentional infliction of emotional distress by "outrageous" conduct. But for reasons heretofore stated this claim cannot, consistently with the First Amendment, form a basis for the award of damages when the conduct in question is the publication of a caricature such as the ad parody involved here. The judgment of the Court of Appeals is accordingly
*Reversed.*

## Bibliography

Post, Robert C. "The Constitutional Concept of Public Discourse: Outrageous Opinion, Democratic Deliberation, and *Hustler Magazine v. Falwell*." *Harvard Law Review* 103 (1990): 603.

Skolnick, Jerome K. "The Sociological Tort of Defamation." *California Law Review* 74 (1986): 677.

Smolla, Rodney A. *Jerry Falwell v. Larry Flynt: The First Amendment on Trial*. Urbana: University of Illinois Press, 1990.

Weaver, Russell L., and Donald E. Lively. *Understanding the First Amendment*. Newark, NJ: LexisNexis, 2012, 64–69.

## Snyder v. Phelps

**Citation: 562 U.S. 443.**

**Issue: Whether the First Amendment shields the members of the Westboro Baptist Church from tort liability for their speech in this case.**

**Year of Decision: 2011.**

**Outcome: Yes. The speech of the church members who picketed near the funeral of a military service member was of "public concern" and therefore was entitled to special protection under the First Amendment.**

**Author of Opinion: Chief Justice Roberts.**

**Vote: 8-1.**

For many years the members of the Westboro Baptist Church have picketed military funerals in order to express their belief, among other things, that God hates the United States for its tolerance of homosexuality, particularly in the military. In March 2006 Westboro founder Fred Phelps and six members of the Church, traveled to Maryland to picket the funeral of Marine Lance Corporal Matthew Snyder, who was killed in the line of duty. The church members obeyed the local ordinances by picketing on public land approximately 1,000 feet from the church where the funeral was held. The church members peacefully displayed their signs, which included such messages as: "Thank God for Dead Soldiers," "Fags Doom Nations," "America is Doomed," "Thank God for IEDs," "God hates you," and "You're Going to Hell." Matthew Snyder's father (Snyder) observed the tops of the picketers' signs when driving to the funeral. Mr. Snyder later learned what was written on the signs while watching a news broadcast later that night. Mr. Snyder sued for emotional damages.

## Chief Justice ROBERTS delivered the opinion of the Court.

. . . Whether the First Amendment prohibits holding Westboro liable for its speech in this case turns largely on whether that speech is of public or private concern, as determined by all the circumstances of the case. "[S]peech on 'matters of public concern' . . . is 'at the heart of the First Amendment's protection.'" The First Amendment reflects "a profound national commitment to the principle that debate on public issues should be uninhibited, robust, and wide-open." That is because "speech concerning public affairs is more than self-expression; it is the essence of self-government." Accordingly, "speech on public issues occupies the highest rung of the hierarchy of First Amendment values, and is entitled to special protection."

"'[N]ot all speech is of equal First Amendment importance,' " however, and where matters of purely private significance are at issue, First Amendment protections are often less rigorous. That is because restricting speech on purely private matters does not implicate the same constitutional concerns as limiting speech on matters of public interest: "[T]here is no threat to the free and robust debate of public issues; there is no potential interference with a meaningful dialogue of ideas"; and the "threat of liability" does not pose the risk of "a reaction of self-censorship" on matters of public import. . . .

Speech deals with matters of public concern when it can "be fairly considered as relating to any matter of political, social, or other concern to the community," or when it "is a subject of legitimate news interest; that is, a subject of general interest and of value and concern to the public." The arguably "inappropriate or controversial character of a statement is irrelevant to the question whether it deals with a matter of public concern." Our opinion in *Dun & Bradstreet,* on the other hand, provides an example of speech of only private concern. In that case we held, as a general matter, that information about a particular individual's credit report "concerns no public issue." The content of the report, we explained, "was speech solely in the individual interest of the speaker and its specific business audience." That was confirmed by the fact that the particular report was sent to only five subscribers to the reporting service, who were bound not to disseminate it further. To cite another example, we concluded in *San Diego v. Roe* that, in the context of a government employer regulating the speech of its employees, videos of an employee engaging in sexually explicit acts did not address a public concern; the videos "did nothing to inform the public about any aspect of the [employing agency's] functioning or operation."

Deciding whether speech is of public or private concern requires us to examine the "'content, form, and context' " of that speech, " 'as revealed by the whole record.' " As in other First Amendment cases, the court is obligated "to 'make an independent examination of the whole record' in order to make sure that 'the judgment does not constitute a forbidden intrusion on the field of free expression.' " . . .

The "content" of Westboro's signs plainly relates to broad issues of interest to society at large, rather than matters of "purely private concern." The placards read "God Hates the USA/Thank God for 9/11," "America is Doomed," "Don't Pray for the USA," "Thank God for IEDs," "Fag Troops," "Semper Fi Fags," "God Hates Fags," "Maryland Taliban," "Fags Doom Nations," "Not Blessed Just Cursed," "Thank God for Dead Soldiers," "Pope in Hell," "Priests Rape Boys," "You're Going to Hell," and "God Hates You." While these messages may fall short of refined social or political commentary, the issues they highlight—the political and moral conduct of the United States and its citizens, the fate of our Nation, homosexuality in the military, and scandals involving the Catholic clergy—are matters of public import. . . .

Westboro's choice to convey its views in conjunction with Matthew Snyder's funeral made the expression of those views particularly hurtful to many, especially to Matthew's father. The record makes clear that the applicable legal term—"emotional distress"—fails to capture fully the anguish Westboro's choice added to Mr. Snyder's already incalculable grief. But Westboro conducted its picketing peacefully on matters of public concern at a public place adjacent to a public street. Such space occupies a "special position in terms of First Amendment protection." . . .

Simply put, the church members had the right to be where they were. Westboro alerted local authorities to its funeral protest and fully complied with police guidance on where the picketing could be staged. The picketing was conducted under police supervision some 1,000 feet from the church, out of the sight of those at the church. The protest was not unruly; there was no shouting, profanity, or violence. . . .

Given that Westboro's speech was at a public place on a matter of public concern, that speech is entitled to "special protection" under the First Amendment. Such speech cannot be restricted simply because it is upsetting or arouses contempt. "If there is a bedrock principle underlying the First Amendment, it is that the government may not prohibit the expression of an idea simply because society finds the idea itself offensive or disagreeable." . . .

For all these reasons, the jury verdict imposing tort liability on Westboro for intentional infliction of emotional distress must be set aside. . . .

Westboro believes that America is morally flawed; many Americans might feel the same about Westboro. Westboro's funeral picketing is certainly hurtful and its contribution to public discourse may be negligible. But Westboro addressed matters of public import on public property, in a peaceful manner, in full compliance with the guidance of local officials. The speech was indeed planned to coincide with Matthew Snyder's funeral, but did not itself disrupt that funeral, and Westboro's choice to conduct its picketing at that time and place did not alter the nature of its speech.

Speech is powerful. It can stir people to action, move them to tears of both joy and sorrow, and—as it did here—inflict great pain. On the facts before us, we cannot react to that pain by punishing the speaker. As a Nation we have chosen a different course—to protect even hurtful speech on public issues to ensure that we do not stifle public debate. That choice requires that we shield Westboro from tort liability for its picketing in this case.

## Justice ALITO, dissenting.

Our profound national commitment to free and open debate is not a license for the vicious verbal assault that occurred in this case.

Petitioner Albert Snyder is not a public figure. He is simply a parent whose son, Marine Lance Corporal Matthew Snyder, was killed in Iraq. Mr. Snyder wanted what is surely the right of any parent who experiences such an incalculable loss: to bury his son in peace. But respondents, members of the Westboro Baptist Church, deprived him of that elementary right. They first issued a press release and thus turned Matthew's funeral into a tumultuous media event. They then appeared at the church, approached as closely as they could without trespassing, and launched a malevolent verbal attack on Matthew and his family at a time of acute emotional vulnerability. As a result, Albert Snyder suffered severe and lasting emotional injury. The Court now holds that the First Amendment protected respondents' right to brutalize Mr. Snyder. I cannot agree.

Respondents and other members of their church have strong opinions on certain moral, religious, and political issues, and the First Amendment ensures that they have almost limitless opportunities to express their views. They may write and distribute books, articles, and other texts; they may create and disseminate video and audio recordings; they may circulate petitions; they may speak to individuals and groups in public forums and in any private venue that wishes to accommodate them; they may picket peacefully in countless locations; they may appear on television and speak on the radio; they may post messages on the Internet and send out e-mails. And they may express their views in terms that are "uninhibited," "vehement," and "caustic."

It does not follow, however, that they may intentionally inflict severe emotional injury on private persons at a time of intense emotional sensitivity by launching vicious verbal attacks that make no contribution to public debate. To protect against such injury, "most if not all jurisdictions" permit recovery in tort for the intentional infliction of emotional distress (or IIED). . . .

. . .

The Court concludes that respondents' speech was protected by the First Amendment for essentially three reasons, but none is sound.

First—and most important—the Court finds that "the overall thrust and dominant theme of [their] demonstration spoke to" broad public issues. As I have attempted to show, this portrayal is quite inaccurate; respondents' attack on Matthew was of central importance. But in any event, I fail to see why actionable speech should be immunized simply because it is interspersed with speech that is protected. The First Amendment allows recovery for defamatory statements that are interspersed with nondefamatory statements on matters of public concern, and there is no good reason why respondents' attack on Matthew Snyder and his family should be treated differently.

Second, the Court suggests that respondents' personal attack on Matthew Snyder is entitled to First Amendment protection because it was not motivated by a private grudge, but I see no basis for the strange distinction that the Court appears to draw. Respondents' motivation—"to increase publicity for its views," —did not transform their statements attacking the character of a private figure into statements that made a contribution to debate on matters of public concern. Nor did their publicity-seeking motivation soften the sting of their attack. And as far as culpability is concerned, one might well think that wounding statements uttered in the heat of a private feud are less, not more, blameworthy than similar statements made as part of a cold and calculated strategy to slash a stranger as a means of attracting public attention.

Third, the Court finds it significant that respondents' protest occurred on a public street, but this fact alone should not be enough to preclude IIED liability. To be sure, statements made on a public street may be less likely to satisfy the elements of the IIED tort than statements made on private property, but there is no reason why a public street in close proximity to the scene of a funeral should be regarded as a free-fire zone in which otherwise actionable verbal attacks are shielded from liability. If the First Amendment permits the States to protect their residents from the harm inflicted by such attacks—and the Court does not hold otherwise—then the location of the tort should not be dispositive. A physical assault may occur without trespassing; it is no defense that the perpetrator had "the right to be where [he was]." And the same should be true with respect to unprotected speech. Neither classic "fighting words" nor defamatory statements are immunized when they occur in a public place, and there is no good reason to treat a verbal assault based on the conduct or character of a private figure like Matthew Snyder any differently.

One final comment about the opinion of the Court is in order. The Court suggests that the wounds inflicted by vicious verbal assaults at funerals will be prevented or at least mitigated in the future by new laws that restrict picketing within a specified distance of a funeral. It is apparent, however, that the enactment of these laws is no substitute for the protection provided by the established IIED tort; according to the Court, the verbal attacks that severely wounded petitioner in this case complied with the new Maryland law regulating funeral picketing. And there is absolutely nothing to suggest that Congress and the state legislatures, in enacting these laws, intended them to displace the protection provided by the well-established IIED tort.

The real significance of these new laws is not that they obviate the need for IIED protection. Rather, their enactment dramatically illustrates the fundamental point that funerals are unique events at which special protection against emotional assaults is in order. At funerals, the emotional well-being of bereaved relatives is particularly vulnerable. Exploitation of a funeral for the purpose of attracting public attention "intrud[es] upon their . . . grief," and may permanently stain their memories of the final moments before a loved one is laid to rest. Allowing family members to have a few hours of peace without harassment does not undermine public debate. I would therefore hold that, in this setting, the First Amendment permits a private figure to recover for the intentional infliction of emotional distress caused by speech on a matter of private concern. . . .

## Bibliography

Zipursky, Benjamin C. "*Snyder v. Phelps,* Outrageousness, and the Open Texture of Tort Law." *DePaul Law Review* 60 (2011): 473.

# OBSCENITY

Obscene expression, like defamation, traditionally has been categorically unprotected by the First Amendment. At the time of the nation's founding, state laws prohibiting vulgar, profane, and obscene expression were commonplace. Federal regulation of obscenity traces back to the *Comstock Act of 1875,* which criminalized dissemination of obscenity through the mail. In its seminal decision on obscenity, *Roth v. United States* (1957), the Supreme Court held that the social value of obscenity was too slight to deserve First Amendment protection. Despite its consistency on this point, the Court has found itself challenged in trying to define obscenity. Reflecting the exasperation experienced by the Court in trying to capture obscenity in an objectifiable manner was Justice Potter Stewart's observation, in *Jacobellis v. Ohio* (1964), that, even if he could not describe obscenity, "I know it when I see it." After years of frustration, the Court in *Miller v. California* (1973) set forth a framework for defining and determining obscenity. In *New York v. Ferber* (1982), the Court determined that child pornography, even if not obscene under *Miller,* could be categorically prohibited without offense to the First Amendment.

## Miller v. California

**Citation: 413 U.S. 15.**

**Issue: Whether expression must be utterly lacking in redeeming social value to be found obscene.**

**Year of Decision: 1973.**

**Outcome: The state is not obligated to demonstrate that allegedly obscene material is "utterly without redeeming social value."**

**Author of Opinion: Chief Justice Earl Warren.**

**Vote: 5-4.**

Obscene expression is entirely without First Amendment protection. This outcast status was established by the Supreme Court's decision, in *Roth v. United States* (1957), when it determined that obscenity had "slight, if any, value." The Court's decision to place obscenity outside the boundaries of constitutionally protected expression has eliminated virtually any barrier to regulating it. It has not, however, foreclosed continuing controversy and litigation. Even though obscenity is not sheltered by the First Amendment, constitutionally significant problems arise in relationship to it. Foremost among these difficulties is the challenge of defining obscenity.

The vexing nature of this problem quickly manifested itself in the aftermath of the *Roth* decision. For more than a decade, the Court struggled to develop a consensus for determining whether expression was obscene. Justice Potter Stewart effectively captured the nature of the task when he suggested that efforts to capture the meaning of obscenity required "trying to define what may be undefinable." Expressing his sense of futility with attempts to define obscenity, Justice Stewart operated on the premise that "I know it when I see it."

In *Memoirs v. Massachusetts* (1966), three justices advocated a test that would require the government to establish that (a) the dominant theme of the material taken as a whole appeals to a prurient interest in sex; (b) the material is patently offensive because it affronts contemporary community standards relating to the description of representation of sexual matters; and (c) the material is utterly without redeeming social value.

As the Court continued to decide obscenity cases without a precise and settled definition, it increasingly was subject to criticism that it was operating without a standard. Chief Justice Warren Burger described the Court's function essentially as "an unreviewable board of censorship for the 50 states, subjectively judging each piece of material brought before us." Against this backdrop, and to reduce the "strain" of a steady flow of obscenity cases into the judicial system, the Court attempted to resolve the definitional problem. The case that led to a majority rule in this regard was *Miller v. California* (1973). In this case, the Court reviewed a criminal conviction based upon mailing advertisements "very explicitly depicting men and women in groups of two or more engaging in a variety of sexual activities, with genitals often prominently displayed." Charges were based upon a California law prohibiting the knowing distribution of obscene materials.

Chief Justice Warren Burger commenced his opinion for a majority of the Court with the premise that state regulation of obscenity "must be carefully limited" and confined "to works which depict or describe sexual conduct." Consistent with this premise, Chief Justice Burger noted that the proscribed conduct must be defined specifically. He then proceeded to announce a definition of obscenity covering "works which, taken as a whole, appeal to the prurient interest in sex, which portray sexual conduct in a patently offensive way, and which, taken as a whole, do not have serious literary, artistic, political, or scientific value." This definition was coupled with guidelines that would aid juries in applying it. The definition of "prurient interest," for example, should be developed from the perspective of "the average person, applying contemporary community standards." Whether a work was patently offensive should be assessed in conjunction with legislation that "specifically defined" the relevant sexual conduct. It also abandoned an inquiry into whether a work was "utterly without redeeming social value" into a determination of whether taken as a whole it "lacked serious literary, artistic, political, or scientific value."

Disclaiming any "function to propose regulatory schemes for the States," the Court stated that the states themselves have the responsibility for specifically defining the type of sexual expression that could be prohibited. Even so, it offered a model regulation that states could use to satisfy the specificity requirement. Pursuant to the Court's formula, portrayal of sexual conduct could be prohibited by specific language barring "[p]atently offensive representations or descriptions of ultimate sexual acts, normal or perverted, actual or simulated" and "[p]atently offensive representation of descriptions of masturbation, excretory functions, and lewd exhibition of the genitals." A critical aspect of the majority's opinion was that "[s]ex and nudity may not be exploited without limit by films and pictures." At a minimum, therefore, prurient and patently offensive depictions of sexual conduct must have serious literary, artistic, political, or scientific value to receive First Amendment protection. An easy example of protected expression in this context would be "medical books for the education of physicians." Despite their "graphic illustrations and descriptions of human anatomy," these publications have obvious scientific value. Arguably, they also do not appeal to the prurient interest and do not contain patently offensive representations of sexual acts or other specifically described sexual conduct.

Use of contemporary community standards, for purposes of assessing prurient interest and patent offensiveness, represented an effort by the Court to move the question of obscenity from a national to a local forum. It also reflected a sense that a universal standard for determining obscenity is difficult in a society that is "too big and too diverse." The Court accordingly concluded that it could not establish a constitutional standard requiring "that the people of Maine or Mississippi accept public depiction of conduct found tolerable in Las Vegas, or New York City." The Court's new model thus was informed by an understanding that "[p]eople in different States vary in their tastes and attitudes, and this diversity is not to be strangled by the absolutism of imposed uniformity." Responding to concern that it was embracing a standard of "repression," the Court maintained that prohibition of obscenity historically had not burdened serious literary, artistic, political, or scientific expression. Given what it saw as the First Amendment's concern with speech critical to informed self-governance, the Court saw no risk that political liberty would be compromised by state efforts to regulate "commercial exploitation of human interest in sex." Rather, the Court concluded that assigning value to obscenity would cheapen "the grand conception of the First Amendment and its high purposes in the historic struggle for freedom."

Despite describing the majority's opinion as "earnest and well intentioned," Justice William O. Douglas reiterated his sense that the First Amendment was an absolute barrier against content-based regulation. From his perspective, the First Amendment unconditionally protected speech and precluded the Court's removal of some speech from its protective reach. Given the operation of the First Amendment as he viewed it, Justice Douglas argued that no "regime of censorship" could be implemented except "by constitutional amendment after full debate by the people." He also found it "astounding" that a judge or jury could punish ideas on grounds they are offensive. This capacity, as Justice Douglas saw it, was "a sharp and radical break with the traditions of a free society" which keep debate open to "offensive" as well as "staid" people. Even if the expression might be described as "garbage," Justice Douglas observed that "so is much of what is said in political campaigns, in the daily press, on TV, or over the radio." In this regard, Justice Douglas's main concern was with the potential for expanding power to regulate speech based upon its capacity to offend. Justice Douglas concluded that judges are without constitutional power to define obscenity, and despite its definitional efforts, still had no guidelines "except our own predilections."

Justice William Brennan, who authored the majority opinion in *Roth* finding that obscenity was constitutionally unprotected, concluded that the Court's case law had become demonstrably misconceived. As he viewed it, the problem of defining obscenity was too great and the constitutional costs of applying vague standards too high. Justice Brennan, in repudiating his original position and the majority's current thinking, suggested that obscenity concerns should be restricted to instances when the interests of children and nonconsenting adults were present.

Despite the dissenting views, the *Miller* decision is a cornerstone of modern obscenity law. Despite the *Miller* Court's objective, the problem of constructing a precise definition of obscenity remains. Justice Antonin Scalia has suggested that "[j]ust as there is no use arguing about taste, there is no use litigating about it." Despite persisting concern that the Court has foreclosed constitutional inquiry in the context of obscenity, some theorists have advocated restrictive regime based not upon obscenity's lack of value but upon the harm that it causes to women. In the 1980s, several communities adopted ordinances pursuant to the premise that pornography facilitates the subordination of women by characterizing them as sex objects and reinforcing harmful ways of viewing women. In striking down an Indianapolis ordinance structured on this premise, a federal appeals court in *American Booksellers, Inc. v. Hudnut* (1985) determined that freedom of speech assumes the risk that insidious expression may "influence the culture and shape our socialization." It further noted that "if a process of [cultural] conditioning were enough to permit governmental regulation, that would be the end of freedom of speech." Despite dissatisfaction from both proponents and opponents of obscenity regulation, the Court's decision in *Miller* has survived the challenges and appears to have evolved doctrine from a very uncertain to a settled status.

More recently, the Court has resisted efforts to expand the categories of unprotected speech generally, even those that may bear some resemblance to an unprotected category such as obscenity. Accordingly, the Court refused to include animal cruelty in the form of "crush videos" as an unprotected category in *United States v. Stevens*, 559 U.S. 460 (2010). The Court in *Brown v. Entertainment Merchants Association*, 131 S.Ct. 2729 (2011) also refused to categorize violence in the form of violent video games purchased by minors as an unprotected category.

### Mr. Chief Justice BURGER delivered the opinion of the Court.

. . . This much has been categorically settled by the Court, that obscene material is unprotected by the First Amendment. We acknowledge, however, the inherent dangers of undertaking to regulate any form of expression. State statutes designed to regulate obscene materials must be carefully limited. As a result, we now confine the permissible scope of such regulation to works which depict or describe sexual conduct. That conduct must be specifically defined by the applicable state law, as written or authoritatively construed. A state offense must also be limited to works which, taken as a whole, appeal to the prurient interest in sex, which portray sexual conduct in a patently offensive way, and which, taken as a whole, do not have serious literary, artistic, political, or scientific value.

The basic guidelines for the trier of fact must be: (a) whether 'the average person, applying contemporary community standards' would find that the work, taken as a whole, appeals to the prurient interest; (b) whether the work depicts or describes, in a patently offensive way, sexual conduct specifically defined by the applicable state law; and (c) whether the work, taken as a whole, lacks serious literary, artistic, political, or scientific value. We do not adopt as a constitutional standard the 'utterly without redeeming social value' test of *Memoirs v. Massachusetts,* that concept has never commanded the adherence of more than three Justices at one time. If a state law that regulates obscene material is thus limited, as written or construed, the First Amendment values applicable to the States through the Fourteenth Amendment are adequately protected by the ultimate power of appellate courts to conduct an independent review of constitutional claims when necessary.

We emphasize that it is not our function to propose regulatory schemes for the States. That must await their concrete legislative efforts. It is possible, however, to give a few plain examples of what a state statute could define for regulation under part (b) of the standard announced in this opinion, supra:

(a) Patently offensive representations or descriptions of ultimate sexual acts, normal or perverted, actual or simulated.
(b) Patently offensive representation or descriptions of masturbation, excretory functions, and lewd exhibition of the genitals.

Sex and nudity may not be exploited without limit by films or pictures exhibited or sold in places of public accommodation any more than live sex and nudity can be exhibited or sold without limit in such public places. At a minimum, prurient, patently offensive depiction or description of sexual conduct must have serious literary, artistic, political, or scientific value to merit First Amendment protection. For example, medical books for the education of physicians and related personnel necessarily use graphic illustrations and descriptions of human anatomy. In resolving the inevitably sensitive questions of fact and law, we must continue to rely on the jury system, accompanied by the safeguards that judges, rules of evidence, presumption of innocence, and other protective features provide, as we do with rape, murder, and a host of other offenses against society and its individual members. . . .

Under the holdings announced today, no one will be subject to prosecution for the sale or exposure of obscene materials unless these materials depict or describe patently offensive 'hard core' sexual conduct specifically defined by the regulating state law, as written or construed. We are satisfied that these specific prerequisites will provide fair notice to a dealer in such materials that his public and commercial activities may bring prosecution. If the inability to define regulated materials with ultimate, god-like precision altogether removes the power of the States or the Congress to regulate, then 'hard core' pornography may be exposed without limit to the juvenile, the passerby, and the consenting adult alike, as, indeed, Mr. Justice Douglas contends. In this belief, however, Mr. Justice Douglas now stands alone. . . .

This may not be an easy road, free from difficulty. But no amount of 'fatigue' should lead us to adopt a convenient 'institutional' rationale—an absolutist, 'anything goes' view of the First Amendment—because it will lighten our burdens. 'Such an abnegation of judicial supervision in this field would be inconsistent with our duty to uphold the constitutional guarantees.' Nor should we remedy 'tension between state and federal courts' by arbitrarily depriving the States of a power reserved to them under the Constitution, a power which they have enjoyed and exercised continuously from before the adoption of the First Amendment to this day.

## Mr. Justice DOUGLAS, dissenting.

Today we leave open the way for California to send a man to prison for distributing brochures that advertise books and a movie under freshly written standards defining obscenity which until today's decision were never the part of any law.

The Court has worked hard to define obscenity and concededly has failed. In *Roth v. United States*, it ruled that '(o)bscene material is material which deals with sex in a manner appealing to prurient interest.' Obscenity, it was said, was rejected by the First Amendment because it is 'utterly without redeeming social importance.' . . .

Today we would add a new three-pronged test: '(a) whether 'the average person, applying contemporary community standards' would find that the work, taken as a whole, appeals to the prurient interest, . . . (b) whether the work depicts or describes, in a patently offensive way, sexual conduct specifically defined by the applicable state law, and (c) whether the work, taken as a whole, lacks serious literary, artistic, political, or scientific value.'

Those are the standards we ourselves have written into the Constitution. Yet how under these vague tests can we sustain convictions for the sale of an article prior to the time when some court has declared it to be obscene?

Today the Court retreats from the earlier formulations of the constitutional test and undertakes to make new definitions. This effort, like the earlier ones, is earnest and well intentioned. The difficulty is that we do not deal with constitutional terms, since 'obscenity' is not mentioned in the Constitution or Bill of Rights. And the First Amendment makes no such exception from 'the press' which it undertakes to protect nor, as I have said on other occasions, is an exception necessarily implied, for there was no recognized exception to the free press at the time the Bill of Rights was adopted which treated 'obscene' publications differently from other types of papers, magazines, and books. So there are no constitutional guidelines for deciding what is and what is not 'obscene.' The Court is at large because we deal with tastes and standards of literature. What shocks me may be sustenance for my neighbor. What causes one person to boil up in rage over one pamphlet or movie may reflect only his neurosis, not shared by others. We deal here with a regime of censorship which, if adopted, should be done by constitutional amendment after full debate by the people.

Obscenity cases usually generate tremendous emotional outbursts. They have no business being in the courts. If a constitutional amendment authorized censorship, the censor would probably be an administrative agency. Then criminal prosecutions could follow as, if, and when publishers defied the censor and sold their literature. Under that regime a publisher would know when he was on dangerous ground. Under the present regime—whether the old standards or the new ones are used—the criminal law becomes a trap. A brand new test would put a publisher behind bars under a new law improvised by the courts after the publication. That was done in *Ginzburg* and has all the evils of an ex post facto law.

My contention is that until a civil proceeding has placed a tract beyond the pale, no criminal prosecution should be sustained. For no more vivid illustration of vague and uncertain laws could be designed than those we have fashioned. . . .

If a specific book, play, paper, or motion picture has in a civil proceeding been condemned as obscene and review of that finding has been completed, and thereafter a person publishers, shows, or displays that particular book or film, then a vague law has been made specific. There would remain the underlying question whether the First Amendment allows an implied exception in the case of obscenity. I do not think it does and my views on the issue have been stated over and over again. But at least a criminal prosecution brought at that juncture would not violate the time-honored void-for-vagueness test.

No such protective procedure has been designed by California in this case. Obscenity—which even we cannot define with precision—is a hodge-podge. To send men to jail for violating standards they cannot understand, construe, and apply is a monstrous thing to do in a Nation dedicated to fair trials and due process. . . .

The idea that the First Amendment permits government to ban publications that are 'offensive' to some people puts an ominous gloss on freedom of the press. That test would make it possible to ban any paper or any journal or magazine in some benighted place. The First Amendment was designed 'to invite dispute,' to induce 'a condition of unrest,' to 'create dissatisfaction with conditions as they are,' and even to stir 'people' to anger.' The idea that the First Amendment permits punishment for ideas that are 'offensive' to the particular judge or jury sitting in judgment is astounding. No greater leveler of speech or literature has ever been designed. To give the power to the censor, as we do today, is to make a sharp and radical break with the traditions of a free society. The First Amendment was not fashioned as a vehicle for dispensing tranquilizers to the people. Its prime function was to keep debate open to 'offensive' as well as to 'staid' people. The tendency throughout history has been to subdue the individual and to exalt the power of government. The use of the standard 'offensive' gives authority to government that cuts the very vitals out of the First Amendment. As is intimated by the Court's opinion, the materials before us may be garbage. But so is much of what is said in political campaigns, in the daily press, on TV, or over the radio. By reason of the First Amendment—and solely because of it—speakers and publishers have not been threatened or subdued because their thoughts and ideas may be 'offensive' to some. . . .

'Conduct that annoys some people does not annoy others. Thus, the ordinance is vague, not in the sense that it requires a person to conform his conduct to an imprecise but comprehensive normative standard, but rather in the sense that no standard of conduct is specified at all.'

How we can deny Ohio the convenience of punishing people who 'annoy' others and allow California power to punish people who publish materials 'offensive' to some people is difficult to square with constitutional requirements.

If there are to be restraints on what is obscene, then a constitutional amendment should be the way of achieving the end. There are societies where religion and mathematics are the only free segments. It would be a dark day for America if that were our destiny. But the people can make it such if they choose to write obscenity into the Constitution and define it.

We deal with highly emotional, not rational, questions. To many the Song of Solomon is obscene. I do not think we, the judges, were ever given the constitutional power to make definitions of obscenity. If it is to be defined, let the people debate and decide by a constitutional amendment what they want to ban as obscene and what standards they want the legislatures and the courts to apply. Perhaps the people will decide that the path towards a mature, integrated society requires that all ideas competing for acceptance must have no censor. Perhaps they will decide otherwise. Whatever the choice, the courts will have some guidelines. Now we have none except our own predilections.

## Bibliography

Brownmiller, Susan. *Against Our Will: Men, Women and Rape.* New York: Bantam Books, 1976.

Posner, Richard. *Sex and Reason.* Cambridge, MA: Harvard University Press, 1992.

Schauer, Frederick. "Causation Theory and the Cases of Sexual Violence." *American Bar Foundation Research Journal* 737 (1987).

Strossen, Nadine. *Defending Pornography.* New York: Scribner, 1995.

# *New York v. Ferber*

**Citation: 458 U.S. 747.**

**Issue: Whether child pornography (e.g., depictions of children engaged in sexual conduct) that is not necessarily obscene can be prohibited consistently with the First Amendment to the United States Constitution.**

**Year of Decision: 1982.**

**Outcome: Child pornography fits in a category of speech that derives no protection under the First Amendment because of the harm to, and exploitation of, children in its production.**

**Author of Opinion: Justice Byron White.**

**Vote: 9-0.**

Although the First Amendment provides broad protection for freedom of speech, there has been much dispute about whether its protections are "absolute" or "qualified." Justice Black, the leading proponent of the absolutist position, argued in *Konigsberg v. State Bar of California,* 366 U.S. 36 (1961), that the "unequivocal command that there shall be no abridgement of the rights of free speech and assembly shows that [those] who drafted our Bill of Rights did all the 'balancing' that was to be done in this field. [The] very object of adopting the First Amendment [was] to put the freedoms protected there completely out of the area of any congressional control that may be attempted through the exercise of precisely those powers that are now being used to 'balance' the Bill of Rights out of existence." Justice Oliver Wendell Holmes disagreed and offered his now famous statement that "[t]he most stringent protection of free speech would not protect a man in falsely shouting fire in a theater and causing a panic." *See Schenck v. United States,* 249 U.S. 47 (1919). Justice Holmes's position ultimately prevailed in the United States Supreme Court.

Once the Court recognized that First Amendment protections were not absolute, the Court then focused on whether particular categories of speech fall outside the parameters of constitutional protection. In *Chaplinsky v. New Hampshire,* 315 U.S. 568 (1942), the Court held that there are "certain well-defined and narrowly limited *classes* of speech, the prevention and punishment of which have never been thought to raise any Constitutional problem. These include the lewd and obscene, the profane, the libelous, and the insulting or 'fighting' words. . . ." While the Court no longer treats all of the *Chaplinsky* classifications as beyond constitutional protection (e.g., defamatory speech is now protected), the Court continues to hold that certain categories of speech receive no constitutional protection.

*New York v. Ferber* concerns one category of unprotected speech: child pornography. *Ferber* involved a New York criminal statute that prohibited persons from knowingly promoting sexual performances by children under the age of 16 through the distribution of such performances. The law was passed in an effort to combat the exploitive use of children in the production of pornography, and applied to both obscene and nonobscene depictions of child pornography. Violations could be prosecuted as class D felonies.

The case arose when Paul Ferber, the proprietor of a Manhattan bookstore specializing in sexually oriented products, sold two films to an undercover police officer that depicted young boys masturbating. Although Ferber was acquitted of possessing obscene materials, he was convicted for possession of nonobscene child pornography. In upholding Ferber's conviction, the United States Supreme Court emphasized that the states have a "compelling" interest in "safeguarding the physical and psychological well-being" of minors, and that the New York law was based on concerns about such exploitation and the proliferation of sexual performances that exploit children. The Court refused to "second-guess this legislative judgment."

In reaching its decision, the Court found that the "distribution of photographs and films depicting sexual activity by juveniles is intrinsically related to the sexual abuse of children in at least two ways." First, the materials themselves constitute a "permanent record of the children's participation, and the harm to the child is exacerbated by their circulation." Second, the "distribution network for child pornography must be closed if the production of material which requires the sexual exploitation of children is to be effectively controlled." The Court found that the "most expeditious if not the only practical method of law enforcement may be to dry up the market for this material by imposing severe criminal penalties on persons selling, advertising, or otherwise promoting the product."

The Court concluded that the state could not be limited to simply prosecuting those who distribute materials that are legally obscene, because children could be harmed physically or psychologically even by the production of nonobscene works. Moreover, the Court concluded that there was an economic motive for the production.

The Court also concluded that, in the hierarchy of free speech values, the value of child pornography (which the Court defined as "lewd sexual conduct") was "*de minimis.*" While the Court conceded that there might be instances in which depictions of children "performing sexual acts or lewdly exhibiting their genitals" might form an "important and necessary part of a literary performance or scientific or educational work," the Court doubted whether this would often be so. Moreover, the Court noted that, if such representation were an "important and necessary" part of a performance, an older person (who appeared younger) could be used in place of a child.

The Court did not hold child pornography was entitled to no protection under the First Amendment. On the contrary, the Court flatly stated that, in order to have a valid prohibition, the "conduct to be prohibited must be adequately defined by the applicable state law, as written or authoritatively construed," that a valid statute must be limited to visual depictions of sexual conduct of children below a specified age, and that the definition of sexual conduct must be "suitably limited and described." Finally, a valid statute must contain an element of scienter. Finally, Court reaffirmed the proposition that other depictions of sexual conduct retain First Amendment protection.

*Ferber* produced a couple of major concurrences. Justice Sandra Day O'Connor argued that the state has a compelling interest in prohibiting child pornography that might allow it to ban child pornography regardless of its social value. However, she would have exempted "depictions that do not actually threaten the harms identified by the Court including clinical pictures of sexuality, such as those that might appear in medical textbooks, if they do not involve sexual exploitation and abuse." She also argued that "pictures of children engaged in rites widely approved by their cultures, such as those that might appear in issues of the National Geographic, might not trigger the compelling interests identified by the Court." Justice

Brennan, joined by Justice Thurgood Marshall, also concurred arguing that the "State has a special interest in protecting the well-being of its youth" and states should have leeway in their regulation unless a depiction has "serious literary, artistic, scientific, or medical value." He viewed child pornography as one of those "limited classes of speech, the suppression of which does not raise serious First Amendment concerns" since it has "slight social value" and since the State has a compelling interest in regulation. However, he distinguished child pornography from "serious contributions" to art, literature, and science."

*Ferber* is a significant contribution to First Amendment jurisprudence. *Ferber* reaffirms *Chaplinsky*'s conclusion that certain categories of speech deserve no constitutional protection, and *Ferber* creates a new category of unprotected speech, child pornography.

### Justice WHITE delivered the opinion of the Court.

At issue in this case is the constitutionality of a New York criminal statute which prohibits persons from knowingly promoting sexual performances by children under the age of 16 by distributing material which depicts such performances. . . .

The *Miller* standard, like its predecessors, was an accommodation between the State's interests in protecting the "sensibilities of unwilling recipients" from exposure to pornographic material and the dangers of censorship inherent in unabashedly content-based laws. Like obscenity statutes, laws directed at the dissemination of child pornography run the risk of suppressing protected expression by allowing the hand of the censor to become unduly heavy. For the following reasons, however, we are persuaded that the States are entitled to greater leeway in the regulation of pornographic depictions of children.

*First.* It is evident beyond the need for elaboration that a State's interest in "safeguarding the physical and psychological well-being of a minor" is "compelling." Accordingly, we have sustained legislation aimed at protecting the physical and emotional well-being of youth even when the laws have operated in the sensitive area of constitutionally protected rights. In *Prince v. Massachusetts,* the Court held that a statute prohibiting use of a child to distribute literature on the street was valid notwithstanding the statute's effect on a First Amendment activity. . . Most recently, we held that the Government's interest in the "well-being of its youth" justified special treatment of indecent broadcasting received by adults as well as children. . . .

*Second.* The distribution of photographs and films depicting sexual activity by juveniles is intrinsically related to the sexual abuse of children in at least two ways. First, the materials produced are a permanent record of the children's participation and the harm to the child is exacerbated by their circulation. Second, the distribution network for child pornography must be closed if the production of material which requires the sexual exploitation of children is to be effectively controlled. Indeed, there is no serious contention that the legislature was unjustified in believing that it is difficult, if not impossible, to halt the exploitation of children by pursuing only those who produce the photographs and movies. While the production of pornographic materials is a low-profile, clandestine industry, the need to market the resulting products requires a visible apparatus of distribution. The most expeditious if not the only practical method of law enforcement may be to dry up the market for this material by imposing severe criminal penalties on persons selling, advertising, or otherwise promoting the product. . . .Respondent does not contend that the State is unjustified in pursuing those who distribute child pornography. Rather, he argues that it is enough for the State to prohibit the distribution of materials that are legally obscene under the *Miller* test. While some States may find that this approach properly accommodates its interests, it does not follow that the First Amendment prohibits a State from going further. The *Miller* standard, like all general definitions of what may be banned as obscene, does not reflect the State's particular and more compelling interest in prosecuting those who promote the sexual exploitation of children. Thus, the question under the *Miller* test of whether a work, taken as a whole, appeals to the prurient interest of the average person bears no connection to the issue of whether a child has been physically or psychologically harmed in the production of the work. Similarly, a sexually explicit depiction need not be "patently offensive" in order to have required the sexual exploitation of a child for its production. In addition, a work which, taken on the whole, contains serious literary, artistic, political, or scientific value may nevertheless embody the hardest core of child pornography. "It is irrelevant to the child [who has been abused] whether or not the material . . . has a literary, artistic, political or social value." We therefore cannot conclude that the *Miller* standard is a satisfactory solution to the child pornography problem.

*Third.* The advertising and selling of child pornography provide an economic motive for and are thus an integral part of the production of such materials, an activity illegal throughout the Nation. . . We note that were the statutes outlawing the employment of children in these films and photographs fully effective, and the constitutionality of these laws has not been questioned, the First Amendment implications would be no greater than that presented by laws against distribution: enforceable production laws would leave no child pornography to be marketed.

*Fourth.* The value of permitting live performances and photographic reproductions of children engaged in lewd sexual conduct is exceedingly modest, if not *de minimis.* We consider it unlikely that visual depictions of children performing sexual acts or lewdly exhibiting their genitals would often constitute an important and necessary part of a literary performance or scientific or educational work. . . .

*Fifth.* Recognizing and classifying child pornography as a category of material outside the protection of the First Amendment is not incompatible with our earlier decisions. Thus, it is not rare that a content-based classification of speech has been accepted because it may be appropriately generalized that within the confines of the given classification, the evil to be restricted so overwhelmingly outweighs the expressive interests, if any, at stake, that no process of case-by-case adjudication is required. When a definable class of material, such as that covered by [the State's law], bears so heavily and pervasively on the welfare of children engaged in its production, we think the balance of competing interests is clearly struck and that it is permissible to consider these materials as without the protection of the First Amendment.

There are, of course, limits on the category of child pornography which, like obscenity, is unprotected by the First Amendment. As with all legislation in this sensitive area, the conduct to be prohibited must be adequately defined by the applicable state law, as written or authoritatively construed. Here the nature of the harm to be combated requires that the state offense be limited to works that *visually* depict sexual conduct by children below a specified age. The category of "sexual conduct" proscribed must also be suitably limited and described. . . .

[The State law's] prohibition incorporates a definition of sexual conduct that comports with the above-stated principles. The forbidden acts to be depicted are listed with sufficient precision and represent the kind of conduct that, if it were the theme of a work, could render it legally obscene: "actual or simulated sexual intercourse, deviate sexual intercourse, sexual bestiality, masturbation, sado-masochistic abuse, or lewd exhibition of the genitals." . . .

We hold that [the State law] sufficiently describes a category of material the production and distribution of which is not entitled to First Amendment protection. It is therefore clear that there is nothing unconstitutionally "underinclusive" about a statute that singles out this category of material for proscription. It also follows that the State is not barred by the First Amendment from prohibiting the distribution of unprotected materials produced outside the State.

### Bibliography

Caughlan, Susan G. "Private Possession of Child Pornography: The Tensions Between *Stanley v. Georgia* and *New York v. Ferber*." 29 *William and Mary Law Review* 187 (1987).

Green, William. "Children and Pornography: An Interest Analysis in System Perspective." *Valparaiso University Law Review* 19 (1985): 441.

Schauer, Frederick. "Codifying the First Amendment: *New York v. Ferber*." *Supreme Court Review* 285 (1982).

Weaver, Russell L., and Donald E. Lively. *Understanding the First Amendment*. Newark, NJ: LexisNexis, 2012, 64–70.

## *United States v. Stevens*

**Citation: 559 U.S. 460.**

**Issue: Whether a Congressional law criminalizing the commercial creation, sale, or possession of certain depictions of animal cruelty violates the First Amendment guarantee of free speech.**

**Year of Decision: 2010.**

**Outcome: Yes. As a restriction upon the content of protected speech, the law was invalid under the First Amendment because Congress could not demonstrate that it passed strict scrutiny.**

**Author of Opinion: Chief Justice John Roberts.**

**Vote: 8-1.**

Congress enacted a law criminalizing the commercial creation, sale, or possession of certain depictions of animal cruelty. The statute addresses only depictions of animal cruelty, not the underlying conduct. The law was aimed primarily at "crush videos," which show the torture and killing of helpless animals and appear to appeal to persons with a certain sexual fetish. Respondent Stevens was indicted under the law for selling videos depicting dogfighting. The Court held that depictions of animal cruelty are not categorically unprotected by the First Amendment. The Court noted those categories of speech that it has recognized as unprotected— obscenity, child pornography, fighting words, defamation, fraud, incitement—and refused to add depictions of animal cruelty to the list. Since the law was directed at the content of the speech in question, the Court subjected it to strict scrutiny and struck it down as failing to satisfy that exacting standard.

## Chief Justice ROBERTS delivered the opinion of the Court.

. . . We read [the Law] to create a criminal prohibition of alarming breadth. To begin with, the text of the statute's ban on a "depiction of animal cruelty" nowhere requires that the depicted conduct be cruel. That text applies to "any . . . depiction" in which "a living animal is intentionally maimed, mutilated, tortured, wounded, or killed." "[M]aimed, mutilated, [and] tortured" convey cruelty, but "wounded" or "killed" do not suggest any such limitation.

The Government contends that the terms in the definition should be read to require the additional element of "accompanying acts of cruelty." . . . But the phrase "wounded . . . or killed" at issue here contains little ambiguity. The Government's opening brief properly applies the ordinary meaning of these words, stating for example that to " 'kill' is 'to deprive of life.'" We agree that "wounded" and "killed" should be read according to their ordinary meaning. Nothing about that meaning requires cruelty.

While not requiring cruelty, [the Law] does require that the depicted conduct be "illegal." But this requirement does not limit [the Law] along the lines the Government suggests. There are myriad federal and state laws concerning the proper treatment of animals, but many of them are not designed to guard against animal cruelty. Protections of endangered species, for example, restrict even the humane "wound[ing] or kill[ing]" of "living animal[s]." Livestock regulations are often designed to protect the health of human beings, and hunting and fishing rules (seasons, licensure, bag limits, weight requirements) can be designed to raise revenue, preserve animal populations, or prevent accidents. The text of [the Law] draws no distinction based on the reason the intentional killing of an animal is made illegal, and includes, for example, the humane slaughter of a stolen cow.

What is more, the application of [the Law] to depictions of illegal conduct extends to conduct that is illegal in only a single jurisdiction. Under subsection (c)(1), the depicted conduct need only be illegal in "the State in which the creation, sale, or possession takes place, regardless of whether the . . . wounding . . . or killing took place in [that] State." A depiction of entirely lawful conduct runs afoul of the ban if that depiction later finds its way into another State where the same conduct is unlawful. This provision greatly expands the scope of [the Law], because although there may be "a broad societal consensus" against cruelty to animals, there is substantial disagreement on what types of conduct are properly regarded as cruel. Both views about cruelty to animals and regulations having no connection to cruelty vary widely from place to place.

In the District of Columbia, for example, all hunting is unlawful. Other jurisdictions permit or encourage hunting, and there is an enormous national market for hunting-related depictions in which a living animal is intentionally killed. Hunting periodicals have circulations in the hundreds of thousands or millions, and hunting television programs, videos, and Web sites are equally popular. The demand for hunting depictions exceeds the estimated demand for crush videos or animal fighting depictions by several orders of magnitude. Nonetheless, because the statute allows each jurisdiction to export its laws to the rest of the country, [the Law] extends to *any* magazine or video depicting lawful hunting, so long as that depiction is sold within the Nation's Capital.

Those seeking to comply with the law thus face a bewildering maze of regulations from at least 56 separate jurisdictions. . . .

. . . We therefore need not and do not decide whether a statute limited to crush videos or other depictions of extreme animal cruelty would be constitutional. We hold only that [this Law] is not so limited but is instead substantially overbroad, and therefore invalid under the First Amendment. . . .

### Justice ALITO, dissenting.

The Court strikes down in its entirety a valuable statute, 18 U.S.C. § 48, that was enacted not to suppress speech, but to prevent horrific acts of animal cruelty—in particular, the creation and commercial exploitation of "crush videos," a form of depraved entertainment that has no social value. The Court's approach, which has the practical effect of legalizing the sale of such videos and is thus likely to spur a resumption of their production, is unwarranted. Respondent was convicted under

§ 48 for selling videos depicting dogfights. On appeal, he argued, among other things, that § 48 is unconstitutional as applied to the facts of this case, and he highlighted features of those videos that might distinguish them from other dog-fight videos brought to our attention. The Court of Appeals—incorrectly, in my view—declined to decide whether § 48 is unconstitutional as applied to respondent's videos and instead reached out to hold that the statute is facially invalid. Today's decision does not endorse the Court of Appeals' reasoning, but it nevertheless strikes down § 48 using what has been aptly termed the "strong medicine" of the overbreadth doctrine.

Instead of applying the doctrine of overbreadth, I would vacate the decision below and instruct the Court of Appeals on remand to decide whether the videos that respondent sold are constitutionally protected. If the question of overbreadth is to be decided, however, I do not think the present record supports the Court's conclusion that § 48 bans a substantial quantity of protected speech. . . .

The First Amendment protects freedom of speech, but it most certainly does not protect violent criminal conduct, even if engaged in for expressive purposes. Crush videos present a highly unusual free speech issue because they are so closely linked with violent criminal conduct. The videos record the commission of violent criminal acts, and it appears that these crimes are committed for the sole purpose of creating the videos. In addition, as noted above, Congress was presented with compelling evidence that the only way of preventing these crimes was to target the sale of the videos. Under these circumstances, I cannot believe that the First Amendment commands Congress to step aside and allow the underlying crimes to continue.

The most relevant of our prior decisions is *Ferber*, which concerned child pornography. The Court there held that child pornography is not protected speech, and I believe that *Ferber*'s reasoning dictates a similar conclusion here.

In *Ferber*, an important factor—I would say the most important factor—was that child pornography involves the commission of a crime that inflicts severe personal injury to the "children who are made to engage in sexual conduct for commercial purposes." The *Ferber* Court repeatedly described the production of child pornography as child "abuse," "molestation," or "exploitation." As later noted in *Ashcroft v. Free Speech Coalition*, in *Ferber* "[t]he production of the work, not its content, was the target of the statute."

It must be acknowledged that § 48 differs from a child pornography law in an important respect: preventing the abuse of children is certainly much more important than preventing the torture of the animals used in crush videos. It was largely for this reason that the Court of Appeals concluded that *Ferber* did not support the constitutionality of § 48. But while protecting children is unquestionably *more* important than protecting animals, the Government also has a compelling interest in preventing the torture depicted in crush videos.

The animals used in crush videos are living creatures that experience excruciating pain. Our society has long banned such cruelty, which is illegal throughout the country. In *Ferber*, the Court noted that "virtually all of the States and the United States have passed legislation proscribing the production of or otherwise combating 'child pornography,' " and the Court declined to "second-guess [that] legislative judgment." Here, likewise, the Court of Appeals erred in second-guessing the legislative judgment about the importance of preventing cruelty to animals.

Section 48's ban on trafficking in crush videos also helps to enforce the criminal laws and to ensure that criminals do not profit from their crimes. We have already judged that taking the profit out of crime is a compelling interest.

In short, *Ferber* is the case that sheds the most light on the constitutionality of Congress' effort to halt the production of crush videos. Applying the principles set forth in *Ferber*, I would hold that crush videos are not protected by the First Amendment. . . .

## Bibliography

Kinsella, Elizabeth. "A Crushing Blow: *United States v. Stevens* and the Freedom to Profit from Animal Cruelty." *University of California-Davis Law Review* 43 (2009): 347.

## *Brown v. Entertainment Merchants Association*

**Citation: 131 S.Ct. 2729.**

**Issue: Whether a California law imposing restrictions on violent video games violates the First Amendment.**

**Year of Decision: 2011.**

**Outcome: Yes. A California law prohibiting the sale or rental of "violent video games" to minors, as a restriction upon content of protected speech, was invalid under the First Amendment because California could not demonstrate that it passed strict scrutiny.**

**Author of Opinion: Justice Antonin Scalia.**

**Vote: 6-3.**

The State of California passed a law restricting the sale or rental of violent video games to minors. The video-game and software industries challenged the law as a violation of the First Amendment. California sought to create a new category of unprotected speech: depictions of violence to children. But the court found that America has no tradition of specially restricting children's access to depictions of violence. The Court also found California's claim that "interactive" video games present special problems, because the player participates in the violent action through the video, to be an unpersuasive argument. Moreover, because the law was directed at suppressing the speech in question due to its content, the Court held the law up to strict scrutiny analysis. The law failed such analysis because, the Court found, psychological studies on the connection between exposure to violent video games and harmful effects on children do not prove that such exposure causes aggressive behavior among minors. Like *Stevens*, *Brown* shows the Court's continued reluctance to expand the categories of unprotected speech.

## Justice SCALIA delivered the opinion of the Court.

We consider whether a California law imposing restrictions on violent video games comports with the First Amendment. . . .

California correctly acknowledges that video games qualify for First Amendment protection. The Free Speech Clause exists principally to protect discourse on public matters, but we have long recognized that it is difficult to distinguish politics from entertainment, and dangerous to try. Like the protected books, plays, and movies that preceded them, video games communicate ideas—and even social messages—through many familiar literary devices (such as characters, dialogue, plot, and music) and through features distinctive to the medium (such as the player's interaction with the virtual world). That suffices to confer First Amendment protection. Under our Constitution, "esthetic and moral judgments about art and literature . . . are for the individual to make, not for the Government to decree, even with the mandate or approval of a majority." . . .

The most basic of those principles is this: "[A]s a general matter, . . . government has no power to restrict expression because of its message, its ideas, its subject matter, or its content." There are of course exceptions. These limited areas—such as obscenity, incitement, and fighting words—represent "well-defined and narrowly limited classes of speech, the prevention and punishment of which have never been thought to raise any Constitutional problem,"

Last Term, in *Stevens,* we held that new categories of unprotected speech may not be added to the list by a legislature that concludes certain speech is too harmful to be tolerated. *Stevens* concerned a federal statute purporting to criminalize the creation, sale, or possession of certain depictions of animal cruelty. . . .

The Government argued in *Stevens* that lack of a historical warrant did not matter; that it could create new categories of unprotected speech by applying a "simple balancing test" that weighs the value of a particular category of speech against its social costs and then punishes that category of speech if it fails the test. We emphatically rejected that "startling and dangerous" proposition. . . .

That holding controls this case. As in *Stevens,* California has tried to make violent-speech regulation look like obscenity regulation by appending a saving clause required for the latter. That does not suffice. Our cases have been clear that the obscenity exception to the First Amendment does not cover whatever a legislature finds shocking, but only depictions of "sexual conduct." . . .

Because speech about violence is not obscene, it is of no consequence that California's statute mimics the New York statute regulating obscenity-for-minors that we upheld in *Ginsberg v. New York*. That case approved a prohibition on the sale to minors of *sexual* material that would be obscene from the perspective of a child. We held that the legislature could "adjus[t] the definition of obscenity 'to social realities by permitting the appeal of this type of material to be assessed in terms of the sexual interests . . .' of . . . minors." And because "obscenity is not protected expression," the New York statute could be sustained so long as the legislature's judgment that the proscribed materials were harmful to children "was not irrational."

The California Act is something else entirely. It does not adjust the boundaries of an existing category of unprotected speech to ensure that a definition designed for adults is not uncritically applied to children. California does not argue that it is empowered to prohibit selling offensively violent works *to adults*—and it is wise not to, since that is but a hair's breadth from the argument rejected in *Stevens*. Instead, it wishes to create a wholly new category of content-based regulation that is permissible only for speech directed at children.

That is unprecedented and mistaken. "[M]inors are entitled to a significant measure of First Amendment protection, and only in relatively narrow and well-defined circumstances may government bar public dissemination of protected materials to them." No doubt a State possesses legitimate power to protect children from harm, but that does not include a free-floating power to restrict the ideas to which children may be exposed. "Speech that is neither obscene as to youths nor subject to some other legitimate proscription cannot be suppressed solely to protect the young from ideas or images that a legislative body thinks unsuitable for them."

California's argument would fare better if there were a longstanding tradition in this country of specially restricting children's access to depictions of violence, but there is none. Certainly the *books* we give children to read—or read to them when they are younger—contain no shortage of gore. Grimm's Fairy Tales, for example, are grim indeed. As her just deserts for trying to poison Snow White, the wicked queen is made to dance in red hot slippers "till she fell dead on the floor, a sad example of envy and jealousy." Cinderella's evil stepsisters have their eyes pecked out by doves. And Hansel and Gretel (children!) kill their captor by baking her in an oven. . . .

Because the Act imposes a restriction on the content of protected speech, it is invalid unless California can demonstrate that it passes strict scrutiny—that is, unless it is justified by a compelling government interest and is narrowly drawn to serve that interest. The State must specifically identify an "actual problem" in need of solving, and the curtailment of free speech must be actually necessary to the solution. That is a demanding standard.

California cannot meet that standard. . . .

## Justice THOMAS, dissenting.

The Court's decision today does not comport with the original public understanding of the First Amendment. The majority strikes down, as facially unconstitutional, a state law that prohibits the direct sale or rental of certain video games to minors because the law "abridg[es] the freedom of speech." U.S. Const., Amdt. 1. But I do not think the First Amendment stretches that far. The practices and beliefs of the founding generation establish that "the freedom of speech," as originally understood, does not include a right to speak to minors (or a right of minors to access speech) without going through the minors' parents or guardians. I would hold that the law at issue is not facially unconstitutional under the First Amendment, and reverse and remand for further proceedings.

When interpreting a constitutional provision, "the goal is to discern the most likely public understanding of [that] provision at the time it was adopted." Because the Constitution is a written instrument, "its meaning does not alter." "That which it meant when adopted, it means now."

As originally understood, the First Amendment's protection against laws "abridging the freedom of speech" did not extend to *all* speech. "There are certain well-defined and narrowly limited classes of speech, the prevention and punishment of which have never been thought to raise any Constitutional problem."

In my view, the "practices and beliefs held by the Founders" reveal another category of excluded speech: speech to minor children bypassing their parents. The historical evidence shows that the founding generation believed parents had absolute authority over their minor children and expected parents to use that authority to direct the proper development of their children. It would be absurd to suggest that such a society understood "the freedom of speech" to include a right to speak to minors (or a corresponding right of minors to access speech) without going through the minors' parents. The founding generation would not have considered it an abridgment of "the freedom of speech" to support parental authority by restricting speech that bypasses minors' parents. . . .

## Bibliography

Clements, Christopher. "Protecting Protected Speech: Violent Video Game Legislation Post-*Brown v. Entertainment Merchants Ass'n.*" *Boston College Law Review* 53 (2012): 661.

# FIGHTING WORDS

First Amendment jurisprudence reflects an understanding that freedom of speech is not an absolute guarantee. Expressive liberty can be abridged on a case-by-case basis when the reasons for regulating it outweigh the freedom interest or categorically when the speech itself possesses inadequate societal value. Obscenity is a primary example of speech that, because it is perceived as mostly valueless, categorically implicates little if any constitutional concern. Another form of expression that is denied First Amendment protection on a categorical basis is "fighting words." The Court, in *Chaplinsky v. New Hampshire* (1942), described fighting words as expression "which by [its] very utterance inflict[s] injury or tend[s] to incite an immediate breach of peace." Like obscenity, fighting words are regarded as inessential to "the exposition of ideas" and having "such slight social value as a step to truth that any benefit which may be derived from them is clearly outweighed by the social interest in order and morality." Also like obscenity, fighting words are difficult to define. Consistent with this reality, the Court has tended to resolve cases on grounds that the pertinent regulation is vague or overbroad. It also has resisted efforts to convert fighting words doctrine into a means of regulating speech that is merely offensive. In *Cohen v. California* (1971), the Court determined that the wearing of a jacket that had "Fuck the Draft" emblazoned may have been offensive. Minus the tendency to induce violent reaction, however, the speech could not be characterized as fighting words.

The notion that fighting words are constitutionally unprotected has become subject to at least one significant qualification. In *R.A.V. v. City of St. Paul* (1992), the Court held that the state could not regulate fighting words on a selective basis. Prohibition based upon whether government agreed or disagreed with an underlying political or social view thus represented an unconstitutional exercise in viewpoint discrimination. In *Virginia v. Black* (2003), the Court upheld a state law that criminalized cross burning. Although cross burning is a form of expressive activity, the Court found that it could be singled out for regulatory purposes because it represented a "true threat" of violence.

## R.A.V. v. City of St. Paul

**Citation: 505 U.S. 377.**

**Issue: Whether an ordinance prohibiting symbols that "arouse anger, alarm or resentment in others on the basis of race, color creed, religion, and or gender" violates the First Amendment.**

**Year of Decision: 1992.**

**Outcome: The ordinance discriminates on the basis of content and viewpoint and thus violates the First Amendment.**

**Author of Opinion: Associate Justice Antonin Scalia.**

**Vote: 9-0.**

A primary driver of expanded First Amendment freedom has been the civil rights movement. As protests and demonstrations spread throughout the South during the 1950s and 1960s, states responded with a variety of measures designed to curb expressive activity. These methods included arrests for disturbing the peace, censorship, arbitrary processes that denied permits for public demonstrations, mandatory disclosure of membership lists of civil rights organizations, and aggressive use of defamation laws. In each of these contexts, First Amendment case law was developed in ways that provided space and opportunity for the civil rights agenda to be heard. So close was the linkage between the civil rights movement and expanded First Amendment freedom that a noted constitutional scholar, Harry Kalven, Jr., credited "the Negro with reclaiming the First Amendment freedom of all Americans."

Notwithstanding the historic relationship between freedom of speech and civil rights, some advocates by the 1980s began to assert that expressive liberty was not always compatible with or facilitative of equality interests. To the contrary, they maintained that speech which disparages persons on the basis of their group status actually is inimical to and undermines those concerns. Consistent with the sense that hate speech represents a verbal assault that harms its victims, many institutions and communities adopted codes that prohibited and punished such expression. Those who favor regulation of hate speech describe it as an "instantaneous slap in the face" that causes immediate and significant injury. Traditional First Amendment principles favor reliance on the marketplace of ideas to put any single viewpoint into perspective. Advocates of hate speech control, however, maintain that hate speech is not motivated by an interest in dialogue or searching for the truth, and the harm it causes is not ameliorated by discussion. They thus view it as an "implement" of racism that "reinforc[es] conditions of domination."

In response to arguments that hate speech diminishes and marginalizes its victims, critics maintain that its regulation chills some important expression and fails to account effectively for equality interests. These competing perspectives eventually came before the Supreme Court in a case concerning a St. Paul, Minnesota, hate speech ordinance. The measure provided that "anyone placing a symbol or object such as a swastika or burning cross on public or private property, with reason to know it would cause anger, alarm or resentment on grounds of race, religion, color, creed or gender, is guilty of disorderly conduct." At issue specifically was its use as the basis for convicting several teenagers who had burned a cross in the yard of an African American family. The Minnesota Supreme Court upheld the ordinance on grounds it targeted fighting words only and thus regulated a category of expression that was not constitutionally protected.

Justice Antonin Scalia, writing for the majority in *R.A.V. v. City of St. Paul* (1992), reversed the state supreme court's decision. Although acknowledging that the expression constituted fighting words, he noted unacceptable risks in allowing government to single out certain types of offending or objection speech for regulation—even if the expression fit into an unprotected category. A key aspect of the decision, therefore, was the Court's determination that traditionally unprotected speech is not "entirely invisible to the Constitution." Even if fighting words may be categorically prohibited for content reasons, the Court concluded that government may not regulate within the category on a selective basis. As the Court put it, government "may not regulate use based on hostility or favoritism toward the underlying message expressed."

This determination thus established a constitutional interest in speech that historically has been denied any constitutional protection.

The Court's gloss on categorically unprotected speech evidenced concern with the consequences of excluding some thoughts and views from the marketplace of ideas. Minus indications that government is favoring a particular view or burdening one that it dislikes, the Court indicated that some selective regulation of offensive expression may be permissible. For purposes of the St. Paul case, however, the majority was concerned that the city was favoring a particular viewpoint. This perception was supported by the law's concern with a narrow range of speech that had the potential to insult or provoke violence. Left untouched by the regulation were other forms of expression "containing abusive invective, no matter how vicious or severe." Referencing the ordinance's selective focus, the Court determined that the city unconstitutionally had "impose[d] special prohibitions on those speakers who express views on disfavored subjects." The Court also viewed the law as an unconstitutional means for advancing the city's preferred viewpoint. An interest in tolerance and equality accordingly may not be the basis for denying expressive freedom to those with a contrary agenda. Allowing members of one group to trade in fighting words, while prohibiting their usage by another, is impermissible. The Court thus found that the city could not "license one side of a debate to fight freestyle, while requiring the other to follow Marquis of Queensbury rules."

Although striking down the ordinance, the Court recognized a community's interest in reckoning with racist behavior and beliefs. The St. Paul ordinance failed, however, because it disregarded the First Amendment's hostility toward regulation constituting a "selective limitation upon speech." The Court stressed that fighting words are categorically excluded from the First Amendment's protection, not because they communicate a particular idea, but because they represent "a particularly intolerable (and socially unnecessary) mode of expressing whatever idea the speaker wishes to convey." Because the city had not identified a "particularly intolerable" mode of fighting words, and regulated on a selective basis, the Court concluded that the enactment aimed "to handicap the expression of particular ideas."

The city had hoped for a different result on grounds the law accounted for some compelling interests, including an effective accounting for "the basic human rights of members of groups that have historically been subjected to discrimination, including the right of such group members to live in peace where they wish." The Court did not reject the proposition that the city's interest was compelling. Rather, it determined that the city could not discriminate on the basis of speech content to achieve the desired objective. Singling out a specific subset of bias or prejudice, from the Court's perspective, "is precisely what the First Amendment forbids." The city thus was left in a position where it could account for its interest but not by regulation that was selective in its application.

In a concurring opinion joined by three others, Justice Byron White maintained that the Court had complicated an otherwise simple case and proposition. He would have invalidated the ordinance on grounds "it criminalized not only unprotected expression but expression protected by the First Amendment." Justice White also found it risky to deny First Amendment status to speech that caused generalized reactions such as "anger, alarm or resentment." As he put it, the capacity of speech to cause "hurt feelings, offense, or resentment" does not render it unprotected.

Justice Harry Blackmun, in a separate concurring opinion, expressed "fear that the Court has been distracted from its proper mission by the temptation to decide the issue over 'politically correct speech' and 'cultural diversity.'" From his perspective, neither of these factors was relevant to the case. Rather, Justice Blackmun viewed the Court's opinion as a manipulative exercise that enabled it to avoid the reality that some fighting words are more harmful than others. He would have permitted lawmakers to single out fighting words reflecting racial prejudice for special regulatory attention. As he put it, First Amendment interests would not be undermined by a law that prohibited "hoodlums from driving minorities out of their homes by burning crosses on their lawns." Justice Blackmun agreed with Justice White, however, that the St. Paul law was constitutionally overbroad because its reach extended beyond fighting words.

The Court's decision invalidated the city's regulation of speech motivated by racial prejudice. In *Wisconsin v. Mitchell* (1993), however, the Court upheld a state law that increased the punishment for certain crimes driven by racial animus. The *Mitchell* ruling thus limited the *R.A.V.* principle to viewpoint selective regulation of unprotected expression. Whether a differentiation between racist speech and racist conduct is sensible remains a subject of debate. Both sides, and the Court itself, would agree that racist expression is a source of harm to persons who are members of groups that historically have been disadvantaged. The consensus breaks down, however, when the issue is how to remedy such injury. Advocates of speech control maintain that racist speech undermines equality, while opponents contend that regulation underestimates the utility of expressive freedom in accounting for this interest.

## Justice SCALIA delivered the opinion of the Court.

. . . The First Amendment generally prevents government from proscribing speech, because of disapproval of the ideas expressed. Content-based regulations are presumptively invalid. From 1791 to the present, however, our society, like other free but civilized societies, has permitted restrictions upon the content of speech in a few limited areas, which are "of such slight social value as a step to truth that any benefit that may be derived from them is clearly outweighed by the social interest in order and morality." We have recognized that "the freedom of speech" referred to by the First Amendment does not include a freedom to disregard these traditional limitations. . . .

We have sometimes said that these categories of expression are "not within the area of constitutionally protected speech," or that the "protection of the First Amendment does not extend" to them. Such statements must be taken in context, however, and are no more literally true than is the occasionally repeated shorthand characterizing obscenity "as not being speech at all." What they mean is that these areas of speech can, consistently with the First Amendment, be regulated *because of their constitutionally proscribable content* (obscenity, defamation, etc.)—not that they are categories of speech entirely invisible to the Constitution, so that they may be made the vehicles for content discrimination unrelated to their distinctively proscribable content. Thus, the government may proscribe libel; but it may not make the further content discrimination of proscribing *only* libel critical of the government. . . .

Our cases surely do not establish the proposition that the First Amendment imposes no obstacle whatsoever to regulation of particular instances of such proscribable expression, so that the government "may regulate [them] freely." That would mean that a city council could enact an ordinance prohibiting only those legally obscene works that contain criticism of the city government or, indeed, that do not include endorsement of the city government. Such a simplistic, all-or-nothing-at-all approach to First Amendment protection is at odds with common sense and with our jurisprudence as well. . . .

The proposition that a particular instance of speech can be proscribable on the basis of one feature (*e.g.,* obscenity) but not on the basis of another (*e.g.,* opposition to the city government) is commonplace and has found application in many contexts. We have long held, for example, that nonverbal expressive activity can be banned because of the action it entails, but not because of the ideas it expresses—so that burning a flag in violation of an ordinance against outdoor fires could be punishable, whereas burning a flag in violation of an ordinance against dishonoring the flag is not. And just as the power to proscribe particular speech on the basis of a noncontent element (*e.g.,* noise) does not entail the power to proscribe the same speech on the basis of a content element; so also, the power to proscribe it on the basis of *one* content element (*e.g.,* obscenity) does not entail the power to proscribe it on the basis of *other* content elements. . . .

When the basis for the content discrimination consists entirely of the very reason the entire class of speech at issue is proscribable, no significant danger of idea or viewpoint discrimination exists. Such a reason, having been adjudged neutral enough to support exclusion of the entire class of speech from First Amendment protection, is also neutral enough to form the basis of distinction within the class. To illustrate: A State might choose to prohibit only that obscenity which is the most patently offensive *in its prurience*—i.e., that which involves the most lascivious displays of sexual activity. But it may not prohibit, for example, only that obscenity which includes offensive *political* messages. And the Federal Government can criminalize only those threats of violence that are directed against the President—since the reasons why threats of violence are outside the First Amendment (protecting individuals from the fear of violence, from the disruption that fear engenders, and from the possibility that the threatened violence will occur) have special force when applied to the person of the President. But the Federal Government may not criminalize only those threats against the President that mention his policy on aid to inner cities. . . .

Applying these principles to the St. Paul ordinance, we conclude that, even as narrowly construed by the Minnesota Supreme Court, the ordinance is facially unconstitutional. Although the phrase in the ordinance, "arouses anger, alarm or resentment in others," has been limited by the Minnesota Supreme Court's construction to reach only those symbols or displays that amount to "fighting words," the remaining, unmodified terms make clear that the ordinance applies only to "fighting words" that insult, or provoke violence, "on the basis of race, color, creed, religion or gender." Displays containing abusive invective, no matter how vicious or severe, are permissible unless they are addressed to one of the specified disfavored topics. Those who wish to use "fighting words" in connection with other ideas—to express hostility, for example, on the basis of political affiliation, union membership, or homosexuality—are not covered. The First Amendment does not permit St. Paul to impose special prohibitions on those speakers who express views on disfavored subjects.

In its practical operation, moreover, the ordinance goes even beyond mere content discrimination, to actual viewpoint discrimination. Displays containing some words—odious racial epithets, for example—would be prohibited to proponents of all views. But "fighting words" that do not themselves invoke race, color, creed, religion, or gender—aspersions upon a person's mother, for example—would seemingly be usable *ad libitum* in the placards of those arguing *in favor* of racial, color, etc., tolerance and equality, but could not be used by those speakers' opponents. One could hold up a sign saying, for example, that all "anti-Catholic bigots" are misbegotten; but not that all "papists" are, for that would insult and provoke violence "on the basis of religion." St. Paul has no such authority to license one side of a debate to fight freestyle, while requiring the other to follow Marquis of Queensberry rules.

What we have here, it must be emphasized, is not a prohibition of fighting words that are directed at certain persons or groups (which would be *facially* valid if it met the requirements of the Equal Protection Clause); but rather, a prohibition of fighting words that contain (as the Minnesota Supreme Court repeatedly emphasized) messages of "bias-motivated" hatred and in particular, as applied to this case, messages "based on virulent notions of racial supremacy." One must wholeheartedly agree with the Minnesota Supreme Court that "[i]t is the responsibility, even the obligation, of diverse communities to confront such notions in whatever form they appear," but the manner of that confrontation cannot consist of selective limitations upon speech. St. Paul's brief asserts that a general "fighting words" law would not meet the city's needs because only a content-specific measure can communicate to minority groups that the "group hatred" aspect of such speech "is not condoned by the majority." The point of the First Amendment is that majority preferences must be expressed in some fashion other than silencing speech on the basis of its content. . . .

Finally, St. Paul and its *amici* defend the conclusion of the Minnesota Supreme Court that, even if the ordinance regulates expression based on hostility towards its protected ideological content, this discrimination is nonetheless justified because it is narrowly tailored to serve compelling state interests. Specifically, they assert that the ordinance helps to ensure the basic human rights of members of groups that have historically been subjected to discrimination, including the right of such group members to live in peace where they wish. We do not doubt that these interests are compelling, and that the ordinance can be said to promote them. But the "danger of censorship" presented by a facially content-based statute, requires that that weapon be employed only where it is "*necessary* to serve the asserted [compelling] interest." The existence of adequate content-neutral alternatives thus "undercut[s] significantly" any defense of such a statute, casting considerable doubt on the government's protestations that "the asserted justification is in fact an accurate description of the purpose and effect of the law." The dispositive question in this case, therefore, is whether content discrimination is reasonably necessary to achieve St. Paul's compelling interests; it plainly is not. An ordinance not limited to the favored topics, for example, would have precisely the same beneficial effect. In fact the only interest distinctively served by the content limitation is that of display-ing the city council's special hostility towards the particular biases thus singled out. That is precisely what the First Amendment forbids. The politicians of St. Paul are entitled to express that hostility—but not through the means of imposing unique limitations upon speakers who (however benightedly) disagree.

Let there be no mistake about our belief that burning a cross in someone's front yard is reprehensible. But St. Paul has sufficient means at its disposal to prevent such behavior without adding the First Amendment to the fire.

### Bibliography

Gates, Henry Louis, Jr., Anthony P. Griffin, Donald E. Lively, Robert C. Post, William R. Rubinstein, and Nadine Strossen. *Speaking of Race, Speaking of Sex*. New York: New York University Press, 1994.

Matsuda, Mari, Charles R. Lawrence III, Richard Delgado, and Kimberle Crenshaw. *Words That Wound*. Boulder, CO: Westview Press, 1993.

Redish, Martin. "Freedom of Thought as Freedom of Expression: Hate Crime Sentencing Enhancement and First Amendment Theory." *Criminal Justice Ethics* 29 (1992).

## *Virginia v. Black*

**Citation: 538 U.S. 343.**

**Issue: Whether cross burning can be criminalized.**

**Year of Decision: 2003.**

**Outcome: Cross burning can be prohibited when it reflects an intent to intimidate.**

**Author of Opinion: Justice Sandra Day O'Connor.**

**Vote: 9-0.**

So-called "hate speech" has generated litigation and controversy in recent years. In general, legislation regulating or proscribing hate speech has the salutary objective of protecting minorities and others who are the targets of such speech. At the same time, whenever government attempts to regulate the content of public discourse, legitimate fears arise regarding the wisdom and propriety of governmental intervention. Historically, when government has been able to regulate speech, it has used that power to prohibit unpopular or objectionable viewpoints. The Court's prior decision in *R.A.V. v. City of St. Paul*, 505 U.S. 377 (1992), involved a St. Paul, Minnesota, ordinance that prohibited the placement of symbols "which one knows or has reasonable grounds to know arouses anger, alarm or resentment in others on the basis of race, color, creed, religion or gender." When the ordinance was used to prosecute teenagers who assembled a crudely made cross and burned it in the front yard of a black family that lived across the street, the Court struck the ordinance down on the basis that the government was discriminating against the teenager's speech based on its content. The Court held that the "First Amendment does not permit St. Paul to impose special prohibitions on those speakers who express views on disfavored subjects." The Court also held that the St. Paul ordinance involved "viewpoint discrimination." In other words, in addressing the topics prohibited by the ordinance, "fighting words" could be used "*in favor* of racial, color, etc., tolerance and equality, but could not be used by those speakers' opponents." The Court offered the following example of how the ordinance applied: one could hold up a sign saying, for example, that all "anti-Catholic bigots" are misbegotten, but not that all "papists" are, for that would insult and provoke violence "on the basis of religion." The Court concluded that "St. Paul has no such authority to license one side of a debate to fight freestyle, while requiring the other to follow Marquis of Queensberry rules."

One argument offered by the City of St. Paul was that the ordinance could be justified by compelling state interests in helping "to ensure the basic human rights of members of groups that have historically been subjected to discrimination, including the right of such group members to live in peace where they wish." While the Court agreed that these interests were compelling, it concluded that the City must achieve its objective without censorship except as "*necessary* to serve the asserted [compelling] interest." The Court concluded that the City of St. Paul could respond to cross burning with content-neutral alternatives. For example, it could punish cross burners under content-neutral arson and trespass statutes. In addition, the City could respond with speech encouraging tolerance.

The question of cross burning came back to the Court in the *Black* case. That case involved a Virginia statute that made it illegal to burn a cross "with the intent of intimidating any person or group of persons." The statute also provided that "Any such burning of a cross shall be prima facie evidence of an intent to intimidate a person or group of persons."

*Black* involved two separate and distinct convictions for violating the cross-burning statute. In the first, Barry Black led a Ku Klux Klan (KKK) rally in Virginia at which a cross was burned on private property. Onlookers testified that speakers talked "real bad about the blacks and the Mexicans," and one speaker stated that "he would love to take a .30/.30 and just random[ly] shoot the blacks." An onlooker testified that the cross burning made her feel "awful" and "terrible." The second incident involved three individuals (Elliott, O'Mara, and a third person) who tried to burn a cross in the yard of James Jubilee, an African American who lived next door to Elliott. Prior to the cross burning, Jubilee had spoken to Elliott's mother inquiring about some gunfire behind Elliott's home, and it appears that the cross was burned to "get back" at Jubilee for complaining about the shooting. After seeing the cross, Jubilee was "very nervous" because he "didn't know what would be the next phase," and because "a cross burned in your yard . . . tells you that it's just the first round."

In reviewing the convictions, the Court noted that burning crosses had been used for various purposes throughout history (e.g., Scottish tribes that used them to signal a call to arms in the fourteenth century). However, in the United States, burning crosses have long been associated with the KKK, which viewed itself as a group of heroes "saving" the South from blacks and the "horrors" of Reconstruction. During the twentieth century, the KKK used violence as an elemental part of its strategy, including murders, floggings, and tar-and-featherings. When cross burnings were directed at particular persons not affiliated with the Klan, the burning cross often involved a "message of intimidation," designed to place the victim in fear of bodily harm. Moreover, because of the KKK's past, "the possibility of injury or death was not just hypothetical." On the contrary, the burning cross conveyed a "serious threat, meant to coerce the victim to comply with the Klan's wishes unless the victim was willing to risk the wrath of the Klan."

In upholding Virginia's cross burning statute, the Court began by recognizing that cross burning can constitute symbolic or expressive speech. However, the Court concluded that the Commonwealth of Virginia could regulate some categories of speech notwithstanding their expressive conduct including "fighting words." The Court concluded that cross burning fit within a category of speech referred to as "true threats"—statements where the speaker communicates an intent to "commit an act of unlawful violence to a particular individual or group of individuals." The Court held that it did not matter whether the speaker actually intended to carry out the threat because the prohibition on true threats protects people from the "fear of violence" and "from the disruption that fear engenders," in addition to protecting them against "the possibility that the threatened violence will occur." The Court viewed cross burning as fitting within the scope of a true threat because "cross burning is often intimidating, intended to create a pervasive fear in victims that they are a target of violence."

The Court rejected the argument that *R.A.V.* required invalidation of the Virginia statute as a content-based restriction on speech. In this regard, it noted that *R.A.V.* did not preclude regulation of "*all* forms of content-based discrimination within a proscribable area of speech." On the contrary, when the basis for the "content discrimination consists entirely of the very reason the entire class of speech at issue is proscribable, no significant danger of idea or viewpoint discrimination exists." Consequently, while *R.A.V.* held that a state may not ban only obscenity based on "offensive *political* messages," or "only those threats against the President that mention his policy on aid to inner cities," the First Amendment permits content discrimination "based on the very reasons why the particular class of speech at issue is prohibitable." The Court viewed cross burning as outside First Amendment protections "because burning a cross is a particularly virulent form of intimidation" given its "long and pernicious history as a signal of impending violence." As a result, "just as a State may regulate only that obscenity which is the most obscene due to its prurient content, so too may a State choose to prohibit only those forms of intimidation that are most likely to inspire fear of bodily harm." The Court went on to emphasize that Virginia's statute did not single out speech directed toward "one of the specified disfavored topics." Moreover, it did not matter whether an individual burns a cross with intent to intimidate because of the victim's race, gender, or religion or because of the victim's "political affiliation, union membership, or homosexuality."

The Court did hold that the "prima facie" evidence portion of Virginia's statute was unconstitutional because it provided that "[a]ny such burning of a cross shall be prima facie evidence of an intent to intimidate a person or group of persons." Va. Code Ann. § 18.2-423 (1996). The Court concluded that the provision permits the Commonwealth to arrest, prosecute, and convict a person based solely on the fact of cross burning itself. The Court concluded that "the provision as so interpreted would create an unacceptable risk of the suppression of ideas." The Court noted that, while a cross burning might involve an attempt to intimidate, it might also involve core political speech. As a result, the Court found that the "provision chills constitutionally protected political speech" by creating a presumption of conviction.

Justice David Souter concurred in part and dissented in part. He agreed with the Court that the Virginia law created a content-based distinction, but he would have applied *R.A.V.* and struck down the law. He feared that the government may have singled out cross burning because "of disapproval of its message of white supremacy, either because a legislature thought white supremacy was a pernicious doctrine or because it found that dramatic, public espousal of it was a civic embarrassment."

Justice Clarence Thomas also dissented. He agreed that it is constitutionally permissible to "ban cross burning carried out with intent to intimidate," but he would even have upheld the prima facie evidence provision noting that "Virginia law still requires the jury to find the existence of each element, including intent to intimidate, beyond a reasonable doubt." He went on to note that cross burning subjects its targets, and, sometimes, an unintended audience, to extreme emotional distress and is virtually never viewed merely as "unwanted communication."

In evaluating *Black*, it is important to realize that the decision did not (as some media accounts suggested) allow states to summarily prohibit all cross burnings. The Court held that Virginia could prohibit only those cross burnings that conveyed a message of violence and intimidation. Consistent with this holding, the Court reversed Black's conviction and dismissed the case against him. Although he burnt a cross in a field, there was no evidence of a direct and imminent threat against any specific person. In this respect, *Black* was consistent with the Court's prior decision in *Brandenburg v. Ohio,* which suggested that cross burners at KKK rallies could not be prosecuted for illegal advocacy unless it could be shown that they intended to produce imminent lawless conduct and that their message was likely to produce such imminent lawless conduct.

Whether *Black* will have much precedential impact outside the cross-burning area is debatable. The decision contains an extensive analysis of cross burning and links that history to violence and intimidation. However, in rendering its decision, the Court did not suggest that any other symbol might convey such a virulent message of hate and violence. In addition, *Black* did not reverse *R.A.V.,* but instead created an exception for situations in which cross burning is used to convey a message of violence and intimidation. In future cases, the Court would still apply its prohibition against content-based and viewpoint-based restriction on speech to other governmental attempts to repress speech and to other less virulent symbols.

### Justice O'CONNOR announced the judgment of the Court and delivered the opinion of the Court in its principal parts.

. . . "True threats" encompass those statements where the speaker means to communicate a serious expression of an intent to commit an act of unlawful violence to a particular individual or group of individuals. The speaker need not actually intend to carry out the threat. Rather, a prohibition on true threats "protect[s] individuals from the fear of violence" and "from the disruption that fear engenders," in addition to protecting people "from the possibility that the threatened violence will occur." Intimidation in the constitutionally proscribable sense of the word is a type of true threat, where a speaker directs a threat to a person or group of persons with the intent of placing the victim in fear of bodily harm or death. Respondents do not contest that some cross burnings fit within this meaning of intimidating speech, and rightly so. As noted in Part II, *supra,* the history of cross burning in this country shows that cross burning is often intimidating, intended to create a pervasive fear in victims that they are a target of violence.

The Supreme Court of Virginia ruled that in light of *R.A.V. v. City of St. Paul,* even if it is constitutional to ban cross burning in a content-neutral manner, the Virginia cross-burning statute is unconstitutional because it discriminates on the basis of content and viewpoint. It is true, as the Supreme Court of Virginia held, that the burning of a cross is symbolic expression. The reason why the Klan burns a cross at its rallies, or individuals place a burning cross on someone else's lawn, is that the burning cross represents the message that the speaker wishes to communicate. Individuals burn crosses as opposed to other means of communication because cross burning carries a message in an effective and dramatic manner. . . .

Similarly, Virginia's statute does not run afoul of the First Amendment insofar as it bans cross burning with intent to intimidate. Unlike the statute at issue in *R.A.V.,* the Virginia statute does not single out for opprobrium only that speech directed toward "one of the specified disfavored topics." It does not matter whether an individual burns a cross with intent to intimidate because of the victim's race, gender, or religion, or because of the victim's "political affiliation, union membership, or homosexuality." Moreover, as a factual matter it is not true that cross burners direct their intimidating conduct solely to racial or religious minorities. Indeed, in the case of Elliott and O'Mara, it is at least unclear whether the respondents burned a cross due to racial animus.

The First Amendment permits Virginia to outlaw cross burnings done with the intent to intimidate because burning a cross is a particularly virulent form of intimidation. Instead of prohibiting all intimidating messages, Virginia may choose to regulate this subset of intimidating messages in light of cross burning's long and pernicious history as a signal of impending violence. Thus, just as a State may regulate only that obscenity which is the most obscene due to its prurient content, so too may a State choose to prohibit only those forms of intimidation that are most likely to inspire fear of bodily harm. A ban on cross burning carried out with the intent to intimidate is fully consistent with our holding in *R.A.V.* and is proscribable under the First Amendment. . . .

The Supreme Court of Virginia has not ruled on the meaning of the prima facie evidence provision. It has, however, stated that "the act of burning a cross alone, with no evidence of intent to intimidate, will nonetheless suffice for arrest and prosecution and will insulate the Commonwealth from a motion to strike the evidence at the end of its case-in-chief." The jury in the case of Richard Elliott did not receive any instruction on the prima facie evidence provision, and the provision was not an issue in the case of Jonathan O'Mara because he pleaded guilty. The court in Barry Black's case, however, instructed the jury that the provision means: "The burning of a cross, by itself, is sufficient evidence from which you may infer the required intent." This jury instruction is the same as the Model Jury Instruction in the Commonwealth of Virginia.

The prima facie evidence provision, as interpreted by the jury instruction, renders the statute unconstitutional. Because this jury instruction is the Model Jury Instruction, and because the Supreme Court of Virginia had the opportunity to expressly disavow the jury instruction, the jury instruction's construction of the prima facie provision "is a ruling on a question of state law that is as binding on us as though the precise words had been written into" the statute. As construed by the jury instruction, the prima facie provision strips away the very reason why a State may ban cross burning with the intent to intimidate. The prima facie evidence provision permits a jury to convict in every cross-burning case in which defendants exercise their constitutional right not to put on a defense. And even where a defendant like Black presents a defense, the prima facie evidence provision makes it more likely that the jury will find an intent to intimidate regardless of the particular facts of the case. The provision permits the Commonwealth to arrest, prosecute, and convict a person based solely on the fact of cross burning itself. . . .

## Bibliography

Bell, Jeannine. "O Say Can You See: Free Expression by the Light of Fiery Crosses." *Harvard Civil Rights–Civil Liberties Law Review* 39 (2004): 335.

Hartley, Roger C. "Cross Burning–Hate Speech as Free Speech: A Comment on *Virginia v. Black*," *Catholic University Law Review* 54 (2004): 1.

Weaver, Russell L., and Donald E. Lively. *Understanding the First Amendment.* Newark, NJ: LexisNexis, 2012, 130–33.

# COMMERCIAL SPEECH

Commercial speech until the late twentieth century categorically was beyond the First Amendment's range of protection. This exclusion was based upon an understanding that expression relating to the speaker's economic interests had no constitutional value. Modern First Amendment jurisprudence reflects a different perspective. Beginning in the 1970s, the Supreme Court began to acknowledge that commercial speech may have significant value for the public. Consistent with this premise, the Court in *Bigelow v. Virginia* (1975) determined that restrictions on abortion advertising violated the First Amendment. In *Virginia State Board of Pharmacy v. Virginia Citizens Consumer Council, Inc.* (1976), the Court placed commercial expression squarely within the zone of constitutionally protected speech.

## *Virginia State Board of Pharmacy v. Virginia Citizens Consumer Council, Inc.*

**Citation: 425 U.S. 748.**

**Issue: Whether commercial expression is protected by the First Amendment.**

**Year of Decision: 1976.**

**Outcome: Speech does not lose First Amendment protection because of its commercial nature.**

**Author of Opinion: Justice Harry Blackmun.**

**Vote: 7-1.**

As the obscenity and fighting words cases evidence, not all expression is protected by the First Amendment. Even among categories of constitutionally safeguarded speech, there are variations with respect to the extent of protection provided. A key premise of modern First Amendment jurisprudence is that speech facilitating informed self-governance has the highest value. Consistent with this proposition, the Supreme Court has been especially protective of political expression. The more distance that is perceived between speech and informed self-governance, however, the more disposed it has been to uphold regulation. As initially regarded by the Court, commercial speech had no significant constitutional currency. During the second half of the twentieth century, as the Court expanded the range of constitutionally protected expression, commercial speech became a primary beneficiary of this evolution.

The process of expanding the spectrum of constitutionally protected expression commenced in the 1960s, as the Court began to recognize that speech beyond the purely political had significant value. The first stage of expansion conferred First Amendment status upon defamatory speech. This development reflected the Court's understanding, expressed in *New York Times Co. v. Sullivan* (1964), "of a profound national commitment to the principle that debate on public issues should be uninhibited, robust, and wide-open, and that it may well include vehement, caustic, and sometimes unpleasantly sharp attacks on government and public officials." Defamation of public officials and public figures thus was afforded constitutional shelter in *Sullivan* and *Curtis Publishing Co. v. Butts* (1968), respectively. Sexually explicit expression, provided it does not rise to the level of obscenity, also is constitutionally protected. Decisions in this context, such as *Federal Communications Commission v. Pacifica Foundation* (1978), have suggested that sexually explicit expression has a lower value and thus may be more susceptible to regulation. Although central to a free market economy, commercial speech had no First Amendment currency until the 1970s. This condition reflected the Supreme Court's decision, in *Valentine v. Chrestensen* (1942), that the First Amendment was not a barrier to regulating "purely commercial advertising."

Three decades after *Valentine v. Chrestensen*, the Court began to rethink its commercial speech doctrine. In *Pittsburgh Press Co. v. Pittsburgh Commission on Human Relations* (1973), it upheld a city ordinance prohibiting newspapers from running gender-based help-wanted advertisements. The *Pittsburgh Press* decision established a first line of protection for commercial speech to the extent states could prohibit advertising only when the underlying activity was illegal. Subsequently, in *Bigelow v. Virginia* (1975), the Court determined that the advertising of legal activities could not be barred. This ruling reversed the conviction of a person who had been prosecuted for violating a state ban on advertisements for abortion. The *Pittsburgh Press* and *Bigelow* decisions prefaced a more comprehensive overhaul of commercial speech doctrine in *Virginia State Board of Pharmacy v. Virginia Consumer Citizens Council, Inc.* (1976). At issue in this case was a state law prohibiting pharmacies from advertising the cost of prescription drugs. In defense of this regulation, the state maintained that it was essential for maintenance of professional standards, safeguarded against competitive pressures that might cause pharmacists to cut corners and thus endanger public health, enabling small pharmacies to remain competitive with drug store chains.

Justice Harry Blackmun wrote the majority's opinion. At the outset, he conceded that the advertisement of prescription drug prices had no political significance and merely provided information as the basis for a commercial transaction. From his perspective, the issue was whether speech that "does 'no more than propose a commercial transaction' is so removed from any 'exposition of ideas' and from 'truth, science, morality, and arts in general'" that it lacks all protection. The Court not only concluded that commercial speech merited First Amendment protection but that the consumer interest in such expression was "as keen, if not keener by far, than his interest in the day's most urgent political debate." It further found a ban on advertising to be at odds with the interests of a free market economy and of consumers wanting to make informed decisions in exercising their purchasing power. The Court accordingly observed that the allocation of resources in a free market economy responds to cumulative private decisions that must be "intelligent and well informed." Within this context, "the free flow of commercial information is indispensable." The Court observed that laws blocking this flow represent a "highly paternalistic" model of regulation. Given a choice, the Court favored a system grounded in the assumption that "people will perceive their own best interests only if they are well enough informed, and that the best means to that end is to open the channels of communication rather than to close them."

Despite finding that commercial speech had significant value and utility, the Court indicated that it could be more prone to regulation. Consistent with earlier case law, the Court reaffirmed that states could prohibit advertising of illegal services or activities. The right to trade in commercial speech also might be conditioned upon disclosures that are state mandated to avoid fraud, injury, or unfair dealing. The lower threshold for regulating commercial speech was grounded in a sense that commercial speech presents risks that can be differentiated from those associated with political expression. The Court thus identified "commonsense differences" that justify a lesser "degree of protection."

The key differentiating factors, as the Court perceived it, are the "hardier" and "more easily verifiable" nature of commercial speech. Neither of these premises is beyond dispute. Arguments that commercial expression is "hardier" may discount the resilience of political speech. Although used in a different context, political speech like commercial speech typically is driven by the powerful force of self-interest. The drive to win an election or promote a particular agenda (which like commercial speech may serve an economic interest) may be as potent a factor as the interest in material enrichment. Debatable too is the premise that the truth of commercial speech is uniquely easier to verify. Whether in the political or commercial context, misleading or false information can be a source of significant public or private harm. Misrepresentation in either context, moreover, may be a function of conscious or calculated thinking. Ease of verification thus depends less upon the category of speech than the speaker's state of mind.

Modern commercial speech doctrine, although expanding the boundaries of the First Amendment, generates concern with the process of classifying speech for constitutional purposes. As defined by the Court, commercial speech is expression that "invites a commercial transaction." The most common form of commercial expression is advertising. The line between commercial speech and more protected forms of expression blurs when it comes to classifying speech in the context of political, social, or charitable fundraising. This difficulty was evidenced in *Schaumburg v. Citizens for a Better Environment* (1980). The majority determined that charitable fund-raising "does more than inform private economic decisions and is not primarily concerned with providing information about the characteristics and costs of goods and services." Justice Rehnquist disagreed with the majority and, in a dissenting opinion, described the expression as purely commercial.

By striking down the regulation of prescription advertising, the Court set a new standard that facilitated regulatory reform in other contexts where commercial speech had been tightly controlled. Restrictions on lawyer advertising and solicitation were among the regulatory barriers that fell soon after the *Virginia Board of Pharmacy* decision. The primary achievement of this ruling was to establish clearly that commercial speech is protected by the First Amendment. Further case law was necessary, however, to establish specific standards for reviewing commercial speech regulation.

This need was met several years later, in *Central Gas and Electric Co. v. Public Service Commission* (1984), when the Court introduced a four-part test for assessing the constitutionality of such regulation. The threshold qualification for First Amendment protection is that the speech neither misleads nor promotes an unlawful activity. If the expression satisfies this first criterion, the analysis turns to whether the regulation is supported by an important governmental interest, whether it directly advances that interest, and whether it is no more extensive than necessary to account for that interest. Subsequent case law has varied the intensity of this review, from more relaxed to more intense. The basic premise that commercial speech merits First Amendment protection, however, appears to be well-settled.

## Mr. Justice BLACKMUN delivered the opinion of the Court.

. . . We begin with several propositions that already are settled or beyond serious dispute. It is clear, for example, that speech does not lose its First Amendment protection because money is spent to project it, as in a paid advertisement of one form or another. Speech likewise is protected even though it is carried in a form that is "sold" for profit, and even though it may involve a solicitation to purchase or otherwise pay or contribute money.

If there is a kind of commercial speech that lacks all First Amendment protection, therefore, it must be distinguished by its content. Yet the speech whose content deprives it of protection cannot simply be speech on a commercial subject. No one would contend that our pharmacist may be prevented from being heard on the subject of whether, in general, pharmaceutical prices should be regulated, or their advertisement forbidden. Nor can it be dispositive that a commercial advertisement is noneditorial, and merely reports a fact. Purely factual matter of public interest may claim protection.

Our question is whether speech which does "no more than propose a commercial transaction," is so removed from any "exposition of ideas," and from " 'truth, science, morality, and arts in general, in its diffusion of liberal sentiments on the administration of Government,' " that it lacks all protection. Our answer is that it is not. . . .

As to the particular consumer's interest in the free flow of commercial information, that interest may be as keen, if not keener by far, than his interest in the day's most urgent political debate. Appellees' case in this respect is a convincing one. Those whom the suppression of prescription drug price information hits the hardest are the poor, the sick, and particularly the aged. A disproportionate amount of their income tends to be spent on prescription drugs; yet they are the least able to learn, by shopping from pharmacist to pharmacist, where their scarce dollars are best spent. When drug prices vary as strikingly as they do, information as to who is charging what becomes more than a convenience. It could mean the alleviation of physical pain or the enjoyment of basic necessities.

Generalizing, society also may have a strong interest in the free flow of commercial information. Even an individual advertisement, though entirely "commercial," may be of general public interest. . . . Obviously, not all commercial messages contain the same or even a very great public interest element. There are few to which such an element, however, could not be added. Our pharmacist, for example, could cast himself as a commentator on store-to-store disparities in drug prices, giving his own and those of a competitor as proof. We see little point in requiring him to do so, and little difference if he does not.

Moreover, there is another consideration that suggests that no line between publicly "interesting" or "important" commercial advertising and the opposite kind could ever be drawn. Advertising, however tasteless and excessive it sometimes may seem, is nonetheless dissemination of information as to who is producing and selling what product, for what reason, and at what price. So long as we preserve a predominantly free enterprise economy, the allocation of our resources in large measure will be made through numerous private economic decisions. It is a matter of public interest that those decisions, in the aggregate, be intelligent and well informed. To this end, the free flow of commercial information is indispensable. . . .

Arrayed against these substantial individual and societal interests are a number of justifications for the advertising ban. These have to do principally with maintaining a high degree of professionalism on the part of licensed pharmacists. Indisputably, the State has a strong interest in maintaining that professionalism. It is exercised in a number of ways for the consumer's benefit. There is the clinical skill involved in the compounding of drugs, although, as has been noted, these now make up only a small percentage of the prescriptions filled. Yet, even with respect to manufacturer-prepared compounds, there is room for the pharmacist to serve his customer well or badly. Drugs kept too long on the shelf may lose their efficacy or become adulterated. They can be packaged for the user in such a way that the same results occur. The expertise of the pharmacist may supplement that of the prescribing physician, if the latter has not specified the amount to be dispensed or the directions that are to appear on the label. . . .

The strength of these proffered justifications is greatly undermined by the fact that high professional standards, to a substantial extent, are guaranteed by the close regulation to which pharmacists in Virginia are subject. And this case concerns the retail sale by the pharmacist more than it does his professional standards. Surely, any pharmacist guilty of professional dereliction that actually endangers his customer will promptly lose his license. . . .

The challenge now made, however, is based on the First Amendment. This casts the Board's justifications in a different light, for on close inspection it is seen that the State's protectiveness of its citizens rests in large measure on the advantages of their being kept in ignorance. The advertising ban does not directly affect professional standards one way or the other. It affects them only through the reactions it is assumed people will have to the free flow of drug price information. There is no claim that the advertising ban in any way prevents the cutting of corners by the pharmacist who is so inclined. . . .

It appears to be feared that if the pharmacist who wishes to provide low cost, and assertedly low quality, services is permitted to advertise, he will be taken up on his offer by too many unwitting customers. They will choose the low-cost, low-quality service and drive the "professional" pharmacist out of business. They will respond only to costly and excessive advertising, and end up paying the price. They will go from one pharmacist to another, following the discount, and destroy the pharmacist-customer relationship. They will lose respect for the profession because it advertises. All this is not in their best interests, and all this can be avoided if they are not permitted to know who is charging what.

There is, of course, an alternative to this highly paternalistic approach. That alternative is to assume that this information is not in itself harmful, that people will perceive their own best interests if only they are well enough informed, and that the best means to that end is to open the channels of communication rather than to close them. . . . If they are truly open, nothing prevents the "professional" pharmacist from marketing his own assertedly superior product, and contrasting it with that of the low-cost, high-volume prescription drug retailer. But the choice among these alternative approaches is not ours to make or the Virginia General Assembly's. It is precisely this kind of choice, between the dangers of suppressing information, and the dangers of its misuse if it is freely available, that the First Amendment makes for us. Virginia is free to require whatever professional standards it wishes of its pharmacists; it may subsidize them or protect them from competition in other ways. But it may not do so by keeping the public in ignorance of the entirely lawful terms that competing pharmacists are offering. In this sense, the justifications Virginia has offered for suppressing the flow of prescription drug price information, far from persuading us that the flow is not protected by the First Amendment, have reinforced our view that it is. We so hold. . . .

What is at issue is whether a State may completely suppress the dissemination of concededly truthful information about entirely lawful activity, fearful of that information's effect upon its disseminators and its recipients. Reserving other questions, we conclude that the answer to this one is in the negative.

The judgment of the District Court is affirmed.

### Bibliography

Baker, C. Edwin. *Advertising and a Democratic Press.* Princeton, NJ: Princeton University Press, 1994.

Morrison, Alan B. "How We Got the Commercial Speech Doctrine: An Originalist's Recollections." *Case Western Reserve Law Review* 54 (2004): 1189.

Rostron, Allen. "Pragmatism, Paternalism, and the Constitutional Protection of Commercial Speech." *Vermont Law Review* 37 (2013): 527.

Smolla, Rodney. "Information, Imagery, and the First Amendment: A Case for Expansive Protection of Commercial Speech." *Texas Law Review* 71 (1993): 777.

# SYMBOLIC SPEECH

Pure speech commonly is understood as the rendering of words through processes of speaking or writing. These methods of expression, however, may be augmented, paralleled, or even superseded by other communicative factors. Message content thus may be influenced by body language, sound amplification, or visual symbols. Political agendas often rely not just upon strength of logic or force of rhetoric but upon conduct that draws attention to or makes a point with heightened emphasis or efficacy. The success of the civil rights movement during the 1960s, for instance, was facilitated by highly visible public protests and demonstrations that depended as much upon symbols as content. Consistent with the utility of symbolic speech in the marketplace of ideas, the Court has acknowledged its First Amendment status. It also has determined that, when government attempts to regulate conduct that is mixed with speech, First Amendment interests diminish somewhat. This premise was established in *United States v. O'Brien* (1968), when the Court upheld the conviction of a protestor who burned his draft card in violation of federal law. The Court determined that the enactment was aimed at protecting the integrity of the selective service system rather than suppressing legitimate expression. It upheld the law on grounds the regulation was supported by a substantial government interest and the incidental burden on expression was no greater than necessary. Had it found Congress's target to be speech itself, the Court would have demanded a compelling government interest and proof that the regulation was the least burdensome means of accounting for that concern. In *Texas v. Johnson* (1989), the Court was called upon to determine whether a law prohibiting flag desecration punished speech or conduct and thus should be reviewed pursuant to an exacting or more relaxed standard.

## Texas v. Johnson

**Citation: 491 U.S. 397.**

**Issue: Whether a conviction for burning the American flag as a political protest abridges the First Amendment.**

**Outcome: Burning an American flag to make a political statement is protected by the First Amendment.**

**Year of Decision: 1989.**

**Author of Opinion: Justice William Brennan.**

**Vote: 5-4.**

Symbolic speech is a form of expression that enhances substitutes for the spoken word. It often represents the speaker's effort to make a point more effectively and increase attention to his or her agenda. Cases concerning symbolic expression tend to arise from contexts that include significant controversy or divisions in public thought. Against this backdrop, it is not surprising that symbolic speech cases provide some of the First Amendment's most dramatic and controversial scenarios.

Squarely within this context are cases concerning desecration of the American flag. For many, the flag is a unique symbol of unity and national definition. It is precisely this symbolism, however, that has made it a favored target for desecration by persons who are alienated or dissatisfied by government policy. Consistent with the notion that the flag is a special symbol that needs to be preserved and protected, numerous stages have enacted laws that prohibit and punish its desecration. Early challenges to these enactments resulted in decisions that struck them down, but with the Court usually not addressing the First Amendment issues. It thus reversed the flag-burning conviction, in *Street v. New York* (1969), of a demonstrator who simultaneously yelled "[w]e don't need no damned flag." Avoidance of the constitutional issue, as related to the flag burning itself, reflected the Court's sense that the conviction may have rested upon the defendant's contemporaneous statement rather than action. In *Spence v. Washington* (1974), the Court reversed a conviction based upon a law prohibiting "improper use" of the flag. This case concerned the taping of a black peace symbol onto a flag for purposes of protesting the Vietnam War. A key turning point for the decision was the fact that the tape did not disfigure the flag permanently. In *Smith v. Goguen* (1974), the Court reversed the conviction of a person whose trousers had a flag sewn into the bottom of them.

The prosecution had been based upon a statute that made it a crime to "publicly mutilate, trample upon, deface, or treat contemptuously the flag of the United States." The Court found the law overbroad and vague.

Speech coupled with conduct constitutes symbolic expression. Government's ability to regulate symbolic speech is dependent upon three factors. First, the state must demonstrate that regulation furthers an important or substantial government interest. Second, the government regulatory interest must be unrelated to suppression of expression. Third, the regulatory impact upon expressive freedom must be no greater than is necessary to account for the government interest. In *United States v. O'Brien,* the Supreme Court applied these principles in reviewing the conviction of an individual who burned his draft card to protest the Vietnam War. In this case, the Court accepted the government's argument that destruction of draft cards undermined the Selective Service System's operational efficiency. It thus found the regulatory interest substantial, unrelated to the content of the message, and no more burdensome than necessary upon First Amendment freedom.

In symbolic speech cases, as the *O'Brien* case illustrates, a primary challenge for lawyers and courts is determining whether the regulation reflects concern with the content of the message or an unrelated interest. The distinction in *O'Brien* was a close call, as evidenced by a 5-4 decision in favor of the government. So, too, was the result when the Court, in *Texas v. Johnson,* determined that a state law prohibiting desecration of the American flag could not be the basis for convicting a protestor who burned it to make a political statement. The flag burning occurred in the context of a political demonstration against the presidential renomination of Ronald Reagan at the 1984 Republican National Convention. As the flag burned, protesters chanted, "American, the red, white, and blue, we sit on you." Johnson was prosecuted under a Texas law that prohibited intentional or knowing desecration of "state or national flag." As defined by the law, desecration "mean[t] deface, damage, or otherwise physically mistreat in a way that the actor knows will seriously offend one or more persons likely to observe or discover his action." Several witnesses testified that the flag burning had "seriously offended" them. Both the state and the defendant agreed that the flag burning was expressive conduct. As the defendant himself testified, "a more powerful statement of symbolic speech, whether you agree with it or not, couldn't have been made at that time."

In justifying the flag desecration law, the state argued that it had two legitimate and significant interests. The first concern related to preventing breaches of peace. The second interest was with regard to maintaining the flag as a symbol of national unity. The Court, in an opinion by Justice Anthony Kennedy, determined that each of these concerns was generated by the content of the message rather than by some factor unrelated to speech. This determination was the key to differentiating the case from *O'Brien* and for applying a stricter standard of review. Because prosecution of the demonstrator was content-based rather than content-neutral, the Court asked not whether the government's interest was merely "substantial" but whether it was "compelling." This chosen terminology is the hallmark of a particularly rigorous standard of review.

With respect to the breach of peace argument, the Court noted that the flag burning generated no disturbance. It accordingly was unmoved by the state's concern with "disorderly action." The Court was unwilling to leap from the premise that an audience offended by the symbolic expression would engage in activity that disturbed the peace. To the contrary, it embraced the proposition that expressive liberty anticipates dispute and disagreement. Freedom of speech actually serves society best, the Court noted, "when it induces a condition of unrest, creates dissatisfaction with conditions as they are, or even stirs people to anger."

Regarding the state's "interest in preserving the flag as a symbol of nationhood and national unity," the Court referenced the "bedrock principle underlying the First Amendment" that government may not curb expression of ideas merely because society finds them "offensive or disagreeable." It also indicated concern with government restricting the use of a symbol to one purpose. Ascertaining which images deserve such special attention would force the Court "to consult our very own political preferences, and impose them on the citizenry, in the very way that the First Amendment forbids us to do." Freedom of speech, as the Court saw it, does not guarantee that "sacred" concepts "will go unquestioned in the marketplace of ideas." Noting that those who authored the First Amendment "were not known for their reverence for the Union Jack," the Court refused "to create for the flag an exception to the joust of principles protected by the First Amendment."

The Court also determined that the state had overstated the likelihood of harm associated with flag burning. Assumptions that a breach of peace would be an incident of flag burning were disproved by the incident at issue. It further noted that the flag's "cherished place" in the national community was fortified by a decision that reaffirmed principles of freedom, inclusiveness, and "the conviction that our toleration of criticism such as Johnson's is a sign and source of our strength." Instead of punishment for flag burning, the Court suggested that the best remedy is speech from a competing perspective—like waving a flag or saluting the flag being destroyed.

In a dissenting opinion joined by two other justices, Chief Justice William Rehnquist argued that the statute and conviction should be upheld. From his perspective, the American flag was not "just another symbol." Chief Justice Rehnquist described it as "the visible symbol embodying our Nation" that transcends the views of any political party or philosophy. Viewing the flag as a symbol that rose above other ideas or views, and noting that 48 of 50 states prohibited burning it in public, he rejected the notion that the First Amendment was a barrier to its protection. In response to the argument that flag burning represented a significant political statement, Chief Justice Rehnquist countered that it "was no essential part of any exposition of ideas." As he saw it, the defendant could have made his point effectively by verbally denouncing the flag, burning it in private, or desecrating other official symbols or effigies of political leaders. Chief Justice Rehnquist thus concluded that flag burning merited no protection under the First Amendment, because (like obscenity and fighting words) it has "such slight social value as a step to truth that any benefit that may be derived from [it] is clearly outweighed" by the public's interest in avoiding a probable breach of the peace.

Justice John Paul Stevens also dissented on grounds the flag is "an important national asset." Given this status, he maintained that it could be protected for the same reason that political graffiti could be banned from national monuments. Justice Stevens viewed the interest in maintaining the flag's unique symbolic value as a legitimate and significant interest. Insofar as "ideas of liberty and equality" are worth fighting for, Justice Stevens concluded that it must be "true that the flag that uniquely symbolized their power is . . . itself worthy of protection from unnecessary desecration."

The Court's decision generated a firestorm among critics who quickly mobilized Congress to enact a federal law prohibiting flag desecration. The statute aimed to protect the flag against action that undermined its symbolic value. The Court found, in *United States v. Eichman* (1990), that this regulatory concern arose only in response to expression which conflicted with the flag's symbolic value. By the same 5-4 vote that yielded the outcome in *Texas v. Johnson*, therefore, the Court struck down the federal law. In so doing, it reinforced the understanding that government's ability to prohibit expressive conduct because of the message is limited. In such instances, regulation is permissible only to the extent the state can demonstrate a compelling interest and employs a method that imposes the least burden on expressive freedom.

The Court's flag-burning decisions have not deterred periodic efforts to enact flag desecration statutes. They also have inspired unsuccessful efforts toward a constitutional amendment. The potential for legislative success is dependent upon the ability to identify a content neutral justification for regulation or the ability to demonstrate a concern that the Court accepts as compelling and minimally invasive of expressive freedom. Given the strong sentiments that drive interest in protecting the flag from desecration, and the narrow margin by which such laws have been invalidated, further legislative initiative would not be unexpected. It is an area where a shift in outcome could be no further away than one resignation from and one new appointment to the Court.

## Justice BRENNAN delivered the opinion of the Court.

. . . The government generally has a freer hand in restricting expressive conduct than it has in restricting the written or spoken word. It may not, however, proscribe particular conduct *because* it has expressive elements. It is, in short, not simply the verbal or nonverbal nature of the expression, but the governmental interest at stake, that helps to determine whether a restriction on that expression is valid. . . .

Texas claims that its interest in preventing breaches of the peace justifies Johnson's conviction for flag desecration. However, no disturbance of the peace actually occurred or threatened to occur because of Johnson's burning of the flag. Although the State stresses the disruptive behavior of the protestors during their march toward City Hall, it admits that "no actual breach of the peace occurred at the time of the flagburning or in response to the flagburning." . . .

The State's position, therefore, amounts to a claim that an audience that takes serious offense at particular expression is necessarily likely to disturb the peace and that the expression may be prohibited on this basis. Our precedents do not countenance such a presumption. On the contrary, they recognize that a principal "function of free speech under our system of government is to invite dispute. It may indeed best serve its high purpose when it induces a condition of unrest, creates dissatisfaction with conditions as they are, or even stirs people to anger." . . .

We thus conclude that the State's interest in maintaining order is not implicated on these facts. The State need not worry that our holding will disable it from preserving the peace. We do not suggest that the First Amendment forbids a State to prevent "imminent lawless action." . . .

The State also asserts an interest in preserving the flag as a symbol of nationhood and national unity. In *Spence,* we acknowledged that the government's interest in preserving the flag's special symbolic value "is directly related to expression in the context of activity" such as affixing a peace symbol to a flag. We are equally persuaded that this interest is related to expression in the case of Johnson's burning of the flag. The State, apparently, is concerned that such conduct will lead people to believe either that the flag does not stand for nationhood and national unity, but instead reflects other, less positive concepts, or that the concepts reflected in the flag do not in fact exist, that is, that we do not enjoy unity as a Nation. These concerns blossom only when a person's treatment of the flag communicates some message, and thus are related "to the suppression of free expression" within the meaning of *O'Brien.* We are thus outside of *O'Brien*'s test altogether. . . .

If there is a bedrock principle underlying the First Amendment, it is that the government may not prohibit the expression of an idea simply because society finds the idea itself offensive or disagreeable. We have not recognized an exception to this principle even where our flag has been involved. . . .

In holding in *Barnette* that the Constitution did not leave this course open to the government, Justice Jackson described one of our society's defining principles in words deserving of their frequent repetition: "If there is any fixed star in our constitutional constellation, it is that no official, high or petty, can prescribe what shall be orthodox in politics, nationalism, religion, or other matters of opinion or force citizens to confess by word or act their faith therein." In *Spence,* we held that the same interest asserted by Texas here was insufficient to support a criminal conviction under a flag-misuse statute for the taping of a peace sign to an American flag. "Given the protected character of [Spence's] expression and in light of the fact that no interest the State may have in preserving the physical integrity of a privately owned flag was significantly impaired on these facts," we held, "the conviction must be invalidated."

In short, nothing in our precedents suggests that a State may foster its own view of the flag by prohibiting expressive conduct relating to it. To bring its argument outside our precedents, Texas attempts to convince us that even if its interest in preserving the flag's symbolic role does not allow it to prohibit words or some expressive conduct critical of the flag, it does permit it to forbid the outright destruction of the flag. The State's argument cannot depend here on the distinction between written or spoken words and nonverbal conduct. That distinction, we have shown, is of no moment where the nonverbal conduct is expressive, as it is here, and where the regulation of that conduct is related to expression, as it is here. In addition, both *Barnette* and *Spence* involved expressive conduct, not only verbal communication, and both found that conduct protected. . . .

It is not the State's ends, but its means, to which we object. It cannot be gainsaid that there is a special place reserved for the flag in this Nation, and thus we do not doubt that the government has a legitimate interest in making efforts to "preserv[e] the national flag as an unalloyed symbol of our country." We reject the suggestion, urged at oral argument by counsel for Johnson, that the government lacks "any state interest whatsoever" in regulating the manner in which the flag may be displayed. Congress has, for example, enacted precatory regulations describing the proper treatment of the flag, and we cast no doubt on the legitimacy of its interest in making such recommendations. To say that the government has an interest in encouraging proper treatment of the flag, however, is not to say that it may criminally punish a person for burning a flag as a means of political protest. "National unity as an end which officials may foster by persuasion and example is not in question. The problem is whether under our Constitution compulsion as here employed is a permissible means for its achievement." . . .

The way to preserve the flag's special role is not to punish those who feel differently about these matters. It is to persuade them that they are wrong. "To courageous, self-reliant men, with confidence in the power of free and fearless reasoning applied through the processes of popular government, no danger flowing from speech can be deemed clear and present, unless the incidence of the evil apprehended is so imminent that it may befall before there is opportunity for full discussion. If there be time to expose through discussion the falsehood and fallacies, to avert the evil by the processes of education, the remedy to be applied is more speech, not enforced silence." And, precisely because it is our flag that is involved, one's response to the flag burner may exploit the uniquely persuasive power of the flag itself. We can imagine no more appropriate response to burning a flag than waving one's own, no better way to counter a flag burner's message than by saluting the flag that burns, no surer means of preserving the dignity even of the flag that burned than by—as one witness here did—according its remains a respectful burial. We do not consecrate the flag by punishing its desecration, for in doing so we dilute the freedom that this cherished emblem represents. . . .

Chief Justice REHNQUIST, with whom Justice WHITE and Justice O'CONNOR join, dissenting.

. . . The American flag, then, throughout more than 200 years of our history, has come to be the visible symbol embodying our Nation. It does not represent the views of any particular political party, and it does not represent any particular political philosophy. The flag is not simply another "idea" or "point of view" competing for recognition in the marketplace of ideas. Millions and millions of Americans regard it with an almost mystical reverence regardless of what sort of social, political, or philosophical beliefs they may have. I cannot agree that the First Amendment invalidates the Act of Congress, and the laws of 48 of the 50 States, which make criminal the public burning of the flag. . .Our Constitution wisely places limits on powers of legislative majorities to act, but the declaration of such limits by this Court "is, at all times, a question of much delicacy, which ought seldom, if ever, to be decided in the affirmative, in a doubtful case." Uncritical extension of constitutional protection to the burning of the flag risks the frustration of the very purpose for which organized governments are instituted. The Court decides that the American flag is just another symbol, about which not only must opinions pro and con be tolerated, but for which the most minimal public respect may not be enjoined. The government may conscript men into the Armed Forces where they must fight and perhaps die for the flag, but the government may not prohibit the public burning of the banner under which they fight. I would uphold the Texas statute as applied in this case. . . .

### Bibliography

Bollinger, Lee. *The Tolerant Society*. New York: Oxford University Press, 1986.
Fletcher, George. *Loyalty*. New York: Oxford University Press, 1993.

# CAMPAIGN FINANCING

Speech that facilitates informed self-governments is the highest priority of the First Amendment. Consistent with this premise, standards of review are most exacting when government attempts to regulate political speech. Experience has demonstrated that money can be a corrupting influence upon the political process. Political expenditures and contributions, however, also are a means of expression. Efforts to regulate them, even for well-intended reasons, thus implicate the freedom of speech clause. In *Buckley v. Valeo* (1976), the Court acknowledged that the reality and perception of corruption may be valid grounds for regulating campaign contributions. Limitations on expenditures by individuals, candidates, and associations would not survive constitutional review, however, because they represented substantial and direct abridgments of political speech. In *McConnell v. Federal Election Commission* (2003), the Court upheld a federal law that imposed new limitations upon political fundraising and contributions.

## McConnell v. Federal Election Commission

**Citation: 124 S. Ct. 619.**

**Issue: Whether the Bipartisan Campaign Reform Act of 2002 (BCRA), which regulates political campaign financing, is constitutional.**

**Year of Decision: 2003.**

**Outcome: In most respects, BCRA is upheld because the Court is concerned about potential circumventions of campaign finance laws.**

**Author of Opinion: Justices John Paul Stevens and Sandra Day O'Connor and Chief Justice William Rehnquist.**

**Vote: 5-4.**

Campaign finance laws have generated much controversy and much litigation in recent decades. In its 1976 decision in *Buckley v. Valeo*, 424 U.S. 1 (1976), the United States Supreme Court recognized that expenditures on political campaigns constitute protected speech within the meaning of the First Amendment because "[d]iscussion of public issues and debate on the qualifications of candidates are integral to the operation of the system of government established by our Constitution." Since the presence or absence of money affects a candidate's ability to speak, the government does not have a free and unfettered right to regulate campaign finance expenditures. Nevertheless, many have argued that campaign finance expenditures are "out of control" and have corruptly and improperly influenced the political process.

In *Buckley*, despite its pro-free-speech rhetoric, the Court held that campaign finance activity is not entitled to absolute constitutional protection. The Court drew a distinction between "expenditure" limitations ("expenditures" are amounts spent by candidates, individuals, and political parties) and "contribution" limitations ("contributions" are amounts donated to candidates or political parties). In the Court's view, expenditure limitations are more objectionable because they directly limit communication about or by candidates and elected officials. By contrast, contribution limitations entail "only a marginal restriction upon the contributor's ability to engage in free communication" because, while contributions serve as "a general expression of support for the candidate and his views," they do not "communicate the underlying basis for the support." The nature of the communication does not change significantly because of the size of the contribution. Moreover, the Court expressed concern that campaign contributions might be given in expectation of a *quid pro quo* vote or action by the candidate, or could create an appearance of corruption. Nevertheless, even restrictions on campaign contributions were subject to review.

Relying on the distinction between contributions and expenditures, the Court struck down *Federal Election Campaign Act of 1971* expenditure limitations, which prohibited individuals from making expenditures "relative to a clearly identified candidate" in excess of $1,000. The Court found that the governmental interest in preventing corruption and the appearance of corruption was inadequate to justify the limitation given the absence of prearrangement and coordination of expenditures with candidates or their agents. The Court rejected the argument that the government has a sufficient interest "in equalizing the relative ability of individuals and groups to influence the outcome of elections." The Court also struck down limitations on expenditures by a candidate "from his personal funds, or the personal funds of his immediate family, in connection with his campaigns during any calendar year." The candidate, no less than any other person, has a First Amendment right to "engage in the discussion of public issues and vigorously and tirelessly to advocate his own election and the election of other candidates. Indeed, the use of personal funds reduces the candidate's dependence on outside contributions and thereby counteracts the coercive pressures and attendant risks of abuse." The Court also struck down limitations on overall campaign expenditures by candidates seeking nomination for election and election to federal office.

In *Buckley,* the Court upheld various disclosure requirements. The Court concluded that there must be a "relevant correlation" or "substantial relation" between the governmental interest and the information required to be disclosed. The Court concluded that disclosure requirements provide the electorate with information regarding the source of contributions. In addition, disclosure requirements "deter actual corruption and avoid the appearance of corruption by exposing large contributions and expenditures to the light of publicity." Finally, disclosure requirements help the government detect contribution violations.

In *McConnell,* the Court was confronted by a challenge to the Bipartisan Campaign Reform Act of 2002 (BCRA), which amended various campaign finance laws including the Federal Election Campaign Act of 1971 (FECA). Following *Buckley,* Congress became concerned about a number of problems in the campaign finance area. First, federal law permitted corporations and unions, as well as individuals who had already made the maximum permissible contributions to federal candidates, to contribute "nonfederal money"—also known as "soft money"—to political parties for activities intended to influence state or local elections. While hard money was limited in various ways, soft money was not. Second, *Buckley* held that FECA's disclosure and reporting requirements, as well as its expenditure limitations, applied only "to funds used for communications that expressly advocate the election or defeat of a clearly identified candidate." As a result, so-called "issue ads" could be financed with soft money even though little difference existed between "an ad that urged viewers to 'vote against Jane Doe'" and one that condemned Jane Doe's record on a particular issue before exhorting viewers to 'call Jane Doe and tell her what you think.'" Finally, the Senate Committee on Governmental Affairs issued [a] report which found that the "soft money loophole" had led to a "meltdown" of the campaign finance system. "[B]oth parties promised and provided special access to candidates and senior Government officials in exchange for large soft-money contributions [and] both parties began to use large amounts of soft money to pay for issue advertising designed to influence federal elections." In addition, national parties frequently transferred soft money to state and local parties for "generic voter activities" that benefitted federal candidates and were effectively controlled by national committees.

In an effort to remedy these problems, BCRA amended federal election laws in a number of ways. First, BCRA prohibited national party committees and their agents from soliciting, receiving, directing, or spending any soft money. In upholding these provisions, the Court in the first majority opinion (the case produced *three* majority opinions) relied on *Buckley* and held that such activities have only a marginal impact on political speech and can "corrupt [or] create the appearance of corruption of federal candidates and officeholders" because "candidates would feel grateful for such donations and that donors would seek to exploit that gratitude." The Court noted that national party committees "peddle access to federal candidates and officeholders in exchange for large soft-money donations and actually furnish their own menus of opportunities for access to would-be soft-money donors."

The Court noted that this rationale applied even to restrictions on the source and amount limits that applied to purely state and local elections in which no federal office is at stake. The Court emphasized "the close relationship between federal officeholders and the national parties, as well as the means by which parties have traded on that relationship, that have made all large soft-money contributions to national parties suspect."

BCRA also prohibited national, state, and local party committees, and their agents or subsidiaries, from "solicit[ing] any funds for, or mak[ing] or direct[ing] any donations" to any organization established under § 501(c) of the Internal Revenue Code that makes expenditures in connection with an election for federal office, and any political organizations established under § 527 (basically, organizations created solely to engage in protected political activity) "other than a political committee, a State, district, or local committee of a political party, or the authorized campaign committee of a candidate for State or local office." Absent the solicitation provision, national, state, and local party committees "had significant incentives to mobilize their formidable fundraising apparatuses, including the peddling of access to federal officeholders, into the service of like-minded tax-exempt organizations that conduct activities benefiting their candidates. The Court used like analysis to extend the ban to § 527 organizations."

BCRA also prohibited federal candidates and officeholders from "solicit[ing], receiv[ing], direct[ing], transfer[ring], or spend[ing]" any soft money in connection with federal elections. It also limited the ability of federal candidates and officeholders to solicit, receive, direct, transfer, or spend soft money in connection with state and local elections. The Court found that large "soft-money donations at a candidate's or officeholder's behest give rise to all of the same corruption concerns."

BCRA also prohibited candidates for state or local office, or state or local officeholders, from spending soft money to fund "public communications"—i.e., a communication that "refers to a clearly identified candidate for Federal office [and] that promotes or supports a candidate for that office, or attacks or opposes a candidate for that office." The Court upheld the provision, noting that it focused "narrowly on those soft-money donations with the greatest potential to corrupt or give rise to the appearance of corruption of federal candidates and officeholders."

The Court also upheld Section II of BCRA, which required political committees to file detailed financial reports with the Federal Election Commission, and a provision that precluded corporations and unions from financing electioneering communications out of their general treasuries within 60 days of an election. In order to engage in such communications, corporations were essentially forced to create new corporations who solicit segregated funds solely for political purposes. The Court concluded that the state interest in this provision was compelling given that "the special characteristics of the corporate structure require particularly careful regulation."

BCRA also contained a provision that excluded from the definition of electioneering communications any "communication appearing in a news story, commentary, or editorial distributed through the facilities of any broadcasting station, unless such facilities are owned or controlled by any political party, political committee, or candidate." The Court noted that this provision applied to news items and commentary only and did not afford *carte blanche* to media companies generally to ignore FECA's provisions.

In the second majority opinion, this one by Chief Justice Rehnquist, the Court BCRA provisions requiring that "certain communications 'authorized' by a candidate or his political committee clearly identify the candidate or committee or, if not so authorized, identify the payor and announce the lack of authorization." The Court held that the provision "bears a sufficient relationship to the important governmental interest of 'shed[ding] the light of publicity' on campaign financing." However, the Court struck down a prohibition that precluded individuals "17 years old or younger" from making contributions to candidates and contributions or donations to political parties. The Court noted that even minors enjoy the protection of the First Amendment and that the asserted governmental interests (protection against corruption by conduit, that is, donations by parents through their minor children to circumvent contribution limits applicable to the parents) were insufficient to sustain the provision. In addition, that interest could be served in other ways (e.g., a restriction on the total amount that could be contributed by a single family).

In the third majority opinion, this one written by Justice Stephen Breyer, the Court upheld BCRA's candidate request requirements [which required broadcast licensees to "keep" a publicly available file "of all requests for broadcast time made by or on behalf of a candidate for public office," along with a notation showing whether the request was granted, and (if granted) a history that includes "classes of time," "rates charged," and when the "spots actually aired"]. The Court held that such requirements were justifiable as part of the government's effort to ensure that broadcasters were satisfying their broadcast obligations under federal law.

Justice Scalia, concurring and dissenting, questioned the Court's decision to uphold BCRA's campaign finance restrictions while previously striking down restrictions on child pornography and sexually explicit cable programming. He argued that campaign finance laws cut "to the heart of what the First Amendment is meant to protect: the right to criticize the government." He also noted that BCRA "*targets* for prohibition" certain categories of campaign speech that are particularly harmful to incumbents and questioned whether it was purely "accidental" that such speech was targeted. He also questioned the decision to ban attack ads. "The premise of the First Amendment is that the American people are neither sheep nor fools, and hence fully capable of considering both the substance of the speech presented to them and its proximate and ultimate source. If that premise is wrong, our democracy has a much greater problem to overcome than merely the influence of amassed wealth." While the Government's briefs [focused] on the horrible "appearance of corruption," the most passionate floor statements [on] this legislation pertained to so-called attack ads.

Justice Thomas also concurred in part and dissented in part, arguing that because "the First Amendment 'has its fullest and most urgent application' to speech uttered during a campaign for political office," the Court is obligated to subject those restrictions to the "strictest scrutiny." He noted that the majority had abandoned the "fundamental principle" that "the best test of truth is the power of the thought to get itself accepted in the competition of the market" in favor of its purported objective of preventing "corruption," or the mere "appearance of corruption." He went on to note that the evidence suggested only that "federal officeholders have commonly asked donors to make soft-money donations to national and state committees solely in order to assist federal campaigns, including the officeholder's own." He concluded that bribery laws could have been used to deal with such abuses.

Justice Kennedy concurred and dissented arguing that only one interest justifies campaign finance laws: "eliminating, or preventing, actual corruption or the appearance of corruption stemming from contributions to candidates." He viewed BCRA as extending far beyond that rationale to "any conduct that wins goodwill from or influences a Member of Congress." He particularly objected to provisions prohibiting corporate communications referring to a candidate for federal office in the weeks immediately before an election. "[To] say [that corporations and unions] cannot alert the public to pending political issues that may threaten the country's economic interests is unprecedented."

In *McConnell's* wake, some have questioned whether there is a meaningful distinction to be made, in terms of campaign finance laws, between media and nonmedia corporations. With regard to advertisements run by nonmedia corporations, the Court upheld restrictions on the basis that candidates and officeholders might look with favor on corporations that run such advertisements. But, in dissent, Chief Justice Rehnquist notes that: "Newspaper editorials and political talk shows *benefit* federal candidates and officeholders every bit as much as a generic voter registration drive conducted by a state party. [T]here is little doubt that the endorsement of a major newspaper *affects* federal elections, and federal candidates and officeholders are surely 'grateful' for positive media coverage." As a result, he asks whether *McConnell* might permit Congress to regulate editorials and political talk shows.

*McConnell* was an important decision because it affirmed broad congressional authority to regulate campaign finance contributions. However, the breadth of the prohibition was staggering and imposed significant restrictions on the ability of individuals to communicate with each other and to participate in the political process.

One of the principle concerns about the *McConnell* decision was addressed by the Court seven years later in *Citizens United v. Federal Election Commission* (2010). In *Citizens United*, the Court held that corporations and unions have free speech rights, and overruled that part of *McConnell* that restricted independent expenditures from corporate and union treasuries. The Court, in an opinion authored by Justice Kennedy, declared that "[T]he Government may not suppress political speech on the basis of the speaker's corporate identity. No sufficient governmental interest justifies limits on the political speech of nonprofit or for-profit corporations." Justice Stevens, joined by Justices Ginsburg, Breyer and Sotomayor, wrote a lengthy dissent arguing that corporations are fundamentally different from human beings, and that the framers never intended the First Amendment to apply to them. The dissent also cautioned about the opportunity for corruption posed by corporate money in the political arena.

### Justice STEVENS and Justice O'CONNOR delivered the opinion of the Court with respect to its principal parts.

. . . The Bipartisan Campaign Reform Act of 2002 (BCRA), contains a series of amendments to the Federal Election Campaign Act of 1971 (FECA or Act), and other portions of the United States Code that are challenged in these cases.

More than a century ago the "sober-minded Elihu Root" advocated legislation that would prohibit political contributions by corporations in order to prevent " 'the great aggregations of wealth, from using their corporate funds, directly or indirectly,' " to elect legislators who would " 'vote for their protection and the advancement of their interests as against those of the public.' " In Root's opinion, such legislation would " 'strik[e] at a constantly growing evil which has done more to shake the confidence of the plain people of small means of this country in our political institutions than any other practice which has ever obtained since the foundation of our Government.' " The Congress of the United States has repeatedly enacted legislation endorsing Root's judgment.

BCRA is the most recent federal enactment designed "to purge national politics of what was conceived to be the pernicious influence of 'big money' campaign contributions." As Justice Frankfurter explained in his opinion for the Court in *Automobile Workers,* the first such enactment responded to President Theodore Roosevelt's call for legislation forbidding all contributions by corporations " 'to any political committee or for any political purpose.' " In his annual message to Congress in December 1905, President Roosevelt stated that " 'directors should not be permitted to use stockholders' money' " for political purposes, and he recommended that " 'a prohibition' " on corporate political contributions " 'would be, as far as it went, an effective method of stopping the evils aimed at in corrupt practices acts.' " . . .

## Justice SCALIA, dissenting in part.

. . . This is a sad day for the freedom of speech. Who could have imagined that the same Court which, within the past four years, has sternly disapproved of restrictions upon such inconsequential forms of expression as virtual child pornography, tobacco advertising, dissemination of illegally intercepted communications, and sexually explicit cable programming, would smile with favor upon a law that cuts to the heart of what the First Amendment is meant to protect: the right to criticize the government. For that is what the most offensive provisions of this legislation are all about. We are governed by Congress, and this legislation prohibits the criticism of Members of Congress by those entities most capable of giving such criticism loud voice: national political parties and corporations, both of the commercial and the not-for-profit sort. It forbids pre-election criticism of incumbents by corporations, even not-for-profit corporations, by use of their general funds; and forbids national-party use of "soft" money to fund "issue ads" that incumbents find so offensive.

To be sure, the legislation is evenhanded: It similarly prohibits criticism of the candidates who oppose Members of Congress in their reelection bids. But as everyone knows, this is an area in which evenhandedness is not fairness. If *all* electioneering were evenhandedly prohibited, incumbents would have an enormous advantage. Likewise, if incumbents and challengers are limited to the same quantity of electioneering, incumbents are favored. In other words, *any* restriction upon a type of campaign speech that is equally available to challengers and incumbents tends to favor incumbents. . . .

## Bibliography

De Figueiredo, John M., and Elizabeth Garrett. "Paying for Politics." *Southern California Law Review* 78 (2005): 591.

Foley, Edward B. "'Smith for Congress' and its Equivalents: An Endorsement Test under Buckley and MCFL." *Election Law Journal* 2 (2003): 3.

Overton, Spencer. "Restraint and Responsibility." *Washington and Lee Law Review* 61 (2004): 663.

Weaver, Russell L., and Donald E. Lively. *Understanding the First Amendment.* Newark, NJ: LexisNexis, 2012, 137–158.

## Citizens United v. Federal Election Commission

Citation: 130 S.Ct. 876.

Issue: Whether limiting corporate campaign finance expenditures violates the First Amendment.

Year of Decision: 2010.

Outcome: Yes. Corporations have free speech rights such that limits on corporate expenditures violate the First Amendment.

Author of Opinion: Justice Kennedy.

Vote: 5-4.

The Bipartisan Campaign Reform Act of 2002 (BCRA) prohibits corporations and unions from using their general treasury funds to spend money for speech that is an "electioneering communication" or for speech that expressly advocates for or against a candidate. The BCRA defines an "electioneering communication" as "any broadcast, cable, or satellite communication" that "refers to a clearly identified candidate for Federal office" and is made within 30 days of a primary election, and that is "publicly distributed." As noted earlier, the Court in *McConnell v. Federal Election Commission* had upheld limits on electioneering communications on the basis that political speech may be banned based on the speaker's corporate identity.

A nonprofit corporation, appellant Citizens United, released a film documentary titled *Hillary* that was critical of then-Senator Hillary Clinton, a candidate for her party's Presidential nomination. Hoping to make *Hillary* available on cable television within 30 days of primary elections, Citizens United created TV ads to run on broadcast and cable television. Based on its concern that these ads might violate BCRA, Citizens United bought suit on the grounds that BCRA's corporate campaign limits were unconstitutional.

Writing for the majority, Justice Kennedy agreed with Citizens United, maintaining that "[T]he Government may not suppress political speech on the basis of the speaker's corporate identity. No sufficient governmental interest justifies limits on the political speech of nonprofit or for-profit corporations." In effect, the majority argued that money is speech, and a healthy democracy must protect such speech, regardless of whether it comes directly from an individual, or from individuals acting in a corporate capacity. However, in an 8-1 ruling, the Court upheld BCRA's disclosure requirements on the grounds that they are important in curbing corruption, or appearance of corruption, from large expenditures of money in political campaigns.

Joined by Justices Ginsburg, Breyer and Sotomayor, Justice Stevens dissented, contending that corporations are fundamentally different from human beings such that they cannot be understood to enjoy free speech rights. Justice Stevens concluded his dissent as follows: "At bottom, the Court's opinion is thus a rejection of the common sense of the American people, who have recognized a need to prevent corporations from undermining self-government since the founding, and who have fought against the distinctive corrupting potential of corporate electioneering since the days of Theodore Roosevelt."

## Justice KENNEDY delivered the opinion of the Court.

. . . The law before us is an outright ban, backed by criminal sanctions. [It] makes it a felony for all corporations—including nonprofit advocacy corporations—either to expressly advocate the election or defeat of candidates or to broadcast electioneering communications within 30 days of a primary election and 60 days of a general election. Thus, the following acts would all be felonies under [the law]: The Sierra Club runs an ad, within the crucial phase of 60 days before the general election, that exhorts the public to disapprove of a Congressman who favors logging in national forests; the National Rifle Association publishes a book urging the public to vote for the challenger because the incumbent U.S. Senator supports a handgun ban; and the American Civil Liberties Union creates a Web site telling the public to vote for a Presidential candidate in light of that candidate's defense of free speech. These prohibitions are classic examples of censorship. . . .

Premised on mistrust of governmental power, the First Amendment stands against attempts to disfavor certain subjects or viewpoints. Prohibited, too, are restrictions distinguishing among different speakers, allowing speech by some but not others. As instruments to censor, these categories are interrelated: Speech restrictions based on the identity of the speaker are all too often simply a means to control content.

Quite apart from the purpose or effect of regulating content, moreover, the Government may commit a constitutional wrong when by law it identifies certain preferred speakers. By taking the right to speak from some and giving it to others, the Government deprives the disadvantaged person or class of the right to use speech to strive to establish worth, standing, and respect for the speaker's voice. The Government may not by these means deprive the public of the right and privilege to determine for itself what speech and speakers are worthy of consideration. The First Amendment protects speech and speaker, and the ideas that flow from each.

The Court has upheld a narrow class of speech restrictions that operate to the disadvantage of certain persons, but these rulings were based on an interest in allowing governmental entities to perform their functions. The corporate independent expenditures at issue in this case, however, would not interfere with governmental functions, so these cases are inapposite. These precedents stand only for the proposition that there are certain governmental functions that cannot operate without some restrictions on particular kinds of speech. By contrast, it is inherent in the nature of the political process that voters must be free to obtain information from diverse sources in order to determine how to cast their votes. At least before *Austin,* the Court had not allowed the exclusion of a class of speakers from the general public dialogue.

We find no basis for the proposition that, in the context of political speech, the Government may impose restrictions on certain disfavored speakers. Both history and logic lead us to this conclusion.

The Court has recognized that First Amendment protection extends to corporations. This protection has been extended by explicit holdings to the context of political speech. Under the rationale of these precedents, political speech does not lose First Amendment protection "simply because its source is a corporation." The Court has thus rejected the argument that political speech of corporations or other associations should be treated differently under the First Amendment simply because such associations are not "natural persons."

There is simply no support for the view that the First Amendment, as originally understood, would permit the suppression of political speech by media corporations. The Framers may not have anticipated modern business and media corporations. Yet television networks and major newspapers owned by media corporations have become the most important means of mass communication in modern times. The First Amendment was certainly not understood to condone the suppression of political speech in society's most salient media. It was understood as a response to the repression of speech and the press that had existed in England and the heavy taxes on the press that were imposed in the colonies. The great debates between the Federalists and the Anti–Federalists over our founding document were published and expressed in the most important means of mass communication of that era—newspapers owned by individuals. At the founding, speech was open, comprehensive, and vital to society's definition of itself; there were no limits on the sources of speech and knowledge. The Framers may have been unaware of certain types of speakers or forms of communication, but that does not mean that those speakers and media are entitled to less First Amendment protection than those types of speakers and media that provided the means of communicating political ideas when the Bill of Rights was adopted. . . .

## Justice STEVENS, with whom Justice GINSBURG, Justice BREYER, and Justice SOTOMAYOR join, concurring in part and dissenting in part.

. . . The basic premise underlying the Court's ruling is its iteration, and constant reiteration, of the proposition that the First Amendment bars regulatory distinctions based on a speaker's identity, including its "identity" as a corporation. While that glittering generality has rhetorical appeal, it is not a correct statement of the law. Nor does it tell us when a corporation may engage in electioneering that some of its shareholders oppose. It does not even resolve the specific question whether Citizens United may be required to finance some of its messages with the money in its PAC. The conceit that corporations must be treated identically to natural persons in the political sphere is not only inaccurate but also inadequate to justify the Court's disposition of this case.

In the context of election to public office, the distinction between corporate and human speakers is significant. Although they make enormous contributions to our society, corporations are not actually members of it. They cannot vote or run for office. Because they may be managed and controlled by nonresidents, their interests may conflict in fundamental respects with the interests of eligible voters. The financial resources, legal structure, and instrumental orientation of corporations raise legitimate concerns about their role in the electoral process. Our lawmakers have a compelling constitutional basis, if not also a democratic duty, to take measures designed to guard against the potentially deleterious effects of corporate spending in local and national races. . . .

## Bibliography

Hasen, Richard L. "*Citizens United* and the Illusion of Coherence." *Michigan Law Review* 109 (2011): 581.

Skrabacz, Jonathan E. "'Leveling the Playing Field': Reconsidering Campaign Finance Reform in the Wake of Arizona Free Enterprise." *St. Louis University Public Law Review* 32 (2013): 487.

## McCutcheon v. Federal Election Commission

**Citation: 134 S.Ct. 1434.**

**Issue: Whether the aggregate campaign contribution limit is constitutional under the First Amendment.**

**Year of Decision: 2014.**

**Outcome: No. Because the aggregate limit fails to meet the government's objective of preventing corruption, it does not survive the "rigorous" standard of review required by this Court and therefore violates the First Amendment.**

**Author of Opinion: Chief Justice Roberts.**

**Vote: 5-4.**

The Federal Election Campaign Act of 1971 (FECA), as amended by the Bipartisan Campaign Reform Act of 2002 (BCRA), imposes two types of limits on campaign contributions. First of all, the law limits how much money a donor may contribute to a particular candidate or committee. Second, certain aggregate limits restrict how much money a donor may contribute in total to all candidates or committees.

Appellant McCutcheon alleged that the aggregate limits prevented him from contributing to 12 additional candidates as well as a number of noncandidate political committees. He also alleged that he wishes to make similar contributions in the future, all within the base limits. McCutcheon filed a complaint asserting that the aggregate limits were unconstitutional under the First Amendment.

In an opinion by Chief Justice Roberts, the plurality held that the aggregate limits did not adequately address the problem of corruption in the electoral process, while at the same time they did limit participation in the democratic process. Because the aggregate limits fail to meet the stated objective of preventing corruption, they do not satisfy the "rigorous" standard of review required by the First Amendment and are therefore unconstitutional.

The limits further prevent a donor from contributing beyond a specific amount to more than a certain number of candidates. This may well result in forcing the donor to choose which interests he can seek to advance in a particular election. This curtails an individual's freedom of speech. The plurality opinion also noted that there are many other means available to the government by which it may fight election corruption without setting an aggregate limit on campaign contributions.

Justice Clarence Thomas wrote an opinion concurring in the judgment in which he argued that *Buckley* itself should be overruled because it undermines the First Amendment's core protection of free speech.

Justice Stephen Breyer, in a dissent joined by Justices Ginsburg, Sotomayor, and Kagan, argued that the plurality's opinion destroys campaign finance laws intended to guard against corruption, resulting in great harm to the democratic process. Justice Breyer maintained that the plurality's opinion was based on a definition of corruption that is far too narrow.

To a significant degree, the disagreement dividing the conservative and liberal members of the Court turns on the extent to which the government should oversee the role of money and its influence in the electoral process. The more conservative members tend to favor fewer restrictions, in the belief that democratic freedoms are better served when the government is not seeking to control speech in the form of monetary contributions. The more liberal members tend to favor greater governmental control, because they are more concerned that money buys influence such that those with greater wealth enjoy disproportionate influence. This philosophic divide is likely to continue shaping the Court's decisions for some time.

**Chief Justice ROBERTS announced the judgment of the Court and delivered an opinion, in which Justice SCALIA, Justice KENNEDY, and Justice ALITO join. THOMAS, J., filed an opinion concurring in the judgment.**

. . . The right to participate in democracy through political contributions is protected by the First Amendment, but that right is not absolute. Our cases have held that Congress may regulate campaign contributions to protect against corruption or the appearance of corruption. At the same time, we have made clear that

Congress may not regulate contributions simply to reduce the amount of money in politics, or to restrict the political participation of some in order to enhance the relative influence of others. . . .

The statute at issue in this case imposes two types of limits on campaign contributions. The first, called base limits, restricts how much money a donor may contribute to a particular candidate or committee. 2 U.S.C. § 441a(a)(1). The second, called aggregate limits, restricts how much money a donor may contribute in total to all candidates or committees. § 441a(a)(3) . . . .

This case does not involve any challenge to the base limits, which we have previously upheld as serving the permissible objective of combatting corruption. The Government contends that the aggregate limits also serve that objective, by preventing circumvention of the base limits. We conclude, however, that the aggregate limits do little, if anything, to address that concern, while seriously restricting participation in the democratic process. The aggregate limits are therefore invalid under the First Amendment. . . .

The First Amendment "is designed and intended to remove governmental restraints from the arena of public discussion, putting the decision as to what views shall be voiced largely into the hands of each of us, . . . in the belief that no other approach would comport with the premise of individual dignity and choice upon which our political system rests." As relevant here, the First Amendment safeguards an individual's right to participate in the public debate through political expression and political association. When an individual contributes money to a candidate, he exercises both of those rights: The contribution "serves as a general expression of support for the candidate and his views" and "serves to affiliate a person with a candidate."

Those First Amendment rights are important regardless whether the individual is, on the one hand, a "lone pamphleteer[ ] or street corner orator[ ] in the Tom Paine mold," or is, on the other, someone who spends "substantial amounts of money in order to communicate [his] political ideas through sophisticated" means. Either way, he is participating in an electoral debate that we have recognized is "integral to the operation of the system of government established by our Constitution."

*Buckley* acknowledged that aggregate limits at least diminish an individual's right of political association. As the Court explained, the "overall $25,000 ceiling does impose an ultimate restriction upon the number of candidates and committees with which an individual may associate himself by means of financial support." But the Court characterized that restriction as a "quite modest restraint upon protected political activity." We cannot agree with that characterization. An aggregate limit on *how many* candidates and committees an individual may support through contributions is not a "modest restraint" at all. The Government may no more restrict how many candidates or causes a donor may support than it may tell a newspaper how many candidates it may endorse.

To put it in the simplest terms, the aggregate limits prohibit an individual from fully contributing to the primary and general election campaigns of ten or more candidates, even if all contributions fall within the base limits Congress views as adequate to protect against corruption. The individual may give up to $5,200 each to nine candidates, but the aggregate limits constitute an outright ban on further contributions to any other candidate (beyond the additional $1,800 that may be spent before reaching the $48,600 aggregate limit). At that point, the limits deny the individual all ability to exercise his expressive and associational rights by contributing to someone who will advocate for his policy preferences. A donor must limit the number of candidates he supports, and may have to choose which of several policy concerns he will advance—clear First Amendment harms that the dissent never acknowledges.

It is no answer to say that the individual can simply contribute less money to more people. To require one person to contribute at lower levels than others because he wants to support more candidates or causes is to impose a special burden on broader participation in the democratic process. And as we have recently admonished, the Government may not penalize an individual for "robustly exercis[ing]" his First Amendment rights.

The First Amendment burden is especially great for individuals who do not have ready access to alternative avenues for supporting their preferred politicians and policies. In the context of base contribution limits, *Buckley* observed that a supporter could vindicate his associational interests by personally volunteering his time and energy on behalf of a candidate. Such personal volunteering is not a realistic alternative for those who wish to support a wide variety of candidates or causes. Other effective methods of supporting preferred candidates or causes without contributing money are reserved for a select few, such as entertainers capable of raising hundreds of thousands of dollars in a single evening.

The dissent faults this focus on "the individual's right to engage in political speech," saying that it fails to take into account "the public's interest" in "collective speech." This "collective" interest is said to promote "a government where laws reflect the very thoughts, views, ideas, and sentiments, the expression of which the First Amendment protects."

But there are compelling reasons not to define the boundaries of the First Amendment by reference to such a generalized conception of the public good. First, the dissent's "collective speech" reflected in laws is of course the will of the majority, and plainly can include laws that restrict free speech. The whole point of the First Amendment is to afford individuals protection against such infringements. The First Amendment does not protect the government, even when the government purports to act through legislation reflecting "collective speech."

Second, the degree to which speech is protected cannot turn on a legislative or judicial determination that particular speech is useful to the democratic process. The First Amendment does not contemplate such "ad hoc balancing of relative social costs and benefits."

Third, our established First Amendment analysis already takes account of any "collective" interest that may justify restrictions on individual speech. Under that accepted analysis, such restrictions are measured against the asserted public interest (usually framed as an important or compelling governmental interest). As explained below, we do not doubt the compelling nature of the "collective" interest in preventing corruption in the electoral process. But we permit Congress to pursue that interest only so long as it does not unnecessarily infringe an individual's right to freedom of speech; we do not truncate this tailoring test at the outset.

With the significant First Amendment costs for individual citizens in mind, we turn to the governmental interests asserted in this case. This Court has identified only one legitimate governmental interest for restricting campaign finances: preventing corruption or the appearance of corruption. We have consistently rejected attempts to suppress campaign speech based on other legislative objectives. No matter how desirable it may seem, it is not an acceptable governmental objective to "level the playing field," or to "level electoral opportunities," or to "equaliz[e] the financial resources of candidates." The First Amendment prohibits such legislative attempts to "fine-tun[e]" the electoral process, no matter how well intentioned.

As we framed the relevant principle in *Buckley,* "the concept that government may restrict the speech of some elements of our society in order to enhance the relative voice of others is wholly foreign to the First Amendment." The dissent's suggestion that *Buckley* supports the opposite proposition, simply ignores what *Buckley* actually said on the matter.

Moreover, while preventing corruption or its appearance is a legitimate objective, Congress may target only a specific type of corruption—"*quid pro quo* " corruption. As *Buckley* explained, Congress may permissibly seek to rein in "large contributions [that] are given to secure a political *quid pro quo* from current and potential office holders." In addition to "actual *quid pro quo* arrangements," Congress may permissibly limit "the appearance of corruption stemming from public awareness of the opportunities for abuse inherent in a regime of large individual financial contributions" to particular candidates.

Spending large sums of money in connection with elections, but not in connection with an effort to control the exercise of an officeholder's official duties, does not give rise to such *quid pro quo* corruption. Nor does the possibility that an individual who spends large sums may garner "influence over or access to" elected officials or political parties. And because the Government's interest in preventing the appearance of corruption is equally confined to the appearance of *quid pro quo* corruption, the Government may not seek to limit the appearance of mere influence or access.

The dissent advocates a broader conception of corruption, and would apply the label to any individual contributions above limits deemed necessary to protect "collective speech." Thus, under the dissent's view, it is perfectly fine to contribute $5,200 to nine candidates but somehow corrupt to give the same amount to a tenth.

It is fair to say, as Justice Stevens has, "that we have not always spoken about corruption in a clear or consistent voice." The definition of corruption that we apply today, however, has firm roots in *Buckley* itself. The Court in that case upheld base contribution limits because they targeted "the danger of actual *quid pro quo* arrangements" and "the impact of the appearance of corruption stemming from public awareness" of such a system of unchecked direct contributions. *Buckley* simultaneously rejected limits on spending that was less likely to "be given as a *quid pro quo* for improper commitments from the candidate." In any event, this case is not the first in which the debate over the proper breadth of the Government's anticorruption interest has been engaged.

The line between *quid pro quo* corruption and general influence may seem vague at times, but the distinction must be respected in order to safeguard basic First Amendment rights. In addition, "[i]n drawing that line, the First Amendment requires us to err on the side of protecting political speech rather than suppressing it."

The dissent laments that our opinion leaves only remnants of FECA and BCRA that are inadequate to combat corruption. Such rhetoric ignores the fact that we leave the base limits undisturbed. Those base limits remain the primary means of regulating campaign contributions—the obvious explanation for why the aggregate limits received a scant few sentences of attention in *Buckley*.

"When the Government restricts speech, the Government bears the burden of proving the constitutionality of its actions." Here, the Government seeks to carry that burden by arguing that the aggregate limits further the permissible objective of preventing *quid pro quo* corruption.

The difficulty is that once the aggregate limits kick in, they ban all contributions of *any* amount. But Congress's selection of a $5,200 base limit indicates its belief that contributions of that amount or less do not create a cognizable risk of corruption. If there is no corruption concern in giving nine candidates up to $5,200 each, it is difficult to understand how a tenth candidate can be regarded as corruptible if given $1,801, and all others corruptible if given a dime. And if there is no risk that additional candidates will be corrupted by donations of up to $5,200, then the Government must defend the aggregate limits by demonstrating that they prevent circumvention of the base limits.

The problem is that they do not serve that function in any meaningful way. In light of the various statutes and regulations currently in effect, *Buckley's* fear that an individual might "contribute massive amounts of money to a particular candidate through the use of unearmarked contributions" to entities likely to support the candidate, is far too speculative. And—importantly—we "have never accepted mere conjecture as adequate to carry a First Amendment burden." . . .

For the past 40 years, our campaign finance jurisprudence has focused on the need to preserve authority for the Government to combat corruption, without at the same time compromising the political responsiveness at the heart of the democratic process, or allowing the Government to favor some participants in that process over others. As Edmund Burke explained in his famous speech to the electors of Bristol, a representative owes constituents the exercise of his "mature judgment," but judgment informed by "the strictest union, the closest correspondence, and the most unreserved communication with his constituents." The Speeches of the Right Hon. Edmund Burke 129–130 (J. Burke ed. 1867). Constituents have the right to support candidates who share their views and concerns. Representatives are not to follow constituent orders, but can be expected to be cognizant of and responsive to those concerns. Such responsiveness is key to the very concept of self-governance through elected officials.

The Government has a strong interest, no less critical to our democratic system, in combatting corruption and its appearance. We have, however, held that this interest must be limited to a specific kind of corruption—*quid pro quo* corruption—in order to ensure that the Government's efforts do not have the effect of restricting the First Amendment right of citizens to choose who shall govern them. For the reasons set forth, we conclude that the aggregate limits on contributions do not further the only governmental interest this Court accepted as legitimate in *Buckley*.

### Justice THOMAS, concurring in the judgment.

I adhere to the view that this Court's decision in *Buckley* denigrates core First Amendment speech and should be overruled.

Political speech is " 'the primary object of First Amendment protection' " and "the lifeblood of a self-governing people." Contributions to political campaigns, no less than direct expenditures, "generate essential political speech" by fostering discussion of public issues and candidate qualifications. *Buckley* itself recognized that both contribution and expenditure limits "operate in an area of the most fundamental First Amendment activities" and "implicate fundamental First Amendment interests." But instead of treating political giving and political spending alike, *Buckley* distinguished the two, embracing a bifurcated standard of review under which contribution limits receive less rigorous scrutiny.

As I have explained before, "[t]he analytic foundation of *Buckley* . . . was tenuous from the very beginning and has only continued to erode in the intervening years." To justify a lesser standard of review for contribution limits, *Buckley* relied on the premise that contributions are different in kind from direct expenditures. None of the Court's bases for that premise withstands careful review. The linchpin of the Court's analysis was its assertion that "[w]hile contributions may result in political expression if spent by a candidate or an association to present views to the voters, the transformation of contributions into political debate involves speech by someone other than the contributor." But that " 'speech by proxy' " rationale quickly breaks down, given that "[e]ven in the case of a direct expenditure, there is usually some go-between that facilitates the dissemination of the spender's message—for instance, an advertising agency or a television station. Moreover, we have since rejected the " 'proxy speech' " approach as affording insufficient First Amendment protection to "the voices of those of modest means as opposed to those sufficiently wealthy to be able to buy expensive media ads with their own resources." . . .

### Justice BREYER, with whom Justice GINSBURG, Justice SOTOMAYOR, and Justice KAGAN join, dissenting.

. . . Without further development of the record, however, I fail to see how the plurality can now find grounds for overturning *Buckley*. The justification for aggregate contribution restrictions is strongly rooted in the need to assure political integrity and ultimately in the First Amendment itself. The threat to that integrity posed by the risk of special access and influence remains real. Even taking the plurality on its own terms and considering solely the threat of *quid pro quo* corruption (*i.e.*, money-for-votes exchanges), the aggregate limits are a necessary tool to stop circumvention. And there is no basis for finding a lack of "fit" between the threat and the means used to combat it, namely the aggregate limits.

The plurality reaches the opposite conclusion. The result, as I said at the outset, is a decision that substitutes judges' understandings of how the political process works for the understanding of Congress; that fails to recognize the difference between influence resting upon public opinion and influence bought by money alone; that overturns key precedent; that creates huge loopholes in the law; and that undermines, perhaps devastates, what remains of campaign finance reform. . . .

## Bibliography

Noe, Mikala. "*Mccutcheon v. Federal Election Commission* and the Supreme Court's Narrowed Definition of Corruption." *Maine Law Review* 67 (2014): 163.

# STUDENT SPEECH

Freedom of expression extends to all persons regardless of age, but maturity may be a factor in determining the degree of the liberty. Government power to restrict access by minors to sexually explicit broadcasting, as discussed later in *Federal Communications Commission v. Pacifica Foundation* (1978), manifests this premise. Public schools are a primary incubator of case law concerning the speech liberties of minors. In *Tinker v. Des Moines Independent School District* (1969), the Court upheld the right of high school students to wear black armbands in protest of the Vietnam War. This ruling hinged in part upon the passive nature of the protest and finding that there was no disruption of school operations. The Court's decision in *Hazelwood School District v. Kuhlmeier* (1988) reaffirmed the proposition that students do not lose "their constitutional rights to freedom of speech or expression at the schoolhouse gate." It also determined, however, that student expression need not be tolerated if it was inconsistent with the school's educational mission. This finding expanded the power of school authorities to determine appropriate speech in the public school setting.

## *Hazelwood School District v. Kuhlmeier*

**Citation: 484 U.S. 260.**

**Issue: Whether a high school principal can censor a school newspaper for inappropriate content.**

**Year: 1988.**

**Outcome: While high school students are protected by the First Amendment, they are not protected against such censorship.**

**Author of Opinion: Justice Byron White.**

**Vote: 6-3.**

In First Amendment jurisprudence, there has been continuing debate about whether students should be accorded free speech rights comparable to those granted to adults. In *Tinker v. Des Moines Independent School District*, 393 U.S. 503 (1969), students wore black armbands to protest United States involvement in the Vietnam War. The Court overturned school official's suspension of the students noting that students have First Amendment rights, but that those rights are tempered by the "special characteristics of the school environment." However, in the Court's subsequent decision in *Bethel School District No. 403 v. Fraser,* 478 U.S. 675 (1986), it held that a student could be disciplined for statements made as part of a school campaign speech.

Student rights issues returned to the Court in the *Hazelwood School District* case, a case involving a student newspaper. In that case, a high school principal withheld from a student newspaper two pages containing student-authored stories about pregnancy and divorce. The decision was based on the principal's concern that the identity of pregnant students might be identifiable from the text, that references to sexual activity and birth control were inappropriate for some of the younger students, and that the parents of a student in the divorce story should be asked for consent to the publication of their daughter's comments about their divorce.

In considering the case, the Court began by recognizing that students do not "shed their constitutional rights [at] the schoolhouse gate." At the same time, the First Amendment rights of students in the public schools "are not automatically coextensive with the rights of adults in other settings." Reaffirming *Tinker,* the Court held that protections for student First Amendment rights must be considered "in light of the special characteristics of the school environment." The Court concluded that a school need not tolerate student speech that is inconsistent with its "basic educational mission," even if the government may not censor comparable speech outside the school environment.

Ultimately, in upholding the principal's actions, the Court held that "educators [may exercise] editorial control over the style and content of student speech in school-sponsored expressive activities so long as their actions are reasonably related to legitimate pedagogical concerns." The Court also noted that "A school may in its capacity as publisher of a school newspaper or producer of a school play 'disassociate itself,' not only from speech that would 'substantially interfere with [its] work [or] impinge on the rights of other students,' but also from speech that is, for example, ungrammatical, poorly written, inadequately researched, biased or prejudiced, vulgar or profane, or unsuitable for immature audiences. A school must be able to set high standards for the student speech that is disseminated under its [auspices]."

In evaluating the principal's actions, the Court found that the principal had legitimate pedagogical concerns in rejecting the articles. In regard to the pregnant students, he legitimately worried that student anonymity was not sufficiently ensured. "In addition, he could reasonably have been concerned that the article was not sufficiently sensitive to the privacy interests of the students' boyfriends and parents, who were discussed in the article but who were given no opportunity to consent to its publication or to offer a response." Moreover, since some of the articles contained frank talk about sexual activity, the principal was legitimately concerned "that such frank talk was inappropriate in a school-sponsored publication distributed to 14-year-old freshmen and presumably taken home to be read by students' even younger brothers and sisters." Finally, the Court concluded that the principal was legitimately concerned about the fact that a divorce was "sharply critical" of a child's father and that the father had not been given the chance to defend himself.

Justice Brennan, joined by Justices Marshall and Blackmun, dissented on grounds a school has no right to censor unless the speech "materially disrupts classwork or involves substantial disorder or invasion of the rights of others." Finding that this standard was not met, he concluded that the principal had engaged in impermissible "censorship authority." He rejected the notion that the school has a right to exercise control over "school-sponsored speech." In addition, he concluded that the school did not have the right to shield impressionable students from the speech: "*Tinker* teaches us that the state educator's undeniable, and undeniably vital, mandate to inculcate moral and political values is not a general warrant to act as 'thought police' stifling discussion of all but state-approved topics and advocacy of all but the official position."

*Hazelwood School District* is an important decision because it recognizes that, even though high school students retain free speech rights, those rights are more limited than the rights of adults. In the context of school-sponsored activities, such as a school newspaper operated as a part of a class activity, school officials retain some power of censorship.

## Justice WHITE delivered the opinion of the Court.

. . . The question whether the First Amendment requires a school to tolerate particular student speech—the question that we addressed in *Tinker*—is different from the question whether the First Amendment requires a school affirmatively to promote particular student speech. The former question addresses educators' ability to silence a student's personal expression that happens to occur on the school premises. The latter question concerns educators' authority over school-sponsored publications, theatrical productions, and other expressive activities that students, parents, and members of the public might reasonably perceive to bear the imprimatur of the school. These activities may fairly be characterized as part of the school curriculum, whether or not they occur in a traditional classroom setting, so long as they are supervised by faculty members and designed to impart particular knowledge or skills to student participants and audiences.

Educators are entitled to exercise greater control over this second form of student expression to assure that participants learn whatever lessons the activity is designed to teach, that readers or listeners are not exposed to material that may be inappropriate for their level of maturity, and that the views of the individual speaker are not erroneously attributed to the school. Hence, a school may in its capacity as publisher of a school newspaper or producer of a school play "disassociate itself," not only from speech that would "substantially interfere with [its] work . . . or impinge upon the rights of other students," but also from speech that is, for example, ungrammatical, poorly written, inadequately researched, biased or prejudiced, vulgar or profane, or unsuitable for immature audiences. A school must be able to set high standards for the student speech that is disseminated under its auspices—standards that may be higher than those demanded by some newspaper publishers or theatrical producers in the "real" world—and may refuse to disseminate student speech that does not meet those standards. In addition, a school must be able to take into account the emotional maturity of the intended audience in determining whether to disseminate student speech on potentially sensitive topics, which might range from the existence of Santa Claus in an elementary school setting to the particulars of teenage sexual activity in a high school setting. A school must also retain the authority to refuse to sponsor student speech that might reasonably be perceived to advocate drug or alcohol use, irresponsible sex, or conduct otherwise inconsistent with "the shared values of a civilized social order," or to associate the school with any position other than neutrality on matters of political controversy. . . .

Accordingly, we conclude that the standard articulated in *Tinker* for determining when a school may punish student expression need not also be the standard for determining when a school may refuse to lend its name and resources to the dissemination of student expression. Instead, we hold that educators do not offend the First Amendment by exercising editorial control over the style and content of student speech in school-sponsored expressive activities so long as their actions are reasonably related to legitimate pedagogical concerns. . . .

We also conclude that Principal Reynolds acted reasonably in requiring the deletion from the May 13 issue of Spectrum of the pregnancy article, the divorce article, and the remaining articles that were to appear on the same pages of the newspaper.

The initial paragraph of the pregnancy article declared that "[a]ll names have been changed to keep the identity of these girls a secret." The principal concluded that the students' anonymity was not adequately protected, however, given the other identifying information in the article and the small number of pregnant students at the school. Indeed, a teacher at the school credibly testified that she could positively identify at least one of the girls and possibly all three. It is likely that many students at Hazelwood East would have been at least as successful in identifying the girls. Reynolds therefore could reasonably have feared that the article violated whatever pledge of anonymity had been given to the pregnant students.

In addition, he could reasonably have been concerned that the article was not sufficiently sensitive to the privacy interests of the students' boyfriends and parents, who were discussed in the article but who were given no opportunity to consent to its publication or to offer a response. The article did not contain graphic accounts of sexual activity. The girls did comment in the article, however, concerning their sexual histories and their use or nonuse of birth control. It was not unreasonable for the principal to have concluded that such frank talk was inappropriate in a school-sponsored publication distributed to 14–year–old freshmen and presumably taken home to be read by students' even younger brothers and sisters.

The student who was quoted by name in the version of the divorce article seen by Principal Reynolds made comments sharply critical of her father. The principal could reasonably have concluded that an individual publicly identified as an inattentive parent—indeed, as one who chose "playing cards with the guys" over home and family—was entitled to an opportunity to defend himself as a matter of journalistic fairness. These concerns were shared by both of Spectrum's faculty advisers for the 1982–1983 school year, who testified that they would not have allowed the article to be printed without deletion of the student's name. . . .

In sum, we cannot reject as unreasonable Principal Reynolds' conclusion that neither the pregnancy article nor the divorce article was suitable for publication in Spectrum. Reynolds could reasonably have concluded that the students who had written and edited these articles had not sufficiently mastered those portions of the Journalism II curriculum that pertained to the treatment of controversial issues and personal attacks, the need to protect the privacy of individuals whose most intimate concerns are to be revealed in the newspaper, and "the legal, moral, and ethical restrictions imposed upon journalists within [a] school community" that includes adolescent subjects and readers. Finally, we conclude that the principal's decision to delete two pages of Spectrum, rather than to delete only the offending articles or to require that they be modified, was reasonable under the circumstances as he understood them. Accordingly, no violation of First Amendment rights occurred. . . .

## Justice BRENNAN, with whom Justice MARSHALL and Justice BLACKMUN join, dissenting.

When the young men and women of Hazelwood East High School registered for Journalism II, they expected a civics lesson. Spectrum, the newspaper they were to publish, "was not just a class exercise in which students learned to prepare papers and hone writing skills, it was a . . . forum established to give students an opportunity to express their views while gaining an appreciation of their rights and responsibilities under the First Amendment to the United States Constitution. . . ." "[A]t the beginning of each school year," the student journalists published a Statement of Policy—tacitly approved each year by school authorities—announcing their expectation that "Spectrum, as a student-press publication, accepts all rights implied by the First Amendment. . . . Only speech that 'materially and substantially interferes with the requirements of appropriate discipline' can be found unacceptable and therefore prohibited." The school board itself affirmatively guaranteed the students of Journalism II an atmosphere conducive to fostering such an appreciation and exercising the full panoply of rights associated with a free student press. "School sponsored student publications," it vowed, "will not restrict free expression or diverse viewpoints within the rules of responsible journalism."

This case arose when the Hazelwood East administration breached its own promise, dashing its students' expectations. The school principal, without prior consultation or explanation, excised six articles—comprising two full pages—of the May 13, 1983, issue of Spectrum. He did so not because any of the articles would "materially and substantially interfere with the requirements of appropriate discipline," but simply because he considered two of the six "inappropriate, personal, sensitive, and unsuitable" for student consumption.

In my view the principal broke more than just a promise. He violated the First Amendment's prohibitions against censorship of any student expression that neither disrupts classwork nor invades the rights of others, and against any censorship that is not narrowly tailored to serve its purpose. . . .

The Court opens its analysis in this case by purporting to reaffirm *Tinker's* time-tested proposition that public school students "do not 'shed their constitutional rights to freedom of speech or expression at the schoolhouse gate.' " That is an ironic introduction to an opinion that denudes high school students of much of the First Amendment protection that *Tinker* itself prescribed. Instead of "teach[ing] children to respect the diversity of ideas that is fundamental to the American system," and "that our Constitution is a living reality, not parchment preserved under glass," the Court today "teach[es] youth to discount important principles of our government as mere platitudes." The young men and women of Hazelwood East expected a civics lesson, but not the one the Court teaches them today.

I dissent.

## Bibliography

Chemerinsky, Erwin. "The Deconstitutionalization of Education." *Loyola University Chicago Law Journal* 36 (2004): 111.

Rosen, Mark D. "The Surprisingly Strong Case for Tailoring Constitutional Principles." *University of Pennsylvania Law Review* 153 (2005): 1513.

Weaver, Russell L., and Donald E. Lively. *Understanding the First Amendment.* Newark, NJ: LexisNexis, 2012, 204–207.

# Chapter 12

# First Amendment: Freedom of Speech (Content-Neutral Regulation)

The concept of content neutrality, during the final decades of the twentieth century, has evolved as a particularly significant limiting principle. Insofar as a regulation is understood to regulate a concern unrelated to or secondary to speech, standards of review are more relaxed than they would be if content itself was regulated. The earliest content neutrality cases arose in the context of accounting for interests such as traffic flow and competing uses in public forums. In the late 1960s, as evidenced in *United States v. O'Brien* (discussed in the subsection on symbolic speech), content neutrality principles expanded beyond the public forum context. The content neutrality concept represents a particularly profound development insofar as it increases space and opportunity for regulation and diminishes the range of constitutional concern.

## PUBLIC FORUMS

The quality of expressive freedom turns in significant part upon opportunity to access a place to speak, communicate, or interact. Consistent with this premise, Justice Owen Roberts in *Hague v. C.I.O.* (1939) observed that "streets and parks . . . have immemorially been held in trust for the use of the public and, time out of mind, have been used for purposes of assembly, communicating thoughts between citizens, and discussing public questions. Such use of the streets and public places has, from ancient time, been a part of the privileges, immunities, rights, and liberties of citizens." Justice Roberts's characterization of the availability of streets and parks for expressive purposes exaggerated the First Amendment tradition associated with them. Less than half a century earlier, the Court in *Davis v. Massachusetts* (1897) rejected the premise that parks or highways "from time immemorial" had been open to speech. It thus found government denial of public access to be no different than a decision by a private property owner.

Although the "time immemorial" understanding may be overstated, it nonetheless has shaped modern understanding of public forums. Two primary First Amendment interests arise in the public forum context. The first is whether a forum actually is accessible to the public. The second concerns the extent to which government may regulate it. With respect to the first issue, access depends upon how the forum is characterized. On the second matter, the constitutionality of regulation hinges upon whether it is content-based or content-neutral. If government aims to control content, its reasons and means will be strictly scrutinized. A diminished standard of review may operate if the speech is perceived as having a low value. Content-neutral regulation typically manifests itself in the form of time, place, or manner restrictions. Typical concerns in this context include management of competing uses, protection of property, maintaining traffic flow, and public safety.

Public forum doctrine has become an increasingly significant and complex aspect of First Amendment jurisprudence. The Court, in *Perry Education Association v. Perry Local Educators' Association* (1983), identified different types of public forums and set forth the basic rules governing each of them. In *Rosenberger v. University of Virginia* (1995), the Court demonstrated the elastic and sometimes abstract nature of a public forum.

## Perry Education Association v. Perry Local Educators' Association

**Citation: 460 U.S. 37.**

**Issue: Whether an interschool mail system and teacher mailboxes were public forums and thus accessible to parties other than those provided for by a collective bargaining agreement.**

**Year of Decision: 1983.**

**Outcome: The mail system and mailboxes were not public forums, so the collective bargaining agreement limiting access to them did not violate the First Amendment.**

**Author of Opinion: Justice Byron White.**

**Vote: 5-4.**

Freedom of speech standards of review are at their peak when government attempts to regulate on the basis of content. Even when regulation is not directed at content, it may have an impact on speech. Under such circumstances, First Amendment interests may abate but they do not disappear. A classic example of this phenomenon arose in *United States v. O'Brien* (1968) when the Court upheld the conviction of an antiwar protester who burned his draft card. Although the demonstrator's symbolic expression became the basis for the prosecution, the Court found that the government was acting primarily upon the content-neutral concern of ensuring the operational efficiency of the selective service system.

Regulation is content-neutral, even if it affects speech, when the law accounts for an interest unrelated to expression. Content neutrality is evidenced, for instance, in symbolic speech regulation that targets conduct rather than expression. It also is manifested when the law attempts to manage those effects of speech that are secondary rather than primary. An example of secondary affects regulation arises when, as in *Young v. American Mini Theatres Inc.* (1976), a city zoning ordinance restricted the location of adult movie theatres pursuant to an interest in neighbor-hood quality. The richest source of content-neutral regulation, however, pertains to governance of public forums on the basis of time, place, or manner.

In public forum cases, the threshold issue is one of definition. Private property implicates no state action and thus is beyond the scope of First Amendment con-cern. Public property may be available for expressive purposes, however, depend-ing upon its use. Certain types of forums must be accessible. In any event, legitimate public forum management must account for interests unrelated to speech content. Typical concerns include protection of property, scheduling competing uses, effi-cient traffic flow, and public safety. These types of interests provide the basis not for regulation of content but of the time, place, and manner of expression.

Public forum doctrine was introduced in the late 1930s, when the Supreme Court in *Hague v. CIO* (1938) determined that streets and parks "immemorially have been held in trust for the use of the public and, time out of mind, have been used for purposes of assembly, communicating thoughts between citizens, and discussing public questions." The characterization of streets and parks as forums that "immemorially" have been reserved for speech may have overstated reality. Four decades previously, in *Davis v. Massachusetts* (1897), the Court specifically had rejected the premise that "from time immemorial," parks had been accessible for public speaking. Notwithstanding the historical glitch, the *Hague* decision rec-ognized what modern case law refers to as the traditional public forum.

The civil rights era was a time of significant growth for public forum doctrine. Official efforts to deter protests in public places during the 1960s affirmed the freedom to speak and assemble on state capitol grounds, *Edwards v. South Caro-lina* (1963), and on public sidewalks, *Cox v. Louisiana* (1965). Decisions like these accounted effectively for speech interests in traditional public forums. In *Brown v. Louisiana* (1966), however, the Court reversed breach of peace convictions of persons who protested silently in a public library. The Court in the same term, in *Adderley v. Florida* (1966), upheld the trespass convictions of demonstrators who protested on jailhouse grounds. These cases indicated uncertainty with respect to the boundaries of traditional public forums. Insofar as a forum's compatibility with speech may be a legitimate state concern, a library might be viewed as an inappro-priate venue for any activity (including speech) that is a distraction. The grounds of a jailhouse like those of "an executive mansion, a legislative chamber, a courthouse, or the statehouse," as Justice William Douglas noted, is a "seat[ ] of government."

Given the need for better definition and clarity, the Court eventually responded with a framework that categorizes public forums and establishes constitutional rules for their governance. This evolution took place in *Perry Educational Association v. Perry Local Educators' Association* (1983). The *Perry* case concerned a rival union's claim that it was entitled to access public school teacher mailboxes. Under a collec-tive bargaining agreement, access was provided exclusively to the union that had been elected to represent the teachers. Access also was permitted for community, civic, and religious groups. Selective access to a public forum entails the risk of abridging not only freedom of speech but equal protection. As the Court concluded in *Police Department of Chicago v. Mosley* (1972), "[o]nce a forum is opened to assembly or speaking by some groups, government may not prohibit others from assembling or speaking on the basis of what they intend to say."

The *Mosley* decision responded to a municipal ordinance that prohibited all picketing near schools except during specified hours and in the context of labor disputes. This regulation, although styled as a time, place, and manner regulation, manifestly discriminated on the basis of content. Minus a compelling reason for differentiating one type of picketing from another, the ordinance was contrary to the First Amendment. Despite arguments that the public schools likewise discriminated on the basis of content, when access to its internal mail system was provided on a selective basis, the Court refused to equate teacher mailboxes with public sidewalks. Finding that teacher mailboxes were not public forums, it concluded that the school system could limit access to organizations engaged in official school business.

The long-term value of the *Perry* decision owes less to its specific result, which critics have questioned, than to its effort to establish an orderly framework for public forum analysis. Toward this end, the Court established three forum categories and the constitutional rules that govern each. The first model is the "quintessential" public forum consisting of those "places which by long tradition or by government fiat have been devoted to assembly and debate." Primary examples of the traditional public forum are parks, streets, and sidewalks. Content-based regulation in this context must be supported by a compelling state interest and must be narrowly drawn in accounting for it.

The second category is the designated public forum. Such a venue is one that government has opened "for use by the public as a place for expressive activity." The designated public forum may consist of a public school auditorium, fairground, or any other property that government has opened to expressive activity. The basis for differentiating it from a traditional forum is that government has no obligation to open it to speech activity and reserves the right to close it. So long as the state opens the forum, however, content-based regulation is subject to the same strict review associated with traditional forums. To the extent that government closes the forum, it must do so on a wholesale rather than selective basis.

The third category is the nonpublic forum, "which is not by tradition or designation for public communication." In this context, government is not bound by prohibitions against content-based regulation or restrictive access. The standard of review for such regulation is not strict scrutiny but whether it is reasonable. For each type of forum, however, government is precluded from conditioning access or punishing expression on the basis of disagreement with the speaker's opinion. This rule against viewpoint discrimination would deny government the ability to control access on the basis of political philosophy or position.

Time, place, and manner regulation, even in the context of a traditional or designated public forum, is subject to a lesser standard of review than for content-based regulation. The general rule is that such content-neutral regulation is consistent with the First Amendment, provided it promotes a substantial government interest and provides speakers an adequate alternative means for communicating their message. Common models of time, place, and manner controls include park and parade permits, limitations on door-to-door solicitation, and restrictions on sidewalk or street use. Since *Perry,* the Court has upheld time controls on the broadcast of indecent programming, place limitations that prohibit picketing in front of a home, and manner restrictions that regulate the volume of amplified music in a public park.

Despite the Court's framing of a more orderly structure for public forum analysis, loose ends and concerns remain. As times and conventions evolve, it is not always easy to determine the boundaries of tradition. Not surprisingly, therefore, the Court, in *International Society for Krishna Consciousness, Inc. v. Lee* (1992), fragmented over whether an airport terminal was a traditional public forum. Since *Perry,* moreover, the Court has reduced analysis of public forum regulation primarily to the question of whether government has a rule because of disagreement with a particular message. So long as government can demonstrate that its objective is unrelated to the content of expression, as the Court observed in *Ward v. Rock Against Racism* (1989), its officially stated purpose "is controlling." Given this relaxed standard of review, critics maintain that the state can accomplish indirectly through public forum regulation what it cannot achieve through direct content control. An ordinance prohibiting residential picketing altogether, which the Court upheld in *Frisby v. Schultz* (1988), can be viewed as a form of prior restraint. As the Court observed in *United States v. New York Times Co.* (1971), "any system of prior restraint carries a heavy burden of justification against its constitutional validity." Diminished standards for reviewing time, place, and manner regulation, so long as government can articulate a credible rationale that is content-neutral, create a potential bypass to this central First Amendment principle.

## Justice WHITE delivered the opinion of the Court.

. . . In places which by long tradition or by government fiat have been devoted to assembly and debate, the rights of the state to limit expressive activity are sharply circumscribed. At one end of the spectrum are streets and parks which "have immemorially been held in trust for the use of the public, and, time out of mind, have been used for purposes of assembly, communicating thoughts between citizens, and discussing public questions." In these quintessential public forums, the government may not prohibit all communicative activity. For the state to enforce a content-based exclusion it must show that its regulation is necessary to serve a compelling state interest and that it is narrowly drawn to achieve that end. The state may also enforce regulations of the time, place, and manner of expression which are content-neutral, are narrowly tailored to serve a significant government interest, and leave open ample alternative channels of communication.

A second category consists of public property which the state has opened for use by the public as a place for expressive activity. The Constitution forbids a state to enforce certain exclusions from a forum generally open to the public even if it was not required to create the forum in the first place. Although a state is not required to indefinitely retain the open character of the facility, as long as it does so it is bound by the same standards as apply in a traditional public forum. Reasonable time, place and manner regulations are permissible, and a content-based prohibition must be narrowly drawn to effectuate a compelling state interest.

Public property which is not by tradition or designation a forum for public communication is governed by different standards. We have recognized that the "First Amendment does not guarantee access to property simply because it is owned or controlled by the government." In addition to time, place, and manner regulations, the state may reserve the forum for its intended purposes, communicative or otherwise, as long as the regulation on speech is reasonable and not an effort to suppress expression merely because public officials oppose the speaker's view. As we have stated on several occasions, "the State, no less than a private owner of property, has power to preserve the property under its control for the use to which it is lawfully dedicated."

The school mail facilities at issue here fall within this third category. The Court of Appeals recognized that Perry School District's interschool mail system is not a traditional public forum: "We do not hold that a school's internal mail system is a public forum in the sense that a school board may not close it to all but official business if it chooses." On this point the parties agree. Nor do the parties dispute that, as the District Court observed, the "normal and intended function [of the school mail facilities] is to facilitate internal communication of school related matters to teachers." The internal mail system, at least by policy, is not held open to the general public. It is instead PLEA's position that the school mail facilities have become a "limited public forum" from which it may not be excluded because of the periodic use of the system by private non-school connected groups, and PLEA's own unrestricted access to the system prior to PEA's certification as exclusive representative.

Neither of these arguments is persuasive. The use of the internal school mail by groups not affiliated with the schools is no doubt a relevant consideration. If by policy or by practice the Perry School District has opened its mail system for indiscriminate use by the general public, then PLEA could justifiably argue a public forum has been created. This, however, is not the case. As the case comes before us, there is no indication in the record that the school mailboxes and interschool delivery system are open for use by the general public. Permission to use the system to communicate with teachers must be secured from the individual building principal. There is no court finding or evidence in the record which demonstrates that this permission has been granted as a matter of course to all who seek to distribute material. We can only conclude that the schools do allow some outside organizations such as the YMCA, Cub Scouts, and other civic and church organizations to use the facilities. This type of selective access does not transform government property into a public forum. . . .

Moreover, even if we assume that by granting access to the Cub Scouts, YMCAs, and parochial schools, the school district has created a "limited" public forum, the constitutional right of access would in any event extend only to other entities of similar character. While the school mail facilities thus might be a forum generally open for use by the Girl Scouts, the local boys' club and other organizations that engage in activities of interest and educational relevance to students, they would not as a consequence be open to an organization such as PLEA, which is concerned with the terms and conditions of teacher employment. . . .

## Justice BRENNAN, with whom Justice MARSHALL, Justice POWELL, and Justice STEVENS join, dissenting.

The Court today holds that an incumbent teachers' union may negotiate a collective bargaining agreement with a school board that grants the incumbent access to teachers' mailboxes and to the interschool mail system and denies such access to a rival union. Because the exclusive access provision in the collective bargaining agreement amounts to viewpoint discrimination that infringes the respondents' First Amendment rights and fails to advance any substantial state interest, I dissent.

The Court properly acknowledges that teachers have protected First Amendment rights within the school context. In particular, we have held that teachers may not be "compelled to relinquish the First Amendment rights they would otherwise enjoy as citizens to comment on matters of public interest in connection with the operation of the public schools in which they work. . . ." We also have recognized in the school context the First Amendment right of "individuals to associate to further their personal beliefs," and have acknowledged the First Amendment rights of dissident teachers in matters involving labor relations. Against this background it is clear that the exclusive access policy in this case implicated the respondents' First Amendment rights by restricting their freedom of expression on issues important to the operation of the school system. As the Court of Appeals suggested, this speech is "if not at the very apex of any hierarchy of protected speech, at least not far below it."

From this point of departure the Court veers sharply off course. Based on a finding that the interschool mail system is not a "public forum," the Court states that the respondents have no right of access to the system, and that the school board is free "to make distinctions in access on the basis of subject matter and speaker identity," if the distinctions are "reasonable in light of the purpose which the forum at issue serves." According to the Court, the petitioner's status as the exclusive bargaining representative provides a reasonable basis for the exclusive access policy.

The Court fundamentally misperceives the essence of the respondents' claims and misunderstands the thrust of the Court of Appeals' well-reasoned opinion. This case does not involve an "absolute access" claim. It involves an "equal access" claim. As such it does not turn on whether the internal school mail system is a "public forum." In focusing on the public forum issue, the Court disregards the First Amendment's central proscription against censorship, in the form of viewpoint discrimination, in any forum, public or nonpublic. . . .

Once the government permits discussion of certain subject matter, it may not impose restrictions that discriminate among viewpoints on those subjects whether a nonpublic forum is involved or not. This prohibition is implicit in the *Mosley* line of cases, in *Tinker v. Des Moines Independent Community School District,* and in those cases in which we have approved content-based restrictions on access to government property that is not a public forum. We have never held that government may allow discussion of a subject and then discriminate among viewpoints on that particular topic, even if the government for certain reasons may entirely exclude discussion of the subject from the forum. In this context, the greater power does not include the lesser because for First Amendment purposes exercise of the lesser power is more threatening to core values. Viewpoint discrimination is censorship in its purest form and government regulation that discriminates among viewpoints threatens the continued vitality of "free speech."

Against this background, it is clear that the Court's approach to this case is flawed. By focusing on whether the interschool mail system is a public forum, the Court disregards the independent First Amendment protection afforded by the prohibition against viewpoint discrimination. This case does not involve a claim of an absolute right of access to the forum to discuss any subject whatever. If it did, public forum analysis might be relevant. This case involves a claim of equal access to discuss a subject that the board has approved for discussion in the forum. In essence, the respondents are not asserting a right of access at all; they are asserting a right to be free from discrimination. The critical inquiry, therefore, is whether the board's grant of exclusive access to the petitioner amounts to prohibited viewpoint discrimination. . . .

## Bibliography

Kalven, Harry, Jr. "The Concept of the Public Forum." *Supreme Court Review* 1 (1965).

Post, Robert. "Between Governance and Management: The History and Theory of the Public Forum." *UCLA Law Review* 34 (1987): 1713.

## *Rosenberger v. University of Virginia*

**Citation: 515 U.S. 819.**

**Issue: Whether a state university's exclusion of a campus religious publication, from a program that funded student organization publications, denied access to a public forum and thus abridged freedom of speech.**

**Year of Decision: 1995.**

**Outcome: The selective exclusion of a student religious publication from the general funding program denied access to a public forum and abridged freedom of speech.**

**Author of Opinion: Justice Anthony Kennedy.**

**Vote: 5-4.**

The First Amendment comprises a set of freedoms that often are bundled together in the same breath. The guarantees of freedom of speech and of the press often merge into the concept of expressive freedom. Religious freedom represents the convergence of the establishment clause and free exercise clause. Although these provisions typically are viewed as mutually enhancing, they sometimes are in conflict with each other. The establishment clause and free exercise clause point in different directions, for instance, when issues such as state aid to parochial schools or public prayer must be reviewed. Prayer or religious displays in public settings may be viewed as official support for religion in derogation of the establishment clause. Exponents and sometimes the Court, however, maintain that these activities should be permitted to accommodate the free exercise of religion.

The establishment clause and free exercise clause are not the only tension in the First Amendment. Conflict also arises between the establishment clause and the freedom of speech clause. The Court initially confronted this clash of constitutional interests in *Widmar v. Vincent* (1981) when it reviewed a state university policy that denied campus facilities access to student religious organizations. Insofar as the university had opened its facilities to some student organizations, the Court determined a designated public forum had been created. Because exclusion of religious groups was driven by content concerns, rather than considerations of time, place, or manner, the Court strictly scrutinized the policy. Although acknowledging that compliance with the establishment clause would constitute a compelling interest, under appropriate circumstances, it determined that restrictive access was not necessary in this instance. Rather, the Court determined that an equal access policy would not have a secular purpose, would not have the primary effect of promoting religion, and would not excessively entangle government and religion. Consistent with modern understanding of the establishment clause, therefore, the Court concluded that the university could accommodate the freedom of speech clause without crossing the establishment clause.

The *Widmar* decision became the basis for invalidating restrictions on church access to school facilities that were open to other groups, *Lamb's Chapel v. Center Moriches Union Free School District* (1993), and allowing the Ku Klux Klan to erect religious symbols on a statehouse plaza, *Capitol Square Review Board v. Pinette* (1995). These cases, arising in designated public forums and traditional public forums, respectively, reaffirmed the principle that equal access to a public forum for speech purposes does not abridge the establishment clause. These decisions were unsatisfactory to critics, such as Justice Ruth Bader Ginsburg, who argued that official disclaimers were necessary to avoid any public perception that government was endorsing religion.

Despite these concerns, the balance between freedom of speech and the establishment clause moved even more decisively toward the accommodation of religious expression. In *Rosenberger v. Rector and Visitors of the University of Virginia* (1995), the Court reviewed a university program for funding student publications. Although providing financial support for "student news, information, opinion, entertainment and academic communications media groups," the program specifically excluded religious publications. This exclusion was based upon the university's concern that funding religious messages would violate the establishment clause.

In an opinion authored by Justice Anthony Kennedy, the Court held that the establishment clause constituted no barrier to public funding of religious publications. From its perspective, the object of university funding was "to open a forum for speech and to support various student enterprises . . . in recognition of the diversity and creativity of student life." The Court thus characterized the funding program as a designated public forum. Consistent with public forum doctrine, and because the denial of funding was content-based, the university was obligated to demonstrate that exclusion of student religious groups was supported by a compelling interest and represented a narrowly tailored means of accounting for it. Noting as it did in *Widmar* that compliance with the establishment clause may represent a compelling interest, the Court nonetheless concluded that a restrictive access policy was not necessary to meet this need. As the Court saw it, "[a]ny benefit to religion is incidental to the government's provision of secular services for secular purposes on a non-religious basis." In other words, it was not necessary to deny funding on the basis of religious views to obey the establishment clause.

For Justice Sandra Day O'Connor, who authored a concurring opinion, the key consideration was whether university funding of the religious publication would constitute an endorsement of religion. Insofar as it received the same assistance provided to other publications, Justice O'Connor was satisfied that its funding would not represent an endorsement of the magazine's religious perspective. Critical to her opinion were requirements that student organizations be independent of the university and provide disclaimers of any association with the university and its responsibility for content. Given the university's objective of a free and diverse market of ideas, and consequent improbability that anyone would perceive its endorsement of a religious message, Justice O'Connor saw exclusion on the grounds of religious viewpoint as a free speech violation.

Justice David Souter, in a dissenting opinion joined by Justices John Paul Stevens, Ruth Bader Ginsburg, and Stephen Breyer, found a clear-cut establishment clause violation. His reading of the majority opinion was that the Court "for the first time, approves direct funding of core religious activities by an arm of the state." From the dissenters' viewpoint, the university's policy against funding religious publications was not only justified but compelled by the establishment clause. Further strengthening the university's position, at least in the dissenters' eyes, was the publication's content, which did not merely discuss religious doctrine but espoused a particular religious view. The use of public money to subsidize religious messages, as Justice Souter saw it, "strikes at what we have repeatedly held to be the heart of the prohibition on establishment."

The *Rosenberger* decision represents a significant expansion of free speech doctrine, insofar as it emphasizes the importance of religious speech and extends the concept of a public forum into a somewhat abstract realm. What the Court characterizes as equal access to funding, however, may be viewed less as a public forum issue than as an economic benefit. If so, the decision is at odds with a long line of cases supporting the proposition that the state cannot abridge basic freedom but is not constitutionally obligated to subsidize them. The trimming of the establishment clause is the inevitable result of a choice between constitutional provisions perceived to be in conflict with each other. Whether the case presented an either-or proposition was debated before and has been debated since the Court's ruling. By making it a choice between constitutional principles, the Court in one decision achieved the dual result of enhancing freedom of speech and subtracting from antiestablishment interests.

## Justice KENNEDY delivered the opinion of the Court.

. . . It does not violate the Establishment Clause for a public university to grant access to its facilities on a religion-neutral basis to a wide spectrum of student groups, including groups that use meeting rooms for sectarian activities, accompanied by some devotional exercises. This is so even where the upkeep, maintenance, and repair of the facilities attributed to those uses are paid from a student activities fund to which students are required to contribute. The government usually acts by spending money. Even the provision of a meeting room, as in *Mergens* and *Widmar*, involved governmental expenditure, if only in the form of electricity and heating or cooling costs. The error made by the Court of Appeals, as well as by the dissent, lies in focusing on the money that is undoubtedly expended by the government, rather than on the nature of the benefit received by the recipient. If the expenditure of governmental funds is prohibited whenever those funds pay for a service that is, pursuant to a religion-neutral program, used by a group for sectarian purposes, then *Widmar, Mergens,* and *Lamb's Chapel* would have to be overruled. Given our holdings in these cases, it follows that a public university may maintain its own computer facility and give student groups access to that facility, including the use of the printers, on a religion neutral, say first-come-first-served, basis. If a religious student organization obtained access on that religion-neutral basis and used a computer to compose or a printer or copy machine to print speech with a religious content or viewpoint, the State's action in providing the group with access would no more violate the Establishment Clause than would giving those groups access to an assembly hall. There is no difference in logic or principle, and no difference of constitutional significance, between a school using its funds to operate a facility to which students have access, and a school paying a third-party contractor to operate the facility on its behalf. The latter occurs here. The University provides printing services to a broad spectrum of student newspapers qualified as CIO's by reason of their officers and membership. Any benefit to religion is incidental to the government's provision of secular services for secular purposes on a religion-neutral basis. Printing is a routine, secular, and recurring attribute of student life.

By paying outside printers, the University in fact attains a further degree of separation from the student publication, for it avoids the duties of supervision, escapes the costs of upkeep, repair, and replacement attributable to student use, and has a clear record of costs. As a result, and as in *Widmar*, the University can charge the SAF, and not the taxpayers as a whole, for the discrete activity in question. It would be formalistic for us to say that the University must forfeit these advantages and provide the services itself in order to comply with the Establishment Clause. It is, of course, true that if the State pays a church's bills it is subsidizing it, and we must guard against this abuse. That is not a danger here, based on the considerations we have advanced and for the additional reason that the student publication is not a religious institution, at least in the usual sense of that term as used in our case law, and it is not a religious organization as used in the University's own regulations. It is instead a publication involved in a pure forum for the expression of ideas, ideas that would be both incomplete and chilled were the Constitution to be interpreted to require that state officials and courts scan the publication to ferret out views that principally manifest a belief in a divine being.

Were the dissent's view to become law, it would require the University, in order to avoid a constitutional violation, to scrutinize the content of student speech, lest the expression in question—speech otherwise protected by the Constitution—contain too great a religious content. The dissent, in fact, anticipates such censorship as "crucial" in distinguishing between "works characterized by the evangelism of Wide Awake and writing that merely happens to express views that a given religion might approve." That eventuality raises the specter of governmental censorship, to ensure that all student writings and publications meet some baseline standard of secular orthodoxy. To impose that standard on student speech at a university is to imperil the very sources of free speech and expression. As we recognized in *Widmar*, official censorship would be far more inconsistent with the Establishment Clause's dictates than would governmental provision of secular printing services on a religion-blind basis.

"[T]he dissent fails to establish that the distinction [between 'religious' speech and speech 'about' religion] has intelligible content. There is no indication when 'singing hymns, reading scripture, and teaching biblical principles' cease to be 'singing, teaching, and reading'—all apparently forms of 'speech,' despite their religious subject matter—and become unprotected 'worship.' . . .

"[E]ven if the distinction drew an arguably principled line, it is highly doubtful that it would lie within the judicial competence to administer. Merely to draw the distinction would require the university—and ultimately the courts—to inquire into the significance of words and practices to different religious faiths, and in varying circumstances by the same faith. Such inquiries would tend inevitably to entangle the State with religion in a manner forbidden by our cases.

To obey the Establishment Clause, it was not necessary for the University to deny eligibility to student publications because of their viewpoint. The neutrality commanded of the State by the separate Clauses of the First Amendment was compromised by the University's course of action. The viewpoint discrimination inherent in the University's regulation required public officials to scan and interpret student publications to discern their underlying philosophic assumptions respecting religious theory and belief. That course of action was a denial of the right of free speech and would risk fostering a pervasive bias or hostility to religion, which could undermine the very neutrality the Establishment Clause requires. There is no Establishment Clause violation in the University's honoring its duties under the Free Speech Clause. . . .

### Justice SOUTER, with whom Justice STEVENS, Justice GINSBURG, and Justice BREYER join, dissenting.

The Court today, for the first time, approves direct funding of core religious activities by an arm of the State. It does so, however, only after erroneous treatment of some familiar principles of law implementing the First Amendment's Establishment and Speech Clauses, and by viewing the very funds in question as beyond the reach of the Establishment Clause's funding restrictions as such. Because there is no warrant for distinguishing among public funding sources for purposes of applying the First Amendment's prohibition of religious establishment, I would hold that the University's refusal to support petitioners' religious activities is compelled by the Establishment Clause. I would therefore affirm.

The central question in this case is whether a grant from the Student Activities Fund to pay Wide Awake's printing expenses would violate the Establishment Clause. Although the Court does not dwell on the details of Wide Awake's message, it recognizes something sufficiently religious in the publication to demand Establishment Clause scrutiny. Although the Court places great stress on the eligibility of secular as well as religious activities for grants from the Student Activities Fund, it recognizes that such evenhanded availability is not by itself enough to satisfy constitutional requirements for any aid scheme that results in a benefit to religion. Something more is necessary to justify any religious aid. Some Members of the Court, at least, may think the funding permissible on a view that it is indirect, since the money goes to Wide Awake's printer, not through Wide Awake's own checking account. The Court's principal reliance, however, is on an argument that providing religion with economically valuable services is permissible on the theory that services are economically indistinguishable from religious access to governmental speech forums, which sometimes is permissible. But this reasoning would commit the Court to approving direct religious aid beyond anything justifiable for the sake of access to speaking forums. The Court implicitly recognizes this in its further attempt to circumvent the clear bar to direct governmental aid to religion. Different Members of the Court seek to avoid this bar in different ways. The opinion of the Court makes the novel assumption that only direct aid financed with tax revenue is barred, and draws the erroneous conclusion that the involuntary Student Activities Fee is not a tax. I do not read Justice O'CONNOR's opinion as sharing that assumption; she places this Student Activities Fund in a category of student funding enterprises from which religious activities in public universities may benefit, so long as there is no consequent endorsement. . . .

Since I cannot see the future I cannot tell whether today's decision portends much more than making a shambles out of student activity fees in public colleges. Still, my apprehension is whetted by Chief Justice Burger's warning in *Lemon*: "in constitutional adjudication some steps, which when taken were thought to approach 'the verge,' have become the platform for yet further steps. A certain momentum develops in constitutional theory and it can be a 'downhill thrust' easily set in motion but difficult to retard or stop."

I respectfully dissent.

### Bibliography

Redish, Martin, and Daryl Kessler. "Government Subsidies and Free Expression." *Minnesota Law Review* 80 (1996): 543.

Werhan, Keith. "The Liberalization of Freedom of Speech on a Conservative Court." *Iowa Law Review* 80 (1994): 51.

## SECONDARY EFFECTS

Regulation may have an impact upon expression that is direct or indirect. When government controls expression because of its content, and the speech is in a constitutionally protected category, standards of review are rigorous. A lesser standard of review operates, however, when government's regulatory interest is unrelated to expression itself. Rules governing access and use of public forums, when properly devised, represent the most established model of content-neutral regulation. Laws targeting the secondary effects of a particular communication mode are a more recently recognized form of content-neutral regulation. In *City of Renton v. Playtime Theatres, Inc.,* the Court reviewed a zoning ordinance restricting the location of adult entertainment businesses. Secondary effects doctrine was the basis for upholding this law.

## City of Renton v. Playtime Theatres, Inc.

**Citation: 475 U.S. 41.**

**Issue: Whether a city may prohibit adult movie theatres from locating in residential neighborhoods.**

**Year: 1986.**

**Outcome: Because of the "secondary effects" of adult movie theatres, specifically their connection with crime and deteriorating property values, their location may be restricted.**

**Author of Opinion: Justice William Rehnquist.**

**Vote: 7-2.**

Obscene expression historically and consistently has been placed beyond the protective range of the First Amendment. Although sexually oriented expression that is not obscene is afforded constitutional protection, much case law views it in a devalued or disfavored manner. The primary challenge to the law of obscenity was defining the term. With respect to sexually explicit expression that falls short of obscenity, the Court has struggled not only with definition but identifying a basis for justifying its regulation.

*Renton* involved a zoning ordinance that prohibited adult movie theatres from locating within 1,000 feet of any residential zone, single- or multiple-family dwelling, church, park, or school. The ordinance was aimed, not at the content of the films shown in the theatres, but rather at the "secondary effects"—such as crime and deteriorating property values—that these theatres fostered: "It is th[e] secondary effect which these zoning ordinances attempt to avoid, not the dissemination of 'offensive' speech."

In deciding the case, the Court treated the Renton ordinance as a "content-neutral" time, place, and manner regulation. This treatment was important because, in a number of prior decisions, the Court has held that content-based speech restrictions should be subjected to strict scrutiny. As a "content-neutral" restriction, the Renton ordinance would be subjected to a lower standard of scrutiny and would be upheld if it was "designed to serve a substantial governmental interest" and did "not unreasonably limit alternative avenues of communication." The Court justified treating the ordinance as content-neutral because it was "aimed not at the *content* of the films shown at 'adult motion picture theatres,' but rather at the *secondary effects* of such theaters on the surrounding community."

The Court readily concluded that the Renton ordinance was designed "to serve a substantial governmental interest and allows for reasonable alternative avenues of communication." The Court concluded that a city's strong "interest in attempting to preserve the quality of urban life is one that must be accorded high respect." The Court noted that Renton had properly relied on the experiences of other cities who had suffered such secondary effects, as well as on expert testimony regarding the effects of adult theatres.

The Court found that Renton's zoning provision was a constitutionally permissible method of dealing with the secondary effects. "Cities may regulate adult theaters by dispersing them, as in Detroit, or by effectively concentrating them, as in Renton." In addition, the Court concluded that the ordinance was "narrowly tailored" to regulate only theatres producing the unwanted secondary effects.

The Court also rejected the argument that the ordinance was "under-inclusive" because it failed to regulate other adult business that might involve similar secondary effects. The Court noted that there were no other adult businesses in the city at the time, and none were trying to locate there. "That Renton chose first to address the potential problems created by one particular kind of adult business in no way suggests that the city has 'singled out' adult theaters for discriminatory treatment." The Court assumed that Renton would deal with other problems as they arose.

Finally, the Court concluded that the ordinance left open "reasonable alternative avenues of communication" because the ordinance left 520 acres of the city, slightly more than five percent of the entire city, available for use by adult theatres. The Court rejected the argument that none of the possible sites were "commercially viable" adult theatre sites.

Justice William Brennan, joined by Justice Thurgood Marshall, dissented. He argued that, since the ordinance imposed limitations based "exclusively on the content of the films shown there," it could not be treated as a content-neutral time, place, and manner restriction. He rejected the argument that, rather than being content-based, the ordinance was based solely on the secondary effects of theatres. As a result, he would have required the government to show that the ordinance served a compelling governmental interest and could be served by less intrusive alternatives. He concluded that the City failed to show that its objectives could not be served by "less intrusive restrictions."

*City of Renton* is an important decision because it gives cities broad authority to "zone" adult movie theatres to places separated from churches and residences.

### Justice REHNQUIST delivered the opinion of the Court.

. . . Describing the ordinance as a time, place, and manner regulation is, of course, only the first step in our inquiry. This Court has long held that regulations enacted for the purpose of restraining speech on the basis of its content presumptively violate the First Amendment. On the other hand, so-called "content-neutral" time, place, and manner regulations are acceptable so long as they are designed to serve a substantial governmental interest and do not unreasonably limit alternative avenues of communication.

At first glance, the Renton ordinance, like the ordinance in *American Mini Theatres,* does not appear to fit neatly into either the "content-based" or the "content-neutral" category. To be sure, the ordinance treats theaters that specialize in adult films differently from other kinds of theaters. Nevertheless, as the District Court concluded, the Renton ordinance is aimed not at the *content* of the films shown at "adult motion picture theatres," but rather at the *secondary effects* of such theaters on the surrounding community. The District Court found that the City Council's "*predominate* concerns" were with the secondary effects of adult theaters, and not with the content of adult films themselves. . . .

The District Court's finding as to "predominate" intent, left undisturbed by the Court of Appeals, is more than adequate to establish that the city's pursuit of its zoning interests here was unrelated to the suppression of free expression. The ordinance by its terms is designed to prevent crime, protect the city's retail trade, maintain property values, and generally "protec[t] and preserv[e] the quality of [the city's] neighborhoods, commercial districts, and the quality of urban life," not to suppress the expression of unpopular views. . . .

In short, the Renton ordinance is completely consistent with our definition of "content-neutral" speech regulations as those that "are *justified* without reference to the content of the regulated speech." The ordinance does not contravene the fundamental principle that underlies our concern about "content-based" speech regulations: that "government may not grant the use of a forum to people whose views it finds acceptable, but deny use to those wishing to express less favored or more controversial views.". . .

The appropriate inquiry in this case, then, is whether the Renton ordinance is designed to serve a substantial governmental interest and allows for reasonable alternative avenues of communication. It is clear that the ordinance meets such a standard. As a majority of this Court recognized in *American Mini Theatres,* a city's "interest in attempting to preserve the quality of urban life is one that must be accorded high respect." Exactly the same vital governmental interests are at stake here.

We hold that Renton was entitled to rely on the experiences of Seattle and other cities, and in particular on the "detailed findings" summarized in the Washington Supreme Court's *Northend Cinema* opinion, in enacting its adult theater zoning ordinance. The First Amendment does not require a city, before enacting such an ordinance, to conduct new studies or produce evidence independent of that already generated by other cities, so long as whatever evidence the city relies upon is reasonably believed to be relevant to the problem that the city addresses. That was the case here. Nor is our holding affected by the fact that Seattle ultimately chose a different method of adult theater zoning than that chosen by Renton, since Seattle's choice of a different remedy to combat the secondary effects of adult theaters does not call into question either Seattle's identification of those secondary effects or the relevance of Seattle's experience to Renton.

We also find no constitutional defect in the method chosen by Renton to further its substantial interests. Cities may regulate adult theaters by dispersing them, as in

Detroit, or by effectively concentrating them, as in Renton. Moreover, the Renton ordinance is "narrowly tailored" to affect only that category of theaters shown to produce the unwanted secondary effects, thus avoiding the flaw that proved fatal to the regulations in *Schad*. Respondents contend that the Renton ordinance is "under-inclusive," in that it fails to regulate other kinds of adult businesses that are likely to produce secondary effects similar to those produced by adult theaters. On this record the contention must fail. There is no evidence that, at the time the Renton ordinance was enacted, any other adult business was located in, or was contemplating moving into, Renton. . . .

## Justice BRENNAN, with whom Justice MARSHALL joins, dissenting.

. . . Renton's zoning ordinance selectively imposes limitations on the location of a movie theater based exclusively on the content of the films shown there. The constitutionality of the ordinance is therefore not correctly analyzed under standards applied to content-neutral time, place, and manner restrictions. But even assuming that the ordinance may fairly be characterized as content neutral, it is plainly unconstitutional under the standards established by the decisions of this Court. Although the Court's analysis is limited to cases involving "businesses that purvey sexually explicit materials," and thus does not affect our holdings in cases involving state regulation of other kinds of speech, I dissent. . . .

The fact that adult movie theaters may cause harmful "secondary" land-use effects may arguably give Renton a compelling reason to regulate such establishments; it does not mean, however, that such regulations are content neutral. Because the ordinance imposes special restrictions on certain kinds of speech on the basis of *content,* I cannot simply accept, as the Court does, Renton's claim that the ordinance was not designed to suppress the content of adult movies. "[W]hen regulation is based on the content of speech, governmental action must be scrutinized more carefully to ensure that communication has not been prohibited 'merely because public officials disapprove the speaker's views.' " "[B]efore deferring to [Renton's] judgment, [we] must be convinced that the city is seriously and comprehensively addressing" secondary-land use effects associated with adult movie theaters. In this case, both the language of the ordinance and its dubious legislative history belie the Court's conclusion that "the city's pursuit of its zoning interests here was unrelated to the suppression of free expression." . . .

## Bibliography

Adler, Amy. "Girls! Girls! Girls! The Supreme Court Confronts the G-String." *New York University Law Review* 80 (2005): 1108.

Fee, John. "Speech Discrimination." *Boston University Law Review* 85 (2005): 1103.

Volokh, Eugene. "Speech as Conduct: Generally Applicable Laws, Illegal Courses of Conduct, 'Situation-Altering Utterances,' and the Uncharted Zones." *Cornell Law Review* 90 (2005): 1277.

Weaver, Russell L., and Donald E. Lively. *Understanding the First Amendment.* Newark, NJ: LexisNexis, 2012, 10, 111–112.

# PROCEDURAL REGULATION

The content neutrality cases illustrate how speech may be burdened for reasons unrelated to its substantive message. In accounting for its interests within their purview, states also employ processes that impose a burden on expression. A system of licensing or permits, for example, may be established to manage competing uses in public forums. Such methods have been upheld to the extent that administrative discretion is minimized and fidelity to content-neutral decision making is maintained. Injunctions are a form of relief that, when entered by a court, prohibit or mandate a specific action. This procedure, when applied to speech, typically constitutes a prior restraint. As discussed in *Nebraska Press Association v. Stuart* (1976), prior restraints are highly disfavored under the First Amendment. The Court distinguishes, however, between injunctions that directly and indirectly burden expression. In *Madsen v. Women's Health Center* (1994), the Court determined that an injunction limiting the place and manner of antiabortion picketing was entered without reference to content. The injunction thus was not subject to the presumption against its constitutionality and strict scrutiny that would apply to a prior restraint.

## *Madsen v. Women's Health Center, Inc.*

**Citation: 512 U.S. 753.**

**Issue: Whether an injunction against abortion protestors involves "viewpoint-based" discrimination against speech and therefore should be subjected to strict scrutiny.**

**Year of Decision: 1994.**

**Outcome: Injunctions against abortion protestors are not necessarily "viewpoint-based" and therefore may be subjected to intermediate scrutiny.**

**Author of Opinion: Chief Justice William Rehnquist.**

**Vote: 5-4.**

Recent United States Supreme Court First Amendment jurisprudence has drawn a distinction between "content-based" and "content-neutral" speech restrictions, as well as between "viewpoint-based" and "viewpoint-neutral" speech restrictions. In a representative democracy, where citizens are expected to vote on candidates and have the right to influence the democratic process, freedom of speech is the engine by which citizens communicate with each other. Content-based restrictions (and, for that matter, viewpoint-based restrictions) are antithetical to democracy because they involve governmental attempts to restrict speech—rather than allowing the people to set the speech agenda.

In Madsen, abortion protestors sought to challenge a court order that limited their ability to protest outside an abortion clinic. The court entered an initial order enjoining petitioners from blocking or interfering with public access to the clinic and from physically abusing persons entering or leaving the clinic. When the protestors violated that injunction, the clinic sought to broaden the injunction because the protestors were impeding access, discouraging potential patients from entering the clinic, and having deleterious physical effects on others. The trial court agreed and issued a broader injunction.

The *Madsen* Court was called upon to determine whether the lower-court's injunction should be subjected to heightened review because it was content-based or viewpoint-based. *See R.A.V. v. City of St. Paul,* 505 U.S. 377 (1992). The Court began by rejecting the argument that, because the injunction restricts only the speech of antiabortion protesters, it is necessarily content-based or viewpoint-based. The Court noted that an injunction, by definition, applies only to an individual, or group of individuals, and regulates the activities of that individual or group. However, the decision to issue the injunction was based on the protestor's past actions, in the context of a specific dispute, and the trial court was simply trying to fashion a remedy to deal with those past actions. As a result, one could not, and would not, expect the injunction to prohibit demonstrations by those who favor abortion. The protestors were enjoined here not because of their message but because "they repeatedly violated the court's original order."

Because the *Madsen* Court concluded that the injunction was not viewpoint-based or content-based, the Court decided not to apply strict scrutiny. Strict scrutiny is the highest standard of review and requires the government to show that its action is supported by a "compelling" or "overriding" governmental interest that is pursued by the least restrictive means possible. At the same time, the Court was unwilling to apply the lower standard of review applicable to statutes imposing so-called time, place, and manner restrictions. This standard inquires whether the injunction is narrowly tailored to serve a significant government interest. The Court concluded that there were "obvious differences" between injunctions and statutes or ordinances. Unlike ordinances, which involve legislative choices and decisions to promote particular societal interests, injunctions "are remedies imposed for violations (or threatened violations) of a legislative or judicial decree." In any event, injunctions "carry greater risks of censorship and discriminatory application than do general ordinances." As a result, the Court formulated a new standard that demanded a "close attention to the fit between the objectives of an injunction and the restrictions it imposes on speech." In particular, the Court required that "the challenged provisions of the injunction burden no more speech than necessary to serve a significant government interest."

Applying this standard, the Court upheld some aspects of the trial court's injunction, but struck down others. For example, the Court upheld a prohibition on chanting and singing outside the clinic, on the basis that the protest could upset women undergoing abortion procedures, but struck down a ban on carrying signs and posters. The Court concluded that the latter restriction burdened more speech than necessary because the clinic could deal with the problem by closing its curtains. In general, the Court upheld a 36-foot no-demonstration zone around the clinic, but struck the ban down as applied to private property that abutted the clinic. The Court also struck down a ban on approaching individuals entering the clinic. The Court concluded that the restriction burdened more speech than necessary by prohibiting all approaches and was not appropriately limited to independently proscribable speech (i.e., "fighting words" or threats). Finally, the Court struck down a prohibition against demonstrations within 300 feet of the residences of clinic staff. In prior cases, the Court had held that it was permissible to prohibit picketing focused on an abortion provider's house. However, the 300-foot limitation burdened more speech than necessary because it was broad enough to prohibit general picketing in the neighborhood.

Justice Stevens, concurring in part and dissenting in part, argued that judicial review of injunctions should be less stringent than judicial review of legislation. In his view, the propriety of an injunction depends on the "character of the violation and the likelihood of its recurrence." As a result, "repeated violations may justify sanctions that might be invalid if applied to a first offender or if enacted by the legislature." Concluding that the protestors in this case had committed repeated violations, Justice Stevens would have deferred to the trial court judge's conclusions.

Justice Antonin Scalia, joined by two other justices, concurred in the judgment in part but dissented in part. He argued that injunctive decrees should be subjected to strict scrutiny because there is a significant risk of discrimination against unpopular groups. He noted that "the injunction in this case was sought against a single-issue advocacy group by persons and organizations with a business or social interest in suppressing that group's point of view." In addition, injunctions against speech "are the product of individual judges rather than of legislatures—and often of judges who have been chagrined by prior disobedience of their orders." As a result, Justice Scalia was uncomfortable with the idea of placing such a "powerful weapon" as injunctive relief in the hands of a single person. "Persons subject to a speech-restricting injunction who have not the money or not the time to lodge an immediate appeal face a Hobson's choice: they must remain silent, since if they speak their First Amendment rights are no defense in subsequent contempt proceedings."

*Madsen* is an important decision because it establishes the standard of review applicable to speech-restricting injunctions. The Court rejects strict scrutiny, and also rejects the more limited standard of review applicable to time, place, and manner regulations, and instead imposes an intermediate standard of review: whether "the challenged provisions of the injunction burden no more speech than necessary to serve a significant government interest."

Chief Justice REHNQUIST delivered the opinion of the Court.

. . . We begin by addressing petitioners' contention that the state court's order, because it is an injunction that restricts only the speech of antiabortion protesters, is necessarily content or viewpoint based. Accordingly, they argue, we should examine the entire injunction under the strictest standard of scrutiny. We disagree. To accept petitioners' claim would be to classify virtually every injunction as content or viewpoint based. An injunction, by its very nature, applies only to a particular group (or individuals) and regulates the activities, and perhaps the speech, of that group. It does so, however, because of the group's past actions in the context of a specific dispute between real parties. The parties seeking the injunction assert a violation of their rights; the court hearing the action is charged with fashioning a remedy for a specific deprivation, not with the drafting of a statute addressed to the general public.

The fact that the injunction in the present case did not prohibit activities of those demonstrating in favor of abortion is justly attributable to the lack of any similar demonstrations by those in favor of abortion, and of any consequent request that their demonstrations be regulated by injunction. There is no suggestion in this record that Florida law would not equally restrain similar conduct directed at a target having nothing to do with abortion; none of the restrictions imposed by the court were directed at the contents of petitioner's message.

Our principal inquiry in determining content neutrality is whether the government has adopted a regulation of speech "without reference to the content of the regulated speech." We thus look to the government's purpose as the threshold consideration. Here, the state court imposed restrictions on petitioners incidental to their antiabortion message because they repeatedly violated the court's original order. That petitioners all share the same viewpoint regarding abortion does not in itself demonstrate that some invidious content- or viewpoint-based purpose motivated the issuance of the order. It suggests only that those in the group *whose conduct* violated the court's order happen to share the same opinion regarding abortions being performed at the clinic. In short, the fact that the injunction covered people with a particular viewpoint does not itself render the injunction content or viewpoint based. Accordingly, the injunction issued in this case does not demand the level of heightened scrutiny set forth in *Perry*. And we proceed to discuss the standard which does govern.

If this were a content-neutral, generally applicable statute, instead of an injunctive order, its constitutionality would be assessed under the standard set forth in *Ward v. Rock Against Racism,* and similar cases. Given that the forum around the clinic is a traditional public forum, we would determine whether the time, place, and manner regulations were "narrowly tailored to serve a significant governmental interest."

There are obvious differences, however, between an injunction and a generally applicable ordinance. Ordinances represent a legislative choice regarding the promotion of particular societal interests. Injunctions, by contrast, are remedies imposed for violations (or threatened violations) of a legislative or judicial decree. Injunctions also carry greater risks of censorship and discriminatory application than do general ordinances. "[T]here is no more effective practical guaranty against arbitrary and unreasonable government than to require that the principles of law which officials would impose upon a minority must be imposed generally. Injunctions, of course, have some advantages over generally applicable statutes in that they can be tailored by a trial judge to afford more precise relief than a statute where a violation of the law has already occurred.

We believe that these differences require a somewhat more stringent application of general First Amendment principles in this context. In past cases evaluating injunctions restricting speech, we have relied upon such general principles while also seeking to ensure that the injunction was no broader than necessary to achieve its desired goals. Our close attention to the fit between the objectives of an injunction and the restrictions it imposes on speech is consistent with the general rule, quite apart from First Amendment considerations, "that injunctive relief should be no more burdensome to the defendant than necessary to provide complete relief to the plaintiffs." Accordingly, when evaluating a content-neutral injunction, we think that our standard time, place, and manner analysis is not sufficiently rigorous. We must ask instead whether the challenged provisions of the injunction burden no more speech than necessary to serve a significant government interest. . . .

In sum, we uphold the noise restrictions and the 36-foot buffer zone around the clinic entrances and driveway because they burden no more speech than necessary to eliminate the unlawful conduct targeted by the state court's injunction. We strike down as unconstitutional the 36-foot buffer zone as applied to the private property to the north and west of the clinic, the "images observable" provision, the 300-foot no-approach zone around the clinic, and the 300-foot buffer zone around the residences, because these provisions sweep more broadly than necessary to accomplish the permissible goals of the injunction.

### Justice SCALIA, with whom Justice KENNEDY and Justice THOMAS join, concurring in the judgment in part and dissenting in part.

. . . The judgment in today's case has an appearance of moderation and Solomonic wisdom, upholding as it does some portions of the injunction while disallowing others. That appearance is deceptive. The entire injunction in this case departs so far from the established course of our jurisprudence that in any other context it would have been regarded as a candidate for summary reversal.

But the context here is abortion. A long time ago, in dissent from another abortion-related case, Justice O'CONNOR, joined by then-Justice REHNQUIST, wrote:

"This Court's abortion decisions have already worked a major distortion in the Court's constitutional jurisprudence. Today's decision goes further, and makes it painfully clear that no legal rule or doctrine is safe from ad hoc nullification by this Court when an occasion for its application arises in a case involving state regulation of abortion. The permissible scope of abortion regulation is not the only constitutional issue on which this Court is divided, but—except when it comes to abortion—the Court has generally refused to let such disagreements, however longstanding or deeply felt, prevent it from evenhandedly applying uncontroversial legal doctrines to cases that come before it."

Today the ad hoc nullification machine claims its latest, greatest, and most surprising victim: the First Amendment.

Because I believe that the judicial creation of a 36-foot zone in which only a particular group, which had broken no law, cannot exercise its rights of speech, assembly, and association, and the judicial enactment of a noise prohibition, applicable to that group and that group alone, are profoundly at odds with our First Amendment precedents and traditions, I dissent.

### Bibliography

Craig, Tracy S. "Abortion Protest: Lawless Conspiracy or Protected Free Speech?" *Denver University Law Review* 72 (1995): 445.

Hersch, Charles. "Five Tellings of an Abortion Clinic Protest: *Madsen v. Women's Health Center* and the Limits of Legal Narrative." *Legal Studies Forum* 19 (1995): 395.

Thomas, Tracy S. "The Prophylactic Remedy: Normative Principles and Definitional Parameters of Injunctive Relief." *Buffalo Law Review* 52 (2004): 301.

Weaver, Russell L., and Donald E. Lively. *Understanding the First Amendment.* Newark, NJ: LexisNexis, 2012, 95–105.

# GOVERNMENT SUBSIDIES AND CONDITIONS

So long as it is acting pursuant to a valid power, and not precluded by a constitutional guarantee, government may exercise discretion with respect to the objectives it targets and how it distributes resources. The First Amendment does not preclude government from communicating a particular message directly or through proxies. In funding expression, however, it may not discriminate on the basis of viewpoint.

In *National Endowment for the Arts v. Finley* (1998), the Court determined that Congress could require the National Endowment for the Arts to factor standards of decency into its processes for distributing grants to artists. The Court also rejected the notion of an unconstitutional condition in *United States v. American Library Association, Inc.* (2004). This case concerned the denial of federal Internet funding to libraries that did not use software that blocked access to obscenity and child pornography.

## *National Endowment for the Arts v. Finley*

**Citation: 524 U.S. 569.**

**Issue: Whether Congress can require the National Endowment for the Arts to consider "general standards of decency and respect for diverse beliefs and values of the American public" in awarding arts grants.**

**Year of Opinion: 1998.**

**Outcome: Congress has the power to compel the National Endowment for the Arts to consider "general standards of decency and respect for the diverse beliefs and values of the American public" in awarding grants.**

**Author of Opinion: Justice Sandra Day O'Connor.**

**Vote: 8-1.**

The United States Supreme Court has repeatedly held that the First Amendment's speech clause protects not only traditional speech, but also art and artistic activity. Indeed, art can sometimes convey ideas more effectively or with the greater emotional and intellectual impact than traditional speech. *National Endowment for the Arts v. Finley* involved the *National Foundation on the Arts and Humanities Act of 1965* (Act) which provided government financial support for art and artistic activity, but which placed restrictions on projects entitled to receive governmental funding. Under the Act, Congress established the National Endowment for the Arts (NEA) and authorized it to provide grants to support artistic activity. The Act specifically articulated the objective of helping to "create and sustain not only a climate encouraging freedom of thought, imagination, and inquiry but also the material conditions facilitating the release of . . . creative talent," and the Act gave the NEA discretion to award grants and identified only broad funding priorities ("artistic and cultural significance, giving emphasis to American creativity and cultural diversity," "professional excellence," and the encouragement of "public knowledge, education, understanding, and appreciation of the arts"). Under the Act, the NEA distributed several billion dollars in grants to individuals and organizations. Grants were made by the NEA's chairperson based on recommendations made by advisory panels.

Although most of the NEA grants were relatively uncontroversial, a few grants produced much controversy. One of the controversial grants was a $15,000 grant that financed "Piss Christ," a photograph that depicted a religious crucifix immersed in urine. A second controversial grant involved a $30,000 grant that was used to finance a retrospective on photographer Robert Mapplethorpe's work composed of homoerotic (allegedly pornographic) photographs.

In response to the "Piss Christ" and Mapplethorpe exhibits, Congress initially considered whether to cut the NEA's budget by the amount spent on those two exhibits ($45,000). However, Congress ultimately decided to amend the governing statute to provide that no NEA funds may be used to promote, disseminate, or produce materials that "may be considered obscene, including but not limited to, depictions of sadomasochism, homoeroticism, the sexual exploitation of children, or individuals engaged in sex acts and which, when taken as a whole, do not have serious literary, artistic, political, or scientific value." The NEA responded by requiring grantees to certify that federal funds would not be used inconsistently with the criteria. However, this restriction was subsequently struck down by a federal district court.

Following the invalidation, Congress considered and rejected a proposal to abolish the NEA. Congress chose, instead, to amend the Act to require the NEA to ensure that "artistic excellence and artistic merit are the criteria by which [grant] applications are judged, taking into consideration general standards of decency and respect for the diverse beliefs and values of the American public." The amendments were challenged by four artists who had applied for grants before the amendments were enacted and had been recommended for funding. However, after the Amendments took effect, the Chairperson's requested reconsideration and all four grants were ultimately denied. The four artists claimed that the NEA had violated their First Amendment rights by rejecting the applications and sought restoration of the recommended grants.

Before the United States Supreme Court, the artists argued that the Amendments constituted "a paradigmatic example of viewpoint discrimination because it rejects any artistic speech that either fails to respect mainstream values or offends standards of decency." The United States Supreme Court disagreed, emphasizing that the amendments merely admonished the NEA to take "decency and respect" into consideration and were aimed at "reforming procedures rather than precluding speech." As a result, the Court rejected the artists' argument that the amendments required the NEA to discriminate against their viewpoints, and expressed uncertainty about how concepts like "decency" and "respect" would be applied in the grant application process.

The Court also rejected the argument that the criteria are so "subjective that the agency could utilize them to engage in viewpoint discrimination." The Court felt that the NEA's general criteria, involving "artistic excellence," already introduced subjectivity into the process, and noted that concepts like "decency" are appropriate criteria, especially in reference to some types of grants (i.e., for schools). Moreover, the Court concluded that the NEA has limited resources, and it must deny the majority of the grant applications that it receives, including many that propose "artistically excellent" projects. As a result, the NEA may fund projects for a wide variety of reasons, "such as the technical proficiency of the artist, the creativity of the work, the anticipated public interest in or appreciation of the work, the work's contemporary relevance, its educational value, its suitability for or appeal to special audiences (such as children or the disabled), its service to a rural or isolated community, or even simply that the work could increase public knowledge of an art form." The "very assumption" of the NEA is that grants will be awarded according to the "artistic worth of competing applicants," and absolute neutrality is simply "inconceivable."

The Court noted that plaintiffs did not allege or show discrimination in regard to any of their funding decisions, and, in fact, two of them later received grants.

Nevertheless, the Court suggested that it might be inclined to step in if the NEA transformed the subjective criteria into a penalty on disfavored viewpoints. The Government may not "ai[m] at the suppression of dangerous ideas." Unless § 954(d)(1) is applied in a manner that raises concern about the suppression of disfavored viewpoints, however, we uphold the constitutionality of the provision.

Justice Scalia, joined by Justice Clarence Thomas, concurred. He disagreed with the majority's conclusion that the Act did not impose content-based restrictions. Justice Souter dissented, arguing that, if "there is a bedrock principle underlying the First Amendment, it is that the government may not prohibit the expression of an idea simply because society finds the idea itself offensive or disagreeable." He would have applied this nondiscrimination principle even to governmental funding decisions: "[A] statute disfavoring speech that fails to respect America's 'diverse beliefs and values' is the very model of viewpoint discrimination; it penalizes any view disrespectful to any belief or value espoused by someone in the American populace."

Finley is important because it grants the government greater power to impose restrictions on government financing of artistic speech. Congress may require the National Endowment for the Arts to take into consideration "general standards of decency and respect for the diverse beliefs and values of the American public."

## Justice O'CONNOR delivered the opinion of the Court.

. . . Respondents argue that the provision is a paradigmatic example of viewpoint discrimination because it rejects any artistic speech that either fails to respect mainstream values or offends standards of decency. The premise of respondents' claim is that  constrains the agency's ability to fund certain categories of artistic expression. The NEA, however, reads the provision as merely hortatory, and contends that it stops well short of an absolute restriction. Section 954(d)(1) adds "considerations" to the grant-making process; it does not preclude awards to projects that might be deemed "indecent" or "disrespectful," nor place conditions on grants, or even specify that those factors must be given any particular weight in reviewing an application. Indeed, the agency asserts that it has adequately implemented § 954(d)(1) merely by ensuring the representation of various backgrounds and points of view on the advisory panels that analyze grant applications. We do not decide whether the NEA's view—that the formulation of diverse advisory panels is sufficient to comply with Congress' command—is in fact a reasonable reading of the statute. It is clear, however, that the text of § 954(d)(1) imposes no categorical requirement. The advisory language stands in sharp contrast to congressional efforts to prohibit the funding of certain classes of speech. When Congress has in fact intended to affirmatively constrain the NEA's grant-making authority, it has done so in no uncertain terms. See § 954(d)(2).

Furthermore, like the plain language of § 954(d), the political context surrounding the adoption of the "decency and respect" clause is inconsistent with respondents' assertion that the provision compels the NEA to deny funding on the basis of viewpoint discriminatory criteria. The legislation was a bipartisan proposal introduced as a counterweight to amendments aimed at eliminating the NEA's funding or substantially constraining its grant-making authority. The Independent Commission had cautioned Congress against the adoption of distinct viewpoint-based standards for funding, and the Commission's report suggests that "additional criteria for selection, if any, should be incorporated as part of the selection process (perhaps as part of a definition of 'artistic excellence'), rather than isolated and treated as exogenous considerations." Report to Congress 89. In keeping with that recommendation, the criteria in § 954(d)(1) inform the assessment of artistic merit, but Congress declined to disallow any particular viewpoints. As the sponsors of § 954(d)(1) noted in urging rejection of the Rohrabacher Amendment: "[I]f we start down that road of prohibiting categories of expression, categories which are indeed constitutionally protected speech, where do we end? Where one Member's aversions end, others with different sensibilities and with different values begin." In contrast, before the vote on § 954(d)(1), one of its sponsors stated: "If we have done one important thing in this amendment, it is this. We have maintained the integrity of freedom of expression in the United States."

That § 954(d)(1) admonishes the NEA merely to take "decency and respect" into consideration and that the legislation was aimed at reforming procedures rather than precluding speech undercut respondents' argument that the provision inevitably will be utilized as a tool for invidious viewpoint discrimination. In cases where we have struck down legislation as facially unconstitutional, the dangers were both more evident and more substantial. In *R.A.V. v. St. Paul*, for example, we invalidated on its face a municipal ordinance that defined as a criminal offense the placement of a symbol on public or private property " 'which one knows or has reasonable grounds to know arouses anger, alarm or resentment in others on the basis of race, color, creed, religion or gender.' " That provision set forth a clear penalty, proscribed views on particular "disfavored subjects," and suppressed "distinctive idea[s], conveyed by a distinctive message."

In contrast, the "decency and respect" criteria do not silence speakers by expressly "threaten[ing] censorship of ideas." Thus, we do not perceive a realistic danger that § 954(d)(1) will compromise First Amendment values. As respondents' own arguments demonstrate, the considerations that the provision introduces, by their nature, do not engender the kind of directed viewpoint discrimination that would prompt this Court to invalidate a statute on its face. Respondents assert, for example, that "[o]ne would be hard-pressed to find two people in the United States who could agree on what the 'diverse beliefs and values of the American public' are, much less on whether a particular work of art 'respects' them"; and they claim that " '[d]ecency' is likely to mean something very different to a septegenarian in Tuscaloosa and a teenager in Las Vegas." The NEA likewise views the considerations enumerated in § 954(d)(1) as susceptible to multiple interpretations. Accordingly, the provision does not introduce considerations that, in practice, would effectively preclude or punish the expression of particular views. Indeed, one could hardly anticipate how "decency" or "respect" would bear on grant applications in categories such as funding for symphony orchestras.

### Justice SCALIA, with whom Justice THOMAS joins, concurring in the judgment.

"The operation was a success, but the patient died." What such a procedure is to medicine, the Court's opinion in this case is to law. It sustains the constitutionality of 20 U.S.C. § 954(d)(1) by gutting it. The most avid congressional opponents of the provision could not have asked for more. I write separately because, unlike the Court, I think that § 954(d)(1) must be evaluated as written, rather than as distorted by the agency it was meant to control. By its terms, it establishes content- and viewpoint-based criteria upon which grant applications are to be evaluated. And that is perfectly constitutional. . . .

In its laudatory description of the accomplishments of the NEA, the Court notes with satisfaction that "only a handful of the agency's roughly 100,000 awards have generated formal complaints." The Congress that felt it necessary to enact § 954(d)(1) evidently thought it much *more* noteworthy that *any* money exacted from American taxpayers had been used to produce a crucifix immersed in urine or a display of homoerotic photographs. It is no secret that the provision was prompted by, and directed at, the funding of such offensive productions. Instead of banning the funding of such productions absolutely, which I think would have been entirely constitutional, Congress took the lesser step of requiring them to be disfavored in the evaluation of grant applications. The Court's opinion today renders even that lesser step a nullity. For that reason, I concur only in the judgment.

### Justice SOUTER, dissenting.

The question here is whether the italicized segment of this statute is unconstitutional on its face: "[A]rtistic excellence and artistic merit are the criteria by which applications [for grants from the National Endowment for the Arts (NEA) ] are judged, *taking into consideration general standards of decency and respect for the diverse beliefs and values of the American public.*" 20 U.S.C. § 954(d) (emphasis added). It is.

The decency and respect proviso mandates viewpoint-based decisions in the disbursement of Government subsidies, and the Government has wholly failed to explain why the statute should be afforded an exemption from the fundamental rule of the First Amendment that viewpoint discrimination in the exercise of public authority over expressive activity is unconstitutional. The Court's conclusions that the proviso is not viewpoint based, that it is not a regulation, and that the NEA may permissibly engage in viewpoint-based discrimination, are all patently mistaken. Nor may the question raised be answered in the Government's favor on the assumption that some constitutional applications of the statute are enough to satisfy the demand of facial constitutionality, leaving claims of the proviso's obvious invalidity to be dealt with later in response to challenges of specific applications of the discriminatory standards. This assumption is irreconcilable with our long-standing and sensible doctrine of facial overbreadth, applicable to claims brought under the First Amendment's speech clause. I respectfully dissent.

## Bibliography

Cunnane, Kristine M. "Maintaining Viewpoint Neutrality for the NEA: *National Endowment for the Arts v. Finley.*" *Connecticut Law Review* 31 (1999): 1445.

Sullivan, Kathleen M. "Unconstitutional Conditions." *Harvard Law Review* 102 (1989): 1413.

Sunstein, Cass R. "Why the Unconstitutional Conditions Doctrine is an Anachronism (with Particular Reference to Religion, Speech and Abortion)." *Boston University Law Review* 70 (1990): 593.

Weaver, Russell L., and Donald E. Lively. *Understanding the First Amendment.* Newark, NJ: LexisNexis, 2012, 211–13.

Yudof, Mark G. *Politics, Law, and Government Expression in America.* Berkeley: University of California Press, 1983.

## *United States v. American Library Association, Inc.*

**Citation: 539 U.S. 194.**

**Issue: Whether libraries can be denied federal funding for Internet access unless they install software that blocks obscenity and child pornography and prevents access to such material by minors.**

**Year of Decision: 2003.**

**Outcome: Libraries can be denied federal Internet funding unless they comply with the stated congressionally imposed requirements.**

**Author of Opinion: Chief Justice William Rehnquist.**

**Vote: 6-3.**

The Internet has enormous potential and capacity for spreading information and knowledge because it enables persons to communicate directly and inexpensively. However, those very characteristics also suggest that the Internet has a great potential for harm. Included on the Internet is a significant amount of potentially objectionable material (e.g., child pornography and sexually explicit material that can be harmful to children).

*United States v. American Library Association, Inc.,* involved a challenge to congressional attempts to control Internet access. In the *Telecommunications Act of 1966* and the *Library Services and Technology Act,* Congress provided financial assistance to help libraries offer Internet access to their patrons. After passing the acts, Congress became concerned that federal funds might be used to facilitate patron access to pornography. To prevent this from happening, Congress passed the *Children's Internet Protection Act* (CIPA), which prohibited public libraries from receiving federal assistance for offering Internet access unless they installed software designed to block images containing obscenity or child pornography and prevented minors from obtaining access to material that is harmful to them. In *American Library Association,* in an opinion by Chief Justice William Rehnquist, the Court upheld the law on the basis that "Congress has wide latitude to attach conditions to the receipt of federal assistance in order to further its policy objectives."

A major issue in the case involved the question of whether Internet access at public libraries should be treated as either a "traditional" or a "designated" public forum. Historically, the Court has treated public streets, parks, and roads as "public fora" on the basis that such venues have been used since "'time immemorial' for purposes of assembly, communication of thoughts between citizens, and discussing public questions." Under the Court's "public forum" doctrine, the Court has held that government has limited authority to restrict the content of speech in such fora. In *American Library Association,* the plurality held that Internet access at public libraries should not be regarded as either a "traditional" or a "designated" public forum. The plurality noted that libraries had not historically been treated as public fora, and it held that the mere addition of Internet terminals did not "create a public forum for Web publishers to express themselves, any more than it collects books in order to provide a public forum for the authors of books to speak." The plurality concluded that libraries provide Internet access, not to "encourage a diversity of views from private speakers," but "to facilitate research, learning, and recreational pursuits by furnishing materials of requisite and appropriate quality."

In rendering its decision, the plurality recognized that libraries have historically exercised broad authority to make qualitative judgments regarding the materials that they choose to include in their collections. For example, since most libraries exclude pornography from their print materials, the plurality concluded that they must also retain the authority to block such material from their Internet sites. However, the Court recognized that it was not possible for libraries to "segregate" materials on the Internet in the way that they segregate or remove unsuitable print materials. If libraries tried to limit Internet access only to sites reviewed and found acceptable by their staff, they would necessarily exclude an enormous amount of material that staff librarians were unable to review. Therefore, the plurality concluded that libraries could use filters to exclude categories of content and thereby avoid the need for making individualized judgments regarding the universe of available Web sites.

Of course, using Internet filtering software ran the risk of blocking "constitutionally protected speech that falls outside the categories that software users intend to block." The reason for this problem is that filters are not precise and sometimes over-block or overfilter. Nonetheless, the plurality upheld the law, noting that it authorizes library officials to disable filters to allow individuals to conduct legitimate research or pursue other permissible research objectives.

The plurality rejected the argument that CIPA imposed an "unconstitutional condition" on the federal Internet grants. The "unconstitutional conditions" doctrine provides that the government may not attach impermissible limitations on a governmental program or subsidy. The plurality held that the Internet subsidy programs were "intended to help public libraries fulfill their traditional role of obtaining material of requisite and appropriate quality for educational and informational purposes," and that Congress had the right to insist that the funds be spent for the purposes for which they were authorized. Moreover, the plurality noted that libraries had already excluded pornographic material from their print collections, and that "Congress could reasonably impose a parallel limitation on its Internet assistance programs." As a result, the plurality concluded that the filtering software restriction imposed a permissible condition.

Because the Court was able to muster only a plurality opinion, the case produced much disagreement among the justices. Justice Kennedy concurred in the judgment because he concluded that the interest in protecting children from inappropriate material is legitimate, if not compelling. He did not believe that CIPA imposed an impermissible burden on the ability of adult library users to access material. Justice Breyer also concurred in the decision. He argued that the Court should have applied "heightened scrutiny," rather than "strict scrutiny," because the higher standard would "unreasonably interfere with the discretion necessary to create, maintain, or select a library's 'collection.'" Under "heightened scrutiny," he would have asked "whether the harm to speech-related interests is disproportionate in light of both the justifications and the potential alternatives," and he would have upheld CIPA because he found that it serves a legitimate, if not compelling, interest in preventing minors from seeing harmful material. Even though software filters tend to "overblock" Internet material, and thereby screen out some "perfectly legitimate material," Justice Breyer noted that an adult patron could request that the filter be disabled or that a particular Web site be unlocked.

*American Library* also produced a number of dissents. Justice Stevens dissented, arguing that CIPA violated the "unconstitutional conditions" doctrine because it "impermissibly conditions the receipt of Government funding on the restriction of significant First Amendment rights." Even though Justice Stevens agreed that libraries could choose to use filtering software, he doubted that Congress could force libraries to install them. He worried that filters tend to "overblock," thereby excluding large quantities of Internet information, as well as "underblock," thereby giving parents a false sense of security regarding the safety of their children. Justice Stevens argued that there were less restrictive alternatives to blocking and filtering, including the imposition of Internet policies that prohibit patrons from accessing illegal speech. In addition, he argued that libraries could use recessed monitors, and place unfiltered Internet terminals outside of sight-lines "to prevent patrons from being unwillingly exposed to sexually explicit content on the Internet."

Justice Souter, who also dissented, agreed with Justice Stevens that the "unconstitutional conditions" doctrine applied. Justice Stevens would have voted to uphold the statute had adult patrons been able to readily obtain unblocked terminals. However, he expressed concern that libraries had discretion about whether to unblock terminals, thereby making adult access dependent on the discretion of library staffs. As a result, adults may be denied access to "nonobscene material harmful to children but lawful for adult examination, and a substantial quantity of text and pictures harmful to no one [because of the] indiscriminate behavior of current filtering mechanisms. . . ." Moreover, he argued that CIPA could have limited children to blocked terminals while providing unblocked terminals for adults. Justice Souter also rejected the plurality's suggestion that CIPA is comparable to a library making acquisition decisions. He noted that, historically, scarce resources had forced libraries to make choices about which books to require, and the acquisition of some materials precluded the choice of others. Internet access, he argued, was different. Once a library spends money for Internet access, it costs nothing to allow patrons to access that material. As a result, he concluded that the "proper analogy" is not "to passing up a book that might have been bought; it is either to buying a book and then keeping it from adults lacking an acceptable 'purpose,' or to buying an encyclopedia and then cutting out pages with anything thought to be unsuitable for all adults." He concluded that filtering amounts to censorship and that a filtering requirement is constitutionally impermissible.

The *American Library* case is important because it allows the government to place restrictions on the use of federal grant money and requires that grantees adhere to those grant requirements. The decision does not provide broad support for government censorship of speech in this limited context. However, the decision probably has limited impact. Outside the context of government-financed Internet connections, the Court has held that the government may not prohibit adults from accessing indecent material. See *Reno v. ACLU,* 521 U.S. 844 (1997).

Chief Justice REHNQUIST announced the judgment of the Court and delivered an opinion, in which Justice O'CONNOR, Justice SCALIA, and Justice THOMAS joined.

. . . The public forum principles on which the District Court relied, are out of place in the context of this case. Internet access in public libraries is neither a "traditional" nor a "designated" public forum. First, this resource—which did not exist until quite recently—has not "immemorially been held in trust for the use of the public and, time out of mind, . . . . been used for purposes of assembly, communication of thoughts between citizens, and discussing public questions." We have "rejected the view that traditional public forum status extends beyond its historic confines." The doctrines surrounding traditional public forums may not be extended to situations where such history is lacking.

Nor does Internet access in a public library satisfy our definition of a "designated public forum." To create such a forum, the government must make an affirmative choice to open up its property for use as a public forum. The District Court likened public libraries' Internet terminals to the forum at issue in *Rosenberger v. Rector and Visitors of Univ. of Va.* In *Rosenberger,* we considered the "Student Activity Fund" established by the University of Virginia that subsidized all manner of student publications except those based on religion. We held that the fund had created a limited public forum by giving public money to student groups who wished to publish, and therefore could not discriminate on the basis of viewpoint.

The situation here is very different. A public library does not acquire Internet terminals in order to create a public forum for Web publishers to express themselves, any more than it collects books in order to provide a public forum for the authors of books to speak. It provides Internet access, not to "encourage a diversity of views from private speakers," but for the same reasons it offers other library resources: to facilitate research, learning, and recreational pursuits by furnishing materials of requisite and appropriate quality. As Congress recognized, "[t]he Internet is simply another method for making information available in a school or library." It is "no more than a technological extension of the book stack." . . .

Appellees mistakenly contend that CIPA's filtering conditions "[d]istor[t] the [u]sual [f]unctioning of [p]ublic [l]ibraries." In *Velazquez,* the Court concluded that a Government program of furnishing legal aid to the indigent differed from the program in *Rust* "[i]n th[e] vital respect" that the role of lawyers who represent clients in welfare disputes is to advocate *against* the Government, and there was thus an assumption that counsel would be free of state control. The Court concluded that the restriction on advocacy in such welfare disputes would distort the usual functioning of the legal profession and the federal and state courts before which the lawyers appeared. Public libraries, by contrast, have no comparable role that pits them against the Government, and there is no comparable assumption that they must be free of any conditions that their benefactors might attach to the use of donated funds or other assistance.

Because public libraries' use of Internet filtering software does not violate their patrons' First Amendment rights, CIPA does not induce libraries to violate the Constitution, and is a valid exercise of Congress' spending power. Nor does CIPA impose an unconstitutional condition on public libraries. . . .

## Justice STEVENS, dissenting.

. . . "To fulfill their traditional missions, public libraries must have broad discretion to decide what material to provide their patrons." Accordingly, I agree with the plurality that it is neither inappropriate nor unconstitutional for a local library to experiment with filtering software as a means of curtailing children's access to Internet Web sites displaying sexually explicit images. I also agree with the plurality that the 7% of public libraries that decided to use such software on *all* of their Internet terminals in 2000 did not act unlawfully. Whether it is constitutional for the Congress of the United States to impose that requirement on the other 93%, however, raises a vastly different question. Rather than allowing local decisionmakers to tailor their responses to local problems, the Children's Internet Protection Act (CIPA) operates as a blunt nationwide restraint on adult access to "an enormous amount of valuable information" that individual librarians cannot possibly review. Most of that information is constitutionally protected speech. In my view, this restraint is unconstitutional.

## Bibliography

Liebler, Raizel. "Institutions of Learning or Havens for Illegal Activities: How the Supreme Court Views Libraries," 25 *Northern Illinois University Law Review* 1 (2004).

Lowenthal, M. Fiske. *Book Selection and Censorship: A Study of School and Public Libraries in California.* Berkeley: University of California Press, 1959, 69–73.

Moon, E. "'Problem' Fiction." Pp. 56–58 in *Book Selection and Censorship in the Sixties*, ed. E. Moon. New York: Bowker, 1969.

Weaver, Russell L., and Donald E. Lively. *Understanding the First Amendment.* Newark, NJ: LexisNexis, 2012, 208–16.

# Chapter 13

# First Amendment: Freedom of Association

Freedom of association is not specifically enumerated by the First Amendment. The Supreme Court, however, has established this liberty as a fundamental incident of freedom of speech. It is a guarantee that is crucial to the ability of individuals to organize, mobilize, or affiliate on the basis of shared views. Freedom to associate thus derives its constitutional stature from an understanding that it is essential to full enjoyment of those guarantees actually specified by the First Amendment. Restrictions on associational freedom, as the Court recognized in NAACP v. Alabama (1958), have the potential to undermine the freedom of speech that the First Amendment contemplates and secures. Over the years, as evidenced by *Roberts v. United States Jaycees* (1984), the concept of freedom of association has expanded.

## *Roberts v. United States Jaycees*

**Citation: 468 U.S. 609.**

**Issue: Whether the constitutional right to freely associate gives the United States Jaycees the right to exclude women from regular membership.**

**Year of Decision: 1984.**

**Outcome: The Jaycees do not have a constitutional right to exclude women.**

**Author of Opinion: Justice William Brennan.**

**Vote: 9-0.**

Since the nation's founding, citizens have "associated" for expressive and intimate purposes. Even though the United States Constitution does not explicitly mention or provide for a right of association, the United States Supreme Court has affirmed this right in numerous decisions. In an early decision, *NAACP v. Alabama*, 357 U.S. 449 (1958), the Court upheld the NAACP's refusal to turn over its membership lists. The NAACP feared that those lists would be used to harass and intimidate its members, thereby impinging their right to freely associate. The Court upheld the NACCP's right to refuse to turn over the lists.

*Roberts* is important because it helps define the outer limits of the right of association. That case involved the United States Jaycees (Jaycees), a nonprofit membership corporation, whose objective was to promote young men and young men's organizations. While the Jaycees had various membership levels, "regular" membership was limited to men between the ages of 18 and 35. Women and older men could apply only for "associate" membership, which meant (among other things) that they could not vote. The Jaycees had approximately 295,000 members in 7,400 local chapters affiliated with 51 state organizations. Of those, only two percent were female associate members. The case arose when the Minneapolis and St. Paul Jaycees chapters began admitting women to regular membership. When the national Jaycees moved to revoke the chapter's charters, the chapters responded by filing a complaint with the Minnesota Department of Human Rights charging a violation of the Minnesota Human Rights Act ("Act"). The Act made it illegal to deny "the full and equal enjoyment of the goods, services, facilities, privileges, advantages, and accommodations of a place of public accommodation because of race, color, creed, religion, disability, national origin or sex." The Minnesota Department of Human Rights concluded that the Jaycees provided a place of public accommodation and found a violation of the Act. The Jaycees challenged the determination in federal court as a violation of their constitutional rights of free speech and association.

In rejecting the Jaycees' associational claim, the United States Supreme Court engaged in an extended discussion of the right. The Court noted that "freedom of association" cases contain two separate and distinct strands. The first strand is based on the concept of "personal liberty." This strand gives individuals the freedom to choose their intimate human relationships and guarantees those relationships against state control or intrusion. The second strand derives from the First Amendment's guarantee of the right to engage in speech and assembly, to petition for the redress of grievances, and to freely exercise religion. This strand of association is guaranteed "as an indispensable means of preserving other individual liberties."

The Court recognized that the strand of association that covers intimate relationships guarantees citizens "a substantial measure of sanctuary from unjustified interference by the State." However, the Court held that a limited number of relationships fit the definition of "intimate" or "highly personal," and these include relationships "that attend the creation and sustenance of a family—marriage, childbirth, the raising and education of children, and cohabitation with one's relatives." The Court characterized family relationships as being unique because they "involve deep attachments and commitments to the necessarily few other individuals with whom one shares not only a special community of thoughts, experiences, and beliefs but also distinctively personal aspects of one's life." Family relationships are "distinguished by such attributes as relative smallness, a high degree of selectivity in decisions to begin and maintain the affiliation, and seclusion from others in critical aspects of the relationship." The Court held that only relationships with the quality of families qualify as "personal liberty" associational interests and would not include large business enterprises. However, as the Court recognized, "a broad range of human relationships" lie between family relationships and business enterprises, and the Court concluded that analysis of these other relationships necessarily "entails a careful assessment of where that relationship's objective characteristics locate it on a spectrum from the most intimate to the most attenuated of personal attachments" including "size, purpose, policies, selectivity, congeniality, and other characteristics that in a particular case may be pertinent." The Court concluded that businesses, especially large businesses, do not fit within the definition of intimate relationships.

Applying these criteria, the Court quickly concluded that the Jaycees did not fit within the category of "intimate" association. The Court noted that local Jaycees chapters are large (the Minneapolis chapter had 400+ members) and relatively unselective groups. The only criteria for membership are age and sex, and new members are admitted without background checks. Even though they were not eligible to be "members," women could attend various meetings, participate in projects, and attend many social functions.

As for the second strand of freedom of association, the strand designed to protect association for speech or religious purposes, the Court recognized "a corresponding right to associate with others in pursuit of a wide variety of political, social, economic, educational, religious, and cultural ends." The Court found that the Minnesota law implicated this right because the right of association includes governmental attempts to interfere with the internal organization or affairs of a protected group, and includes the right not to associate. In other words, freedom of association is implicated by a law requiring an advocacy group to accept members that it does not want.

Even though the Court recognized that the Jaycees are protected by the right of expressive association, the Court held that the Jaycees' rights can be infringed by "regulations adopted to serve compelling state interests, unrelated to the suppression of ideas, that cannot be achieved through means significantly less restrictive of associational freedoms." The Court found that Minnesota had a compelling interest in eradicating discrimination against women and held that this interest was sufficient to justify the law's impact on the associational rights of the Jaycees' male members. The Court noted that government was legitimately concerned about discrimination based on "archaic and overbroad assumptions about the relative needs and capacities of the sexes" that "forces individuals to labor under stereotypical notions that often bear no relationship to their actual abilities." The Court found that such discrimination "deprives persons of their individual dignity and denies society the benefits of wide participation in political, economic, and cultural life." The Court also found "compelling" the state's interest in ensuring access to the provision of purely tangible goods and services.

In addition to holding that the Minnesota law was supported by a compelling governmental interest, the Court also found that Minnesota had advanced its compelling interests by the least restrictive means. The Court found that the Jaycees remained able to engage in protected activities and to disseminate its preferred views, including its creed of promoting the interests of young men. In addition, the Court concluded that, notwithstanding the Minnesota nondiscrimination law, the Jaycees remained free to exclude women who disagree with that goal. However, the Court rejected the notion that women would inevitably have different views than men on these issues. As a result, the Court concluded that: "[E]ven if enforcement of the Act causes some incidental abridgment of the Jaycees' protected speech, that effect is no greater than is necessary to accomplish the State's legitimate purposes. Like violence or other types of potentially expressive activities that produce special harms distinct from their communicative impact, such practices are entitled to no constitutional protection."

Justice Sandra Day O'Connor, concurring in the judgment, argued that the Jaycees is essentially a commercial organization, and therefore should be treated as a "commercial" association rather than an organization devoted to "protected expressive activity." She went on to note that the "Jaycees itself refers to its members as customers and membership as a product it is selling."

*Roberts* is an extremely important decision because it distinguishes between different types of association and suggests that different standards of review should be applied to different categories. The decision is also important because it holds that the Jaycees, being a large and unselective group, does not fit within the protections for so-called "intimate" activities or "highly personal" relationships. The Jaycees do associate for expressive purposes, but the Court concluded that the government had a "compelling" interest in prohibiting the Jaycees from discriminating against women.

## Justice BRENNAN delivered the opinion of the Court.

The right to associate for expressive purposes is not, however, absolute. Infringements on that right may be justified by regulations adopted to serve compelling state interests, unrelated to the suppression of ideas, that cannot be achieved through means significantly less restrictive of associational freedoms. We are persuaded that Minnesota's compelling interest in eradicating discrimination against its female citizens justifies the impact that application of the statute to the Jaycees may have on the male members' associational freedoms.

On its face, the Minnesota Act does not aim at the suppression of speech, does not distinguish between prohibited and permitted activity on the basis of viewpoint, and does not license enforcement authorities to administer the statute on the basis of such constitutionally impermissible criteria. Nor does the Jaycees contend that the Act has been applied in this case for the purpose of hampering the organization's ability to express its views. Instead, as the Minnesota Supreme Court explained, the Act reflects the State's strong historical commitment to eliminating discrimination and assuring its citizens equal access to publicly available goods and services. That goal, which is unrelated to the suppression of expression, plainly serves compelling state interests of the highest order.

The Minnesota Human Rights Act at issue here is an example of public accommodations laws that were adopted by some States beginning a decade before enactment of their federal counterpart, the Civil Rights Act of 1875. Indeed, when this Court invalidated that federal statute in the Civil Rights Cases, it emphasized the fact that state laws imposed a variety of equal access obligations on public accommodations. In response to that decision, many more States, including Minnesota, adopted statutes prohibiting racial discrimination in public accommodations. These laws provided the primary means for protecting the civil rights of historically disadvantaged groups until the Federal Government reentered the field in 1957. Like many other States, Minnesota has progressively broadened the scope of its public accommodations law in the years since it was first enacted, both with respect to the number and type of covered facilities and with respect to the groups against whom discrimination is forbidden. In 1973, the Minnesota Legislature added discrimination on the basis of sex to the types of conduct prohibited by the statute.

By prohibiting gender discrimination in places of public accommodation, the Minnesota Act protects the State's citizenry from a number of serious social and personal harms. In the context of reviewing state actions under the Equal Protection Clause, this Court has frequently noted that discrimination based on archaic and overbroad assumptions about the relative needs and capacities of the sexes forces individuals to labor under stereotypical notions that often bear no relationship to their actual abilities. It thereby both deprives persons of their individual dignity and denies society the benefits of wide participation in political, economic, and cultural life. These concerns are strongly implicated with respect to gender discrimination in the allocation of publicly available goods and services. Thus, in upholding Title II of the Civil Rights Act of 1964, which forbids race discrimination in public accommodations, we emphasized that its "fundamental object . . . was to vindicate 'the deprivation of personal dignity that surely accompanies denials of equal access to public establishments.'" That stigmatizing injury, and the denial of equal opportunities that accompanies it, is surely felt as strongly by persons suffering discrimination on the basis of their sex as by those treated differently because of their race. . . .

In any event, even if enforcement of the Act causes some incidental abridgment of the Jaycees' protected speech, that effect is no greater than is necessary to accomplish the State's legitimate purposes. As we have explained, acts of invidious discrimination in the distribution of publicly available goods, services, and other advantages cause unique evils that government has a compelling interest to prevent—wholly apart from the point of view such conduct may transmit.

Accordingly, like violence or other types of potentially expressive activities that produce special harms distinct from their communicative impact, such practices are entitled to no constitutional protection. In prohibiting such practices, the Minnesota Act therefore "responds precisely to the substantive problem which legitimately concerns" the State and abridges no more speech or associational freedom than is necessary to accomplish that purpose. . . .

## Bibliography

Inazu, John D. "The Unsettling 'Well-Settled' Law of Freedom of Association." *Connecticut Law Review* 43 (2010): 149.

Karst, Kenneth. "Freedom of Intimate Association." *Yale Law Journal* 89 (1980): 624.

Linder, Douglas. "Freedom of Association after *Roberts v. United States Jaycees.*" *Michigan Law Review* 82 (1984): 1878.

Raggi, Reena. "An Independent Right to Freedom of Association." *Harvard Civil Rights-Civil Liberties Law Review* 12 (1977): 1.

# Chapter 14

# First Amendment: Freedom of the Press

Freedom of the press in the United States emerged against a centuries-old backdrop of official suppression. Introduction of the printing press in the fifteenth century presented a threat to established political and religious orders accustomed to controlling the stream of information. Responding to the perils they perceived in mass disseminated information, authorities strictly controlled access to print technology and imposed harsh sanctions for criticism of church or state. Although intolerance of speech challenged established centers of power carried over to the American colonies, resentment of royal policies and privileges fueled and facilitated interest in a system of press liberty. Prior to and during the American Revolution, the press played a critical role in defining and mobilizing anti-British sentiment. Widespread mob violence against pro-British publishers, however, demonstrated that appreciation of a free press was often selective rather than universal. This tension between freedom of the press and suppressive instincts outlived the colonial experience. Abolitionists were largely unheard from in the South, for instance, where they were subject to punishment if they distributed antislavery literature. Publications criticizing American participation in World War I triggered prosecutions and resulted in harsh sentences under federal espionage laws. During the 1950s, anticommunist fervor similarly daunted mass dissemination of expression advocating radical political change. Although the terms of the press clause have remained unchanged since the republic's founding, the press itself has redefined itself dramatically. Communications technologies, such as broadcasting, cable, satellite, and networked computers, did not exist when the First Amendment was framed and ratified. A constitutional response to their emergence, however, has become a primary preoccupation of modern First Amendment review.

## PRIOR RESTRAINT

Central to a system of freedom of expression is the notion that prior restraints are generally impermissible. Concern with the chilling consequences of official censorship relates back to the late seventeenth-century England. Pursuant to the English Licensing Act, printing was tightly controlled by the Crown. This enactment empowered the Crown to determine who could publish. The Act was repealed in 1694, but the legacy of prior restraint extended into the American colonies and beyond the founding of the republic. Systems of prior restraint, ranging from prohibition of antislavery literature in southern states to movie censorship boards, have operated with limited or no constitutional constraint. The notion that prior restraints generally are inconsistent with the First Amendment, however, was affirmed in *Near v. Minnesota* (1931). In *New York Times Co. v. United States* (1971), the Court established two key propositions. The first is that prior restraints have a strong presumption of unconstitutionality. The second is that government has a heavy burden of justifying any system of prior restraint. Against this backdrop, the Court in *Nebraska Press Association v. Stuart* (1976) examined prior restraint in the context of the judicial process. At issue specifically was the constitutionality of gag orders designed to control pretrial publicity and limit risks to a defendant's right to a fair trial.

## Nebraska Press Association v. Stuart

**Citation: 427 U.S. 539.**

**Issue: Whether a trial judge may prohibit reporting on a criminal trial in an effort to protect the defendant against excessive and prejudicial publicity.**

**Year of Decision: 1976.**

**Outcome: The national commitment to free speech, and the aversion against prior restraints, precludes a trial court judge from imposing restraints on publication provided that adequate alternatives exist for protecting a defendant's right to a fair trial.**

**Author of Opinion: Chief Justice Warren Burger.**

**Vote: 9-0.**

Press coverage of criminal trials can result in tension between the Fifth and Fourteenth Amendments to the United States Constitution, which guarantee criminal defendants the right to due process of law including the right to a fair trial, and the First Amendment right to free speech and a free press. In some instances, media publicity regarding criminal cases can be so intrusive that it creates the potential for an unfair and prejudicial impact on a criminal trial.

Illustrating the tension between the defendant's right to a fair trial and the media's right to report is the United States Supreme Court's landmark decision in *Sheppard v. Maxwell*, 384 U.S. 333 (1966). In *Sheppard*, the defendant was convicted of murdering his wife and children in a trial at which "bedlam reigned at the courthouse." Much of the material printed or broadcast was never presented at the trial, including charges that Sheppard had purposely impeded the murder investigation, that he must be guilty since he hired a prominent criminal lawyer, that he was a perjurer, that he had sexual relations with numerous women, that his slain wife had characterized him as a "Jekyll-Hyde," that he was "a bare-faced liar," and that a woman convict claimed Sheppard to be the father of her illegitimate child. The Court assumed that some of this material must have reached members of the jury because the trial judge did not protect Sheppard from "inherently prejudicial publicity" and did not control disruptive influences in the courtroom. In granting Sheppard's habeas petition, the Court concluded that no one may be convicted without "a charge fairly made and fairly tried in a public tribunal free of prejudice, passion, excitement, and tyrannical power."

After *Sheppard,* trial courts were obligated to protect a defendant's right to due process, but there were questions about how this goal was to be achieved. In *Nebraska Press Association,* the trial court confronted its obligation in the context of a sensational multiple murder trial (six victims) that attracted widespread media publicity. In an effort to ensure that the defendant received a fair trial, the trial judge entered an order restraining the media from publishing or broadcasting accounts of confessions or admissions made by the defendant to either law enforcement officers or third parties, except members of the press. It also prohibited them from publishing other facts "strongly implicative" of the defendant.

Petitioners—several press and broadcast associations, publishers, and individual reporters—challenged the order. The trial judge rejected the challenge, noting that, "because of the nature of the crimes charged in the complaint that there is a clear and present danger that pre-trial publicity could impinge upon the defendant's right to a fair trial." The judge continued the order, which specifically prohibited petitioners from reporting on five topics: (1) the existence or contents of a confession Simants had made to law enforcement officers, which had been introduced in open court at arraignment; (2) the fact or nature of statements Simants had made to other persons; (3) the contents of a note he had written the night of the crime; (4) certain aspects of the medical testimony at the preliminary hearing; and (5) the identity of the victims of the alleged sexual assault and the nature of the assault. It also prohibited reporting the exact nature of the restrictive order itself. Like the County Court's order, this order incorporated the Nebraska Bar-Press Guidelines. Finally, the order set out a plan for attendance, seating, and courthouse traffic control during the trial.

In striking down the gag order, the United States Supreme Court began by noting that "prior restraints on speech and publication are the most serious and the least tolerable infringement on First Amendment rights," especially when they involve the "communication of news and commentary on current events." The Court emphasized that truthful reporting about judicial proceedings has been accorded special protection, especially reports on criminal proceedings, because the press is regarded as "the handmaiden of effective judicial administration, especially in the criminal" justice context. "The press does not simply publish information about trials but guards against the miscarriage of justice by subjecting the police, prosecutors, and judicial processes to extensive public scrutiny and criticism."

Although the trial court order only postponed the publication of relevant information, the Court questioned whether the delay was constitutionally permissible. The Court concluded that the element of time is important if "press coverage is to fulfill its traditional function of bringing news to the public promptly," and the Court doubted whether it was permissible for government "to insinuate itself into the editorial rooms of this Nation's press."

Despite the important public interest in prompt reporting, the Court recognized that a prior restraint might be justifiable if the "gravity of the evil" were high enough. As a result, in evaluating the *Nebraska Press* restrictions, the Court inquired "whether the record supports the entry of a prior restraint on publication, one of the most extraordinary remedies known to our jurisprudence." Even though the Court expressed concern regarding the impact of "intense and pervasive pretrial publicity" on the case, the Court concluded that the trial court had other means at its disposal for protecting the defendant's right to a fair trial. The trial court judge could have taken any of the following actions: (1) ordered a change of venue to "a place less exposed to the intense publicity"; (2) it could postpone the trial until public attention subsided; (3) it could ask searching questions of jurors designed to ensure that they are capable of fairly and impartially assessing the evidence; (4) it could clearly and emphatically instruct jurors regarding their sworn duty to decide the issues only on evidence presented in open court; and (5) the judge could sequester the jury to insulate them from the impact of pretrial publicity.

The Court also raised other questions regarding the trial court's order. For example, the Court questioned the trial court's ability to enforce its order, especially against media interests outside its jurisdiction. Moreover, the Court doubted that press reports would necessarily be more damaging than the alternatives. Even without media reports, rumors regarding the defendant's guilt were likely to circulate in the community. *Nebraska Press* is an important decision because it reaffirms the nation's commitment to free speech, and the general impermissibility of prior restraints. While the Court was sensitive to the important governmental interest in ensuring that criminal defendants receive fair trials, untainted by the threat of excessive and prejudicial publicity, the Court concluded that a trial court has other means, besides prior restraints, for ensuring the right to a free trial.

## Mr. Chief Justice BURGER delivered the opinion of the Court.

. . . The problems presented by this case are almost as old as the Republic. Neither in the Constitution nor in contemporaneous writings do we find that the conflict between these two important rights was anticipated, yet it is inconceivable that the authors of the Constitution were unaware of the potential conflicts between the right to an unbiased jury and the guarantee of freedom of the press. The unusually able lawyers who helped write the Constitution and later drafted the Bill of Rights were familiar with the historic episode in which John Adams defended British soldiers charged with homicide for firing into a crowd of Boston demonstrators; they were intimately familiar with the clash of the adversary system and the part that passions of the populace sometimes play in influencing potential jurors. They did not address themselves directly to the situation presented by this case; their chief concern was the need for freedom of expression in the political arena and the dialogue in ideas. But they recognized that there were risks to private rights from an unfettered press. Jefferson, for example, writing from Paris in 1786 concerning press attacks on John Jay, stated:

"In truth it is afflicting that a man who has past his life in serving the public . . . should yet be liable to have his peace of mind so much disturbed by any individual who shall think proper to arraign him in a newspaper. It is however an evil for which there is no remedy. Our liberty depends on the freedom of the press, and that cannot be limited without being lost. . . ." 9 Papers of Thomas Jefferson 239 (J. Boyd ed. 1954). . . .

The Sixth Amendment in terms guarantees "trial, by an impartial jury . . ." in federal criminal prosecutions. Because "trial by jury in criminal cases is fundamental to the American scheme of justice," the Due Process Clause of the Fourteenth Amendment guarantees the same right in state criminal prosecutions. "In essence, the right to jury trial guarantees to the criminally accused a fair trial by a panel of impartial, 'indifferent' jurors. . . . 'A fair trial in a fair tribunal is a basic requirement of due process.' In the ultimate analysis, only the jury can strip a man of his liberty or his life. In the language of Lord Coke, a juror must be as 'indifferent as he stands unsworne.' His verdict must be based upon the evidence developed at the trial."

In the overwhelming majority of criminal trials, pretrial publicity presents few unmanageable threats to this important right. But when the case is a "sensational" one tensions develop between the right of the accused to trial by an impartial jury and the rights guaranteed others by the First Amendment. The relevant decisions of this Court, even if not dispositive, are instructive by way of background. . . .

The First Amendment provides that "Congress shall make no law . . . abridging the freedom . . . of the press," and it is "no longer open to doubt that the liberty of the press and of speech, is within the liberty safeguarded by the Due Process Clause of the Fourteenth Amendment from invasion by state action." The Court has interpreted these guarantees to afford special protection against orders that prohibit the publication or broadcast of particular information or commentary orders that impose a "previous" or "prior" restraint on speech. None of our decided cases on prior restraint involved restrictive orders entered to protect a defendant's right to a fair and impartial jury, but the opinions on prior restraint have a common thread relevant to this case. . . .

The thread running through all these cases is that prior restraints on speech and publication are the most serious and the least tolerable infringement on First Amendment rights. A criminal penalty or a judgment in a defamation case is subject to the whole panoply of protections afforded by deferring the impact of the judgment until all avenues of appellate review have been exhausted. Only after judgment has become final, correct or otherwise, does the law's sanction become fully operative. . . .

Our analysis ends as it began, with a confrontation between prior restraint imposed to protect one vital constitutional guarantee and the explicit command of another that the freedom to speak and publish shall not be abridged. We reaffirm that the guarantees of freedom of expression are not an absolute prohibition under all circumstances, but the barriers to prior restraint remain high and the presumption against its use continues intact. We hold that, with respect to the order entered in this case prohibiting reporting or commentary on judicial proceedings held in public, the barriers have not been overcome; to the extent that this order restrained publication of such material, it is clearly invalid. To the extent that it prohibited publication based on information gained from other sources, we conclude that the heavy burden imposed as a condition to securing a prior restraint was not met and the judgment of the Nebraska Supreme Court is therefore

Reversed.

## Bibliography

Bernabe-Riefkohl, Alberto. "Another Attempt to Solve the Prior Restraint Mystery: Applying the Nebraska Press Standard to Media Disclosure Attorney-Client Communications." *Cardozo Arts & Entertainment Law Journal* 18 (2000): 307.

Freedman, Warren. *Press and Media Access to the Criminal Courtroom*. New York: Quorum, 1988.

Weaver, Russell L., Leslie W. Abramson, John M. Burkoff, and Catherine Hancock. *Principles of Criminal Procedure*. St. Paul, MN: Thomson/West, 2004, 359–69.

Weaver, Russell L., and Donald E. Lively. *Understanding the First Amendment*. Newark, NJ: LexisNexis, 2012, 225–29.

# THE NEWSGATHERING FUNCTION

Although protecting freedom of the press, the First Amendment provides nothing in the way of a definition for "the press." The modern press consists of much more than the print media that existed at the time of the First Amendment's framing. An understanding of its boundaries is important, therefore, for purposes of determining the scope of the press clause.

The Supreme Court, despite the definitional void, has made no concerted effort to fill it. During the 1970s, some members of the Court engaged in a debate over the nature of the press. Justice Potter Stewart, for instance, argued that the press consists largely of organized media that provide the public with access to information necessary for informed self-government. Given this important proxy function, he would have protected the press not just in its publishing but in its newsgathering role.

Over the years, the Supreme Court largely has rejected this premise. In *Branzburg v. Hayes* (1972), for instance, it rejected the notion of a First Amendment privilege that would protect journalists from revealing confidential sources or testifying to a grand jury. Likewise, in *Zurcher v. Stanford Daily* (1979), the Court spurned arguments that the press's unique role immunizes it from otherwise legitimate police searches and seizures.

The notion that the press has no special standing under the First Amendment was reaffirmed in *Globe Newspaper Co. v. Superior Court* (1982). Although acknowledging that court proceedings typically are open and the press may cover them, the Court in *Globe* emphasized that the press had no greater right of access than the public.

## *Zurcher v. Stanford Daily*

**Citation: 436 U.S. 547.**

**Issue: Whether the search of a newsroom for criminal evidence violated the Fourth Amendment.**

**Year of Decision: 1978.**

**Outcome: The First Amendment is no barrier to an otherwise valid search for criminal evidence.**

**Author of Opinion: Justice Byron White.**

**Vote: 5-3.**

Freedom of speech and freedom of the press are set forth explicitly and separately in the First Amendment. For some constitutional experts, separation of the speech and press clauses means that the provisions have independent significance. Whether this differentiation was intended or real has been a continuing topic of debate. Although not officially resolved, case law largely has been consistent with the notion that the press clause adds no further meaning to the speech clause.

Freedom of expression sometimes has been referred to as occupying a "preferred position" in relationship to other constitutional provisions. Exponents of this proposition have maintained that liberty of expression is more important than any constitutional interest that may be in competition with it. Some, such as Justices William Douglas and Hugo Black, maintained that freedom of expression is of such significance that it cannot be abridged for any reason. The Supreme Court has resisted an understanding of the First Amendment in absolute terms, either in its relationship with other constitutional provisions or other policy interests that the Court may view as overriding.

The Court's interpretation of the press clause has reflected a similar reluctance to give it special force. Arguments that the press clause has relevance above and beyond the speech clause are based upon the media's special role in informing the public. A leading advocate of this position was Justice Potter Stewart. He maintained that the speech clause protected individuals, but the press clause gives "protection to an institution." As Justice Stewart saw it, the gathering of news was essential to the public's interest in being well-informed. Given the close relationship between the role of the press and the imperative of informed self-government, he urged protection not only for the process of publishing but newsgathering itself. When the Court held that the First Amendment did not shield reporters from having to reveal confidential sources to a grand jury, in *Branzburg v. Hayes* (1972), Justice Stewart predictably dissented.

Although his rationale has not been officially repudiated, the Court generally has been guided by the competing reasoning of Chief Justice Warren Burger in *First National Bank of Boston v. Bellotti* (1978). In this decision, Chief Justice Burger could find no difference "between the right of those who seek to disseminate ideas by way of a newspaper and those who give lectures or speeches." This understanding, that the media do not have special status through the press clause, was the basis for the Court's ruling on the claim that a police search of a newsroom violated the First Amendment. The search aimed to locate and seize photographs taken by a campus newspaper photographer, who had shot pictures of a demonstration at Stanford University. The newspaper had run a story detailing a clash between protesters and police. Following normal procedures, law enforcement officials obtained a warrant to search for photographs that would enable them to identify demonstrators. Justice Byron White, writing for a majority, found that the case implicated both the First Amendment and Fourth Amendment (which guarantees against "unreasonable searches and seizures"). The key question was whether First Amendment interests outweighed Fourth Amendment concerns.

The Court's answer was that the search of a newsroom was governed exclusively by the Fourth Amendment. Although indicating that the First Amendment was not a factor in this context, the Court noted that procedures for an otherwise constitutional search and seizure must be adhered to "with 'scrupulous exactitude'" in a newsroom search. As in any search context, a warrant allowing police to rummage through records, documents, and papers would violate the Fourth Amendment. The Court restated the well-established principle that search warrants should "leave as little as possible to the discretion or whim of the officer in the field." It also referenced the historical struggle between "Crown and press," and what it regarded as the framers' consequent awareness of the need to safeguard against official intrusion with the editorial process.

In particular, the Court noted that the framers did not preclude the use of search warrants in the context of newsgathering. Even in a newsroom, the Fourth Amendment standards for a search warrant—"probable cause, specificity with respect to the place to be searched and the things to be seized, and overall reasonableness"—provided sufficient protection. The risk of official overreaching could be managed, moreover, by the Fourth Amendment requirement that the objects of a search be specifically defined in the warrant. By insisting upon satisfaction of this specificity requirement, the Court was convinced that no additional constitutional protection was necessary.

Justice Lewis Powell concurred with the majority. He was similarly influenced by the lack of historical evidence that the "Framers had believed that the press was entitled to a special procedure." Justice Powell suggested, however, that a judicial officer issuing a warrant to search a newsroom should be mindful "of the independent values protected by the First Amendment."

In a dissenting opinion, Justice Stewart was more specific with respect to what those factors should be. As he saw it, police searches of newspapers manifestly burdened freedom of the press. Among the burdens was the interference with editorial processes (newsgathering, writing, and publishing) during the search itself. More significant, from Justice Stewart's perspective, was the possibility that confidential information or sources might be revealed. A search provides the opportunity for police to read "each and every documental until they have found the one named in the warrant." Without more than the standard Fourth Amendment protection, however, the end result was "a diminishing flow of potentially important information to the public." Such an outcome, as Justice Stewart viewed it, was inimical to First Amendment interests.

Justice Stewart also thought it relevant that there were no emergency circumstances requiring immediate investigative action or evidence of criminal activity by the newspaper. Minus such exigencies, he believed that the evidence should have been obtained by less intrusive means. Specifically, Justice Stewart maintained that the appropriate methodology would have been a *subpoena duces tecum* that required the newspaper to produce the photographs by a specific date. This procedure would not have disrupted editorial operations or entailed the risk of chilling information sources.

Justice Stewart's reasoning did not carry the day for constitutional purposes. It nonetheless was reflected in a legislative response to the decision. Two years after the ruling, Congress passed the *Privacy Protection Act of 1980*. This enactment bars newsroom searches except when there is probable cause that the evidence sought is in the possession of a person who committed a crime or it is necessary to prevent death or serious bodily harm. Minus such conditions, law enforcement officers must obtain evidence by means of a *subpoena duces tecum*. Among the grounds for challenging such a process is that it is unconstitutional or the evidence sought is confidential. The aftermath of *Zurcher* is a classic illustration of how the political process sometimes accounts for constitutional values that the Court itself has denied.

## Mr. Justice WHITE delivered the opinion of the Court.

. . . As the Fourth Amendment has been construed and applied by this Court, "when the State's reason to believe incriminating evidence will be found becomes sufficiently great, the invasion of privacy becomes justified and a warrant to search and seize will issue." [Earlier] we indicated that in applying the "probable cause" standard "by which a particular decision to search is tested against the constitutional mandate of reasonableness," it is necessary "to focus upon the governmental interest which allegedly justifies official intrusion" and that in criminal investigations a warrant to search for recoverable items is reasonable "only when there is 'probable cause' to believe that they will be uncovered in a particular dwelling." Search warrants are not directed at persons; they authorize the search of "place[s]" and the seizure of "things," and as a constitutional matter they need not even name the person from whom the things will be seized. . . .

The net of the matter is that "[s]earches and seizures, in a technical sense, are independent of, rather than ancillary to, arrest and arraignment." The Model Code provides that the warrant application "shall describe with particularity the individuals or places to be searched and the individuals or things to be seized, and shall be supported by one or more affidavits particularly setting forth the facts and circumstances tending to show that such individuals or things are or will be in the places, or the things are or will be in possession of the individuals, to be searched." There is no suggestion that the occupant of the place to be searched must himself be implicated in misconduct.

Against this background, it is untenable to conclude that property may not be searched unless its occupant is reasonably suspected of crime and is subject to arrest. And if those considered free of criminal involvement may nevertheless be searched or inspected under civil statutes, it is difficult to understand why the Fourth Amendment would prevent entry onto their property to recover evidence of a crime not committed by them but by others. As we understand the structure and language of the Fourth Amendment and our cases expounding it, valid warrants to search property may be issued when it is satisfactorily demonstrated to the magistrate that fruits, instrumentalities, or evidence of crime is located on the premises. The Fourth Amendment has itself struck the balance between privacy and public need, and there is no occasion or justification for a court to revise the Amendment and strike a new balance by denying the search warrant in the circumstances present here and by insisting that the investigation proceed by subpoena *duces tecum*, whether on the theory that the latter is a less intrusive alternative or otherwise.

This is not to question that "reasonableness" is the overriding test of compliance with the Fourth Amendment or to assert that searches, however or whenever executed, may never be unreasonable if supported by a warrant issued on probable cause and properly identifying the place to be searched and the property to be seized. We do hold, however, that the courts may not, in the name of Fourth Amendment reasonableness, prohibit the States from issuing warrants to search for evidence simply because the owner or possessor of the place to be searched is not then reasonably suspected of criminal involvement. . . .

We accordingly reject the reasons given by the District Court and adopted by the Court of Appeals for holding the search for photographs at the Stanford Daily to have been unreasonable within the meaning of the Fourth Amendment and in violation of the First Amendment. Nor has anything else presented here persuaded us that the Amendments forbade this search. It follows that the judgment of the Court of Appeals is reversed.

### Mr. Justice STEWART, with whom Mr. Justice MARSHALL joins, dissenting.

Believing that the search by the police of the offices of the Stanford Daily infringed the First and Fourteenth Amendments' guarantee of a free press, I respectfully dissent.

It seems to me self-evident that police searches of newspaper offices burden the freedom of the press. The most immediate and obvious First Amendment injury caused by such a visitation by the police is physical disruption of the operation of the newspaper. Policemen occupying a newsroom and searching it thoroughly for what may be an extended period of time will inevitably interrupt its normal operations, and thus impair or even temporarily prevent the processes of news-gathering, writing, editing, and publishing. By contrast, a subpoena would afford the newspaper itself an opportunity to locate whatever material might be requested and produce it.

But there is another and more serious burden on a free press imposed by an unannounced police search of a newspaper office: the possibility of disclosure of information received from confidential sources, or of the identity of the sources themselves. Protection of those sources is necessary to ensure that the press can fulfill its constitutionally designated function of informing the public, because important information can often be obtained only by an assurance that the source will not be revealed. And the Court has recognized that " 'without some protection for seeking out the news, freedom of the press could be eviscerated.' "

Today the Court does not question the existence of this constitutional protection, but says only that it is not "convinced . . . that confidential sources will disappear and that the press will suppress news because of fears of warranted searches." This facile conclusion seems to me to ignore common experience. It requires no blind leap of faith to understand that a person who gives information to a journalist only on condition that his identity will not be revealed will be less likely to give that information if he knows that, despite the journalist's assurance his identity may in fact be disclosed. And it cannot be denied that confidential information may be exposed to the eyes of police officers who execute a search warrant by rummaging through the files, cabinets, desks, and wastebaskets of a newsroom. Since the indisputable effect of such searches will thus be to prevent a newsman from being able to promise confidentiality to his potential sources, it seems obvious to me that a journalist's access to information, and thus the public's will thereby be impaired.

A search warrant allows police officers to ransack the files of a newspaper, reading each and every document until they have found the one named in the warrant, while a subpoena would permit the newspaper itself to produce only the specific documents requested. A search, unlike a subpoena, will therefore lead to the needless exposure of confidential information completely unrelated to the purpose of the investigation. The knowledge that police officers can make an unannounced raid on a newsroom is thus bound to have a deterrent effect on the availability of confidential news sources. The end result, wholly inimical to the First Amendment, will be a diminishing flow of potentially important information to the public.

One need not rely on mere intuition to reach this conclusion. The record in this case includes affidavits not only from members of the staff of the Stanford Daily but also from many professional journalists and editors, attesting to precisely such personal experience. Despite the Court's rejection of this uncontroverted evidence, I believe it clearly establishes that unannounced police searches of newspaper offices will significantly burden the constitutionally protected function of the press to gather news and report it to the public.

## Bibliography

LaFave, Wayne R., Jerold H. Israel, and Nancy J. King. *Criminal Procedure*. St. Paul, MN: Thomson/West, 2004.

Levy, Leonard W. *Emergence of a Free Press*. New York: Oxford University Press, 1985.

## *Globe Newspaper Co. v. Superior Court*

**Citation: 457 U.S. 596.**

**Issue: Whether closure of trial under state law, when testimony is provided by the victim of an alleged sex offense, violates the First Amendment.**

**Year of Decision: 1982.**

**Outcome: A mandatory closure rule abridges the First Amendment; denial of public access is permissible only when supported by a compelling government interest and when the law is narrowly tailored to account for that concern.**

**Author of Opinion: Justice William Brennan.**

**Vote: 6-3.**

Speech essential for informed self-government historically has been given the highest value under the First Amendment. Consistent with this premise, the Supreme Court has been particularly protective of political speech. State and federal legislation, in the form of freedom of information and open meeting laws, reflects this imperative. Central also to a free flow of politically relevant speech is access to government proceedings and information. Like other First Amendment interests, such access is not absolutely guaranteed. Even when having a constitutional basis, it may be outweighed by competing interests that are found to be more compelling under the circumstances. Norms of open proceedings or access to information thus may give way, for instance, in light of national security concerns, law enforcement interests, privacy considerations, or other countervailing factors.

Generally speaking, the judiciary historically has been the least accessible branch of government. Through most of the twentieth century, strict limits were placed upon media coverage of judicial proceedings. Even today, cameras are barred from federal courts except for designated ceremonial events. Gag orders were commonly used to manage the risk of prejudicial publicity, until the Court restricted their use in *Nebraska Press Association v. Stuart* (1976). Equally strong as a remedy is the closure of proceedings to press and public. Controlling the flow of information through these strict measures typically aims to preserve the right of a fair trial, and thus requires a balancing of competing constitutional concerns. Specifically at odds with the First Amendment in these contexts is the guarantee of a fair trial incident to due process and the right to a public trial.

In *Gannett, Inc. v. DePasquale* (1979), the Court referenced the Sixth Amendment guarantee of a public trial in support of a trial court's order to close a pretrial hearing. This decision reflected an understanding that the right was personal to the defendant and could not be claimed by the press or public. Noting that the Court provided transcripts of the proceeding after the risk of prejudicial publicity had abated, the Court determined that the impact upon any First Amendment interest was inconsequential. The *Gannett* decision was written in rather imprecise terms and thus raised concern that the rule for closing pretrial proceedings might extend to actual trials. Many critics urged a narrow reading of it and hoped the Court would find an opportunity to limit and clarify its reach.

The Court responded to this concern the following term. In *Richmond Newspapers, Inc. v. Virginia* (1980), it determined that a right for the public and press to attend and cover trials was grounded in the First Amendment. By doing so, it extended the First Amendment beyond the protection of expression itself to the securing of access to a critical government process. Noting that trials had a tradition of being open, and that closed proceedings carried inherent risks of abuse, the Court limited the power of judges to operate beyond public view. Although the result was supported by a strong majority, the Court split on a supporting rationale. Two years later, in *Globe Newspaper Co. v. Superior Court,* the Court settled on a premise that has provided a long-term guide for review.

At issue in the *Globe Newspaper* case was a state law authorizing closed proceedings when a minor was called to testify as a sex offense victim. As the Court saw it, the enactment's goal of protecting sex offense victims from embarrassment or injury was laudable. So too was the objective of encouraging them to testify in criminal proceedings. The statute's mandatory nature, however, made it constitutionally problematic. In particular, it excessively discounted the public's and press's interest in attendance. The Court was sensitive to the possibility that victims of child sex abuse may be harmed further if called upon to testify in open court. It also was alert to the reality, however, that factors such as age, maturity, family preferences, and the nature of the crime may cut against closure. The Court thus concluded that decisions on closure in such circumstances should be made not on a wholesale basis but pursuant to standards that drove resolution on a case-by-case basis.

Justice William Brennan, Jr., who wrote the majority opinion, announced the premise that the First Amendment protects not only expressive freedom but interests that facilitate this liberty. Pursuant to this understanding, the right to attend a criminal trial was crucial to the "free discussion of public affairs." The Court's recognition of a First Amendment right of access was grounded in two key premises. First, criminal trials historically (and even before the Constitution) have been open to the press and public. In support of this observation, the Court noted its inability "to find a single instance of a criminal trial conducted *in camera* in any federal, state, or municipal court during the history of this country." Beyond the historical significance of this reality was what the Court identified as "the favorable judgment of experience." The Court's second point was that open trials represented an important safeguard of quality and integrity. The ability of the press and public to access trials, in the Court's view, "fosters an appearance of fairness, thereby heightening public respect for the judicial process." Open proceedings also constitute an important "check upon the judicial process."

The Court, although invalidating the state law, did not altogether preclude the possibility of closed trials. It limited closure, however, to instances when the government presented such a remedy that was a "narrowly tailored" means of accounting for "a compelling governmental interest." Press and public might be excluded from a trial, therefore, when the state can show that the child would experience real injury if required to testify in open court.

Although setting a clear standard for the closure of trials, the *Globe Newspaper* decision gave no clear indication of whether it applied to other types of judicial proceedings. The scope of the ruling was particularly important, in light of the high volume of criminal cases that are resolved prior to trial. In *Press Enterprise Co. v. Superior Court* (1986), the Court expanded First Amendment access rights to preliminary hearings. Consistent with the Globe Newspaper premise, it noted the historical and unbroken preference for open proceedings. It also characterized the *Gannett* decision as a departure from this norm and emphasized that access to criminal proceedings was not restricted to any particular phase or event. Connecting its decision with overarching First Amendment values, the Court embraced the proposition that open proceedings ensure that the "constitutionally protected discussion of governmental affairs is an informed one."

Unlike simpler times, modern life imposes demands that limit the opportunity for citizens to attend judicial or other proceedings in person. Information that leads to understanding of and perspective on important government processes thus depends upon intermediaries that can access and disseminate relevant information. Media largely perform this function and, although the Court protects their ability to do so, the right of access extends equally to the public. The constitutional parity of press and public, with respect to accessing information, is consistent with the Court's sense that the press has no preferred or privileged constitutional status. Whatever the media's right of access, as noted in *Branzburg v. Hayes* (1972), it does not extend beyond information "available to the public generally." The media, as the Court observed in *Pell v. Procunier* (1974), may be "free to seek out sources of information not available to members of the general public." The Court's interpretation of the First Amendment, however, does not "impose upon government the affirmative duty to make available to journalists sources of information not available to members of the public generally." Even if the media play a critical role in facilitating the citizenry's ability to make informed judgments about government, therefore, case law consistently has made the point that they are to have no constitutional advantage beyond the people that they inform.

### Justice BRENNAN delivered the opinion of the Court.

. . . The Court's recent decision in *Richmond Newspapers* firmly established for the first time that the press and general public have a constitutional right of access to criminal trials. Although there was no opinion of the Court in that case, seven Justices recognized that this right of access is embodied in the First Amendment, and applied to the States through the Fourteenth Amendment.

Of course, this right of access to criminal trials is not explicitly mentioned in terms in the First Amendment. But we have long eschewed any "narrow, literal conception" of the Amendment's terms, for the Framers were concerned with broad principles, and wrote against a background of shared values and practices. The First Amendment is thus broad enough to encompass those rights that, while not unambiguously enumerated in the very terms of the Amendment, are nonetheless necessary to the enjoyment of other First Amendment rights. Underlying the First Amendment right of access to criminal trials is the common understanding that "a major purpose of that Amendment was to protect the free discussion of governmental affairs." By offering such protection, the First Amendment serves to ensure that the individual citizen can effectively participate in and contribute to our republican system of self-government. Thus to the extent that the First Amendment embraces a right of access to criminal trials, it is to ensure that this constitutionally protected "discussion of governmental affairs" is an informed one. . . .

Although the right of access to criminal trials is of constitutional stature, it is not absolute. But the circumstances under which the press and public can be barred from a criminal trial are limited; the State's justification in denying access must be a weighty one. Where, as in the present case, the State attempts to deny the right of access in order to inhibit the disclosure of sensitive information, it must be shown that the denial is necessitated by a compelling governmental interest, and is narrowly tailored to serve that interest. We now consider the state interests advanced to support Massachusetts' mandatory rule barring press and public access to criminal sex-offense trials during the testimony of minor victims.

The state interests asserted to support [the law], though articulated in various ways, are reducible to two: the protection of minor victims of sex crimes from further trauma and embarrassment; and the encouragement of such victims to come forward and testify in a truthful and credible manner. We consider these interests in turn.

We agree with appellee that the first interest—safeguarding the physical and psychological well-being of a minor—is a compelling one. But as compelling as that interest is, it does not justify a *mandatory* closure rule, for it is clear that the circumstances of the particular case may affect the significance of the interest. A trial court can determine on a case by case basis whether closure is necessary to protect the welfare of a minor victim. Among the factors to be weighed are the minor victim's age, psychological maturity and understanding, the nature of the crime, the desires of the victim, and the interests of parents and relatives. [The law], in contrast, requires closure even if the victim does not seek the exclusion of the press and general public, and would not suffer injury by their presence. In the case before us, for example, the names of the minor victims were already in the public record, and the record indicates that the victims may have been willing to testify despite the presence of the press. If the trial court had been permitted to exercise its discretion, closure might well have been deemed unnecessary. In short, [the law] cannot be viewed as a narrowly tailored means of accommodating the State's asserted interest: That interest could be served just as well by requiring the trial court to determine on a case-by-case basis whether the State's legitimate concern for the well-being of the minor victim necessitates closure. Such an approach ensures that the constitutional right of the press and public to gain access to criminal trials will not be restricted except where necessary to protect the State's interest.

Nor can [the law] be justified on the basis of the Commonwealth's second asserted interest—the encouragement of minor victims of sex crimes to come forward and provide accurate testimony. The Commonwealth has offered no empirical support for the claim that the rule of automatic closure contained in [the law] will lead to an increase in the number of minor sex victims coming forward and cooperating with state authorities. Not only is the claim speculative in empirical terms, but it is also open to serious question as a matter of logic and common sense. Although [the law] bars the press and general public from the courtroom during the testimony of minor sex victims, the press is not denied access to the transcript, court personnel, or any other possible source that could provide an account of the minor victim's testimony. Thus [the law] cannot prevent the press from publicizing the substance of a minor victim's testimony, as well as his or her identity. If the Commonwealth's interest in encouraging minor victims to come forward depends on keeping such matters secret, [the law] hardly advances that interest in an effective manner. And even if [the law] effectively advanced the State's interest, it is doubtful that the interest would be sufficient to overcome the constitutional attack, for that same interest could be relied on to support an array of mandatory closure rules designed to encourage victims to come forward: Surely it cannot be suggested that minor victims of sex crimes are the *only* crime victims who, because of publicity attendant to criminal trials, are reluctant to come forward and testify. The State's argument based on this interest therefore proves too much, and runs contrary to the very foundation of the right of access recognized in *Richmond Newspapers*: namely, "that a presumption of openness inheres in the very nature of a criminal trial under our system of justice."

For the foregoing reasons, we hold that [the law], as construed by the Massachusetts Supreme Judicial Court, violates the First Amendment to the Constitution.

### Chief Justice BURGER, with whom Justice REHNQUIST joins, dissenting.

Historically our society has gone to great lengths to protect minors *charged* with crime, particularly by prohibiting the release of the names of offenders, barring the press and public from juvenile proceedings, and sealing the records of those proceedings. Yet today the Court holds unconstitutional a state statute designed to protect not the *accused*, but the minor *victims* of sex crimes. In doing so, it advances a disturbing paradox. Although states are permitted, for example, to mandate the closure of all proceedings in order to protect a 17-year-old charged with rape, they are not permitted to require the closing of part of criminal proceedings in order to protect an innocent child who has been raped or otherwise sexually abused.

The Court has tried to make its holding a narrow one by not disturbing the authority of state legislatures to enact more narrowly drawn statutes giving trial judges the discretion to exclude the public and the press from the courtroom during the minor victim's testimony. I also do not read the Court's opinion as foreclosing a state statute which mandates closure except in cases where the victim agrees to testify in open court.1 But the Court's decision is nevertheless a gross invasion of state authority and a state's duty to protect its citizens—in this case minor victims of crime. I cannot agree with the Court's expansive interpretation of our decision in *Richmond Newspapers, Inc. v. Virginia*, or its cavalier rejection of the serious interests supporting Massachusetts' mandatory closure rule. Accordingly, I dissent. . . .

### Bibliography

LaFave, Wayne R., and Jerold H. Israel. *Criminal Procedure*. St. Paul, MN: Thomson/West, 2004.

Lively, Donald E., Allen S. Hammond IV, Blake D. Morant, and Russell L. Weaver. *Communications Law*. Cincinnati, OH: Anderson Publishing Co., 1997.

## MEDIUM-SPECIFIC STANDARDS

The First Amendment was framed at a time when mass communication consisted of the published word. Since then, numerous new technologies have evolved and presented challenges to how the First Amendment should be understood. For any new medium, the threshold question has been whether it falls within the purview of the First Amendment. When initially confronted with this question in *Mutual Film Co. v. Burstyn* (1915), the Supreme Court determined that motion pictures were more in the nature of "spectacle" and "entertainment" and thus did not fit within the boundaries of freedom of press.

By the middle of the twentieth century, when broadcasting had emerged as a significant medium, the Court's thinking had evolved and its view of the First Amendment had become more expansive. Although the new media that grew and developed over the course of the twentieth century achieved First Amendment status, the Court established different standards of review and thus varying levels of protection for each of them. This resulting model of medium specific analysis begins with the premise that each medium presents unique problems that require a customized definition and application of the First Amendment. As Justice Robert Jackson put it, in *Kovacs v. Cooper* (1949), "[t]he moving picture screen, the radio, the newspaper, the handbill, the sound truck and the street orator have differing natures, abuses, and dangers. Each . . . is a law unto itself." Consistent with this analytical method, the Court in *Miami Herald Publishing Co. v. Tornillo* (1974) established that print media have the highest level of First Amendment protection. Broadcasting, as the Court found in *Federal Communications Commission v. Pacifica Foundation* (1978), has the least First Amendment protection despite being the nation's dominant medium.

Within these constitutional extremes, and often with analogies to print or broadcasting, the Court has attempted to fix the appropriate level of security for other media. During the final decades of the twentieth century, cable television emerged as a significant medium. The Court has recognized that cablecasters are protected by the First Amendment. In *Turner Broadcasting System, Inc. v. Federal Communications Commission* (1994), it determined that federal rules requiring them to carry the signals of local broadcasters were content-neutral rather than content-based (and thus subject to a less rigorous standard of review).

Efforts to extend the *Pacifica* ruling to other media have been unsuccessful, as evidenced by the Court's decision in *Sable Communications of California, Inc. v. Federal Communications Commission* (1989). This decision struck down a federal law that would have prohibited access to pornography through telephone dial-up services. A similar outcome was achieved in *Reno v. American Civil Liberties Union* (1997), when the Court determined that a federal law prohibiting indecent and patently offensive material on the Internet violated the First Amendment. The Court in *New York v. Ferber* (1982), as discussed previously, determined that child pornography could be criminalized even though it did not rise to the level of obscenity. In *Ashcroft v. Free Speech Coalition* (2002), however, the Court determined that Congress could not ban virtual child pornography.

## *Miami Herald Publishing Co. v. Tornillo*

**Citation: 418 U.S. 241.**

**Issue: Whether a state law giving political candidates a right to reply to an editorial violates the First Amendment.**

**Year of Decision: 1974.**

**Outcome: The right of access provision abridged the publisher's editorial freedom.**

**Author of Opinion: Chief Justice Warren Burger.**

**Vote: 9-0.**

The First Amendment was framed and ratified in an environment of intense debate between political factions that had sharply different views over the nation they were founding. A key medium for this debate was the press.

Publishers in the late eighteenth century typically reflected and were motivated by strong partisan sentiments. Consistent with this reality, they traded in pointed criticism over government officials and policy. In addition to their partisanship, early newspapers tended to have limited circulation with respect to readership and geography. This limited reach reflected underdeveloped distribution methods and literacy. As the national economy evolved and modernized, and mass production and dissemination became possible, the newspaper business grew into a major industry. The introduction of photojournalism in the late nineteenth century expanded the dimensions and influence of newspapers and heightened the impact of a medium that traditionally had relied upon print and drawings.

So disturbing were some changes in the newspaper industry that critics suggested the need for a legal response to its impact. Louis Brandeis, two decades before being appointed to the United States Supreme Court, coauthored an influential law review article that expressed concern with increasingly aggressive and intrusive news reporting. From Brandeis's perspective, media that a century ago had been facilitators of partisan debate had become instrumentalities of intrusion and gossip that appealed to people's lower instincts. Media emphasis upon sensationalism and entertainment, as Brandeis saw it, diverted space from "matters of genuine community concern" to the interests of "the indolent." With the press "overstepping in every direction the obvious bounds of propriety and decency," through "[i]nstantaneous photographs" and "newspapers enterprise," Brandeis believed the law must shore up the individual's "right 'to be let alone.'"

Change was not limited to the media's interests, the tone of its coverage, and its means of reporting. A primary trend of the newspaper industry, especially over the course of the twentieth century, has been the emergence of chains that have resulted in many publications being operated by group ownership. Another phenomenon has been the decline of the total number of daily newspapers. In 1910, a total of 2,600 daily newspapers were published in American metropolitan areas. By the final decade of the century, that number had diminished to fewer than 1,750. Cities with more than one newspaper, which had been a common feature at the beginning of the century, were a rarity by its end. As the Supreme Court observed in the early 1970s, one-newspaper towns "have become the rule, with effective competition operating in only four percent of our large cities." With increasingly concentrated ownership of newspapers, and a shrinking market for them, concern has been expressed that power to inform the American people and influence public opinion rests in the hands of a relative few. Whether this circumstance affects the meaning of freedom of the press, however, has been a question that the Court has answered in the negative.

The issue with respect to whether concentrated ownership necessitates constitutional doctrine that ensures not just a free but balanced flow of information arose in connection with a Florida "right to respond law." Under the terms of the statute, political candidates had "a right to equal space to reply to criticism and attacks on [their] record by a newspaper." In determining whether this provision undermined press freedom, the Court acknowledged how the newspaper industry increasingly had become characterized by concentrated ownership and diminished competition. Because editorial output was a function of centralized and homogenized opinion, commentary, and analysis, the argument for a right of response was that "the public has lost any ability to respond to or contribute in a meaningful way to the debate on issues." A public right of access to the media, to ensure broad and balanced coverage of important public concerns, thus was advocated as a constitutional check against "the vast accumulations of unreviewable power in the modern media empires."

The Court noted that economic facts had altered the right of free public expression as initially experienced in the society. Editorial competition, which had been common at the nation's outset, was difficult if not impossible to achieve because entry into the publishing business had become prohibitively expensive. Despite these profound changes, and their impact on First Amendment circumstances, the Court rejected the notion that the state might attempt to secure a publisher's fairness, accuracy, or accountability. Writing for the majority, Chief Justice Warren Burger indicated that "a responsible press" might be a "desirable goal," but it could not be achieved by constitutional interpretation without offending the First Amendment. The core issue presented by Florida's right to response law was whether government can force "editors to publish that which 'reason tells them should not be published.'" To the extent that news coverage is officially mandated or directed, the impact upon the editorial process is notable. As the Court observed, a public right of access requires a setting aside of "space that could be devoted to other material the newspaper may have preferred to print." Viewing the law not only as impermissible because it compromised editorial autonomy, which is the essence of press freedom, the Court noted that it might encourage editors to shy away from controversy so that they do not trigger a right to reply. Such a result would be detrimental not only to editorial freedom but to the needs of the information marketplace.

The constitutional bottom line for the Court was the state law was unacceptable "because of its intrusion into the function of editors." Because it compelled printing of a reply, the statute was viewed as extracting a penalty on the basis of content. The costs included "printing and composing time and materials and . . . space" that might be used for other stories. Even if it did not impose additional costs, a right of reply was unacceptable because it intruded into the function of editors. As the Court described them, newspapers are "more than a passive receptacle or conduit for news, comment, and advertising." The content of a newspaper and decisions concerning size and attitude toward persons and policy "constitute the exercise of editorial control and function." Whether editorial judgment is "fair or unfair," it is a central aspect of press freedom. Recognizing the importance of editorial autonomy, the Court stressed that it has not yet been "demonstrated how governmental regulation of this crucial process can be exercised consistent with First Amendment guarantees as they have evolved to this time."

The Court's decision reflects an appreciation of the role that the press plays as a check on government and how that function might be undermined if the state were to assume responsibility for fairness and balance. It reflects a philosophy faithful to founding sentiments expressed by John Adams, who drafted the free press clause of the Massachusetts Constitution. Adams penned the observation that "liberty of the press is essential to the security of the state, . . . [and] the relevant metaphor . . . is the metaphor of the Fourth Estate." The "Fourth Estate" is a term coined in pre-Revolutionary England in reference to the "Reporters' Gallery" that observed the "Three Estates in Parliament." Justice Byron White in a concurring opinion reinforced the value of this role in referring to "the unhappy experiences of other nations where government has been allowed to meddle in the internal editorial affairs of newspapers." No matter how well-intentioned the regulation might be, Justice White stressed the need to "remain intensely skeptical about those measures that would allow government to insinuate itself into the editorial rooms of this Nation's press." For him, a right of reply law advanced an important interest but ignored how "[w]oven into the fabric of the First Amendment is the unexceptional, but nonetheless timeless, sentiment that 'liberty of the press is in peril as soon as the government tries to compel what is to go into a newspaper.'" Modern circumstances of concentrated ownership and declining numbers of newspapers have challenged the ability of press freedom to achieve fairness and balance. By striking down Florida's right to reply law, the Court conclusively repudiated the notion that the First Amendment either permits or requires government to promote fairness and evenhandedness through official regulation.

## Mr. Chief Justice BURGER delivered the opinion of the Court.

. . . The appellee and supporting advocates of an enforceable right of access to the press vigorously argue that government has an obligation to ensure that a wide variety of views reach the public. The contentions of access proponents will be set out in some detail. It is urged that at the time the First Amendment to the Constitution was ratified in 1791 as part of our Bill of Rights the press was broadly representative of the people it was serving. While many of the newspapers were intensely partisan and narrow in their views, the press collectively presented a broad range of opinions to readers. Entry into publishing was inexpensive; pamphlets and books provided meaningful alternatives to the organized press for the expression of unpopular ideas and often treated events and expressed views not covered by conventional newspapers. A true marketplace of ideas existed in which there was relatively easy access to the channels of communication.

Access advocates submit that although newspapers of the present are superficially similar to those of 1791 the press of today is in reality very different from that known in the early years of our national existence. In the past half century a communications revolution has seen the introduction of radio and television into our lives, the promise of a global community through the use of communications satellites, and the spectre of a 'wired' nation by means of an expanding cable television network with two-way capabilities. The printed press, it is said, has not escaped the effects of this revolution. Newspapers have become big business and there are far fewer of them to serve a larger literate population. . . .

The elimination of competing newspapers in most of our large cities, and the concentration of control of media that results from the only newspaper's being owned by the same interests which own a television station and a radio station, are important components of this trend toward concentration of control of outlets to inform the public.

The result of these vast changes has been to place in a few hands the power to inform the American people and shape public opinion. Much of the editorial opinion and commentary that is printed is that of syndicated columnists distributed nationwide and, as a result, we are told, on national and world issues there tends to be a homogeneity of editorial opinion, commentary, and interpretive analysis. The abuses of bias and manipulative reportage are, likewise, said to be the result of the vast accumulations of unreviewable power in the modern media empires. In effect, it is claimed, the public has lost any ability to respond or to contribute in a meaningful way to the debate on issues. . . .

The obvious solution, which was available to dissidents at an earlier time when entry into publishing was relatively inexpensive, today would be to have additional newspapers. But the same economic factors which have caused the disappearance of vast numbers of metropolitan newspapers, have made entry into the marketplace of ideas served by the print media almost impossible. It is urged that the claim of newspapers to be 'surrogates for the public' carries with it a concomitant fiduciary obligation to account for that stewardship. From this premise it is reasoned that the only effective way to insure fairness and accuracy and to provide for some account-ability is for government to take affirmative action. The First Amendment interest of the public in being informed is said to be in peril because the 'marketplace of ideas' is today a monopoly controlled by the owners of the market. . . .

However much validity may be found in these arguments, at each point the implementation of a remedy such as an enforceable right of access necessarily calls for some mechanism, either governmental or consensual. If it is governmental coercion, this at once brings about a confrontation with the express provisions of the First Amendment and the judicial gloss on that Amendment developed over the years. . . .

Appellee's argument that the Florida statute does not amount to a restriction of appellant's right to speak because 'the statute in question here has not prevented the Miami Herald from saying anything it wished' begs the core question. Compel-ling editors or publishers to publish that which "reason' tells them should not be published' is what is at issue in this case. The Florida statute operates as a com-mand in the same sense as a statue or regulation forbidding appellant to publish specified matter. Governmental restraint on publishing need not fall into familiar or traditional patterns to be subject to constitutional limitations on governmental powers. The Florida statute exacts a penalty on the basis of the content of a news-paper. The first phase of the penalty resulting from the compelled printing of a reply is exacted in terms of the cost in printing and composing time and materials and in taking up space that could be devoted to other material the newspaper may have preferred to print. It is correct, as appellee contends, that a newspaper is not subject to the finite technological limitations of time that confront a broadcaster but it is not correct to say that, as an economic reality, a newspaper can proceed to infinite expansion of its column space to accommodate the replies that a govern-ment agency determines or a statute commands the readers should have available.

Faced with the penalties that would accrue to any newspaper that published news or commentary arguably within the reach of the right-of-access statute, edi-tors might well conclude that the safe course is to avoid controversy. Therefore, under the operation of the Florida statute, political and electoral coverage would be blunted or reduced. Government-enforced right of access inescapably 'dampens the vigor and limits the variety of public debate."

Even if a newspaper would face no additional costs to comply with a compul-sory access law and would not be forced to forgo publication of news or opinion by the inclusion of a reply, the Florida statute fails to clear the barriers of the First Amendment because of its intrusion into the function of editors. A newspaper is more than a passive receptacle or conduit for news, comment, and advertising. The choice of material to go into a newspaper, and the decisions made as to limitations on the size and content of the paper, and treatment of public issues and public officials—whether fair or unfair—constitute the exercise of editorial control and judgment. It has yet to be demonstrated how governmental regulation of this crucial process can be exercised consistent with First Amendment guarantees of a free press as they have evolved to this time. Accordingly, the judgment of the Supreme Court of Florida is reversed.

## Bibliography

Brandeis, Louis D., and Samuel D. Warren. "The Right to Privacy." *Harvard Law Review* 4 (1890): 193.

Campbell, Angela J. "A Historical Perspective on the Public's Right of Access to the Media." *Hofstra Law Review* 35 (2007): 1027.

Chafee, Zechariah. *Government and Mass Communications.* Chicago: University of Chicago Press, 1947.

Emery, Edward. *The Press and America.* Englewood Cliffs, NJ: Prentice-Hall, 1962.

Sunstein, Cass. *Democracy and the Problem of Free Speech.* New York: The Free Press, 1993.

## *Federal Communications Commission v. Pacifica Foundation*

**Citation: 438 U.S. 726.**

**Issue: Whether the First Amendment bars the Federal Communications Commission from prohibiting sexually indecent but not obscene expression on radio and television.**

**Year of Decision: 1978.**

**Outcome: The First Amendment does not preclude regulation of sexually indecent expression.**

**Author of Opinion: Justice John Paul Stevens.**

**Vote: 5-4.**

Broadcasting is the primary source of information for Americans. Despite its dominance, the Supreme Court has given it the least protection under the First Amendment. This diminished status reflects in part the sense that broadcasting is a "scarce medium." Pursuant to an understanding that there are more persons wanting to broadcast than available frequencies, the Court has upheld regulations requiring broadcasters to balance their coverage of controversial issues or make time available for a specific use in the public interest.

Regulation of broadcasting flows from the general premise that, as the Court observed in *Metromedia, Inc. v. San Diego* (1981), "[e]ach method of communicating is a 'law unto itself,' reflecting the 'differing natures, values, abuses, and dangers' of each method." Beyond the concerns that drove efforts to promote fairness and balance in the coverage of controversial public issues, regulatory authorities have been particularly concerned with radio and television's impact upon children. Government power to regulate on these grounds was tested, in *Federal Communications Commission v. Pacifica Foundation* (1978), when the Supreme Court reviewed the use of profane and sexually explicit language over the airwaves.

At issue specifically was a comedian's (George Carlin's) monologue concerning "words you couldn't say on the public . . . airwaves." The presentation, entitled "Filthy Words" had been recorded before a live audience. It was broadcast during the middle of a weekday by a New York radio station that specialized in "alternative" programming. It was preceded by warnings that the language might offend some listeners.

The program generated a complaint to the Federal Communications Commission (FCC) by a listener who heard it while riding in a car with his 15-year-old son. The complainant was an official in an organization called "Morality in Media." Despite the radio station's argument that the humorist was a "significant social satirist," and no other complaints were received, the FCC determined that federal indecency standards had been violated.

Although vested with regulatory authority over broadcasting, the FCC under federal law is prohibited from "interfer[ing] with the right of free speech by means of radio communication." Congress, however, also has prohibited broadcasters from airing "any obscene, indecent, or profane language." Obscene speech is constitutionally unprotected regardless of the medium that propagates it. Indecent or profane language, however, typically is within the scope of First Amendment protection. Because the monologue was not obscene, the radio station argued that the FCC could not prohibit it without violating the First Amendment. The question, therefore, was "whether the First Amendment denies government any power to restrict the public broadcast of indecent language in any circumstances."

In an opinion by Justice John Paul Stevens, the Court acknowledged that the speech was protected by the First Amendment. Nonetheless, it considered whether there were important reasons for prohibiting such programming on radio or television.

The Court began by restating the general proposition that speech cannot be regulated merely because it is "offensive." It further noted that the First Amendment was a bar to any regulation based upon political content. Having stated these premises, however, the Court determined that First Amendment interests were not significant. From the Court's perspective, the monologue was offensive "for the same reasons that obscenity offends." Although the First Amendment interest was found to be minimal, the Court noted that this reading could change depending upon context. It thus contrasted "a two-way radio conversation between a cab driver and a dispatcher, or a telecast of an Elizabethan comedy." Describing the programming as "vulgar," "offensive," and "shocking," the Court focused upon the actual setting in which it was broadcast. As a starting point, the Court observed that "of all forms of communication, it is broadcasting that has received the most limited First Amendment protection." The starting point for analysis thus reflected a dual sense that the monologue had slight social value and the medium that broadcast it had limited First Amendment standing.

Broadcasting's devalued constitutional status was explained on two grounds. First, as the Court put it, the medium has "a uniquely pervasive presence in the lives of all Americans." In this regard, a central concern was with the listener's privacy—particularly in the home where "the right to be left alone plainly outweighs the First Amendment rights of an intruder." A well-established line of cases holds that, when confronted with offensive expression in public contexts, a person can simply ignore what he or she finds offensive.

With respect to broadcasting, however, the Court found it insufficient that viewers or listeners can change a station or turn off the offending medium. Placing total responsibility upon the viewer or listener, the Court observed, is "like saying that the remedy for an assault is to run away after the first blow." Even if the broadcaster provided warnings, the Court thought them insufficient for a broadcast audience that is "constantly tuning in and out."

The Court also identified the medium's unique accessibility to children as a reason for downgrading its First Amendment status. Differentiating broadcasting from print media, it noted that "even [for] those too young to read" the monologue would "have enlarged a child's vocabulary in an instant." Although the content might be prohibited in broadcasting, it could be disseminated without constraint in other media and, in fact, was set forth in an appendix to the Court's opinion. Nonetheless, the easy access children have to radio and television led the Court to conclude that regulation advanced the state's interest in "the well-being of its youth."

The Court closed its opinion by comparing indecent broadcasting to a nuisance. Building upon this premise, it noted that regulation depended upon several factors, including the time of day, the makeup of the audience, and whether indecent content was disseminated over the air or by closed circuit. The Court described a nuisance as "merely a right thing in the wrong place—like a pig in the parlor instead of the barnyard." Consistent with this observation, it held "that when the [FCC] finds that a pig has entered the parlor, the exercise of its regulatory power does not depend on proof that the pig is obscene."

Justice William Brennan authored a pointed dissenting opinion alleging that the Court misconceived the privacy interests at stake and undervalued the interests of expressive diversity, particularly as this interest relates to consenting viewers and listeners. As Justice Brennan saw it, the Court actually undercut the authority of parents to make decisions pursuant to their sense of what is in the best interests of their children. He described the Court's opinion as an effort "to unstitch the warp and woof of First Amendment law in an effort to reshape its fabric to cover [a] patently wrong result." In this regard, he perceived a "depressing inability to appreciate that in our land of cultural pluralism, there are many who think, act, and talk differently from the Members of this Court, and who do not share their fragile sensibilities."

The opinion thus represented, at least for Justice Brennan, "an acute ethnocentric myopia that enables the Court to approve the censorship of communications solely because of the words they contain." Reality from Justice Brennan's perspective was that the words at issue were "the stuff of everyday conversations" in many of the nation's subcultures. Banning them would burden those who dispute or challenge the "dominant culture." For Justice Brennan, the ruling established a preferred "way of thinking, acting and speaking" that was inconsistent with the First Amendment.

The aftermath of *Pacifica* consisted of nearly two decades of interplay between the FCC and the courts with respect to indecency regulation. After several failed efforts, the FCC adopted rules that provide a safe harbor for indecent programming between the hours of 10 PM and 6 AM. A federal appeals court, in *Action for Children's Television v. Federal Communications Commission* (1995), upheld this time channeling provision. In so doing, it recognized a compelling interest in protecting children under the age of 18. The court also was satisfied that the adult audience was not denied access altogether to a constitutionally protected form of expression.

Efforts to extend indecency regulation to other contexts largely have failed on grounds that media, like cable, provide better means for viewers and listeners to block unwanted programming. Technology's utility in other settings highlights how relevant differences among media may drive different First Amendment results. At a time when most broadcast signals are carried to the audience by cable, however, the different outcomes also evidence how technology ultimately may break down the logic of medium-specific analysis.

### Mr. Justice STEVENS delivered the opinion of the Court.

. . . When the issue is narrowed to the facts of this case, the question is whether the First Amendment denies government any power to restrict the public broadcast of indecent language in any circumstances. For if the government has any such power, this was an appropriate occasion for its exercise.

The words of the Carlin monologue are unquestionably "speech" within the meaning of the First Amendment. It is equally clear that the Commission's objections to the broadcast were based in part on its content. The order must therefore fall if, as Pacifica argues, the First Amendment prohibits all governmental regulation that depends on the content of speech. Our past cases demonstrate, however, that no such absolute rule is mandated by the Constitution.

The classic exposition of the proposition that both the content and the context of speech are critical elements of First Amendment analysis is Mr. Justice Holmes' statement for the Court in *Schenck v. United States*:

"We admit that in many places and in ordinary times the defendants in saying all that was said in the circular would have been within their constitutional rights. But the character of every act depends upon the circumstances in which it is done. . . . The most stringent protection of free speech would not protect a man in falsely shouting fire in a theatre and causing a panic. It does not even protect a man from an injunction against uttering words that may have all the effect of force. . . . The question in every case is whether the words used are used in such circumstances and are of such a nature as to create a clear and present danger that they will bring about the substantive evils that Congress has a right to prevent." . . .

The question in this case is whether a broadcast of patently offensive words dealing with sex and excretion may be regulated because of its content. Obscene materials have been denied the protection of the First Amendment because their content is so offensive to contemporary moral standards. But the fact that society may find speech offensive is not a sufficient reason for suppressing it. Indeed, if it is the speaker's opinion that gives offense, that consequence is a reason for according it constitutional protection. For it is a central tenet of the First Amendment that the government must remain neutral in the marketplace of ideas. If there were any reason to believe that the Commission's characterization of the Carlin monologue as offensive could be traced to its political content—or even to the fact that it satirized contemporary attitudes about four-letter words—First Amendment protection might be required. But that is simply not this case. These words offend for the same reasons that obscenity offends. Their place in the hierarchy of First Amendment values was aptly sketched by Mr. Justice Murphy when he said: "Such utterances are no essential part of any exposition of ideas, and are of such slight social value as a step to truth that any benefit that may be derived from them is clearly outweighed by the social interest in order and morality."

Although these words ordinarily lack literary, political, or scientific value, they are not entirely outside the protection of the First Amendment. Some uses of even the most offensive words are unquestionably protected. Indeed, we may assume, *arguendo*, that this monologue would be protected in other contexts. Nonetheless, the constitutional protection accorded to a communication containing such patently offensive sexual and excretory language need not be the same in every context.

In this case it is undisputed that the content of Pacifica's broadcast was "vulgar," "offensive," and "shocking." Because content of that character is not entitled to absolute constitutional protection under all circumstances, we must consider its context in order to determine whether the Commission's action was constitutionally permissible.

We have long recognized that each medium of expression presents special First Amendment problems. And of all forms of communication, it is broadcasting that has received the most limited First Amendment protection. Thus, although other speakers cannot be licensed except under laws that carefully define and narrow official discretion, a broadcaster may be deprived of his license and his forum if the Commission decides that such an action would serve "the public interest, convenience, and necessity." Similarly, although the First Amendment protects newspaper publishers from being required to print the replies of those whom they criticize, it affords no such protection to broadcasters; on the contrary, they must give free time to the victims of their criticism.

The reasons for these distinctions are complex, but two have relevance to the present case. First, the broadcast media have established a uniquely pervasive presence in the lives of all Americans. Patently offensive, indecent material presented over the airwaves confronts the citizen, not only in public, but also in the privacy of the home, where the individual's right to be left alone plainly outweighs the First Amendment rights of an intruder. Because the broadcast audience is constantly tuning in and out, prior warnings cannot completely protect the listener or viewer from unexpected program content. To say that one may avoid further offense by turning off the radio when he hears indecent language is like saying that the remedy for an assault is to run away after the first blow. One may hang up on an indecent phone call, but that option does not give the caller a constitutional immunity or avoid a harm that has already taken place.

Second, broadcasting is uniquely accessible to children, even those too young to read. Although Cohen's written message might have been incomprehensible to a first grader, Pacifica's broadcast could have enlarged a child's vocabulary in an instant. Other forms of offensive expression may be withheld from the young without restricting the expression at its source. Bookstores and motion picture theaters, for example, may be prohibited from making indecent material available to children. . . .

It is appropriate, in conclusion, to emphasize the narrowness of our holding. This case does not involve a two-way radio conversation between a cab driver and a dispatcher, or a telecast of an Elizabethan comedy. We have not decided that an occasional expletive in either setting would justify any sanction or, indeed, that this broadcast would justify a criminal prosecution. The Commission's decision rested entirely on a nuisance rationale under which context is all-important. The concept requires consideration of a host of variables. The time of day was emphasized by the Commission. The content of the program in which the language is used will also affect the composition of the audience, and differences between radio, television, and perhaps closed-circuit transmissions, may also be relevant. As Mr. Justice Sutherland wrote a "nuisance may be merely a right thing in the wrong place,—like a pig in the parlor instead of the barnyard." We simply hold that when the Commission finds that a pig has entered the parlor, the exercise of its regulatory power does not depend on proof that the pig is obscene. . . .

### Mr. Justice BRENNAN, with whom Mr. Justice MARSHALL joins, dissenting.

I agree with Mr. Justice STEWART that the word "indecent" in 18 U.S.C. § 1464 (1976 ed.) must be construed to prohibit only obscene speech. I would, therefore, normally refrain from expressing my views on any constitutional issues implicated in this case. However, I find the Court's misapplication of fundamental First Amendment principles so patent, and its attempt to impose *its* notions of propriety on the whole of the American people so misguided, that I am unable to remain silent.

For the second time in two years, the Court refuses to embrace the notion, completely antithetical to basic First Amendment values, that the degree of protection the First Amendment affords protected speech varies with the social value ascribed to that speech by five Members of this Court. Moreover, as do all parties, all Members of the Court agree that the Carlin monologue aired by Station WBAI does not fall within one of the categories of speech, such as "fighting words," or obscenity, that is totally without First Amendment protection. This conclusion, of course, is compelled by our cases expressly holding that communications containing some of the words found condemnable here are fully protected by the First Amendment in other contexts.

Yet despite the Court's refusal to create a sliding scale of First Amendment protection calibrated to this Court's perception of the worth of a communication's content, and despite our unanimous agreement that the Carlin monologue is protected speech, a majority of the Court nevertheless finds that, on the facts of this case, the FCC is not constitutionally barred from imposing sanctions on Pacifica for its airing of the Carlin monologue. This majority apparently believes that the FCC's disapproval of Pacifica's afternoon broadcast of Carlin's "Dirty Words" recording is a permissible time, place, and manner regulation. Both the opinion of my Brother STEVENS and the opinion of my Brother POWELL rely principally on two factors in reaching this conclusion: (1) the capacity of a radio broadcast to intrude into the unwilling listener's home, and (2) the presence of children in the listening audience. Dispassionate analysis, removed from individual notions as to what is proper and what is not, starkly reveals that these justifications, whether individually or together, simply do not support even the professedly moderate degree of governmental homogenization of radio communications—if, indeed, such homogenization can ever be moderate given the pre-eminent status of the right of free speech in our constitutional scheme—that the Court today permits.

Without question, the privacy interests of an individual in his home are substantial and deserving of significant protection. In finding these interests sufficient to justify the content regulation of protected speech, however, the Court commits two errors. First, it misconceives the nature of the privacy interests involved where an individual voluntarily chooses to admit radio communications into his home. Second, it ignores the constitutionally protected interests of both those who wish to transmit and those who desire to receive broadcasts that many—including the FCC and this Court—might find offensive.

"The ability of government, consonant with the Constitution, to shut off discourse solely to protect others from hearing it is . . . dependent upon a showing that substantial privacy interests are being invaded in an essentially intolerable manner. Any broader view of this authority would effectively empower a majority to silence dissidents simply as a matter of personal predilections." I am in wholehearted agreement with my Brethren that an individual's right "to be let alone" when engaged in private activity within the confines of his own home is encompassed within the "substantial privacy interests" to which Mr. Justice Harlan referred in *Cohen*, and is entitled to the greatest solicitude. However, I believe that an individual's actions in switching on and listening to communications transmitted over the public airways and directed to the public at large do not implicate fundamental privacy interests, even when engaged in within the home. Instead, because the radio is undeniably a public medium, these actions are more properly viewed as a decision to take part, if only as a listener, in an ongoing public discourse. Although an individual's decision to allow public radio communications into his home undoubtedly does not abrogate all of his privacy interests, the residual privacy interests he retains vis-à-vis the communication he voluntarily admits into his home are surely no greater than those of the people present in the corridor of the Los Angeles courthouse in *Cohen* who bore witness to the words "Fuck the Draft" emblazoned across Cohen's jacket. Their privacy interests were held insufficient to justify punishing Cohen for his offensive communication.

Even if an individual who voluntarily opens his home to radio communications retains privacy interests of sufficient moment to justify a ban on protected speech if those interests are "invaded in an essentially intolerable manner," the very fact that those interests are threatened only by a radio broadcast precludes any intolerable invasion of privacy; for unlike other intrusive modes of communication, such as sound trucks, "[t]he radio can be turned off,"—and with a minimum of effort. As Chief Judge Bazelon aptly observed below, "having elected to receive public air waives, the scanner who stumbles onto an offensive program is in the same position as the unsuspecting passers-by; he can avert his attention by changing channels or turning off the set." Whatever the minimal discomfort suffered by a listener who inadvertently tunes into a program he finds offensive during the brief interval before he can simply extend his arm and switch stations or flick the "off" button, it is surely worth the candle to preserve the broadcaster's right to send, and the right of those interested to receive, a message entitled to full First Amendment protection. To reach a contrary balance, as does the Court, is clearly to follow Mr. Justice STEVENS' reliance on animal metaphors, "to burn the house to roast the pig."

The Court's balance, of necessity, fails to accord proper weight to the interests of listeners who wish to hear broadcasts the FCC deems offensive. It permits majoritarian tastes completely to preclude a protected message from entering the homes of a receptive, unoffended minority. No decision of this Court supports such a result. Where the individuals constituting the offended majority may freely choose to reject the material being offered, we have never found their privacy interests of such moment to warrant the suppression of speech on privacy grounds. *Rowan v. Post Office Dept.*, relied on by the FCC and by the opinions of my Brothers POWELL and STEVENS, confirms rather than belies this conclusion. In *Rowan*, the Court upheld a statute, 39 U.S.C. § 4009, permitting householders to require that mail advertisers stop sending them lewd or offensive materials and remove their names from mailing lists. Unlike the situation here, householders who wished to receive the sender's communications were not prevented from doing so. Equally important, the determination of offensiveness *vel non* under the statute involved in

*Rowan* was completely within the hands of the individual householder; no governmental evaluation of the worth of the mail's content stood between the mailer and the householder. In contrast, the visage of the censor is all too discernible here. . . .

## Bibliography

Kaneb, Michael. "Neither Realistic nor Constitutionally Sound: The Problem of the FCC's Community Standard for Broadcast Indecency Determinations." *Boston College Law Review* 49 (2008): 1081.

Meiklejohn, Alexander. *Free Speech and Its Relation to Self-Government.* New York: Harper, 1948.

Powe, Lucas A., Jr. *American Broadcasting and the First Amendment.* Berkeley: University of California Press, 1987.

Spitzer, Matthew. *Seven Dirty Words and Six Other Stories.* New Haven, CT: Yale University Press, 1986.

## *Sable Communications of California, Inc. v. Federal Communications Commission*

**Citation: 492 U.S. 115.**

**Issue: Whether a congressional ban on indecent commercial telephone messages violated freedom of speech.**

**Year of Decision: 1989.**

**Outcome: The federal ban was not narrowly tailored in its effort to protect minors and thus abridged freedom of speech.**

**Author of Opinion: Justice Byron White.**

**Vote: 8-1.**

First Amendment case law establishes that expression which may be fit for one medium is not necessarily acceptable in another medium. Sexually explicit content that may be published in a book or magazine, therefore, may not be permissible on radio or television. This result reflects a basic premise, as the Supreme Court noted in *Federal Communications Commission v. Pacifica Foundation* (1978), that "each medium of expression presents specific First Amendment problems." The starting point for reviewing the constitutionality of a content-based regulation, therefore, is to determine whether it responds to a unique or identifiable problem that the medium presents.

Finding that radio and television had a "uniquely pervasive presence" and were "uniquely accessible to children," the *Pacifica* Court upheld federal regulation of indecent programming. With this precedent established, it was only a matter of time before the Court would confront the same issue in the context of other electronic media. Barely a decade after its *Pacifica* ruling, the Court reviewed a federal law banning both indecent and obscene commercial telephone messages. At issue, in *Sable Communications of California, Inc. v. Federal Communications Commission,* were the sexually oriented telephone recordings of a dial-a-porn service. To access this service, users were required to dial a particular number and pay a fee. Drawing upon the rationale for regulating indecent expression in broadcasting, the government maintained that the regulation was necessary to protect against access by children.

In a majority opinion authored by Justice Byron White, the Court found that the *Pacifica* decision was easily distinguished because it did not demand a total prohibition of indecent programming. Rather, it required a channeling of such content to times of the day when children were less likely to be exposed to it. Even if the ban was not absolute, the Court observed that the characteristics of broadcasting that provided a basis for concern in *Pacifica* were not present in telephone communications. The uniquely pervasive presence problem that affects broadcasting, as the Court explained, is that a viewer or listener may not receive a warning with respect to program content that enables him or her to avoid it. This issue does not arise in connection with the use of telephones, insofar as the user must take affirmative steps to access the service. The decision to use the service, moreover, indicates a state of mind that is "manifestly different from a situation in which a listener does not want to receive the message."

With respect to concern with access by children, the government maintained that nothing could account for this interest short of a total ban of the expression. The Court found this argument to be "quite unpersuasive." It noted that the Federal Communications Commission, in its own rule making proceedings, had found credit card, access codes, and scrambling rules to be sufficient barriers to access by minors. In response to the government's contention that enterprising youngsters could bypass these safeguards, the Court found no evidence to justify the concern. To the contrary, the record as the Court read it could support the inference that technology was an "extremely effective" means for balancing the interests of consenting adults and the state's concern with protecting children.

In a concurring opinion, Justice Antonin Scalia agreed that the First Amendment prohibits Congress from banning the type of indecent telephone communications at issue. At the same time, he noted that telephone companies were not obligated to provide or contract for such services. Justice Scalia's observation restates two important principles. First, the First Amendment like other constitutional rights governs only action by the government. Second, telephone companies typically are public utilities and typically have no First Amendment interests. To the contrary, they are common carriers and thus are obligated to provide access on a nondiscriminatory basis to any user willing to pay the designated tariff. This rule does not apply insofar as telephone companies develop other lines of business, such as video programming that competes with cable. When functioning in such a capacity, the company is a content provider and protected by the First Amendment.

Justice William Brennan, in a concurring opinion joined by Justices Thurgood Marshall and John Paul Stevens, maintained that the prohibition of indecent telephone communication was "patently unconstitutional." He departed from the Court's determination, however, that the law as applied to obscene expression should stand. This conclusion was consistent with Justice Brennan's evolution since authoring the majority opinion in *Roth v. United States* (1958) that defined obscenity as unprotected speech. In *Paris Adult Theatre I v. Slaton* (1973), as a dissenting justice, he expressed his sense that obscenity should be protected to the extent that the interests of children and unconsenting adults were not implicated. The circumstances of *Sable,* in which dial-a-porn services were restricted to consenting adults and generally inaccessible to children, represented a logical opportunity for reaffirming this principle. It is a premise, however, that has not commanded a majority of the Court, which continues to regard obscenity as unprotected speech.

The *Sable* decision represents an important boundary of government's ability to regulate indecent expression. The *Pacifica* Court itself emphasized that its holding was narrow. Despite this express limitation, the ruling became a basis for regulatory initiative that attempted to impose similar restrictions upon other electronic media. In *Denver Area Educational Telecommunications Consortium v. Federal Communications Commission* (1996), the Court examined a federal law regulating the availability of "patently offensive" programming on cable television. Among the provisions of the law that the Court struck down was one that required cable operators to route all sexually explicit programming to a single channel and block access to it minus written consent by the subscriber. Borrowing heavily from its decision in *Sable,* the Court noted that technology can provide viewers with the ability to block or code access to unwanted programming.

The *Sable* ruling is notable also because of the rigorous standard of review it employed. Specifically, the Court insisted upon a compelling government interest to support the regulation and evidence that the rule was a narrowly tailored means of achieving its end. Although acknowledging that the interest in protecting children was compelling, the Court referenced technology as a solution that was effective and did not compromise First Amendment freedom. To decide otherwise, as the Court put it, would "reduce the adult population . . . to only what was fit for children."

## Justice WHITE delivered the opinion of the Court.

. . . Sexual expression which is indecent but not obscene is protected by the First Amendment; and the federal parties do not submit that the sale of such materials to adults could be criminalized solely because they are indecent. The Government may, however, regulate the content of constitutionally protected speech in order to promote a compelling interest if it chooses the least restrictive means to further the articulated interest. We have recognized that there is a compelling interest in protecting the physical and psychological well-being of minors. This interest extends to shielding minors from the influence of literature that is not obscene by adult standards. The Government may serve this legitimate interest, but to withstand constitutional scrutiny, "it must do so by narrowly drawn regulations designed to serve those interests without unnecessarily interfering with First Amendment freedoms. It is not enough to show that the Government's ends are compelling; the means must be carefully tailored to achieve those ends. . . .

The federal parties nevertheless argue that the total ban on indecent commercial telephone communications is justified because nothing less could prevent children from gaining access to such messages. We find the argument quite unpersuasive. The FCC, after lengthy proceedings, determined that its credit card, access code, and scrambling rules were a satisfactory solution to the problem of keeping indecent dial-a-porn messages out of the reach of minors. The Court of Appeals, after careful consideration, agreed that these rules represented a "feasible and effective" way to serve the Government's compelling interest in protecting children.

The federal parties now insist that the rules would not be effective enough—that enterprising youngsters could and would evade the rules and gain access to communications from which they should be shielded. There is no evidence in the record before us to that effect, nor could there be since the FCC's implementation of § 223(b) prior to its 1988 amendment has never been tested over time. In this respect, the federal parties assert that in amending § 223(b) in 1988, Congress expressed its view that there was not a sufficiently effective way to protect minors short of the total ban that it enacted. The federal parties claim that we must give deference to that judgment.

To the extent that the federal parties suggest that we should defer to Congress' conclusion about an issue of constitutional law, our answer is that while we do not ignore it, it is our task in the end to decide whether Congress has violated the Constitution. This is particularly true where the Legislature has concluded that its product does not violate the First Amendment. "Deference to a legislative finding cannot limit judicial inquiry when First Amendment rights are at stake." The federal parties, however, also urge us to defer to the factual findings by Congress relevant to resolving the constitutional issue; they rely on *Walters v. National Association of Radiation Survivors*. Beyond the fact that whatever deference is due legislative findings would not foreclose our independent judgment of the facts bearing on an issue of constitutional law, our answer is that the congressional record contains no legislative findings that would justify us in concluding that there is no constitutionally acceptable less restrictive means, short of a total ban, to achieve the Government's interest in protecting minors.

There is no doubt Congress enacted a total ban on both obscene and indecent telephone communications. But aside from conclusory statements during the debates by proponents of the bill, as well as similar assertions in hearings on a substantially identical bill the year before, H.R. 1786, that under the FCC regulations minors could still have access to dial-a-porn messages, the congressional record presented to us contains no evidence as to *how* effective or ineffective the FCC's most recent regulations were or might prove to be. It may well be that there is no fail-safe method of guaranteeing that never will a minor be able to access the dial-a-porn system. The bill that was enacted, however, was introduced on the floor; nor was there a committee report on the bill from which the language of the enacted bill was taken. No Congressman or Senator purported to present a considered judgment with respect to how often or to what extent minors could or would circumvent the rules and have access to dial-a-porn messages. On the other hand, in the hearings on H.R. 1786, the Committee heard testimony from the FCC and other witnesses that the FCC rules would be effective and should be tried out in practice. Furthermore, at the conclusion of the hearing, the Chairman of the Subcommittee suggested consultation looking toward "drafting a piece of legislation that will pass constitutional muster, while at the same time providing for the practical relief which families and groups are looking for." The bill never emerged from Committee.

For all we know from this record, the FCC's technological approach to restricting dial-a-porn messages to adults who seek them would be extremely effective, and only a few of the most enterprising and disobedient young people would manage to secure access to such messages. If this is the case, it seems to us that § 223(b) is not a narrowly tailored effort to serve the compelling interest of preventing minors from being exposed to indecent telephone messages. Under our precedents, § 223(b), in its present form, has the invalid effect of limiting the content of adult telephone conversations to that which is suitable for children to hear. It is another case of "burn[ing] the house to roast the pig."Because the statute's denial of adult access to telephone messages which are indecent but not obscene far exceeds that which is necessary to limit the access of minors to such messages, we hold that the ban does not survive constitutional scrutiny.

### Bibliography

Farber, Daniel A. "Civilizing Public Discourse: An Essay on Professor Bickel, Justice Harlan, and the Enduring Significance of *Cohen v. California.*" *Duke Law Journal* 283 (1980).

Lively, Donald E., William D. Araiza, Phoebe A. Haddon, John C. Knechtle, and Dorothy E. Roberts. *First Amendment Law*. Cincinnati, OH: Anderson Publishing Co., 2003.

## *Turner Broadcasting System, Inc. v. Federal Communications Commission*

**Citation: 512 U.S. 622.**

**Issue: Whether federal rules requiring cable television operators to carry broadcast signals were content-based or content-neutral.**

**Year of Decision: 1994.**

**Outcome: The must-carry rules were content-neutral and subject to less exacting constitutional review than if they were content- based.**
**Author of Opinion: Justice Anthony Kennedy.**
**Vote: 5-4.**

The cable television industry originated as a means for distributing broadcast signals into regions that, because of topography or distance, had difficulty accessing television. By the late twentieth century, cable television had become a dominant medium in its own right. Instead of merely enhancing broadcast television, modern cable systems provide multiple channels of programming from other sources. With cable penetrating approximately three-quarters of the nation's households by the beginning of the twenty-first century, it was a medium that no longer was ancillary to, but rather in competition with, traditional broadcasting.

As cable became a more powerful presence, the Federal Communications Commission (FCC) grew concerned with the medium's potential for causing economic harm to broadcasters. Television's revenue stream flows from advertisers whose interest in purchasing time for commercials depends upon the ability to reach an audience. With cable having become the primary gateway for delivering broadcast programming, the FCC became increasingly worried by the possibility that cable operators might drop local television stations from their systems.

To avoid the possibility that cable might use its market power to displace broadcasters, and thus destroy an industry that provides service with no direct charge to users, Congress included provisions in the *Cable Television Consumer Protection and Competition Act of 1992* that required operators to carry most if not all local broadcast signals. Twice during the 1980s, the FCC had proposed must-carry regulations only to have them invalidated by lower courts. Congressional action reflected a growing sense, however, that economic power was becoming concentrated in the cable industry to a point that broadcasting's ability to compete was becoming endangered. Must-carry regulation thus rested upon findings that, without them, there was a "substantial likelihood" that cable would erode the advertising revenue base that sustains free local television and its economic viability.

The cable industry, in *Turner Broadcasting System, Inc. v. Federal Communications Commission* (1994), challenged the must-carry provisions on grounds that they abridged the freedom of speech and freedom of the press secured by the First Amendment. Its primary arguments were that must carriage invaded the editorial discretion of cable operators and burdened the ability of other programming sources to obtain channel access.

From the cable industry's standpoint, the must-carry requirement constituted content-based regulation and thus should be subject to a high standard of review. Pursuant to this strict scrutiny model, which applies when a fundamental right has been burdened, the Court would be required to ask whether the regulation was narrowly tailored toward achieving a compelling interest. The government, however, maintained that must carriage was nothing more than antitrust legislation. It thus pushed for a relaxed standard of review consistent with precedent that governs constitutional analysis of economic regulation. Further supporting its argument for judicial deference, the government maintained that cable regulation should be reviewed under the less rigorous standards that apply to broadcast regulation.

Justice Anthony Kennedy commenced the majority's analysis with the proposition that cable programmers and operators are safeguarded by the First Amendment. Their constitutional protection responds to two primary communicative interests—the origination of programming and exercise of editorial discretion in selecting the content that is carried on their systems. In factoring these concerns, the Court rejected the notion that the less rigorous standard of review governing broadcasting should apply to cable. Radio and television are more vulnerable to regulation because, as noted in *Red Lion Broadcasting Co. v. Federal Communications Commission* (1969), there is a scarcity of broadcast signals. Cable, by way of contrast, is characterized by a multiplicity of channels and the potential for unlimited access and use.

Having explained why it would not use the relaxed standard of review governing broadcasting, the Court then turned its attention to the cable industry's argument for strict scrutiny. Insofar as the must carriage requirement singled out cable for special treatment, by imposing unique burdens upon it, the Court determined that some degree of heightened First Amendment scrutiny was necessary. To the extent that the regulation burdened expression on account of its content, it would have found a basis for particularly rigorous review. The Court concluded, however, that the regulation was unrelated to the content of speech. As the Court saw it, Congress's purpose was not to favor a particular type or source of programming but to preserve access to free television for those persons without cable. Finding the must-carry requirement to be content-neutral, the Court opted for a level of review that was more intense than the deferential model advocated by the government but more relaxed than the strict scrutiny urged by the cable industry.

The intermediate standard of review that the Court applied was the same criterion introduced in *United States v. O'Brien* (1968), a case that concerned the conviction of an individual who burned his draft card to protest the Vietnam War. Consistent with *O'Brien,* the Court inquired into whether the regulation advanced "a substantial government interest" and "burden[ed] substantially more speech than is necessary to further [its] legitimate interests." Having announced the appropriate standard of review, the Court declined to apply it pending further development of the record.

Based upon the evidence presented by the government, the Court found a lack of evidence indicating that cable would deny carriage to broadcasters and that such denial would endanger the television industry. Missing too were findings regarding the actual impact of must carriage on the speech of cable operators and programmers. Without such information, the Court concluded that it could not determine whether the regulation suppressed "'substantially more speech than . . . necessary' to ensure the viability of broadcast television." Given these unresolved factual questions, the Court remanded the case for further proceedings at the district court level.

Justice Sandra Day O'Connor, joined by three other justices, authored an opinion that concurred in part with and dissented in part from the majority. Although concurring with the Court that content-neutral regulations need not be strictly scrutinized, she disagreed with its determination that the must carriage provisions were not content-based. In support of the proposition that the regulation was referenced to content, Justice O'Connor cited congressional findings that favored diversity of views through multiple media, educational programming, and locally originated programming, particularly with respect to news and public affairs. She maintained that these preferences, which Congress had cited in support of protecting broadcasting from the risk that cable operators might exclude them from their systems, represented content considerations. Insofar as must carriage was justified with reference to content, Justice O'Connor argued that it could not be justified unless "narrowly tailored to a compelling state interest." Although recognizing diversity, educational programming, and local service and educational programming as "important" interests, she maintained that they fell short of being "compelling." From her perspective, these concerns should be managed not by government but by market shaped by the interaction of private speakers and listeners. In a separate concurrence and dissent, Justice Ruth Bader Ginsburg criticized the must-carry requirement as "an unwarranted content-based preference [that] hypothesizes a risk to local stations that remains imaginary."

Three years later, after further review by the district court, the Court revisited the case. In *Turner Broadcasting System, Inc. v. Federal Communications Commission II* (1997), it found that a more fully developed factual record supported the must-carry provisions. The Court thus accepted Congress's judgment that cable systems would drop broadcasters in many instances without must carriage and, as a consequence, local broadcasting would become financially imperiled. It also identified important regulatory interests in the form of preserving free broadcasting, multiple sources of information, and fair competition. Applying the intermediate standard of review that it referenced in the preceding case, it found that must-carry regulation was content-neutral, directly advanced important government interests, was unrelated to the suppression of expression, and burdened substantially no more speech than necessary to account for the government interests.

Although not prevailing in the context of the must carriage controversy, cable operators actually scored significant First Amendment points. The *Turner Broadcasting* decision not only reaffirmed that cable has First Amendment interests but that the standard for reviewing content-based or content-neutral regulation is not the deferential model that governs broadcasting.

Although a victory for broadcasters with respect to must carriage, therefore, the *Turner Broadcasting* decision is significant for placing cable operators in a more favorable position under the First Amendment. It is a position that is likely to endure pending a rethinking of underlying rationales or the long-standing preference for developing each medium's constitutional status in isolation from other media.

### Justice KENNEDY announced the judgment of the Court and delivered the opinion of the Court.

. . . There can be no disagreement on an initial premise: Cable programmers and cable operators engage in and transmit speech, and they are entitled to the protection of the speech and press provisions of the First Amendment. Through "original programming or by exercising editorial discretion over which stations or programs to include in its repertoire," cable programmers and operators "see[k] to communicate messages on a wide variety of topics and in a wide variety of formats."

By requiring cable systems to set aside a portion of their channels for local broadcasters, the must-carry rules regulate cable speech in two respects: The rules reduce the number of channels over which cable operators exercise unfettered control, and they render it more difficult for cable programmers to compete for carriage on the limited channels remaining. Nevertheless, because not every interference with speech triggers the same degree of scrutiny under the First Amendment, we must decide at the outset the level of scrutiny applicable to the must-carry provisions.

We address first the Government's contention that regulation of cable television should be analyzed under the same First Amendment standard that applies to regulation of broadcast television. It is true that our cases have permitted more intrusive regulation of broadcast speakers than of speakers in other media. But the rationale for applying a less rigorous standard of First Amendment scrutiny to broadcast regulation, whatever its validity in the cases elaborating it, does not apply in the context of cable regulation. . . .

As a general rule, laws that by their terms distinguish favored speech from disfavored speech on the basis of the ideas or views expressed are content based. By contrast, laws that confer benefits or impose burdens on speech without reference to the ideas or views expressed are in most instances content neutral. . . .

The design and operation of the challenged provisions confirm that the purposes underlying the enactment of the must-carry scheme are unrelated to the content of speech. The rules, as mentioned, confer must-carry rights on all full power broadcasters, irrespective of the content of their programming. They do not require or prohibit the carriage of particular ideas or points of view. They do not penalize cable operators or programmers because of the content of their programming. They do not compel cable operators to affirm points of view with which they disagree. They do not produce any net decrease in the amount of available speech. And they leave cable operators free to carry whatever programming they wish on all channels not subject to must-carry requirements. . . .

In short, Congress' acknowledgment that broadcast television stations make a valuable contribution to the Nation's communications system does not render the must-carry scheme content based. The scope and operation of the challenged provisions make clear, in our view, that Congress designed the must-carry provisions not to promote speech of a particular content, but to prevent cable operators from exploiting their economic power to the detriment of broadcasters, and thereby to ensure that all Americans, especially those unable to subscribe to cable, have access to free television programming-whatever its content. . . .

In short, the must-carry provisions are not designed to favor or disadvantage speech of any particular content. Rather, they are meant to protect broadcast television from what Congress determined to be unfair competition by cable systems. In enacting the provisions, Congress sought to preserve the existing structure of the Nation's broadcast television medium while permitting the concomitant expansion and development of cable television, and, in particular, to ensure that broadcast television remains available as a source of video programming for those without cable. Appellants' ability to hypothesize a content-based purpose for these provisions rests on little more than speculation and does not cast doubt upon the content-neutral character of must-carry. . . .

The must-carry provisions, as we have explained above, are justified by special characteristics of the cable medium: the bottleneck monopoly power exercised by cable operators and the dangers this power poses to the viability of broadcast television. Appellants do not argue, nor does it appear, that other media—in particular, media that transmit video programming such as MMDS and SMATV—are subject to bottleneck monopoly control, or pose a demonstrable threat to the survival of broadcast television. It should come as no surprise, then, that Congress decided to impose the must-carry obligations upon cable operators only.

In addition, the must-carry provisions are not structured in a manner that carries the inherent risk of undermining First Amendment interests. The regulations are broad based, applying to almost all cable systems in the country, rather than just a select few. As a result, the provisions do not pose the same dangers of suppression and manipulation that were posed by the more narrowly targeted regulations in *Minneapolis Star* and *Arkansas Writers' Project*. For these reasons, the must-carry rules do not call for strict scrutiny. . . .

Thus, in applying *O'Brien* scrutiny we must ask first whether the Government has adequately shown that the economic health of local broadcasting is in genuine jeopardy and in need of the protections afforded by must-carry. Assuming an affirmative answer to the foregoing question, the Government still bears the burden of showing that the remedy it has adopted does not "burden substantially more speech than is necessary to further the government's legitimate interests." On the state of the record developed thus far, and in the absence of findings of fact from the District Court, we are unable to conclude that the Government has satisfied either inquiry. . . .

## Justice GINSBURG, concurring in part and dissenting in part.

Substantially for the reasons stated by Circuit Judge Williams in his opinion dissenting from the three-judge District Court's judgment, I conclude that Congress' "must-carry" regime, which requires cable operators to set aside just over one-third of their channels for local broadcast stations, reflects an unwarranted content-based preference and hypothesizes a risk to local stations that remains imaginary.

The "must-carry" rules Congress has ordered do not differentiate on the basis of "viewpoint," and therefore do not fall in the category of speech regulation that Government must avoid most assiduously. The rules, however, do reflect a content preference, and on that account demand close scrutiny.

The Court has identified as Congress' "overriding objective in enacting must-carry," the preservation of over-the-air television service for those unwilling or unable to subscribe to cable, and has remanded the case for further airing centered on that allegedly overriding, content-neutral purpose. But an intertwined or even discrete content-neutral justification does not render speculative, or reduce to harmless surplus, Congress' evident plan to advance local programming.

As Circuit Judge Williams stated:

"Congress rested its decision to promote [local broadcast] stations in part, but quite explicitly, on a finding about their content—that they were 'an important source of local news and public affairs programming and other local broadcast services critical to an informed electorate.' "

Moreover, as Judge Williams persuasively explained, "[the] facts do not support an inference that over-the-air TV is at risk," "[w]hatever risk there may be in the abstract has completely failed to materialize." "The paucity of evidence indicating that broadcast television is in jeopardy," if it persists on remand, should impel an ultimate judgment for the appellants.

### Bibliography

Brenner, Daniel. "Cable Television and the Freedom of Expression." *Duke Law Journal* 329 (1988).

Powe, Lucas A., Jr. *American Broadcasting and the First Amendment*. Berkeley: University of California Press, 1987.

## *Reno v. American Civil Liberties Union*

**Citation: 521 U.S. 844.**

**Issue: Whether a congressional prohibition of indecent and patently offensive material on the Internet abridged freedom of speech.**

*(Continued)*

**Year of Decision: 1997.**

**Outcome: The restrictions on indecent and patently offensive material abridged freedom of speech.**

**Author of Opinion: Justice John Paul Stevens.**

**Vote: 7-2.**

The First Amendment has developed in the context of technological change that has evolved media beyond print formats into a variety of electronic methods for disseminating information. In response to these changes that have occurred since the First Amendment was framed and ratified, the Supreme Court has developed different models of review. The utility of this medium specific basis of analysis depends upon the existence of real differences among media. It is for this reason that the emergence of the Internet poses significant challenges to traditional constitutional thinking.

Instead of being characterized by differences from other media, the Internet represents the convergence of various media. It is an international network of computers connected by telephone lines that provides access to and interaction with information sources and on-line services. A primary Internet feature is the World Wide Web, which enables users to search, read, view, research, publish, communicate, and purchase. Unlike mass media such as publishing, broadcasting, and cablecasting, the Internet is characterized by its decentralization. Any person connected to the Internet, therefore, can be a publisher.

Studies of Internet utilization indicate that sites providing access to sexually explicit material are among its most popular attractions. With Internet use growing rapidly, along with concern that children might be exposed to obscene and indecent content, Congress enacted the *Communications Decency Act of 1996* (CDA). This enactment prohibited anyone from knowingly using a telecommunications device to make, create, or solicit and transmit any "obscene or indecent" communication to persons under the age of 18. It also barred the use of interactive computer services for knowingly sending any "patently offensive" communication to persons under the age of 18 or displaying it in a manner making it available to them. Exempted from the prohibitions were those who took "good faith, reasonable, effective, and appropriate actions" to restrict access by minors.

In support of the enactment, Congress cited the need to protect children from obscene and indecent communications. Although acknowledging the legitimacy and importance of this objective, a federal district court found that the law violated the First Amendment. In *Reno v. American Civil Liberties Union,* the Supreme Court considered the government's appeal for reversal of the lower court. The government's case consisted of three primary arguments. First, it maintained that

Congress had the power to define obscenity for children differently than for adults. Second, the government argued that the same principles governing indecency in broadcasting should apply to the Internet. Third, it contended that the CDA merely operated as a zoning ordinance like regulations that govern the placement and availability of adult movie theaters.

The Court found each of the government's arguments unpersuasive and struck down the law. With respect to the first point, it acknowledged a state's power to differentiate materials that were obscene to minors even if not obscene for adults. For this proposition, it cited the nearly three-decades-old case of *Ginsberg v. New York* (1968). The Court distinguished the statute upheld in *Ginsberg* from the CDA on grounds the former did not deny availability of the material to adults. Because the law swept so broadly as to impact protected speech, the Court determined that it was fatally overbroad on its face. Absent a meaningful definition of the term "indecent," it also was unconstitutionally vague.

The Court also found significant differences between indecency controls upheld in broadcasting and the CDA. Contrary to the government's argument that the Court's decision in *Federal Communications Commission v. Pacifica Foundation* supported a like outcome with respect to the Internet, the Court found significant differences in the circumstances. First, unlike the CDA, regulation of broadcast indecency pertained not to whether but to when indecent programming could be aired. Second, and also different from the CDA, the regulatory order reviewed in *Pacifica* was an exercise in agency action rather than criminal prosecution. Third, indecency regulation in the context of broadcasting operates against a medium that has "received the most limited First Amendment protection."

With respect to the government's contention that the CDA was akin to a zoning ordinance that kept adult-themed enterprises out of residential neighborhoods, the Court found that the law swept more broadly. Rather than "cyberzoning" the Internet, the law was found to apply to the entire cyberspace universe. Because the CDA aimed to protect children from "indecent" and "patently offensive" speech, moreover, it was clear to the Court that content was a primary rather than secondary legislative concern.

In structuring an appropriate standard of review for the Internet, the Court reaffirmed as its starting point the premise that "each medium of expression . . . may present its own problems" that justify a customized regulatory response. It thus referenced case law that justified broadcasting controls on grounds the medium had a "tradition of extensive government regulation," frequencies were scarce, and its nature was "invasive." None of these factors, from the Court's perspective, applied to the Internet. Contrary to being grounded in tradition, the CDA represented the first regulatory initiative relating to the Internet. Unlike the scarcity phenomenon in broadcasting, the Internet provides "relatively unlimited, low-cost capacity for communication of all kinds." Finally, because access to the Internet requires affirmative steps by the user, it does not carry the risk of intrusion that inheres in "turning on a radio and being taken by surprise by an indecent message." Based upon these differentiating considerations, the Court concluded that the CDA should not be evaluated pursuant to the relaxed standard of review urged by the government.

Using a strict scrutiny standard of review instead, the Court agreed with the district court that protecting children from indecent material was a compelling interest. Because the CDA could not be enforced against foreign sites and age is difficult to verify, it determined that the legislation would not achieve its purpose. The law also denied large amounts of speech to adults, who have a First Amendment right to receive or disseminate indecent expression. Against this backdrop, and if there were less constitutionally burdensome means of achieving Congress's objectives, the Court determined that the CDA was wanting. In this regard, it cited favorably the district court's finding that user-based filtering software would "soon be widely available."

Justice Sandra Day O'Connor, joined by Chief Justice William Rehnquist, concurred in part and dissented in part. Her primary objection was that the majority based its decision upon the hope rather than the reality of technology. She thus agreed with the Court that the "display" provision of the CDA was unconstitutional, insofar as a speaker could avoid liability only by refraining from indecent speech altogether. Because such expression is protected in relationship to adults, the law unconstitutionally would "reduce[ ] the adult population [on the Internet] to reading only what is fit for children." With respect to the provision prohibiting knowing transmission of indecent material to minors, Justice O'Connor would have reached a different result. She would have upheld the law as it related to e-mails knowingly addressed to minors and on-line chats between an adult and minor, but not in connection with interaction with other adults even when there is a risk that minors may be present.

In response to the Court's decision, Congress enacted the Child On Line Pornography Act (COPA). This legislation, like the CDA, was designed to protect children from indecent materials on the World Wide Web. The COPA prohibits knowing communication for commercial purposes of any material that appeals to the "prurient interest" of or is "patently offensive" to minors. It also establishes "community standards" as the basis for determining whether these factors are present. In *Ashcroft v. Free Speech Coalition* (2002), the Court found that this provision was not unconstitutionally overbroad. It did not rule on other constitutional issues, however, and remanded the case to the federal district court for further development. The lower court entered a preliminary injunction against the COPA on grounds it was likely that the statute was unconstitutional. In *Ashcroft v. American Civil Liberties Union II,* the Court affirmed on grounds there appeared to be less restrictive means for achieving the regulatory objectives.

Even if the COPA were to be enjoined permanently, it is unlikely that such a ruling would deter further legislative efforts to regulate indecency on the Internet.

The Court itself has acknowledged that limiting access to children is a compelling interest. The challenge for legislators, however, is to regulate in a manner that restricts access to minors but not adults. Given the Internet's nature and easy accessibility, such selective control may be more attainable through technology than by regulation. Pending widespread availability and real efficacy of filtering software, however, indecency on the Internet is likely to be of continuing interest to regulators.

### Justice STEVENS delivered the opinion of the Court.

. . . In *Renton,* we upheld a zoning ordinance that kept adult movie theaters out of residential neighborhoods. The ordinance was aimed, not at the content of the films shown in the theaters, but rather at the "secondary effects"—such as crime and deteriorating property values—that these theaters fostered: " 'It is th[e] secondary effect which these zoning ordinances attempt to avoid, not the dissemination of "offensive" speech.' " According to the Government, the CDA is constitutional because it constitutes a sort of "cyberzoning" on the Internet. But the CDA applies broadly to the entire universe of cyberspace. And the purpose of the CDA is to protect children from the primary effects of "indecent" and "patently offensive" speech, rather than any "secondary" effect of such speech. Thus, the CDA is a content-based blanket restriction on speech, and, as such, cannot be "properly analyzed as a form of time, place, and manner regulation." . . .

Finally, unlike the conditions that prevailed when Congress first authorized regulation of the broadcast spectrum, the Internet can hardly be considered a "scarce" expressive commodity. It provides relatively unlimited, low-cost capacity for communication of all kinds. The Government estimates that "[a]s many as 40 million people use the Internet today, and that figure is expected to grow to 200 million by 1999." This dynamic, multifaceted category of communication includes not only traditional print and news services, but also audio, video, and still images, as well as interactive, real-time dialogue. Through the use of chat rooms, any person with a phone line can become a town crier with a voice that resonates farther than it could from any soapbox. Through the use of Web pages, mail exploders, and newsgroups, the same individual can become a pamphleteer. As the District Court found, "the content on the Internet is as diverse as human thought." We agree with its conclusion that our cases provide no basis for qualifying the level of First Amendment scrutiny that should be applied to this medium. . . .

In evaluating the free speech rights of adults, we have made it perfectly clear that "[s]exual expression which is indecent but not obscene is protected by the First

Amendment." Indeed, *Pacifica* itself admonished that "the fact that society may find speech offensive is not a sufficient reason for suppressing it."

It is true that we have repeatedly recognized the governmental interest in protecting children from harmful materials. But that interest does not justify an unnecessarily broad suppression of speech addressed to adults. As we have explained, the Government may not "reduc[e] the adult population . . . to . . . only what is fit for children." "[R]egardless of the strength of the government's interest" in protecting children, "[t]he level of discourse reaching a mailbox simply cannot be limited to that which would be suitable for a sandbox." . . .

In this Court, though not in the District Court, the Government asserts that—in addition to its interest in protecting children—its "[e]qually significant" interest in fostering the growth of the Internet provides an independent basis for upholding the constitutionality of the CDA. The Government apparently assumes that the unregulated availability of "indecent" and "patently offensive" material on the Internet is driving countless citizens away from the medium because of the risk of exposing themselves or their children to harmful material.

We find this argument singularly unpersuasive. The dramatic expansion of this new marketplace of ideas contradicts the factual basis of this contention. The record demonstrates that the growth of the Internet has been and continues to be phenomenal. As a matter of constitutional tradition, in the absence of evidence to the contrary, we presume that governmental regulation of the content of speech is more likely to interfere with the free exchange of ideas than to encourage it. The interest in encouraging freedom of expression in a democratic society outweighs any theoretical but unproven benefit of censorship.

## Bibliography

Barrage, Rafic H. "*Reno v. American Civil Liberties Union*: First Amendment Free Speech Guarantee Extended to the Internet." *Mercer Law Review* 49 (1998): 625.

Katsh, Ethan M. *The Electronic Media and the Transformation of Law.* New York: Oxford University Press, 1989.

## *Ashcroft v. Free Speech Coalition*

**Citation: 535 U.S. 234.**

**Issue: Whether Congress may prohibit "virtual" child pornography (pornography produced by computer without the participation of any real children).**

**Year of Decision: 2002.**

**Outcome: Virtual child pornography cannot be prohibited consistently with the First Amendment.**

**Author of Opinion: Justice Anthony Kennedy.**

**Vote: 7-2.**

As technology has advanced, it has become possible for pornographers to simulate real sexual conduct on the computer. So-called "virtual pornography" has been controversial to the extent that it has been used to create virtual child pornography. In *United States v. Ferber,* 458 U.S. 747 (1982), the United States Supreme Court held that child pornography (pornography depicting children involved in lewd sexual conduct) was not protected under the First Amendment. In *Ashcroft v. Free Speech Coalition,* 535 U.S. 564 (2002), the Court was forced to decide whether virtual child pornography could be included within the ban.

*Ashcroft* involved the constitutionality of the Child Pornography Prevention Act of 1996 (CPPA). CPPA extended the federal prohibition against child pornography to sexually explicit images that appear to depict minors but are produced without using any real children (also known as "virtual child pornography). Section 2256(8)(B) prohibited "any visual depiction, including any photograph, film, video, picture, or computer or computer-generated image or picture" that "is, or appears to be, of a minor engaging in sexually explicit conduct." The literal terms of the statute were broadly defined to include not only classical paintings but also movies (including older actors who appeared to be minors engaged in sexual intercourse). The CPPA applied not only to obscene depictions of virtual child pornography but also to nonobscene depictions.

The Court was not asked to decide whether Section 2256(8)(C), dealing with morphed images (images of real children that have been altered), was constitutional. However, the Court indicated that it would have upheld the antimorphing provision because such images "implicate the interests of real children and are in that sense closer to the images in *Ferber.*"

As for the remainder of the Act, in an opinion by Justice Kennedy, the Court struck down most of the CPPA. The Court invalidated Section 2256(8)(D), which defined child pornography to include any sexually explicit image that was "advertised, promoted, presented, described, or distributed in such a manner that conveys the impression" it depicts "a minor engaging in sexually explicit conduct." The Court expressed concern that the provision applied not only to those who pander child pornography, but also "those possessors who took no part in pandering. Once a work has been described as child pornography, the taint remains on the speech in the hands of subsequent possessors, making possession unlawful even though the content otherwise would not be objectionable." The Court was especially concerned about the fact that the law imposed serious criminal penalties (15 years in prison for the first offense and 30 years in prison for second or later offenses).

In striking down Section 2256(8)(D), the Court reaffirmed *Ferber* in noting that "sexual abuse of a child is a most serious crime and an act repugnant to the moral instincts of a decent people," and the Court recognized that there "are subcultures of persons who harbor illicit desires for children and . . . trade pictures and written accounts of sexual activity with young children." However, the Court noted that

Congress is free to enact laws protecting children against sexual abuse. Moreover, the Court distinguished *Ferber*, which was based on the Court's recognition of the State's compelling interest in stamping out child sexual abuse. Since virtual child pornography does not involve a "record of sexual abuse," and does not record a crime or create victims by its production, *Ferber* did not necessarily permit its prohibition.

In striking down the ban on virtual child pornography, the Court rejected the government's argument that "child pornography rarely can be valuable speech." The Court noted that *Ferber* did not hold that child pornography lacked value, but instead focused on the manner in which it was created. On the contrary, the Court concluded that, when child pornography is not obscene and does not result from sexual abuse, it can have value. Indeed, in *Ferber*, itself, the Court recognized that some examples of child pornography may have value, but concluded that virtual images could be used to create that speech without using actual children. Of course, the CPPA would have prohibited those images as well.

The Court also rejected the government's claim that virtual pornography imposes specific harms on society, specifically that it can be used to seduce children or to whet the appetites of pedophiles. The Court noted that there are many things that can be used to seduce children (e.g., candy and video games), but concluded that "we would not expect those to be prohibited because they can be misused." The Court concluded that any restriction must be narrowly drawn, and the Court noted that the "mere tendency of speech to encourage unlawful acts is not a sufficient reason for banning it." The Court concluded that the State had "shown no more than a remote connection between speech that might encourage thoughts or impulses and any resulting child abuse."

In the final analysis, the Court focused on the values underlying the First Amendment and concluded that "the First Amendment bars the government from dictating what we see or read or speak or hear." The Court was also concerned that the CPPA applies without regard to whether the work has serious literary, artistic, political, or scientific value. In addition, the CPPA prohibits the "visual depiction of an idea—that of teenagers engaging in sexual activity—that is a fact of modern society and has been a theme in art and literature throughout the ages." The Court noted that both themes (teenage sexual activity and child sex abuse) "have inspired countless literary works." The Court specifically referenced Shakespeare's famous play, *Romeo and Juliet* (which involved a thirteen-year-old girl), and the movie *Traffic* (nominated for best picture). The Court noted that, if such films "contain a single graphic depiction of sexual activity within the statutory definition, the possessor of the film would be subject to severe punishment without inquiry into the work's redeeming value." In the Court's view, this result would be inconsistent with an essential First Amendment rule: The artistic merit of a work does not depend on the presence of a single explicit scene. Under *Miller*, the First Amendment requires that redeeming value be judged by considering the work as a whole."

Finally, the Government argued that the possibility of producing images by using computer imaging makes it very difficult for it to prosecute those who produce pornography by using real children. In other words, experts might have difficulty determining whether a given set of pictures was made using real children or by using computer imaging. The Court rejected this argument noting that the government may not suppress lawful speech as a means of suppressing unlawful speech.

Justice O'Connor, joined by Chief Justice Rehnquist and Justice Scalia, concurred in part and dissented in part. She emphasized the "compelling interest" in protecting children and noted that even virtual images "whet the appetites of child molesters who may use the images to seduce young children." In addition, she feared that possessors of "actual child pornography may evade liability by claiming that the images attributed to them are in fact computer-generated," and she feared that this problem would only grow worse as technology improved.

Chief Justice Rehnquist, joined by Justice Scalia, dissented. He argued that the government has a "compelling interest" in prohibiting actual child pornography, and he expressed concern that "rapidly advancing technology soon will make it all but impossible" to distinguish between actual pornography and child pornography. Nevertheless, he concluded that he would have serious "First Amendment concerns" if someone were prosecuted for possession or distribution of a film with serious literary or artistic value. He avoided that problem by construing the CPPA to apply only to hard-core pornography.

*Ashcroft* is an important contribution to First Amendment jurisprudence. It distinguishes *Ferber* in holding that "virtual child pornography," which does not depict any real children, still qualifies for constitutional protection provided that it is not obscene.

## Justice KENNEDY delivered the opinion of the Court.

. . . By prohibiting child pornography that does not depict an actual child, the statute goes beyond *New York v. Ferber,* which distinguished child pornography from other sexually explicit speech because of the State's interest in protecting the children exploited by the production process. As a general rule, pornography can be banned only if obscene, but under *Ferber,* pornography showing minors can be proscribed whether or not the images are obscene under the definition set forth in *Miller v. California. Ferber* recognized that "[t]he *Miller* standard, like all general definitions of what may be banned as obscene, does not reflect the State's particular and more compelling interest in prosecuting those who promote the sexual exploitation of children." While we have not had occasion to consider the question, we may assume that the apparent age of persons engaged in sexual conduct is relevant to whether a depiction offends community standards. Pictures of young children engaged in certain acts might be obscene where similar depictions of adults, or perhaps even older adolescents, would not. The CPPA, however, is not directed at speech that is obscene; Congress has proscribed those materials through a separate statute. Like the law in *Ferber,* the CPPA seeks to reach beyond obscenity, and it makes no attempt to conform to the *Miller* standard. For instance, the statute would reach visual depictions, such as movies, even if they have redeeming social value.

The principal question to be resolved, then, is whether the CPPA is constitutional where it proscribes a significant universe of speech that is neither obscene under *Miller* nor child pornography under *Ferber.* . . .

As we have noted, the CPPA is much more than a supplement to the existing federal prohibition on obscenity. Under *Miller,* the Government must prove that the work, taken as a whole, appeals to the prurient interest, is patently offensive in light of community standards, and lacks serious literary, artistic, political, or scientific value. The CPPA, however, extends to images that appear to depict a minor engaging in sexually explicit activity without regard to the *Miller* requirements. The materials need not appeal to the prurient interest. Any depiction of sexually explicit activity, no matter how it is presented, is proscribed. The CPPA applies to a picture in a psychology manual, as well as a movie depicting the horrors of sexual abuse. It is not necessary, moreover, that the image be patently offensive. Pictures of what appear to be 17-year-olds engaging in sexually explicit activity do not in every case contravene community standards.

The CPPA prohibits speech despite its serious literary, artistic, political, or scientific value. The statute proscribes the visual depiction of an idea—that of teenagers engaging in sexual activity—that is a fact of modern society and has been a theme in art and literature throughout the ages. Under the CPPA, images are prohibited so long as the persons appear to be under 18 years of age. This is higher than the legal age for marriage in many States, as well as the age at which persons may consent to sexual relations. It is, of course, undeniable that some youths engage in sexual activity before the legal age, either on their own inclination or because they are victims of sexual abuse.

Both themes—teenage sexual activity and the sexual abuse of children—have inspired countless literary works. William Shakespeare created the most famous pair of teenage lovers, one of whom is just 13 years of age. In the drama, Shakespeare portrays the relationship as something splendid and innocent, but not juvenile. The work has inspired no less than 40 motion pictures, some of which suggest that the teenagers consummated their relationship. Shakespeare may not have written sexually explicit scenes for the Elizabethan audience, but were modern directors to adopt a less conventional approach, that fact alone would not compel the conclusion that the work was obscene. . . .

The CPPA, for reasons we have explored, is inconsistent with *Miller* and finds no support in *Ferber.* The Government seeks to justify its prohibitions in other ways. It argues that the CPPA is necessary because pedophiles may use virtual child pornography to seduce children. There are many things innocent in themselves, however, such as cartoons, video games, and candy, that might be used for immoral purposes, yet we would not expect those to be prohibited because they can be misused. The Government, of course, may punish adults who provide unsuitable materials to children, and it may enforce criminal penalties for unlawful solicitation. The precedents establish, however, that speech within the rights of adults to hear may not be silenced completely in an attempt to shield children from it. . . .

## Chief Justice REHNQUIST, with whom Justice SCALIA joins in part, dissenting.

. . . To the extent the CPPA prohibits possession or distribution of materials that "convey the impression" of a child engaged in sexually explicit conduct, that prohibition can and should be limited to reach "the sordid business of pandering" which lies outside the bounds of First Amendment protection. This is how the Government asks us to construe the statute, and it is the most plausible reading of the text, which prohibits only materials *advertised, promoted, presented, described, or distributed in such a manner* that conveys the impression that the material is or contains a visual depiction of a minor engaging in sexually explicit conduct."

The First Amendment may protect the video shopowner or film distributor who promotes material as "entertaining" or "acclaimed" regardless of whether the material contains depictions of youthful looking adult actors engaged in nonobscene but sexually suggestive conduct. The First Amendment does not, however, protect the panderer. Thus, materials promoted as conveying the impression that they depict actual minors engaged in sexually explicit conduct do not escape regulation merely because they might warrant First Amendment protection if promoted in a different manner. I would construe "conveys the impression" as limited to the panderer, which makes the statute entirely consistent with *Ginzburg* and other cases.

The Court says that "conveys the impression" goes well beyond *Ginzburg* to "prohibi[t][the] possession of material described, or pandered, as child pornography by someone earlier in the distribution chain." The Court's concern is that an individual who merely possesses protected materials (such as videocassettes of Traffic or American Beauty) might offend the CPPA regardless of whether the individual actually intended to possess materials containing unprotected images.

This concern is a legitimate one, but there is, again, no need or reason to construe the statute this way. In *X–Citement Video,* we faced a provision of the Protection of Children Against Sexual Exploitation Act of 1977, the precursor to the CPPA, which lent itself much less than the present statute to attributing a "knowingly" requirement to the contents of the possessed visual depictions. We held that such a requirement nonetheless applied, so that the Government would have to prove that a person charged with possessing child pornography actually knew that the materials contained depictions of real minors engaged in sexually explicit conduct. In light of this holding, and consistent with the narrow class of images the CPPA is intended to prohibit, the CPPA can be construed to prohibit only the knowing possession of materials actually containing visual depictions of real minors engaged in sexually explicit conduct, or computer-generated images virtually indistinguishable from real minors engaged in sexually explicit conduct. The mere possession of materials containing only suggestive depictions of youthful looking adult actors need not be so included.

In sum, while potentially impermissible applications of the CPPA may exist, I doubt that they would be "substantial . . . in relation to the statute's plainly legitimate sweep." The aim of ensuring the enforceability of our Nation's child pornography laws is a compelling one. The CPPA is targeted to this aim by extending the definition of child pornography to reach computer-generated images that are virtually indistinguishable from real children engaged in sexually explicit conduct. The statute need not be read to do any more than precisely this, which is not offensive to the First Amendment.

For these reasons, I would construe the CPPA in a manner consistent with the First Amendment, reverse the Court of Appeals' judgment, and uphold the statute in its entirety.

## Bibliography

Dugan, Kate. "Regulating What's Not Real: Federal Regulation in the Aftermath of *Ashcroft v. Free Speech Coalition*." *St. Louis University Law Journal* 48 (2004): 1063.

Milstead, Virginia F. "*Ashcroft v. Free Speech Coalition*: How Can Virtual Child Pornography Be Banned Under the First Amendment?" *Pepperdine Law Review* 31 (2004): 825.

Weaver, Russell L., and Donald E. Lively. *Understanding the First Amendment*. Newark, NJ: LexisNexis, 2012, 64–70.